AFRICA AND THE SECOND WORLD WAR

AFRICA AND THE SECOND WORLD WAR

Edited by
David Killingray
and
Richard Rathbone

St. Martin's Press New York

Scholarly & Reference Division,
St. Martin's Press, Inc., 175 Fifth Avenue, New York, NY 10010

First published in the United States of America in 1986

Printed in Hong Kong

ISBN 0-312-00941-0

Library of Congress Cataloging-in-Publication Data
Main entry under title:
Africa and the Second World War.
Bibliography: p.
Includes index.
1. World War, 1939-1945—Africa—Congresses.
I. Killingray, David II. Rathbone, Richard.
D754.A34A34 1986 940.54'496 85-27911
ISBN 0-312-00941-0

Contents

List of Maps

List of Tables

Preface

This collection of essays grew out of an international conference hosted by the Centre of African Studies of the University of London and held at the School of Oriental and African Studies. Reactions to the announcement of a forthcoming conference on the Second World War and Africa to be held in the summer of 1984 frankly surprised the organisers. In the event over 100 scholars attended the conference and, even more impressively, nearly forty colleagues offered and delivered papers, the bulk of which we were able to distribute in advance. Although, as we stress in our introduction, Africa has been rather neglected during the war period by historians, it was abundantly clear that a great deal of good work was being undertaken to redress that situation in Africa, in Europe, in the United States and Australasia. Given the richness of what we were offered at the conference, the task of selection was both daunting and to some extent tragic, as much of that material that we had perforce to exclude was excellent and exciting. In selecting the pieces for this volume we endeavoured to present a reasonable continental spread, combined with various treatments of many of the major themes that emerged at the conference.

Our greatest debt is to the very large number of first-rate historians of Africa who managed to get funding, no easy task in these hard times, and sacrificed the time to make this a stimulating, intimate (though large) and entirely constructive conference. The notable absence of prima donnas, the openness of discussion and the good humour throughout a series of very taxing sessions proved once again that historians of Africa are an unusually nice bunch of people.

The editors would like to register their gratitude for the financial assistance of the Group Research Committee of the School of Oriental and African Studies and especially to Michael Strange, a good man in a crisis. We are also grateful for the assistance of Annette Percy, Marion Swiny and Jean Waring.

DAVID KILLINGRAY
RICHARD RATHBONE

Notes on the Contributors

Michael Brett is Lecturer in the History of North Africa at the School of Oriental and African Studies, University of London.

Michael Cowen was born in Zimbabwe and attended the University College of Rhodesia and Nyasaland before going on to Cambridge. He has taught at the Universities of Nairobi and Swansea and is now a Senior Lecturer at the City of London Polytechnic. He is the author of a number of papers and articles on the peasantry in Kenya; he is currently working on a study of the colonial policy of the Labour Government, 1945–51.

Louis Grundlingh teaches at the Rand Afrikaans University in Johannesburg. He studied at the University of the Orange Free State and was until late 1983 a Lecturer at Potchefstroom University in the Western Transvaal. He is completing a doctoral dissertation on 'The Role of the South African Blacks in the Second World War'.

Mohamed Khenouf was born in Constantine, Algeria. He studied at the University of Constantine, where he now teaches history. He has recently completed research on Algerian nationalism during the Second World War at the School of Oriental and African Studies, University of London.

David Killingray has taught at Goldsmiths' College, University of London, for the last fourteen years. He has written on various aspects of modern African history and imperial relations and is currently preparing a book on Africa and the First World War. In 1986 he became an editor of *African Affairs*.

John Lonsdale is a Lecturer in history at the University of Cambridge and a Fellow of Trinity College. He is the author of a number of articles on Kenyan and East African history and a contributor to the *Cambridge History of Africa. Vol. 6, 1870–1905*, edited by R. Oliver and J. D. Fage.

Brian Mokopakgosi III was born in southern Botswana, in which country he received his secondary and undergraduate education. In 1983 he gained an MA degree in European History from The Johns Hopkins University, returning to the University of Botswana as a lecturer in history. He is now on study leave working for a doctorate at the School of Oriental and African Studies in London.

Anthony Ndi attended school in Cameroon and then studied at Ibadan University. From there he went to the School of Oriental and African Studies in London, where he gained a doctorate in African history. He has taught history in several secondary schools in Cameroon and is currently Vice-Principal of Lycée de Wum, Bamenda, Cameroon.

Richard Rathbone has taught at the School of Oriental and African Studies since 1969. He edited *African Affairs* with Alison Smith in the early 1970s. He has written on modern West African political history, population history, and the social history of South Africa, and more recently upon slavery and the slave trade. He is currently finishing a book on European colonialism in Africa.

Gilbert A. Sekgoma was born and studied in Botswana, graduating from the University in 1979 to become a Staff Development Fellow in the Department of History. He went to Dalhousie University, Nova Scotia, where he is now completing a doctoral thesis on the history of Sierra Leone.

Nicholas Westcott studied history at the University of Cambridge, undertook research in Tanzania from 1979 to 1980 and in 1982 completed a PhD thesis on 'The Impact of the Second World War on Tanganyika, 1939–49'. He is in the process of publishing a number of studies of the period. He now works for the Foreign and Commonwealth Office in London.

1 Introduction

DAVID KILLINGRAY and
RICHARD RATHBONE

To say that the Second World War was important is to make the last uncontroversial statement in African studies. Everyone knows that it was either the end of the beginning or the beginning of the end of European colonialism in Africa and that the huge global upheaval it unleashed had far-reaching effects upon politics, and economic and social life. The beginning of the war provides innumerable studies with a terminal date, just as 1945 has been a convenient opening for a similar number of influential works. But if this is so, it is remarkable that so little attention has been paid to the war both as a savage process and as a period in the history of Africa. Like the Great Depression and the influenza pandemic before it, it remains one of those sets of events and one of those eras that has been widely acknowledged to have been of immense significance and yet has attracted very little systematic study.[1] It is hard to account for this. Many of the most affected metropolitan countries and their ex-dependencies in Africa have permitted archival access to some, if not all, of the documentation for the period and have done so for nearly a decade now. It is, moreover, a period in which the United States' archives become increasingly important for historians of Africa. In addition, the oral information which so usefully augments the written record is a resource that is steadily declining. The period is not a distant one, blocked-off to us by myth and the mists of time. But, despite this, the war has remained more of an assumption than a reality. Few modern historians of Africa have not invoked it as an explanation for the termination of certain policies, the initiation of others, for the ushering in of the circumstances giving rise to modern mass nationalism, for the acceleration or slowing down of class formation and so forth. But much of this has been an almost incantatory invocation, the convenient use of a *deus ex machina*. There is little need for either energetic breast-beating or elaborate pleas in mitigation. The enormous complexity of the events, the fact that they are not neatly contained, concern all parts of the globe, and persist well after 1945, makes heavy demands on scholars.

A starting point in a volume which seeks to suggest that the war, its effects and the general period of the 1940s constitute a real cornucopia must be an insistence on the absolute significance of that period. Manifestly little of the military action took place south of the Sahara, although North and North East Africa were crucial theatres of war.[2] But, in the absence of a re-run of the dramatic events that ravaged so much of east and central Africa in the First World War, it would be tempting to see the Second as essentially external to Africa. While 1939–45 might remain as dates as resonant with meaning and implication as 1789 or 1848, they could be presented as a period in which the Far East, Eastern Europe and the Near and Middle East are profoundly altered but one that only had tangential significance for Africa. Beyond those many thousands of Africans who served in the armed forces of the colonial powers, the war was something that Africans read about in newspapers or heard about on the wireless, a series of desperate but distant struggles in which the balance of international power was being fundamentally altered, in which millions of fellow human beings were dying, but essentially something removed and remote, 'a white man's war' yet again. Manifestly this was not so.

There was scarcely a level of life, both material and less tangible, that was not fundamentally affected from the Cape to Cairo. Few Africans remained untouched by the great events taking place for the most part thousands of kilometres from their homes, whether they recognised the war as the ultimate author of those changes or not. To begin with the obvious, it is clear that the ultimate victory for the Allies was in many senses a Pyrrhic victory. The Second World War finally brought home to Britain and to France that their claim to be world powers was essentiallly spurious. The latter was left in the unenviable position of being partly occupied and in partly collaborating with the continental power which had humiliated her in 1870 and which she had humiliated in a railway carriage in 1918. Britain had maintained her integrity at great cost; while the islands themselves resisted, sizeable portions of the Empire On Which The Sun Never Set were lost rapidly, and perhaps ironically, to the land of the Rising Sun, and few could doubt that victory in Europe and the eventual repossession of the eastern empire would have been impossible to achieve without Russian resistance and American intervention. None of the colonial powers would be likely to dominate future international bodies and to be able to stand aloof from the criticism of colonialism as they had after 1918. Above all, neither of Africa's major colonial powers could claim that in the event they had proved more able than the Dutch to protect sizeable sections of their overseas territories. They were weakened by war and it could certainly be additionally maintained that the war had uncovered many of the frailties of those powers that, with hindsight, had their origins in the final quarter of the nineteenth century. If colonial power in Africa had always rested on a mixture of bluff and force, the bluff proved to be a busted flush and the force more questionable than it had appeared before 1939.[3]

The major shifts in world power ushered in by the war similarly sapped at colonialism. On the one hand, the long established hostility of the Soviet Union to that colonialism carried out by capitalist powers became an organising principle of her external relations after the cessation of hostilities. For the colonial powers this far more assertive stance proved nightmarish, for now the local opposition to alien rule, more marked, it is true, outside Africa, could manipulate the threat of the support of one of the two great powers. Although this threat proved to be more of an apprehension than a reality in Africa, it indubitably sapped imperial confidence; unsurprisingly, some of the most powerful echoes of McCarthyism were to be found in post-war colonial territories, where reds were perceived under even the most bourgeois of beds.

Such might have been tolerable if the United states had demonstrated a more eager support for the future of colonialism. Manifestly it did not. Its inherent anti-colonialism might be traced at the level of ideas to her undoubted status as the first self-liberating colony of modern times. Far more significant, however, were her economic and strategic concerns. Now the most powerful economy in the West, and the creditor through Lend Lease and war loans to much of the free world, the demands of war had brought America to a new pitch of economic efficiency. Understandably, her dominance proved to be the foundation for a strident doctrine of free trade; either formally or informally colonies were antithetical to that ideal in that they had constituted protected markets for colonial powers whose competitiveness had long since declined. Moreover, in the elaborate schemes of pooling colonial production during the war, America had begun to enjoy access to colonial production and was not enamoured with the thought of the restoration of the pre-war market system. If free markets were forced upon colonies by the sheer power of the United States, a great deal of the rationale of colonialism would, of course, disappear. Secondly, the United States was less than impressed by the capacity of its allies to defend its overseas territories, which were now threatened not by Japanese imperialism but by that of the Soviet Union. The initial willingness of colonial people in South East Asia and the Far East to welcome the Japanese as liberators was instructive. Colonial rule could itself be seen as a pretty efficient recruiting officer for the 'other side'. While the strategic shivering in the Cold War was less of an issue within sub-Saharan Africa than it was to prove in the eastern empires, the distaste of the State Department for the maintainance of colonial rule *ad infinitum* added to an international environment which was decidedly less disinterested and uncaring than that of the period following the First World War.[4]

The obvious fragility of the European powers produced paradoxical results for Africa in terms of policy. It is clear that the major powers perceived, though in different ways, that the forces of nationalism, which had to some extent been muted by the war, itself could not be simply outfaced by shows of force. As with the history of much colonial policy, it appears that cost rather than straight humanity was the organising principle behind such reasoning. The deployment of significant levels of force in colonial contexts was immensely costly, and the French abandonment of this penny-pinching logic in Indo-China and Algeria proved the point handsomely. Great strides were made in techniques of modern propaganda.[5] Belgium, Britain, France, and to a lesser degree Portugal, all attempted a measure of incorporation within the colonial state by the creation of more representative governmental systems. It was hoped thereby that the largely middle-class opponents of colonialism would be contained. Clearly this tactic met with varied degrees of success: by and large the British experience suggested that limited constitutional reform merely turned up the volume of protest; the French story after 1944 is markedly uneven, ranging from the largely successful avoidance of serious trouble in West Africa, other than in Guinea and the Ivory Coast, to the serious insurrection in Madagascar in 1947. But the objectives of the frequently pusillanimous reforms were not solely the relatively obvious ones of political containment. They also related to the growing significance of colonial production for metropolitan economies.

The recovery in prices from the troughs of the late 1920s and the 1930s had occurred during the latter stages of the Second World War and, despite the parallel upward drift of inflation, many tropical products demonstrated real gains. Manifestly a world literally rebuilding itself after the devastation of a war that had destroyed towns, industrial areas and infrastructure as well as lives had a long shopping list of raw materials. Such commodities were sold on world markets, and in post-war Europe the siege-economies of the war period were understandably slow to get back into export-earning capacity. Colonial production could therefore be seen as a highly significant foreign-exchange earner. The capacity of colonial governments to control production, so powerfully entrenched during the particular circumstances of the war itself, took on a new significance. Extensive controls adopted in war-time and rationalised as 'war effort' were to some extent recast as 'development programmes'. Attempts were made to utilise expertise and materials to expand African production, resulting in an odd combination of relative liberalism in the fields of politics and labour with the active intervention of government as never before in the generality of the market. That dirigisme has a great deal of explanatory force in showing how nationalism acquired its wider base in the post-war period. But its origins and its mechanisms belong to the period of the war itself; it is surely arguable that the exploitative (in the economists' sense of the word) role of colonial government, so often ascribed to the relatively powerless regimes of Africa before 1939, is more readily ascertained after 1940. It comes as a surprise to some that the assumption of direct economic control occurs under metropolitan regimes which are rightly seen as more politically concessive than most of their predecessors.

The more obviously concessive stance of colonial regimes in a period of centrally directed production and extraction is, of course, no paradox. British policy in the labour field, which was gradually to extend the enabling legislation permitting the legal foundation of labour unions, can assuredly be viewed as a welcome liberalisation of a previously restrictive and even repressive stance. Yet its roots lay in the reaction to major disturbances in the Caribbean and Asian territories in the 1930s, and in the African context could and should be seen as pre-emptive. But these reforms were also underlined by a new stress on efficiency generated by war-time imperatives. Labour unions, helped on their way by government funded and controlled Labour Departments and aided by the experience of the British Trades Union Congress, created organisations that were aids to productivity. Through regulated negotiating machinery, the prospect of preventing the phenomenon of 'wild-cat' strikes, which had caused major war-time disruptions, was infinitely more likely. Unions could also be regarded as training initiatives, improving as they would safety at work, time-keeping and 'proper' shop-floor hierarchies and chains of command. Although the additional intention of dividing the essentially economistic interests of organised labour from those of nationalism pure and simple has received far more attention in the scholarly literature, changes in labour regulation, the introduction of reasonably policed shops, hours' regulations and the rest are significant symptoms of the way in which the war effort altered a previously rather agnostic relation between government and economic institutions.[6] Just as the First World War had ushered in a new and more intensive colonial regime in much of Africa, so too did the demands of the Second World War create far more interventionist regimes following a palpable slackening of colonial commitment by the powers in the course of and immediately after the Depression years.

After the drastic reductions in colonial staffs in the early 1930s, the war saw first an immediate reduction and then a dramatic increase in personnel. And in the wake of that war, the nature of such people had undergone significant change. Unwelcome as it is to all decent people, it is an inescapable aspect of modern war that its demands act as a catalyst in the development of new technologies. Similarly the vastly altered pace of government in a period of such dire emergency generates radically altered styles of management and human organisation. The Second World War was an experts' war, a conflict in which scientists ceased to be viewed as eccentric 'boffins' and were, rather, drawn into the very heart of planning at the highest levels. In the replanning of post-war Europe, a prospect in train well before the cessation of hostilities, town-planners, sociologists, educational theorists, agronomists and economists were central figures in the free or newly liberated liberal democracies, ushering in a social revolution of major proportions. There is, of course, a natural elision between the notions of central planning, the co-option of experts and directive government deployed in war-time circumstances and its successor forms of government, which are very radically different from their pre-war equivalents. Colonial governments were no less subjected to technicist notions of rational administration. In easily demonstrated fashion, the enthusiasms, hobby-horses and schemes of technical departments, research institute scientists and other newly respected pundits rapidly and sometimes disastrously became policies and practices.[7]

The positive aspects of the new emphasis on research and development were legion. Immediate and long-overdue attention was given to health and education policies, and, ambiguous as we might now find it, the recognition that 'start-up' finance would be necessary for any reasonable degree of minor industrialisation and even crop diversification were all welcome retreats from the earlier hard-nosed insistence upon a dependence on locally raised revenue. The price was, however, high. The functions of colonial states and hence the states themselves grew. The radically slimmed-down colonial states of the pre-war period gave way to physically enlarged apparatuses taking on a wide variety of roles that vastly exceeded the rather simpler functions of control and regulation of earlier times. Despite the maintenance of a devolutionary rhetoric, more and more decision-making fell into the hands of, or was, rather, seized by, the councils of state in capital cities. Economies in particular were seen as too important to be left in the hands of unpredictable evolutionary forces.

The logic of this is of considerable significance to the understanding of the eventual politics of decolonisation. Put very simply, it is clear that governments' assumption of greater and greater responsibility in education, health care, infrastructural development, and agricultural and industrial development created not only large but also expensive states. If policy were geared to economic expansion and political containment, the costs would assuredly over-run returns. Only the most bullish of the planners could envisage returns on such investment being sufficient for, let alone exceeding, the price of 'modernisation'. Although economic advance could be 'sold' as precisely that, it was clear that 'development' was a major item on the political agenda. Such was, after all, a major component of the nationalist demand, and its consummation served two ends in chief. It could, at a stroke, effectively 'buy-off' all but the most extreme activists and at the same time would remove many of the underlying social conditions that gave nationalism 'street credibility'. Such assumptions were in the forefront of discussion between the British (and the Free French) and representatives of the African elite in war-time. They were to some extent expressed at the epic Brazzaville meetings in 1944, in the constitutional reforms of the mid-1940s, in labour law and in the commitment to long-range economic planning. The net effect of pressure from both the metropolitan and the nationalist side was the creation of the modern, massively directive and interventionist colonial and post-colonial state. Inevitably the increasing costs of the colonial state weighed heavily in the balance when colonial powers were faced with the essential problems of the nature and timing of decolonisation.

The immediate social, economic and political effects of the war upon Africa were immense. The remarkable recovery in commodity prices, which was, through the 1940s and 1950s, to provide economic planners with more confidence than subsequent events have warranted, proved an ambiguous advantage. War-time booms in colonial territories provide easily understood case-studies of rapid inflation. As seldom before, money poured into the colonies, especially during and after 1942. But there were few outlets for it. Consumption patterns in colonial states had come to depend heavily upon imported consumer and capital goods. Outside South Africa, a state which had already undergone an industrial revolution unique in Africa, there is little evidence of a strong surge of import-substituting industry on any scale, not least because of the sheer impossibility of acquiring capital goods in war-time. Thus a great deal of money chased a severely restricted supply of goods. War-time shipping shortages, the perils of high-seas navigation in a period dominated by the deadly skills of the submariner, coupled with the diversion of much of the industrial world's capacity towards 'war production', conspired to reduce severely the volume and often the quality of goods off-loaded in Africa. Very rapidly the goods available became increasingly costly. Black markets thrived throughout Africa. The 'knock-on' effect of inflation in the consumer goods sector was quickly felt in the food sector; the 5-year period between 1942 and 1947 saw massive increases in the general cost of living for all Africans. In West Africa the rocketing costs of foodstuffs in rural as well as urban markets were exacerbated at the end of the war by serious rain failures whose impact may well have been worsened by the absence of relatively large numbers of men in the forces or in the southern urbanities, particularly as those men were drawn almost inevitably from the poorer and more marginal regions.

In the realm of employment the war effort had momentarily eased the burden of work-seekers in opening up a new range of activities, from conscription in the armed forces to the building of aircraft runways or military installations and the informal sector activities generated by the presence of local and foreign troops in large concentrations. Men were being laid off in large numbers before the ending of hostilities with Japan. By the end of 1947 the work-seekers, the recently laid-off and the new urban drifters were supplemented by the demobilisation of the extra battalions recruited in war-time. For the latter, the payment of war-time bonuses, large sums in pre-war terms, proved shockingly parsimonious in the light of inflation. Many of the skills they had been introduced to in the military, from the driving of heavy goods vehicles to the operating of wireless telegraphy equipment, were redundant in colonies with few new motor vehicles and primitive local communications systems.

In the countryside no less than in the towns inflation reduced the value of earnings and remittances. The developmental demands of government increased the burdens of required communal labour on local roads. Pressures to enhance production, to change to new crops, to improve drainage, to experiment with new strains were coupled with the denial to the primary producer in many parts of Africa of the choice of who he or she sold produce to as the state began to take over this role.

The burden of a great deal of the enforcement of new policies and new techniques fell upon the shoulders of chiefs and headmen, either traditional or appointed. For many such government agents the war period and its attendant stresses presented them with the most severe test of their political skills, and many were found wanting. They were all too frequently faced with the potential wrath of the local administrator for failing to deliver the goods, and the simmering resentment and sometimes violence of their subjects for the adoption of coercive methods. The ensuing crisis in many local authorities in part accounts for the increasingly ready acceptance of national political leadership in areas long deemed conservative, as well as the growing disenchantment of colonial authority with the capacities of local agencies to serve as useful auxiliaries in the demanding work of enhancing productivity.

The collapse of France and the entry of Italy into the war in mid-1940 brought Africa directly into the firing line. The major theatres of conflict were North Africa (1940–3), Ethiopia and Somalia (1940–1), with smaller actions which successfully wrested control of Madagascar from Vichy in 1942. From 1940 onwards the Free French held Chad, from where they extended their control over Equatorial Africa. However, the Vichy regime maintained its authority over French West Africa until 1943, to the constant anxiety of the British. In North and North East Africa much of the fighting took place in relatively arid and thinly populated country. Nevertheless, this caused widespread destruction and disruption to commercial activities. Egypt, for example, was effectively under British military occupation throughout the war, its government subverted, and the country turned into a major base for Middle East Command. Cape Town, Freetown and Kenya also became vital bases guarding trade routes and supply lines for war material and essential foodstuffs for the army. The West Africa supply route ferried aircraft from the Americas via Takoradi and Kano to the Middle East, while tons of food and equipment were moved north from Kenya to Egypt along the Africa Line of Communication (AFLOC) route.

Europe's war-time relation with Africa is essentially one of increased economic exploitation. As in the First World War, Africa proved its value to the imperial powers and the word exploitation begins to have an authentic ring about it. In the first 18 months of the war Africa's trade was reduced and redirected, and the colonial territories bore the burden of small losses of manpower and of financial gifts to the metropoles. In the British territories non-sterling imports were reduced to a minimum and shipping was increasingly in short supply. The loss of the South East Asian tropical products, especially rubber and tin, in early 1942 increased Allied interest in the resources of Africa. By then the United States had developed an active commercial and strategic interest in sub-Saharan Africa. Before the war US trade with Africa was negligible, amounting to 3 per cent per annum; official acknowledgement of the continent merited no more than a desk in the State Department. War in Europe, and the fall of France, altered US policy, and by early 1941 Roosevelt had committed his country to an active role in supplying aircraft to the British in the Middle East via the West African supply route. That interest increased after 1942 and focused increasingly on the rubber production of Liberia, where the United States also had air bases, and the mineral resources of Central Africa. By the end of the war United States trade and investment in sub-Saharan Africa had grown greatly, particularly in the Belgian Congo, which, amongst other things, supplied minerals vital to the new atomic programme.[8]

The defeat and occupation of France and Belgium radically altered the position of those countries' African colonies. Most French territories maintained an allegiance to the Vichy regime, but Chad, under the governorship of the Guyanese Felix Eboué, adhered to the cause of De Gaulle's Free French. From this central African base De Gaulle was able to consolidate Free French control over Equatorial Africa and open a new front against the Axis in southern Libya. An Anglo-French attempt to seize Dakar failed in September 1940, and thereafter the frontiers between Vichy and British-held territory in West Africa remained closed, the two colonial powers regarding each other with a watchful wariness. The US landings in Morocco in November 1942 altered the position of the Vichy colonies and brought about the gradual ascendancy of the Free French to effective political control.[9] A Belgian government in exile in London attempted, with few resources and limited authority, to continue the tradition of centralised control over the Belgian Congo, but real economic and political power lay in the Congo itself. There an increased European population, swollen by refugees, was able to assert a new measure of autonomy from the inheritors of metropolitan authority as well as a more concerted control over the economy of the Belgian Congo.[10]

The post-war years have been described as those of a 'second colonial occupation of Africa', a time when the colonial powers extended their economic and welfare interests in Africa. This process began in some respects in the war years. Up to early 1942 colonial bureaucracies were further reduced as administrative manpower was withdrawn for war service and colonial budgets were pared down. Thereafter the interventionist role of the colonial state rapidly increased as African raw materials and manpower were mobilised for the war effort. The war resulted in the colonial state managing substantial sectors of the economy, seeking new sources of taxation and, attempting to direct labour, investment, mineral and agricultural production, and Africa's exports. As a result of this, by the end of the war there can have been few people, or areas, in Africa that had not been brought into contact, by one way or another, with the direct influence and authority of the colonial state.

Increased production of vital primary goods in the colonies would help to reduce British dependence upon the United States, uphold the international value of sterling, and enable the country to earn dollars. British officials at the time were not only concerned with the state of the war-time economy and the continued ability of Britain to maintain a major belligerent role, but also with the vital question of the international economic and political position of the country vis-à-vis a greatly strengthened United States in the post-war world. War-time controls, such as bulk purchases, marketing monopolies, fixed prices, rigid exchange controls, import licensing schemes and shipping management, were organised through a variety of newly established official bodies – the Resident Minister's office, Governors' Conferences, War Councils, Economic Councils, Allied Combined Boards, the East African Production and Supply Council, and the Ministry of War Transport, to name but a few. The machinery for these bodies was often hastily created and not very sophisticated. Smooth operations were also hampered by shortages of skilled personnel and inter-departmental rivalries.[11] In addition to the increased role of civil government, the military forces established extensive controls over aspects of the colonial economies, especially labour supply, food production and transport. Large areas of North and North East Africa were subject to direct military administration both during and after the war.

Such war-time controls, although extensive, were usually aimed at specific sectors of the colonial economy or problems associated with the changes brought about by the war. Certain economic problems seemed to be beyond the control of government either because of limited official resources or an inability to establish effective regulatory controls. Inflation is a case in point. Prices of most basic foodstuffs and consumption commodities increased in the war years by as much as 75–100 per cent, or more, and although governments were aware of the difficulties that this caused and the potential for social unrest, attempts to control prices were rarely successful other than in a limited way or over a short term. Equally administrations proved incapable of regulating the movement of people to the urban areas and effectively controlling the growth of shanty towns on the edges of the rapidly growing towns.[12] Even in South Africa the carefully constructed legislation of the inter-war years which attempted to regulate population movement and racial segregation began to break apart in war-time. The black industrial labour force not only increased but moved into jobs formerly reserved for whites and began to organise in labour unions, not least in a rapidly expanding manufacturing sector.[13]

During the First World War the colonial powers had organised the raw materials and labour of Africa for war purposes. In the Second World War the process was repeated more systematically and thoroughly. In order to increase the output of raw materials, new sources of manpower had to be tapped and thousands of peasants were forced into a state-regulated wage-labour system. As a result of the Depression of the 1930s, the prices of most African minerals and cash crops had been reduced. The increased demands of war-time led to a rise in the volume of output and dramatically raised the prices of primary products. The mineral resources of South Africa, the Belgian Congo and Northern Rhodesia, and to a lesser extent of Sierra Leone and the Gold Coast, became vital to Allied war-time production.

As the United States geared up for war production, she increased her demand for minerals from Latin America and also Africa. The Belgian Congo was the main area of her sub-Saharan interests, providing industrial diamonds, cobalt, chromite, vanadium and copper. By 1945 US finance capital dominated the Congo mining industry and a large proportion of that colony's trade. In West Africa the production of manganese and bauxite was started or extended during the war, and after 1942 ruthless, and largely ineffective, efforts were made to increase the output of Nigerian tin by using conscripted labour. In the years following the war Africa's mineral production remained strategically important to the Western powers. These resources were not only useful as dollar earners to the impoverished colonial powers but also vital to the industries that had expanded largely as a result of the war – the aeronautical industry, the high technology industries that required high grade alloys and steels, and the atomic programme.[14]

Agricultural output increased in many colonies because of war-time demands and new markets. Government controls over production and marketing in the first two years of the war were mainly a selective response to aid those industries, such as sisal,[15] which had lost their traditional markets. The great transformation followed Pearl Harbor and Japanese conquest of the South East Asian imperial possessions, with their essential raw materials. The colonial state in Africa now promoted the production of crops such as rubber and cotton, which helped save dollars and also contributed to war requirements. Parallel to this were measures to encourage the production of more foodstuffs to fulfil the requirements of the army and the urban areas. Much of this new increased production – for example, crops such as maize – came from white farmers in East and Central Africa, although some African producers also benefited from the expanding demand and higher prices. Generally, however, African peasant producers saw little positive gain during the war, as prices, particularly of imports, rose above the fixed prices given for primary produce. Increased war-time agricultural production and guaranteed prices rescued many marginal white farmers in Kenya and Southern Rhodesia, who emerged from the war with a greatly strengthened political and economic control over the settler states.[16]

Attempts to increase agricultural output were hindered in many areas by military and labour recruiting programmes, which removed young able-bodied men from the land. In some parts of East, Central and West Africa peasant production of food fell, and additional labour burdens were placed on women and children. Further severe restrictions on food production came with the severe droughts in central Tanganyika in 1942–3 and in the southern sahelian region in 1943–4. Famine marched close behind the loss of manpower and failed rains. In Northern Nigeria, and elsewhere on the continent, government food allocation policies and price controls often discouraged peasant farmers from growing food crops and failed to prevent famine.[17] Where farmers did earn more cash from higher crop and cattle prices, their new wealth was invariably eroded by inflation; additionally, import controls and shortages of fertilisers, seeds and tools meant that investment and improvement in African agriculture was slight, with increased money incomes being expended largely on a limited range of consumer goods.

Africa's volume of trade increased considerably during the war, but trade, like production, was distorted as colonial economies were fashioned to the economic and political interests of the metropoles and the value of money fell. Small-scale import substitution industries, developed, for example, in the Belgian Congo, contributed little to African development. Industrialisation was most rapid in South Africa, where manufacturing output more than doubled in the years 1939–45.

The exploitation engendered by the war continued in peace-time. The African colonies became economic assets to aid metropolitan recovery and reconstruction, and a source of foreign-revenue-earning exports. As the Cold War heated up, Africa also acquired a strategic as well as an economic significance. Commodity control boards, quotas and fixed prices, part of the apparatus of war-time economic control, were maintained and extended. Grandiose imperial agricultural schemes, such as the groundnut scheme in southern Tanganyika, were launched to reap abundant surpluses, which proved to be chimerical. Behind such British ideas was an attempt to retain a position as a world power against the ascendant United States.[18] That colonial Africa's economy continued to expand after the war and to earn increased funds for development owed more to the commodity boom attendant on rapid post-war European recovery, aided by the increased demands for raw materials generated by the Cold War and the Korean War, than to the investment programmes, such as Fonds d'Investissement et de Développement Economique et Social (FIDES) and the Colonial Development and Welfare Acts, introduced in the 1940s by the French and British.

The other area of war-time exploitation was African labour. Manpower in large numbers was required by the armed forces as combatants and also as non-combatant labour, and to expand war-time production on plantations, farms and public works. Most parts of the continent experienced the effects of the direct or indirect search for labour. No comprehensive figures exist for the total number of people enlisted for the war effort but throughout the continent it must have amounted to many millions of men, women and children. On the outbreak of war the small colonial armies rapidly expanded. French colonial troops fought in Europe in 1939–40 but British policy initially restricted African soldiers to campaigns within the continent. Under the terms of the armistice of June 1940 the French colonial army was reduced. Italy's entry into the war and the emergence of the Vichy regime accelerated British military recruiting in the colonies. African troops from the Sudan, East and West Africa, and also South Africa, were successfully employed against a largely black Italian colonial army in Somalia and Ethiopia. From 1942 to 1947 African soldiers, including units from the Belgian Congo, helped to garrison North Africa. The King's African Rifles and the Royal West African Frontier Force fought the Japanese in Burma and served as back-up forces in India and Ceylon. By mid-1945 nearly 400 000 African soldiers were employed by the British; the French and Italians also had large African armies.[19]

Most men in uniform had non-combatant roles as labourers, drivers, guards and orderlies. South Africa attempted to confine non-European recruits to non-combatant roles but by 1944 the Union Defence Force included blacks and coloureds bearing arms. The peace-time French colonial army had been conscripted, mainly in West Africa and Madagascar; the Italians also used conscripts. Up to 1939 the British and Belgian forces employed volunteers. Indeed, the military forces in British Africa were little more than a lightly armed gendarmerie. Conscription was introduced on the outbreak of war and extended in 1940 and again in 1943–4 as manpower was required for the campaigns in North Africa and Asia. Recruiting followed the well tried and traditional pattern: propaganda, area quotas, pressure on chiefs and various methods of compulsion ranging from sudden round-ups to statutory conscription. Generally African soldiers proved to be both loyal and effective. The few mutinies that occurred, mostly towards the end of the war, were occasioned by the slow processes of demobilisation resulting from shipping shortages and the priority given to white soldiers required as civil labour in the metropoles. The most serious mutinies happened in 1944 in British Somaliland, the Belgian Congo and Senegal.[20]

Alongside the military demands for labour was the civil authorities' use of forced labour to increase output in the mines and docks, on farms and plantations. The Italians, Belgians, French and Portuguese customarily used forced labour, often disregarding the international convention of 1930. The British acted more cautiously. During the war emergency forced labour increased in most parts of Africa. The British Colonial Office only reluctantly agreed to the introduction of forced labour schemes in certain territories and for specific industries. These included the Nigerian tin mines on the Jos Plateau and agricultural production in East and Central Africa. Altogether several million people were forcibly employed as labourers on schemes connected directly or indirectly with the war.

In Africa the war acted as a catalyst for social and economic change. Urbanisation, rising costs of living, new levels of expectation by Africans, many of whom had enjoyed the welfare system of the armed forces, the growth of labour unions, and high levels of post-war unemployment placed new pressures on the colonial state. The limited accommodationist steps of the late 1930s and early 1940s were accentuated. Colonial bureaucracies expanded to service new social welfare infrastructures, to develop agriculture and transport systems under the direct management of the colonial state. Investment came from metropolitan funds and also from the foreign revenue earned by the commodity export boom of the late 1940s and early 1950s. Economic development, even of the relatively meagre kind experienced by sub-Saharan economies in this period, spawned a rising demand for further social welfare expenditure, which in a very short period of time made colonies increasingly costly possessions in which expenditure was beginning to outpace returns. In such circumstances decolonisation became in the 1950s both a politically and economically sensible policy to pursue, though with caution. However, this was barely perceived by Europeans or Africans during or immediately after the war. The intention of the colonial rulers was to remain in charge for decades. Indeed the French policy proclaimed at Brazzaville in 1944 was clearly integrationist. Africa had proved its value in war-time and would have a vital economic role to play in aiding French recovery and in reasserting her position as a great power. States that think of themselves as great do not willingly abandon territory or empire.

To what extent did the war stimulate nationalism in Africa? By 1945 a more militant nationalism had emerged in North Africa, prepared to confront the *pieds noires* minority in Algeria who resisted reform. In South Africa the expansion of war-time manufacturing industry had led to an increase in the black working force, had eroded white–black wage differentials, and promoted black labour unions. Younger men challenged the older, more passive politics of acceptance long pursued by the ANC leadership, and advocated that black numerical strength be used to pressure the white regime towards greater social and economic equity. Faced with a crisis that threatened to undermine the segregationist legislation of the past three decades, the whites responded in 1948 by electing a government pledged to turn back any liberalising impulse and to harden race boundaries with a policy of apartheid.[21]

Elsewhere in sub-Saharan Africa the post-war constitutional reforms of the British and the French represented an attempt to forge new alliances. The educated elite was enlisted as a partner of the colonial state; traditional rulers and the systems of authority slowly assembled in the inter-war years were abandoned and gradually wound down. But even modest measures of reform encouraged further pressure on the cautious reformers. It came from the educated elite, who demanded a greater share of power and who found a measure of popular support from the urban population, many of whom were unemployed or under-employed, from farmers disgruntled at fixed commodity prices and government policies, and from peasants protesting against the alienation of land by white settlers.[22] Resistance to colonial rule in Madagascar, Algeria, the Ivory Coast, Cameroon and Kenya was met with firm and often fearsome repression by the metropoles' military might. The large-scale operations in Indo-China, and later in Algeria, indicated the extent to which the French were prepared to go to counter serious challenge to their colonial rule. The British were more pragmatic and generally avoided military confrontation, although in the late 1940s, when Cold War fears grew, they saw even West African bourgeois nationalist politics as part of the 'red menace'.

At the end of the war the global position of the European imperial powers was greatly weakened. Defeat in Europe and Asia emphasised their decline, while the war had been fought largely with United States credits and Soviet manpower. The world of 1945 was a vastly different place to that of 1939. Western Europe was now dwarfed by the two super-powers, both avowedly anti-colonial, and the United States eager to see the colonial markets opened to her trade goods. Sub-Saharan Africa had an enhanced economic value for the United States, as the Cold War developed, her anti-colonialism became muted while her capitalist penetration increased. And yet the war that weakened the colonial powers globally also resulted, paradoxically, in the strengthening of the colonial state in Africa. This newly acquired power lasted for little more than a decade and a half and in that time it was steadily assailed by indigenous political forces demanding a transfer of the levers of political power to African hands. That increased power of the colonial state became the inheritance of the new rulers of Africa's independent states from the late 1950s onwards.

NOTES

1. Michael Crowder (ed.), *The Cambridge History of Africa, vol. 8, c.1940–1975* (Cambridge, 1984), ch. 1. John Shuckburgh, 'Colonial Civil History of the War', 4 vols (unpub. typescript, 1949) is a useful survey of British policy and practice during the war, and copies are available in the Public Record Office, Kew; the Institute of Commonwealth Studies, University of London; and in the Library of the Royal Commonwealth Society, London. By contrast with Africa, there are studies on the impact of the war on the American continent: R. A. Humphreys, *Latin America and the Second World War, Vol. 1 1939–1942* (London, 1981), and Ken Post, *Strike the Iron, A Colony at War, Jamaica 1939–1945* (New Jersey, 1981).
2. See the British official war histories, e.g. I. S. O. Playfair, *The Mediterranean and Middle East*, vol. 2 (London 1956).
3. See Rudolf von Albertini, *Decolonization. The Administration and Future of the Colonies 1919–1963* (1966, 2nd ed.; and Eng. trs., New York, 1982); Henri Grimal, *Decolonization: the British, French, Dutch and Belgian Empires 1919–1965* (1965; Eng. trs., London, 1978); John Hargreaves, *The End of Colonial Rule in West Africa* (London, 1979); Prosser Gifford and Wm Roger Louis (eds), *The Transfer of Power in Africa* (New Haven, 1982).
4. Wm Roger Louis, *Imperialism at Bay, 1941–1945* (Oxford, 1977).

5. Rosaleen Smyth, 'The Development of Government Propaganda in Northern Rhodesia up to 1953' (unpub. PhD thesis, Univ. of London, 1983); and 'War Propaganda during the Second World War: Northern Rhodesia', *Afr. Affairs*, 83, 332 (July 1984).
6. John Iliffe, *A Modern History of Tanganyika* (Cambridge, 1979), and also his 'A History of the Dockworkers of Dar es Salaam', *Tanzania Notes and Records*, 71 (1970). Anthony Clayton and D. C. Savage, *Government and Labour in Kenya 1895–1963* (London, 1974), ch. 7. Wale Oyemakinde, 'Michael Imoudu and the Emergence of Militant Trade Unionism in Nigeria, 1940–1942', *J. Hist. Soc. Nigeria*, 3 (Dec. 1974).
7. J. M. Lee and Martin Petter, *The Colonial Office and Development Policy: Organization and Planning of a Metropolitan Initiative 1939–1945* (London, 1982).
8. D. W. Ray, 'The Takoradi Route: Roosevelt's pre-war venture beyond the Western Hemisphere', *J. Am. History* , LXII, 2 (Sept. 1975); Lloyd N. Beecher, 'The Second World War and United States politico-expansionism and the case of Liberia, 1938–1945', *Diplomatic History*, 3 (Fall 1979); J. Donald Miller, 'The United States and Colonial Sub-Saharan Africa, 1939–1945' (Ph.D. thesis, Univ. of Connecticut, 1981).
9. Michael Crowder, 'The 1939–45 War and West Africa', in J. F. A. Ajayi and Crowder (eds), *History of West Africa*, vol. 2 (London, 1974); Jean Suret-Canale, *French Colonialism in Tropical Africa 1900–1945* (London, 1971), pp. 462–90; Brian Weinstein, *Eboué* (New York, 1972); James Giblin, 'The Vichy Years in French Africa: A Period of African Resistance to Capitalism' (MA thesis, McGill Univ., 1978).
10. See the essays in *Le Congo Belge Durant la Seconde Guerre Mondiale* (Académie Royale des Sciences D'Outre-Mer, Brussels, 1983).
11. P. T . Bauer, *West African Trade* (London, 1963), particularly chs 11, 19 and 20. A. Olurunfemi, 'Effects of Wartime Trade Controls on Nigerian Cocoa Traders and Producers, 1939–45'. A Case Study of the Hazards of a Dependent Economy', *Int. J. Afr. Hist. Stud.*, 13, 4 (1980). W. Oyemakinde, 'The Pullen Marketing Scheme: A Trial in Food Price Control, 1941–47', *J. Hist. Soc. Nigeria*, IV (1973). See also N. A. Cox-George, *Studies in Finance and Development 1914–50* (London, 1973).
12. Bruce Fetter, 'Elizabethville and Lubumbashi: The Segmentary Growth of a Colonial City 1910—1945' (unpub. PhD thesis, Univ. of Wisconsin, 1968), ch. V and Appendix; Roger Anstey, *King Leopold's Legacy. The Congo under Belgian Rule 1908–1960* (London, 1966), ch. VIII.
13. John Lewis, *Industrialisation and Trade Union Organisation in South Africa 1925–1955* (Cambridge, 1984).
14. Raymond E. Dumett, 'Africa's Strategic Minerals During the Second World War', *J. Afr. Hist.*, 26, 4 (1985).
15. Nicholas Westcott, 'The East African Sisal Industry, 1929–1949: The Marketing of a Colonial Commodity During Depression and War', *J. Afr. Hist.*, 25, 4 (1984).
16. Ian Spencer, 'Settler Dominance, Agricultural Production and the Second World War in Kenya', *J. Afr. Hist.*, 21, 4 (1980).
17. Michael Watts, *Silent Violence: Food, famine and Peasantry in Northern Nigeria* (Berkeley, 1983), pp. 327–35.

18. Hugh Dalton, Chancellor of the Exchequer in the post-war Labour Government, argued that the British aim should be 'to organize the middle of the planet – Western Europe, the Middle East, the Commonwealth . . . If we pushed on and developed Africa, we could have the United States dependent upon us, and eating out of our hand in four or five years. Two great mountains of manganese are in Sierra Leone, etc. U.S. is very barren of essential minerals, and in Africa we have them all.' Quoted by Yusef Bangura, *Britain and Commonwealth Africa. The Politics of Economic Relations 1951–75* (Manchester, 1983, pp. 19–20.
19. Rita Headrick, 'African Soldiers in World War II', *Armed Forces and Society*, 4, 3 (May 1978).
20. Myron Echenberg, 'Tragedy at Tiaroye: the Senegalese Soldiers' Uprising of 1944', in Peter G. W. Gutkind, Robin Cohen and Jean Copans (eds), *African Labour History* (Berkeley and London, 1979).
21. G. O. Olusanya, *The Second World War and Politics in Nigeria 1939–1945* (London, 1973). Peter Walshe, *The Rise of Nationalism in South Africa. The ANC 1912–52* (London, 1971). Tom Lodge, *Black Politics in South Africa since 1945* (London, 1983).
22. For a cautionary note about the role of ex-servicemen in African nationalism see David Killingray, 'Soldiers, Ex-Servicemen and Politics in the Gold Coast, 1939–1950', *J. Mod. Afr. Stud.*, 21, 3 (1983).

2 British Imperial Economic Policy During the War*

MICHAEL COWEN and NICHOLAS WESTCOTT

> Hands off the British Empire is our maxim and it [will] not be weakened or smirched to please sob-stuff merchants at home or foreigners of any hue. W. S. CHURCHILL, 1944[1]

> I feel sure you (Beaverbrook) cannot have looked into the extraordinary and possibly mortal consequences of our coming out of this war owing India a bigger debt, after having defended her, than we owed to the United States at the end of the last war. Your note does not seem at all to take into consideration these frightful consequences.
> W. S. CHURCHILL, 1944[2]

This chapter examines the extent to which both the principle of total war and the experience of the Second World War reduced colonial autonomy and centralised imperial economic policy around the entity of a British national economy. The argument here is that British centralisation was accentuated during the war as the British government deliberately tried to regulate the use of sterling for international payments. If the use of international money within the Empire could be regulated through the British state, then it was hoped that a changed pattern of trade and production might be determined to conform to a distinct British national advantage. Control over sterling was a means of controlling the distribution of productive resources within the Empire without directly controlling colonial production itself.

British imperial policy was faced during the war not only with fending

* Research for parts of this chapter was financed by the ESRC.

off threats, whether from national enemies or allies, from without but also from preventing collapse from within the Empire. War did not simply increase the degree of colonial attachment to Britain; British desperation and resulting imperial dirigisme was supposed to increase British dependence on the colonies.

Lee and Petter, for instance, argue a prevailing view thus:

> Never had a periphery been expected to keep in such close step with metropolitan decrees. The colonial system became more regularised and colonial societies more regulated. Yet in a paradoxical way wartime centralisation had the effect of introducing a greater degree of remoteness into relationships between London and 'the man on the spot'.[3]

If the conditions for constructing a British national economy are spelt out, then it will become apparent that 'a greater degree of remoteness' was entailed by a greater degree of centralisation, and that there is no paradox between British regulation and colonial autonomy.

Prewar colonial autonomy was registered by the Treasury injunction to make the Colonial Office ensure that each colony be financially self-sufficient on each government's current account. This principle was dropped by the acceptance of the terms of the Moyne Report and the 1940 Colonial Development and Welfare Act, implementation of which was suspended during the war.[4] Furthermore, for the inter-war period at any rate, colonial autonomy was reinforced in terms of British state regulation, by the manner in which investment in colonial raw material production was guided by the profitability criteria of individual firms, whether or not of British origin, and little determined by the prerequisites of British national need.[5] And if investment in colonial industrial production was constrained by the British national desire to protect employment in Britain, then colonial governments were not subject to the pressure which enforced industrialisation might have imposed on the premise of administration – to insulate colonial subjects politically from the economic subjection of becoming a proletariat.[6]

The construction of a British national economy, it has been argued, owed much to the inter-war depression and the Ottawa agreements of 1932. National self-sufficiency is registered for the specific period between 1931 and 1950, in which 'British trade shifted significantly towards an exchange of British manufactures for primary products from the Empire' and in which the import share of the British domestic market for manufactures fell from a 24 per cent peak in 1931 to 11 per cent in 1937.[7] Furthermore, this expansion of intra-imperial trade followed the evolution of the sterling area, as a bloc of countries whose governments deliberately chose to prefer sterling as international money, after 1931, when British sterling went off the gold standard.[8]

However, the argument here is that the construction of the idea of a British national economy was separate from the attempt to evolve an integrated trading bloc in the name of the British Empire.[9] Ideas of a British economy and of the British Empire were distinct. It was precisely the squeezing of Britain as an entity, of money and production, between the United States and the Empire that led Keynes and others to articulate a specific national economic interest.

With the inception of Lend Lease in March 1941, British production was directed to the war effort as part of a combined system of production and allocation with the United States. Between 1940 and 1945 one-third of British imports came from the US, but at the peak of the war, 1942–4, 55 per cent of imports came as part of operations of combined boards.[10] In view of production constraints, largely raw materials for the US but labour and equipment for Britain, the combined boards centralised production decisions and allocated commodities across national boundaries. In this sense the degree to which colonial production may be said to have been centralised was dependent upon the way in which production in Britain was integrated with that of the United States. However, the international payments of money for commodities, which were allocated centrally across national boundaries, were not centralised in any combined system of finance. Otto Clarke (a Treasury official who played a major part in drawing up post-war ideas for implementing colonial development to recapture British economic independence from the US) has made a fundamental distinction between Britain fighting a combined war, on account of production and supply, and a debtor's war, on account of finance: 'The debtor system for running the "finance and national economy" half of the war, was an important cause of paradox that we "won" the war, but at the same time "lost" it'.[11] But the kernel of the construction of a national economy lay in the independent control over money through the nation state, and the ability to provide self-sufficiency, independently of the United States, was premised upon the independent control over finance for international payments. Keynes, as we show, successfully urged that external war financial policy was to be orientated around the principle that dollar debt be minimised and sterling debt be maximised. If sterling debt was maximised, then it would be through the British state that external claims by countries holding sterling would be minimised.

External claims would be claims on British productive resources for use in the Empire and the British Treasury would subject the claim to scrutiny and regulation according to the terms of the political relation between each country of the Empire and the British state itself.

The combined system of production and allocation developed around the doctrine of Reciprocal Aid, which, as Sayers explains, rested on two conflicting principles. The first was that each allied nation directed its productive resources to the war effort and maximised the use of resources for war. This principle entailed that consumption within each country would be equally minimised and thus all countries would equally bear sacrifice for total war. The second principle was that no allied nation should end the war bearing a burden of net financial debt to any other as a result of the total war effort. This entailed that were a country to maximise production but not be subject to immediate internal input constraints, then countries supplying inputs externally, as exports, would meet the cost of resources free of charge, and without a counter claim against future imports. Thus, the US supplied exports to Britain worth some £4 billion during Lend Lease but (with Canada to the UK alone) provided £5 billion worth of grants to cover dollar imports.[12] The principles conflicted with each other because the grants for imports were conditional upon the degree it could be shown that the 'debtor' country was bearing sacrifice for war by maximising production and minimising civilian consumption.

Clarke's objection to the debtor part of war, in the British case, was that the US government confined and circumscribed the use of US imports for immediate war objectives. It was able to do so because finance, as grants, was allocated unilaterally by the US administration and Congress and not subject to international negotiation as under the combined system of commodity production and allocation. 'Any rational purpose (if such existed),' for allocating grants, Clarke concludes, 'was to ensure that at the war's end the British economy would be crippled.'[13] US circumscription reduced the ability of any British government to reduce consumption any further in the post-war period and to direct productive capacity towards increasing industrial capacity for the post-war period. As such, Britain ended the war disadvantaged and this negated the equality of sacrifice principle.

Conflict between the principles of equality of sacrifice and no net national advantage could only be worked out through the experience of war and not by altering the principles of total war. Firstly, it was appreciated that there was no equality, in any material form, between Britain and the US as national entities. In the colonial connection, Law of the Foreign Office argued: 'We can only work with the Americans upon a basis of partnership. And we must realise that on paper, we shall not appear as the senior partner. That position must go to the US by virtue of their resources and their population. We, for our part, can hope to redress the balance – and more – by virtue of our experience and our greater political sagacity'.[14] Keynes pushed cleverness to its limit in external finance but only within Reciprocal Aid terms. Secondly, the British Cabinet, and particularly Keynes and Churchill, applied the terms of Reciprocal Aid against the Empire, and India in particular. Sterling debt, owed to the Empire, was to be treated not as debt but as, in effect, a grant to Britain because India, for instance, had not and could not bear equality of sacrifice with Britain.

Through pressing colonial governments to increase taxation and local borrowing, to improve import controls and increase duties,[15] the Colonial Office hoped to show that the reduction in consumption would approach that rate of decrease which was being achieved in Britain and so fulfil the equality of sacrifice principle. But aside from the fact that colonies in Africa were part of total war, by extension, rather than in war theatres, the equal sacrifice principle could not be applied directly through state controls because the balance of class forces was so different from that which was expressed within British state power. Local capitalist interests, whether of associated estate owners or as traders and merchants, became well organised through the state without facing, as in Britain, any form of organised labour at the level of state power. In Britain, the Labour Party part of war government could demand the promise of increased social consumption after the war in return for acquiescing in direct and immediate sacrifice.[16] In the colonies consumption was reduced by consumer-good price inflation as part of the experience of war and not because of the direct application of the principles of total war. And, in any case, and following from this, no general principle could govern the terms on which equality of sacrifice could be established. As Sayers asks, 'how were the pains and penalties of the Bengal famine to be weighed against fire and blast in London's East End?'[17] Finance, through the issue of sterling balances, came to establish the terms of equal sacrifice but only as national terms of exchange.

To conceive of equality of sacrifice in national terms did not easily meet the presumption of total war. Milward shows that for the German state, war was an instrument of economic policy to dissolve the economic boundaries of the nation state, a residue of nineteenth-century liberalism, through creating *Grossraumwirtschaft*, the economy of large areas.[18] However, under the British conception of total war, economic policy is an instrument of war. In Milward's terms, the absolute economic potential for war is realised in so far as the sole criterion of economic policy becomes the maximisation of production for war. However, where the threat of human and physical destruction is relatively uncertain and national state power does not face immediate annihilation, then the relative economic potential for war is directed towards specific strategic objectives. The maximisation of war production and minimisation of civilian consumption are not objectives of economic policy as part of the relative potential for war.[19] However formally they were meant to be part of the total British war effort, colonies in Africa faced conditions for the relative rather than absolute economic potential for war. If Africa's colonial resources were not marginal to the British national interest after the war, the British Empire in Africa was marginal to total war for Britain. Even after the fall of France, Churchill reckoned sub-Saharan Africa to be of little strategic or economic significance. Cranborne (as Colonial Secretary) pointed out that there was no strategic plan to deal with possible war, in Africa, against Spain and Vichy France:

> The magnitude of our African interests is out of all proportion to our defences ... [African] resources [60 million persons, minerals, food, fats] are of immense value to us in war: and it is essential not only that we should continue to command them for ourselves but also that we should be in a position to deny them to the enemy ... [Africa] may turn out to be the decisive [war] theatre. Our defensive positions there are lamentably weak.[20]

Churchill took three weeks to reply and dismissed any prospect of war with Spain or Vichy France or that South Africa would go neutral or pro-German. He suggested that the Colonial Office develop its own plans for the War Cabinet but through the Middle East Committee: 'I should deprecate setting up a Special [African] Committee. We are overrun by them, like the Australians were by the rabbits'.[21] When an Africa committee was established in 1942 to superintend regional authorities of supply, it was so remote from the presumed colonial production drive that it could not decide, for Kenya, whether food production should have priority over cotton export production.[22] Earl

Winterton (a former minister in Baldwin's cabinet and large landowner in Northern Rhodesia) campaigned along Cranborne's lines and pleaded for a Commons debate, which took 6 weeks to arrange: 'Even then, after two excellent speeches by Mr Amery in regard to India's war effort, and by Mr Hall (Labour Colonial spokesman and 1945 Colonial Secretary) about the corresponding one of the British Colonial Empire, the debate developed into a discussion on the position of the Government of India vis-à-vis the Congress Party'.[23] He put colonial distance down to residues of 'Little Britain' Baldwinism, which differed from the imperial one-nation design of Disraeli because it made the Tory party suffer from 'self-reproach, amounting almost to masochism' about the Empire and imperial power.[24] Churchillism was clearly a welcome reaction against Baldwinism for the likes of Winterton, but Churchill was constrained from conflating the Imperial delusion with the material and strategic worth of different parts of Empire.

During 1940 Churchill pressed for offensive action against the Italian army in Abyssinia and accused the British generals of lacking 'obstinacy and vigour in resistance' in their claims that the Italian army possessed 'hopeless superiority' over the British army in eastern Africa.[25] The Italian army was estimated at twenty-seven brigades against ten British brigades, which included two from West Africa and one from South Africa. Unlike the Italian army, British formations had no AA or AT guns and no tanks and were 'kept at a low scale of equipment'.[26] Anthony Eden (as Foreign Secretary) undertook a military review of Africa and suggested that irregular war was the most effective means of combat against German and Italian forces: 'We are not strong enough to launch sustained offensives on the approved scale, but it should be possible for us to harass the enemy in subject countries where he temporarily holds sway'.[27] It is on these grounds that the defeat of the Italian army in Abyssinia created the belief in the moral superiority of British heroism in overcoming and vanquishing Italian cowardice. The fall of British Malaya, however, possibly and similarly could be explained by material and regular strategic inadequacies, but if racial criteria were invoked as part of the explanation, it was because of the mythology of ingrained British superiority that the enemy were so underestimated.

The fall of Malaya and Pearl Harbor switched the focus of imperial defence in Africa eastwards through fear of Japanese advance and occupation across the Indian Ocean. If the Japanese war threat had been officially underestimated before the end of 1941, it was overestimated thereafter in the popular mind. But in the minds of imperial defence, the maximum possible scale of Japanese attack on Africa was estimated to be generous but not grossly threatening. On the assumption that one-third of the total Japanese battle fleet could be committed to the Indian Ocean in March 1942 (before Midway and Coral Sea), the maximum threat was reckoned to be a brigade force of 5000, which could only seize and hold relatively lightly defended ports such as Mombasa.[28] The German threat to West Africa was then reported as being 'token'.[29] Japanese strategy, like German blitzkrieg strategy, was directed at short campaigns, and even before 1942 supply lines in the Pacific were overstretched.[30] It was not on strategic grounds that colonial Africa became less marginal to total war after 1942. As we indicate below, it was the threat to India and the collapse of Far East sources of colonial supply that indirectly created sources of military demand for African colonial production.

For the war period as a whole, the colonial capacity to supply materials should not be overemphasised. Unlike the post-war period, Africa was no potential *Grossraum* for Britain. It was estimated that in 1937 only three colonially produced commodities, cocoa, rubber and tin, separately accounted for more than 40 per cent of world production; cotton, coffee, tobacco, sugar, and copper accounted for 1, 2, 1, 6, and 12 per cent respectively of world output.[31] Between 1941 and 1945 the above accounted as *Empire* commodities for 60, 27, 20, 35, and 63 per cent of the volume of British imports. But only in the cases of cocoa and cotton (and, to a lesser extent, tea) was there a substantial increase in imports from African colonies.[32] Equally, in 1936, nominal British investment, of all forms, in East and West Africa accounted for 2 per cent of total British investment overseas; sub-Saharan Africa, including South Africa, accounted for 16 per cent of British investment in the *Empire* as opposed to 22 per cent for India or 33 per cent for Australia and New Zealand.[33] In short, in the words of Hancock and Gowing, 'the economic and social structure of the Colonial dependencies could not sustain a ponderous mobilisation' in 1941.[34] India was to experience just this, and between 1942 and 1944 accounted for one-half of British military expenditure in the sterling area, as opposed to 6 per cent for East and West Africa, 5 per cent for South Africa and 2.5 per cent for Australia and New Zealand.[35] And as India was to account for one-third of wartime sterling balances, the measure of British debt to the Empire, so it was to be focus and object of British imperial economic policy. Whatever the experience of war for specific colonies, as part of total war and by virtue of material and strategic significance, the African colonial empire was a remote extension of policy towards India.

STERLING BALANCES

Sterling balances are formally defined as external short-term liabilities which are held in London for countries trading with the use of sterling as an international currency. The balances represented the surplus of sterling earnings over expenditures for a wide range of countries but were significantly largest for a selected number of Empire countries. 'It has been a prime object of policy on the part of the Treasury and the Bank of England', wrote Keynes, 'so as to conduct their technical tasks that we should end the war in a financial position which did not leave us hopelessly at the mercy of the United States'.[36] In view of Clark's distinction between a combined and debtor war, Keynes's statement was sanguine, because his purpose was to show that the corollary of minimising British external dollar debt was to maximise sterling debt. He approved that 'by cunning and kindness, we have persuaded the outside world to lend us upwards of the prodigious total of £3,000 million. The very size of these external debts is itself a protection. The old saying holds. Owe your banker £1,000 and you are at his mercy; owe him £1 million and the position is reversed.'[37] The 'outside world' to which Keynes referred was that of the colonial empire, the Middle East of Egypt, Iraq and Palestine and, above all, of India. A financial bloc of the sterling area, the inner circle of which centred on these areas, was not in this view part of a British national economy as Keynes and the other war-time mandarins understood a national economy to be. The financial sterling bloc, of variegated territorial units, was held at arm's length from the British national economic core precisely to permit the British Treasury to determine whether and by what means and by how much the sterling debt would be repaid.

In the case of British internal war finance, state expenditure was financed by taxation and borrowing under the explicit premise and with the expressed promise that forced saving, increasingly extracted out of current wages, would be realised post-war as increased consumption. The Beveridge plan for welfare expenditure was framed to realise the promise.[38] By refusing to extend the promise to realise forced saving to the sterling bloc, it would be easier to satisfy the expectations which war sacrifice imposed upon British wage-earners. Keynes was explicit on this: 'It is pretty well understood by those concerned (the sterling bloc) that they are in our hands and cannot successfully claim to use this sterling except in accordance with principles to be agreed with us hereafter.[39] Within this restricted sense of a national economy, the imperialist ideas, as portrayed by Hobson and Lenin, in maintaining

TABLE 2.1 *Financing the British balance of payments current account deficit, 1939–45 (£ billion)*

	Current account deficit	*Overseas disinvest-ment*	*Net drawings (+) from gold and dollar reserves £ billion*	*Net dollar grants*	*Sterling balances*	*%*
	1	*2*	*3*	*4*	*5*	*5/1*
1939[a]	0.2	0.1	0	—	0.1	50
40	0.8	0.2	+0.4	—	0.2	25
41	1.1	0.3	−0.1	0.3	0.6	55
42	1.7	0.2	−0.1	1.1	0.5	30
43	2.1	0.2	−0.2	1.4	0.7	33
44	2.5	0.1	−0.1	1.8	0.7	28
45	1.6	0.1	0	0.8	0.7	44
1939–45	10.0	1.2	−0.1	5.4	3.5[b]	35

[a] September–December
[b] Includes dollar liabilities but only £0.4 of total £3.5 bill.

SOURCES Sayers, p. 499; Moggeridge (1972), p. 1032.

that Empire sustained the material expectations of British Labour, had merit for Keynes and Churchill only providing that Empire was of the outside world and not of Britain.

The sterling debt was termed sterling balances for countries which held them but 'quick liabilities' to ameliorate American concern. Table 2.1 shows the extent to which sterling balances helped to finance the British current account balance of payments deficit. Until United States Lend Lease appeared in March 1941, sterling balances financed about one-half of the deficit, which rose rapidly until 1944. During the period of the phoney war and until the fall of France exports were maintained at not far less than 1938 levels, but during the period of total war, until 1944, they slumped to 30 per cent of the 1938 volume level. In current cost terms, exports covered nearly 60 per cent of British imports in 1938; this proportion fell to one-third in 1941 and 15 per cent by 1944.[40] Exports were deliberately restrained to direct the use of labour power and resources towards war production. The chronic shortage of merchant shipping after 1940 and the disinvestment of overseas marketable securities, insurance company and other assets, reduced invisible earnings, the traditional source of cover for the balance of trade deficit.

Whereas the British government was forced to increase the British import surplus deliberately, sterling bloc governments contrived to reduce import surpluses by expanding exports and restricting imports. Colonial governments were urged by London to restrict consumption by raising taxes and cutting imports. Their experience was uneven but some colonies, particularly in Africa, cut imports so drastically as to entail real hardship. For instance, Kenya's and Uganda's pre-war import surplus was cut by one half. And this was accompanied by a substantial shift in the pattern of trade, with India and South Africa replacing Britain and Japan as major sources of supply for imports. For instance, East African rubber was exported to South Africa in return for imports of tyres produced in South Africa; cotton, which was previously exported to Japan, went to India, which supplied cotton piece goods, previously imported from Japan, to East and West African markets. Tables 2.2 and 2.3 show the extent to which trade patterns changed as a result of war experience. For the most part, and except for the dramatic increase in post-war West African export surpluses, the change was a once and for all replacement of trade with Germany, German-occupied Europe and Japan with that of other Empire countries, particularly India and South Africa. The scale of the reduction of the import surplus (as for East Africa) is understated because export prices for the colonies were closely tied to production costs through supply controls, but the British and Indian governments refused to control their export and colonial import prices. Thus, whereas the total value of cotton piece good imports into African colonies remained roughly constant throughout the war, the average unit price rose between 1939 and 1945 from 4 to 14 shillings and the quantity imported fell accordingly by two-thirds. For East Africa, international terms of trade declined from 109 in 1939 (1938 = 100) to 49 in 1943 and 75 in 1945. Likewise, in West Africa, terms of trade declined to between 50 and 70 per cent of the pre-war level.[41] The reduction in colonial consumption, resulting from restrictive imports and price inflation, showed itself as an increase in real export surpluses and thus sterling balances.

Table 2.3 shows the extent to which, even in current prices, exports to exceeded imports from Britain. This was counteracted by growing import surpluses from elsewhere, particularly India, which also faced a substantial reduction in imports from Britain. It is of interest to note that whereas the war-time share of total British exports for Australia, for instance, doubled to 12 per cent (from 7 per cent, 1935–9) and for South Africa increased from 7 to 9 per cent, India's share remained constant at 7 per cent.[42] As the extent of the British import surplus determined one part of the growth of sterling balances, Amery (Secretary of State for India) argued that sterling balances were 'a blessing in disguise' because

TABLE 2.2 *Export and import surplus and direction of trade, Kenya–Uganda and Nigeria, 1935–51*

	Average annual export (import) surplus		*Proportions of exports (imports) to and from*				
	£ million	*% of total trade*	*UK*	*India*	*S.Africa*	*US*	*Other*
					%		
KENYA–UGANDA							
1935–39	(2260)	(3)	30	30	2	5	33
			(41)	(5)	(2)	(9)	(43)
1940–45	(2400)	(1.6)	23	31	11	10	25
			(25)	(21)	(13)	(12)	(29)
1946–51	(12665)	(15)	29	24	5	7	35
			(48)	(10)	(4)	(7)	(31)
NIGERIA							
1935–39	3045	1.3	47	n.a.	n.a.	10	43
			(55)	(6)	(0.01)	(7)	(32)
1940–45	3070	1.2	83	n.a.	n.a.	10	7
			(44)	(16)	(2)	(13)	(25)
1946–51	35500	33.3	77	—	0.05	13	10
			(55)	(6)	(0.05)	(8)	(30)

SOURCES Kenya, *Blue Books* 1945, 1946, Nairobi, Section 20, Tables 1,2; Kenya and Uganda, *Annual Trade Reports* 1946, Nairobi, Tables 1,2; HMSO, *Statistical Abstract of the British Commonwealth,* 1933–9, 1945–7, 1951, London.

TABLE 2.3 *Trade of British African colonies,*[a] *1938–45, current prices*

	Exports to				*Imports from*			
	UK	*Other Empire countries*	*Non-British countries*	*Total*	*UK*	*Other Empire countries*	*Non-British countries*	*Total*
	%	%	%	£ mill.	%	%	%	£ mill.
1938	41	17	42	51	48	14	38	53
39	46	20	34	51	43	20	37	49
40	58	19	23	58	40	29	31	53
41	41	43	16	64	35	39	26	60
42	55	26	19	67	32	38	30	67
43	57	27	16	72	33	40	27	73
44	53	29	18	77	33	41	26	83
45	43	28	29	92	37	36	27	82

[a]Includes Sudan and S. Rhodesia but excludes S. Africa and B. Somaliland.

SOURCE *Statistical Abstract of the British Commonwealth 1936–45* (Cmd 7224), London, 1947.

they registered the good fact that war-time exports had been reduced and promised the good omen that post-war British exports would be increased.[43] Keynes referred to Amery as 'a dangerous lunatic' in that any attempt to facilitate British exports on these grounds paid no attention to the probable consequences of a post-war deflationary world.[44] More specifically, Keynes's argument was that post-war British exports had to be requited in terms of imports which would increase productive capacity in Britain, and not increased on the grounds that the Empire had supplied non-productive imports for the British war effort.

This contention was to spill over into the second, and most important, cause of the growth of sterling balances, that of British military expenditure overseas. The Indian export surplus accounted for one-quarter of Indian sterling balances in March 1944 but munitions and war materials, which were produced in India but purchased by the British government, accounted for over one-half of Indian-held sterling balances.[45] Likewise, for East, Central and West Africa, British military expenditure totalled nearly £100 million (between 1942 and 1944) and this represented more than one-half of the roughly estimated accumulations of sterling balances held by colonies in these areas at the end of 1944.[46] During 1943 the army in India comprised thirty divisions, including ten for internal security and including forces in Ceylon and on the Burmese frontiers. At the same time, forces in Africa amounted to eight brigades of 65,000 with another six brigades serving in India and the East.[47] Therefore the Indian army of 600,000 was ten-fold that of forces in Africa, and this difference approximated to the difference between the Indian and African colonial holdings of sterling balances. Under the terms of the 1940 India Defence Agreement, which revised pre-war agreements and passed through the Commons without any discussion, the Indian government met the local costs of Indian forces in India plus the cost of special defence measures 'in India's interests' overseas.[48] But the cost of the bulk of Indian defence expenditure outside India and expenditure on war materials in India by British forces was met by the British government. As we show below, the war cabinet, at Keynes's beckoning, tried to contest the terms of this agreement by arguing that British military expenditure for the overseas defence of India, in South East Asia and particularly Burma, was 'in India's interests' and not simply a specific aspect of total war.

It was not merely the scale of sterling balances that was at issue for Churchill. The scale of British military expenditure in India was such that it was nearly equal to Indian government *total* expenditure in 1942–3. Indian Government revenue from taxation and other receipts covered barely one-half of civil and defence expenditure; after local borrowing, the Indian budget deficit amounted to one-half of total Indian and British government expenditure and some 15 per cent of GNP.[49] This increase in the British component of military expenditure was financed by the Indian government borrowing rupees on behalf of the British government, which credited the borrowings as sterling held in London for the Indian government. Industrial production in India was estimated to have grown in real terms by 60 per cent to 1943 in response to the direct and derived demand for military expenditure.[50] But from the British vantage point of Keynes, and like the post-war significance of the export surpluses, the accumulation of sterling balances out of war expenditure represented a deadweight loss for British productive capacity. Military expenditure was not merely deemed to be unproductive but its financing overseas represented a colonial claim on productive British assets. The object of imperial economic policy became one of freezing and isolating colonial claims from the core of the British national economy.

Retrospectively in 1945 Keynes had welcomed the contribution that sterling balances had played in minimising British debt to the United States. However, we have noted that the caveat in this paean was the concern for the extent to which British military expenditure overseas had grown and was expected to grow further in the post-war period without the counteracting assistance of United States Lend Lease grants. In fact, the concern for the extent to which military expenditure had contributed towards building up sterling balances was forcibly expressed by Keynes in July 1942 and conveyed to Churchill:

> Lord Keynes mentioned to me (Churchill) the other night (at the Other Club) that we were incurring enormous indebtedness to India. Are we on the other hand charging India for the defence services we are giving? . . . In my opinion all out-of-pocket charges by Great Britain for defending India or any other Colony must be set off against these book figures which are piling up.[51]

A year later, he returned to the attack and insisted to sceptical Cabinet colleagues that the accumulated balances will 'result in putting an unbearable burden on the backs of the British work people'.[52] And in 1944, the annual outburst continued: Britain saved India from invasion and he 'felt strongly that the principle of a counter-claim (against India) was justified on merits, and hoped that he would have the support of his colleagues in maintaining this attitude'.[53] The attitude, which he claimed was not understood by Parliament or the British public, was that India was exercising a claim on future British production because the India government's financial contribution towards the war effort was inconsistent with Roosevelt's principle of Reciprocal Aid.

Reciprocal Aid, to repeat, was designed to ensure that each allied nation contribute the maximum of its resources to the war effort and that no allied nation would be forced to incur debt to any other allied nation. The mechanism for executing the principle was that of Mutual Aid. Each country would meet the local money costs of war within its boundaries no matter what was the national origin of the allied forces and materials in the country in question. However, the nation supplying the forces and or materials would meet the foreign exchange costs of war where local money (for instance, rupees for US forces' wages) and local resources could not service and supply the war effort. India posed a problem not merely because it became the arsenal of eastern war theatres, including the Middle East after 1941, but because it was not deemed to be an equal allied nation.

It is now well documented that American pressures on the British War Cabinet made a declaration of British colonial policy necessary as an adjunct to the Atlantic Charter and a condition for Lend Lease but that the War Cabinet refused to accept a commitment to national freedom and self-government outside Europe.[54] A Foreign Office official rhetorically asked whether freedom meant personal freedom or political freedom and came up with the definition of freedom as 'freedom from fear and want'. If the US government would accept this definition, he suggested, they would be rid of their own 'highly dangerous definition of freedom – the idea that freedom is, in essence, nineteenth century nationalism'.[55] The cabinet committee (under Attlee) which eventually drew up the Colonial Charter laid down three principles as a general statement of post-war colonial policy: The United States must be involved in a general scheme for colonial defence and that the principle of trusteeship for colonies be accepted but, thirdly, that the US must equally be committed to the principle that colonial powers would have the right to administer 'their own territories'. But, equally, the cabinet was adamant that it could not accept the suggestion of the US Secretary of State, Cordell Hull, that the criteria for self-government were to be invoked by 'a fitness and willingness to fight for freedom': 'It would be unfortunate to suggest that any colony which had contributed men to, for instance, the KAR, had qualified for self-government by that alone'.[56]

The converse, that the absence of self-government might determine the extent to which 'a fitness and willingness to fight for freedom' was present, was the kernel of the Indian problem for Churchill. In April 1942, under pressure from both Attlee and Roosevelt, Churchill agreed to Stafford Cripps' mission to India to negotiate for full self-government, and the mission foundered on the Viceroy's insistence that the Indian Defence Council, unlike the Financial Council, be subject to Indian rather than British control. Churchill explained earlier that:

> The idea that we should 'get more out of India' by putting the Congress in charge at this juncture seems ill founded . . . Bringing hostile political element into the defence machine will paralyse action. Merely picking and choosing friendly Indians will . . . not in any way meet political demands. The Indian troops are fighting splendidly, but it must be remembered that their allegiance is to the King Emperor, and that the rule of the Congress and Hindoo Priesthood machine would never be tolerated by a fighting race. I do not think you [Attlee] will have any trouble with American opinion.[57]

Total war was not fighting alone and India was not merely of a fighting race. Keynes's 'lunatic', Amery, reported to Cabinet in August 1942 that the 'whole body of Indian industrialists, financiers and commercial men are united in opposition to the idea that India's share of the financial burden of the war should be substantially increased'.[58]

Linlithgow, the Viceroy, who stood with Churchill on constitutional policy towards defence, rapidly turned against him on the matter of economic relations with the independent part of Indian government. The Viceroy would refuse to accept any notice of Churchill's right to revise the 1940 Indian Defence Agreement and to make a British counter claim against India's sterling balances. When Raisman, the Indian Financial Secretary, attempted to negotiate a compromise whereby the Indian government would pay all rupee costs of the RAF, airport construction costs for the USAF and one-half of capital expenditure on war industrial development, the Viceroy's Council rejected the compromise out of hand. The council would not 'allow India to swallow such an unpalatable pill, and that having supported firm action against Congress they had done enough unpopular things for the time being'.[59] Amery pointed out that if Churchill's counter claim went forward, Indian capital would be withdrawn from industrial production for the war effort and that the British cabinet had no means to force Indian capitalists to invest in the production of materials for the armed forces.[60] These points were absorbed by mandarins, ministers and officials. Kingsley Wood (Chancellor of the Exchequer) and his Financial Adviser, Lord Catto, said that there was no escaping from 'criticism in India in her present mood' and that financial relations were subsumed by the contingent political objection in the form of political agitation that India is in the war against her own consent and therefore should bear the least possible financial burden'.[61] Rowe Dutton, an influential Treasury official on overseas and colonial finance in the post-war period, put the survival of the sterling area down to political relations: 'I should not expect any difficulty from Australia or New Zealand. We can be firm with the Colonial Empire and with Eire. We need not fear Iraq and the really unpleasant possibility is Egypt'.[62] In fact, Catto proved to be the most prescient. As long as war was going against Britain in the Far East, the indigenous bourgeoisie would hold out against a British national interest since it held command over the economic instruments of state power. In the conjuncture of war, the British interest would have to be expressed imperially and British power in India would have to be exercised militarily against the Indian bourgeoisie. But if Japan was to be militarily defeated, concluded Catto, the sterling balance problem could then be negotiated, nationally, between Britain and India.[63] In this case, war could be an instrument of economic policy rather than the other way around, the postulate of total war.

If Churchill was thwarted by the indigenous bourgeoisie in India because he was forced to accede to these points, then it was ultimately because the US government was exercising the right to claim against British dollar balances which started to emerge after the inception of Lend Lease. Britain started out the war with net gold and dollar reserves of $2455m. At the end of 1940, as war materials were purchased on a 'cash and carry' basis from US arms manufacturers, the reserves had been whittled down to $300m. Thereafter, under the combined system of production and allocation, US government departments procured arms by way of grant.[64] Table 2.1 shows that British reserves rose by $2000m (£500m) between 1941 and 1944 and ended up in 1945 at $1900m. The US Treasury, through Morgenthau and White, pressed the argument in 1943 that the accumulation of dollar balances showed that the British foreign exchange position was 'really very healthy' and Britain could do with less grant, through Lend Lease, and pay more for imports from the US. Catto and Keynes were 'horrified' and replied that British dollar balances did not represent claims against American resources but were quick liabilities, cover for sterling balances which were held by the sterling bloc, some of whose countries, such as India, might insist on the conversion of sterling into dollars.[65] Keynes's protest was remarkably similar to that issued by the Viceroy on behalf of the Indian bourgeoisie;

> The British government ask the US Administration to agree with them that the present arrangements are not open to criticism; and that it cannot fairly be represented by anyone acquainted with the complete facts, that the growth of [dollar] balances represents a net improvement of the British position which justifies a call upon her to a larger share of the common financial burden than at present.[66]

The size of dollar balances were linked to the size of sterling balances in two ways. Firstly, dollar outlays by US forces throughout the Empire were converted into sterling and the increment in dollar reserves were thus accompanied by an accumulation of sterling balances which were a claim on British and not American resources.

As we have pointed out, these sterling claims were contested by Churchill and Keynes. Secondly, the conversion of dollars into sterling was centred upon the City of London as the mechanism for dollar pooling, the bedrock of the sterling area. Each country's dollars would be converted into sterling but reallocated as dollars according to the minimum requirements which each country could claim as being necessary for dollar imports.[67] Import controls, against dollar imports, were exercised by virtue of the evolution of the sterling area itself. War-time import controls, to reduce civilian consumption within the sterling area, were designed as a form of British export control in the name of total war and were distinct from the pre-war controls, which were exercised through dollar pooling.

The conversion of dollars into sterling through the City of London was jealously guarded by the Bank of England, which was insistent that one proposed solution to the Indian problem, the separate allocation of dollars for India, would establish a precedent for other countries and thus kill the sterling system.[68] More importantly, to return dollars to India would remove the benefit which accrued to the City as dollar–sterling dealer. Catto estimated that other than the causes of export surplus and India as eastern arsenal, dollar–sterling conversion accounted for 15 per cent of the growth of Indian sterling balances.[69] More generally, we note that the build-up of £500m of dollar balances between 1941 and 1944 accounted for just over 15 per cent of the £3.5bn accumulated sterling balances shown in Table 4.1.

Roosevelt placed an upper limit on British dollar reserves of £250m

TABLE 2.4 *Composition of accumulated sterling balances for specific countries, 1938–45 and 1948*

	1938	*1939*	*1940*	*1941*	*1942*	*1943*	*1944*	*1945*	*1948*
					£ million				
India[1]	45	85	142	217	390	664	955	1265	1026
[2]	n.a.	48	107	108	213	385	713	1023	n.a.
Australia	54	36	69	48	62	76	146	132	275
New Zealand	8	13	19	20	32	33	42	75	70
South Africa	8	9	2	2	0	14	24	59	115
Eire	125	75	79	97	117	138	159	1943	188
Egypt	n.a.	45	80	125	180	280	350	404	n.a.
Palestine	n.a.	20	25	30	55	80	95	115	n.a.
Ceylon	14	n.a.	n.a.	20	25	33	48	79	53
Malaya	n.a.	n.a.	n.a.	100	100	100	100	115	105
West Africa	n.a.	n.a.	n.a.	45	60	80	90	100	180
East Africa	n.a.	n.a.	n.a.	40	50	70	80	100	105
Rhodesia	4	n.a.	n.a.	7	10	10	15	23[3]	29
All Colonies	[76]							446	556
Total[1]	760[3]	560	735	1300	1820	2470	3170	3660[3]	3820

[1]Gross of sterling debt repatriation } and including Pakistan.
[2]Net of sterling debt repatriation }
[3]Estimates adjusted by Bell, p. 23.

SOURCES: H. A. Shannon, 'The Sterling Balances of the Sterling Area', *Economic Journal*, 60 (3), 1950 pp. 532–3, 539, 550; P. W. Bell, *The Sterling Area in the Postwar World* (Oxford, 1958), p. 22.

($1bn) in 1943, beyond which Lend Lease grants would be cut, but this formal directive, to assuage Congress, was not directly implemented. The British claimed, for instance, that the Soviet Union had accumulated $1.6bn worth of dollar reserves without penalty and that US reserves were eighteen times the British level or that Britain incurred liabilities and sales of $10 billion worth ($3bn of disinvestment of overseas assets, $2bn of gold and dollar sales, $5bn of sterling balances) of assets and claims. These claims were sufficient to prevent action without removing the American threat.[70] It was ingenious to attempt to maximise the accumulation of sterling balances vis-à-vis the US but to minimise it when confronting India. But this ingenuity signalled the ambiguity behind the attempt to construct and protect a specifically British national economy within the pretext that total war extended the defence and residual elements of British imperial power.

The 1940 Indian Defence Agreement was not renegotiated. In 1943, when confronted with rising consumption prices in India which reduced real wages, particularly of agricultural workers, and gave rise to the Bengal famine and some 3 million deaths,[71] the only British-inspired solution to rising sterling balances was undertaken. Gold worth £55m was sold to the Indian government to reduce Indian SB by some £100m.[72] This transaction was a feature of London-centred financial dealing, which could realise an Indian price well above the official (and thus dollar-equivalent price) of gold. No significant attempt (other than the 'token' shipment of one-tenth of India's 1943–4 demand for wheat of 100 000 tons) was made in London to reduce the Indian export surplus by increasing imports and reducing the rate of price inflation. Rising British military expenditure in India was ameliorated by the gold sales, which realised more rupees per pound credited to the sterling balances, and rupee payments to Indian defence contractors were controlled more tightly.[73] Otherwise, solutions to the sterling balances problem, proposed by Catto, Henderson, Cherwell and Keynes, remained to be taken up in the post-war period, and only then did an African context appear to have significance.

Keynes originally had proposed that the balances be blocked (and effectively thus confiscated) after the war or that India be directed to reduce its claim by £75m (in 1943) by whatever means the Indian government preferred. Later, in the twilight zone of 1945 between the defeats of Germany and Japan (Stage II), Keynes insisted that the general SB problem could only be resolved within the general framework of Anglo-American financial negotiations which separately culminated in Bretton Woods and the 1946 US loan to Britain of $3.75bn.[74] Sterling balances were to be divided into three groups of claims. One part of the balances were to be fully convertible into dollars for current transactions but the British Treasury would ration dollars between holders according to each's current dollar earnings. The second part would be made over to Britain as Churchill's counter claim for a contribution towards the war effort. The third and most substantial part would be funded or capitalised at no or nominal rate of interest and released 5 years after the end of war over 40 to 50 years for British exports.[75] A zero rate of interest was proposed by Keynes because the balances did not give rise to productive assets against which the claim for British resources was justified.[76] The Bank of England, however, was hostile to the second and third parts and wanted all balances to be run down freely. Keynes retorted that this was 'reckless gambling in the shape of assuming banking undertakings beyond what we have any means to support as soon as anything goes wrong, coupled with a policy, conceived in the interests of the old financial traditions, which pays no regard to the inescapable requirements of domestic politics'.[77] The third part conflicted with the US demand for non-discrimination against dollar imports. No specific agreement with the US government could be reached and as Moggeridge concludes: 'These plans were submerged in the failure of the bid for convertibility in 1947 (as required by the terms of the 1945 US Loan). And after that, through the long years before and after convertibility in 1958, the only attitude consistently followed by the British authorities was one of defensive drift'.[78] Sterling debt, as sterling balances, was the major contribution which the Empire made to the British war effort. It was the means by which colonies in Africa felt the brunt of total war and in the post-war period was to provide the argument that colonial development should be regarded as some kind of reward for war-time colonial sacrifice.

RAW MATERIALS AND SUPPLY

There is little evidence to show that the Colonial Office or any of the combined board production agencies systematically directed change in the *forms* of colonial production. We show, below, that state enterprise sponsored import-substituting industrialisation but that the impetus for this came from regional authorities of supply and import control. With few exceptions, no direct attempts were made to change production relations between peasant producers, estate or plantation owners and capitalist enterprise. In Kenya's Central Province, all landholders under tha authority of the Karatina dry vegetable project were forced to produce a given quota of vegetables for a state-owned factory; in Tanganyika, the Northern Province wheat scheme was funded entirely through the state and managed by an American settler. And in Nigeria and Tanganyika, for instance, colonial governments conscripted workers to increase labour supply for tin and sisal enterprises. However, all these cases involved production directly for the war effort with only half an eye directed at post-war production possibilities.

It was the enforced change in the pattern of international trade in conjunction with the centralisation of sterling which determined change in market conditions for raw material production. Colonial external trade was controlled to serve the war-time needs of the British war economy. The production and marketing of raw material exports was controlled by both the British and colonial governments through bulk purchase and other arrangements which served to change supply and quantities supplied rather than relations and conditions of production.

In considering the production and supply of raw materials the war falls clearly into two periods, that before and that after Pearl Harbor, although in some cases the fall of the Far East and America's entry into the war merely accentuated existing trends. When war broke out, the British government rather lethargically introduced the planned arrangements for war supply until the fall of France precipitated a crisis that required more drastic action. Building on the experience of the First World War, the Cabinet established ministries of Supply, Food, Shipping and Economic Warfare to ensure the most efficient procurement and allocation of the supplies Britain needed. A number of controls were created, manned mainly by seconded staff from City of London shipping companies, to purchase government's requirement of essential materials either through normal trade channels or direct from producers. If British needs exceeded supply, the controls were empowered to buy everything available at a fixed 'fair' price (usually the pre-war average price plus demonstrable increases in costs); otherwise they bought only as much as Britain required and allowed the rest to be sold on the (rather erratic) free market.[79] Most important were the basic materials for war production – iron ore, timber, machinery, cloth – and food, especially grains and protein. At the outset supply was dominated by the need to save dollars and all possible resources were drawn from within the sterling area – mainly from the dominions and Far East, as few of the necessary materials could be found in Africa. In November 1939 British supply authorities agreeed to buy the total wool production of Australia and New Zealand and the whole colonial sugar output for the duration of the war and one year thereafter; authorities contracted on an annual basis to buy the whole output of Northern Rhodesian copper. After the fall of France, however, the rapid procurement of physical supplies took priority over dollar-saving, and the British government turned increasingly to American sources of supply. This was reinforced by an unanticipated shortage of shipping, which resulted in a concentration of convoys on the North Atlantic route. The proportion of British ships using this route rose from one-third to over a half during 1940.[80]

The effect of these early pressures on the African colonies was threefold. They reduced the supply of dollars for colonial imports; reduced the supply of British exports to the colonies because as many as possible were diverted to dollar markets, particularly in Latin America; and reduced the markets and shipping available for colonial exports. The resulting reduction in import supplies forced all African colonies to introduce import-licensing and occasionally rationing. Licensing and the restriction on dollar imports also served one of the Board of Trade's interests in preventing American suppliers replacing British trading channels in colonial markets while British exports were restricted.[81]

More serious, however, was the problem of surplus colonial commodities. For many colonial primary producers the sudden disappearance of markets and shipping meant disaster. Before the war well over 40 per cent of exports from British African territories had gone to non-Commonwealth markets, mainly in Europe and the USA. By mid-1940 the first was closed by occupation, the other by lack of shipping. Few tropical products were priority items for the war effort, nor important enough to be bought by the United Kingdom Commercial Corporation to deny them to Axis nations, and the added cost of war risks insurance made them unprofitable for the merchants still in operation. Estate and peasant producers of bananas and citrus fruit in the West Indies, citrus fruit in Palestine and sugar in Fiji, cocoa and bananas in West Africa and sisal and cotton in East Africa found that much of their produce remained unshipped and unsold. Colonial governments warned London that there would be a grave danger of political unrest unless something was done to bail out producers, as these exports directly or indirectly accounted for a relatively large part of state revenues.

The Colonial Office approached the buying ministries and Treasury and after much hard bargaining persuaded them to guarantee to buy, one by one, any unsold surpluses of the worst hit commodities – Palestinian citrus, Fijian sugar, West Indian bananas, West African cocoa and East African sisal. This was done mainly on the grounds that the immediate economic cost was less than the potential post-war social cost of putting down riots and reconstructing colonial economies. The prices offered were not generous, being fixed to cover only the costs of production plus a small allowance for 'standard pre-war profits' (which had been low by any reckoning) for settler products or, more simply, the average pre-war price (also hardly generous) for peasant output.[82]

Bulk purchase by the British government required local administrations to arrange and organise bulk sale. State marketing controls were therefore created to bring all available supplies under administrative direction. For the 1939–40 season West African cocoa was bought in bulk by the Ministry of Food direct from the merchants. During 1940, however, the ministry refused to continue buying surpluses not required in Britain, and responsibility for marketing cocoa passed to the Colonial

Office's West African Cocoa Control Board (WACCB). The Board bought all available cocoa at the fixed official price, sold to the ministry whatever it required for British needs and disposed of the rest on the open market for the best price it could get. The funds were provided by the British government but the board was staffed jointly by Colonial Office officials and the West African merchant companies, who were also employed as its agents. The companies were thus able to maintain the pre-war status quo, their profits and their interests.[83] In East Africa a Sisal Control – in the person of Sir W. Lead (Chairman of the Tanganyika Sisal Growers Association) – was created to buy the Ministry of Supply's requirements from the growers, though initially this requirement was only 62 per cent of production distributed among estates by a quota system; the remainder was left for merchant companies to sell. Sisal control was firmly in the hands of the East African growers' associations, which aimed to wrest complete control of marketing from the merchants. They therefore tried to persuade the Ministry of Supply to buy the whole crop but it was only after the fall of France that the Treasury agreed. Thereafter, although the merchants continued to be employed as agents, price and marketing were dealt with directly between the Ministry and the producers. The beneficiaries of bulk purchase therefore varied from case to case, depending largely on the different balances of political forces in London and different colonies. Where producing companies were well organised, they fulfilled control functions; where and when they could not collude and cooperate to control, colonial state officials moved in to control directly.

At this stage, however, government purchase was introduced only for the worst hit commodities. By January 1941 it was felt necessary to set up an official committee on export surpluses in Whitehall and a Colonial Office representative was sent to Washington to persuade the United States to buy some of the colonial surpluses.[84] But for many colonial governments it seemed as if the inter-war depression was returning with a vengeance, because there were not only no markets for their exports but no imports for their markets. For Britain these colonial problems were a minor irritant. Its own war supply problems continued and despite the efforts to find supplies within the sterling area it became ever more dependant on the US. This problem was only overcome with the introduction of Lend Lease in March 1941. Though slow to get off the ground, this effectively provided the British government with whatever war supplies it needed, subject only to the constraint of US production. Initially Lend Lease applied only to Britain but by July 1941 it had been extended to the dominions and colonies as well. As a result the Colonial

Supply Liaison Office was established in Washington to handle all allocations of Lend Lease supplies for the colonies.[85]

The Japanese conquest of the Far East and America's entry into the war transformed the supply situation; demand for raw materials rose just as supplies were cut off. In March 1942 Cranborne was able to impress his long-held view about the significance of African resources:

> Now that we have lost Malaya the main problem before our African Administrations, after defence, is to make good as far as the resources of their Territories allow the commodities formerly drawn from the Far East and to intensify all forms of local production which assist the war effort . . . the foodstuffs and minerals of the African dependencies have become a vast armoury for the war effort. There is a new call to producers in Africa to do their utmost to serve the needs of the United Nations.[86]

From the imperial perspective this change had three important effects: the growth of Anglo-American economic coordination and its implications for Commonwealth cooperation; the effect of raw material supply arrangements on colonial commodity marketing; and the strengthening of regional coordination for production and supply in the colonies.

The basis of Anglo-American cooperation was the pooling of all available material resources and their allocation to the greatest benefit of the combined war effort. This was achieved through the machinery established in Washington in early 1942. The existing informal cooperation was formalised in a series of combined boards for munitions, food, raw materials (the CRMB) and production. Each board had only two representatives, an American representing the whole Western Hemisphere, and a British member representing the Commonwealth and Empire.[87] All Empire demands for supplies therefore passsed through London and were coordinated by the Empire Clearing House (later the Commonwealth Supply Council). The colonial and dominion governments notified London of their supply requirements, which were met where possible from Britain or other sterling sources and then residually from orders placed in the US. Most dominion governments also had representatives in Washington and in 1942 a strengthened Colonial Supply Mission, headed by J. Huggins, replaced the Liaison. The Colonial Office, however, never resorted to bulk ordering or long-term contracts for colonial supplies, because of its desire to preserve pre-war trade channels. This and the restrictions on dollar imports meant that when African colonies were unable to obtain supplies from Britain (whose exports fell to 30 per cent of their pre-war level) they turned mainly to other Empire sources, which by 1944 supplied 40 per cent of their needs compared to 14 per cent before the war.[88] (See Table 2.3.)

If the Empire had to go cap in hand to the US for supplies of manufactures, for raw materials the opposite was true, and this gave British representatives on the CRMB more leverage. The Board controlled only those raw materials in shortest supply: hard fibres, tin, rubber, and oilseeds. Most of these were produced within the Empire and all, to a varying extent, in Africa. The CRMB agreed the priorities for production and distribution of available supplies, and the colonies were expected simply to fulfil the agreed requirements. Some of these raw materials were provided to the US under Reciprocal Aid (or reverse Lend Lease), which began in February 1942 under the Mutual Aid Agreement as part of the general pooling of resources. Most reciprocal aid, however, was in the form of goods and services provided by the UK and dominions, and the US government continued to buy colonial raw material supplies from the British government for dollars.[89] The combined approach to production and supply is well illustrated by the case of sisal. United States agencies, when faced by a strong demand for the commodity, gave privileged access to sisal companies for scarce machinery and shipping space to secure an increased quantity of sisal output for the US as soon as possible. The increased control over raw material supplies after 1942 provided Britain with an increasing dependence upon Empire sources of supply. After 1942 Britain was entirely dependent on Empire sources for bauxite, chrome ore, sisal and rubber and more heavily dependent than before for flax, silk, tin and tungsten.[90] The effects of the change in the pattern of trade were disguised during the war by combined purchase and free exchange of materials between Britain and the US. As soon as war ended, the significance of Empire for preserving the idea of a British national economy became all too apparent.

The most important long-term effect of this second phase of the war was on colonial commodity marketing. After 1942 local administrations were instructed to become the sole buyers of many colonial export crops, either to allow their allocation under the Combined Boards or simply to guarantee British supplies at reasonable prices in a situation of world shortage. For the first time therefore commodity marketing came almost exclusively under state control. There were three important aspects of this change. Firstly, the machinery constructed to operate state monopoly purchasing tended to be established by the local balance of political and social forces acting through the colonial state. In West

Africa the marketing apparatus preserved the domination of merchant companies. But in East Africa, and Kenya in particular, the gains which settler estate owners had made in the inter-war period were consolidated in their command over state marketing controls. Estate owners became insulated, through the state, from the potential threat which Asian merchant capital (in commanding purchases of output) and indigenous competitive enterprise (in commanding labour power for a larger market share of commodity output) posed for estate production.[91] Secondly, the price of commodities no longer bore much relation to market forces. Despite the pressure for increased production, it was considered that higher prices would fuel inflation rather than encourage more output because of the restriction on imported consumer goods. In many cases the British government laid down what producer prices should be on the basis of what it was prepared to pay colonial governments for British needs. In other cases colonial governments themselves kept producer prices down in line with the policy prescribed in Lord Moyne's despatch to the colonies of June 1941, which encouraged the restriction of consumption and compulsory saving by every means possible in the colonies as in Britain.[92] Thirdly, state control over marketing gave colonial authorities the initiative in planning to stabilise commodity prices in the future. In London, Washington and colonial capitals, schemes were hatched to prevent the market fluctuations that had plagued producers during the depression. This was part of the wider process of planning for the post-war world, and though of little direct relevance to the experience of war, it casts a useful light on the different views within the British government of the purpose of control.[93]

The first two points can be best illustrated by describing the experience of marketing in East and West Africa. In 1942 the WACCB was expanded to become the West African Produce Control Board, which dealt with exports of oilseeds and palm oil, now subject to Ministry of Food purchase, as well as cocoa. The WAPCB bought and shipped all marketed produce, but continued to employ the pre-war merchant companies (such as the UAC) as its buying agents, giving each firm a quota to buy based on its past performance. This petrified the pre war division of the market, preventing new merchant capitalists entering to compete for trade while guaranteeing comfortable profits for the old established firms. The demands for market access by African merchants were recognised in the Colonial Office, but a proposed scheme to allow greater flexibility was rejected on the grounds that it would arouse too much hostility from the European companies, who were thereby saved from any degree of uncomfortable competition by their effective political pressure in London.[94] The WAPCB also operated a price policy that enabled it to build up substantial surpluses. Producer prices were kept considerably below the average price obtained from the Ministry of Food and sales on the New York market, mainly in order to restrict local demand and prevent inflation, but also with an eye to building up surpluses in these good years for use later as a price stabilisation fund, when, as was expected, post-war prices fell.

The Ministry of Food obtained by bulk purchase almost the whole oilseed and palm oil crop but only a third of the cocoa crop, and there is no doubt that through the cost-plus pricing system which was established early in the war they were able to obtain supplies far more cheaply than they could from non-colonial producers. From the Ministry of Food's vantage point of subsidising the British consumer during the war, the price paid to colonial producers had to be kept low to compensate for and balance out the higher prices paid to, for example, Indian oilseed producers. And although the Board's surplus, being kept in London, contributed to the wartime sterling policy, producer pricing policy was effectively in the hands of the local administration, whose main aim was to contain inflation through market rather than direct controls over consumption and production.[95]

In East Africa, settlers as estate producers were aligned alongside colonial officials to turn the political balance of power against the merchant companies and the British Ministry of Supply. Thus, in the case of cotton, which was produced by peasants rather than estates, the Ministry of Supply required only a small proportion of East African production, but insisted in November 1942 that local governments became the sole buyers of the whole crop. This enabled the Ministry to control the price of the cotton they did need and prevent East African prices, pulled by the Bombay market, rising above the price Britain was paying Egypt and Sudan, which was kept as low as possible to subsidise clothing for the British consumer. In establishing the regional machinery to control marketing, the East African governments were guided by four principles:

(a) a reasonable price level to the producer
(b) the ensurance of supplies to the UK consumer at these reasonable price levels
(c) the maintenance in business of the recognised and reputable exporters of cotton who will continue to carry out their normal functions freed from all risk, and be able to use their ability

collectively in disposing of any surplus available in the 'free market' in India

(d) the refund to the Governments concerned of any profits made in the 'free market' for the benefit directly or indirectly, of the cotton producers of East Africa.[96]

The merchants were formed into an Exporters' Group and, as in West Africa, allocated quotas on the basis of past performance, on the assumption that normal trade would be resumed as soon as the war ended. The producer price had to be based on that offered by the Ministry of Supply for its fraction of the crop, with the result that the producers' return fell to 30 per cent of the real export value of their cotton.[97] An exporters' group was also formed for coffee, produced by estates in Kenya, and government controls set up to buy the peasant-produced robustas in Uganda and Tanganyika; but, for the higher quality arabicas, local purchasing was in the hands of the producers' own organisations, who kept control over the surplus that accrued from the difference between the producer and export prices.[98] The same applied to other predominantly settler crops, such as pyrethrum and sisal, and in the latter case producers used the war-time market controls to secure better prices and more control over the marketing of their crops than they had got before the war.[99]

The bulk purchase of metals such as tin, iron ore and copper from West and Central Africa was rather different from that of peasant or settler production. As production and trade were dominated by a very few large companies, the Ministry of Supply bought direct from them. Prices and output were settled directly between company and Ministry. When the Ministry of Supply suddenly required far less copper in 1944, Northern Rhodesian production fell accordingly.[100] There were those in the Colonial Office and colonies themselves who believed that:

> The big mining groups concerned with the various competing base metals do real disservice to the countries whose assets they are realising by competing with one another to drive down prices as low as possible, and that in any international discussions ... and in any particular arrangements which we make in regard to particular colonial mineral developments, we should give a much more prominent position to the interests of the colonial territory concerned than has hitherto been customary.[101]

The Colonial Secretary even suggested the nationalisation of the mining companies. But the hopes came to nothing because the colonial authorities had been unable to insert themselves into the marketing process. When the Treasury decided to reopen the London Metal Exchange after the war, the hopes of nationalising mining evaporated.[102]

War-time controls over intra-imperial trade amounted to the rationalisation of trade in so far as market forces and profitability criteria may have run counter to what was constructed as the dictates of a British national economy. In the case of minerals, where profitability did not run counter to British need, British state intervention had no premise for action. But in any case in which colonial trade would have run counter to the British conception of total war, and thus the equality of sacrifice principle, state intervention determined the pattern and terms of trade. Within the framework of combined production and allocation, British state authorities were to dictate the place and price at which all the main commodities and manufactured goods imported and exported by the colonies would be purchased and sold. The changed patterns of trade made imperial preference irrelevant. As Caine noted: 'Imperial preference really ceased to exist during the war because the prices paid for colonial produce became in due course lower not higher than the prices for foreign supplies ... The Imperial preference ... became a *minus* quantity'.[103] But equally the combined system limited British state intervention more generally because it involved either the immediate presence of the American state in combined decisions or else the threat of unilateral US action to compete with Britain in hitherto protected markets. British intervention was also limited by the balance of political forces, which was expressed by local colonial administration. The limits of central British intervention were encapsulated by the war-time experience of regional authorities which mediated between British demands and local production capacities.

REGIONALISATION

The accumulation of sterling balances, which were centred upon Britain, held the Empire at arm's length from immediate and expected demands upon the resources of a British national economy. But, equally, the development of the combined system of production and allocation between the US and the UK after 1941 reduced any unilateral ability for a British government to direct the pattern and trade for colonial territories. When the use of commodities was pooled by combined boards of British and US governments, then any attempt by the Colonial Office or Board of Trade in London to change direction of commodity production in any colony, and so fulfil a specific British demand, could be nullified by the direct claim which the US agency could exercise over a particular commodity. However, there was a wide gap between the production of commodities in individual and specific British colonies and allocative decisions of the combined boards in Washington and London. The combined boards could directly allocate commodity stocks on the basis of direct and derived war material demand but could not directly ensure that any existing pattern of supply would meet established demand. By 1942 institutions were created to attempt to fill the gap between central allocation and local production. The institutions, such as the Middle East Supply Centre (MESC), East African Production and Supply council (EAPSC), West African Supply Council (WASC), were both supra-territorial and, depending upon the extent of American strategic and economic interest in the area, subject to the supra-national terms of Anglo-American control.

Although Americans might have seen Anglo-American Authorities as the means to extend US control over the resources and policies of specific colonial governments, the British saw them as a way of keeping British control over colonial resources and containing US pressure for colonial self-government. The origin of the Anglo-American Caribbean Commission did lie in the express desire for the US State Department to establish an advisory committee to express an American interest on labour and welfare policy for British West Indies colonies. In early 1942, although the Colonial Office could not refuse to entertain the desire, officials were 'mystified' and 'perplexed' about American enthusiasm for the Commission.[104] But whatever the British doubts about the West Indies case, there was no lack of British enthusiasm for Anglo-American regional authorities in Africa. Regional authorities were to be the means of containing American and local pressures for self-government while serving to meet American demands for international trusteeship. It was thought, within the Foreign Office, for instance, that 'backward peoples' might reach self-government through Regional Commissions rather than by independent statehood – 'a conception which, in any case, may be meaningless a generation or two from now. We must avoid undertaking, here and now, that every backward people is going to be, at some point in the future, an independent Sovereign State.'[105] Earlier a Colonial Office official had specified cases, such as Aden, Gibraltar, Gambia, Falklands, Fiji, Hong Kong, which were deemed to be 'too small or too important strategically ever to become independent self governing units'.[106] Oliver Stanley (as Colonial Secretary) announced in Parliament in July 1943 that commissions were to be established for each colonial region in 'close cooperation with neighbouring and friendly nations' (the US, South Africa, Australia) but that, to repeat, 'the administration of British colonies must continue to be the sole responsibility of Great Britain'.[107] The principle of regionalism was so well established by 1945, from an exclusively British vantage point, that whatever the political reservations which made it difficult to conceive of reviving proposals for closer union or colonial fusion in East Africa, the decision to turn the Governors' Conference into a Common Services Organisation was taken on the nod in the British Cabinet in 1945 and settled by discussion between the Colonial Secretary and Lord President.[108] Regional policy, then, was no simple American construction to determine the terms of British colonial policy.

Lee and Petter pinpoint regionalism as a general means of implementing the 1940 Colonial Development and Welfare Act, to promote 'social and economic development' as a general aspect of colonial policy. War-time regionalisation was accentuated for areas where British and American military bases had been established:

> As a result an incompatibility was identified between a highly centralised military command structure on the one hand, and a civil arm composed of a collection of separate (territorial) units on the other . . . in an emergency it would be imperative for the military commander-in-chief to work in close conjunction with a single civilian counterpart for the area in question.[109]

To pre-empt direct militarisation of the economy and administration of areas such as the Middle East and West Africa, resident ministers of state, as part of the full British cabinet, were civilian counterparts to military chiefs, and the regional economic councils were developed around their offices. But there was even more to regionalism than this.

In the Middle East it became apparent during the phoney war of 1939–40 that British war-time expenditure spawned a multiplied volume of international trade that neither bore a relation to the war effort nor to the British export drive to earn dollars to pay for war materials: 'United States exporters worked feverishly to cash in on the elimination of their German, French, and Italian competitors from the Middle East'.[110] This was despite the fact that the US Neutrality Act of 1939 banned American-owned shipping from the Red Sea and the Gulf. With the inception of Lend Lease, the British fear was that the United States administration might negotiate directly with particular nation states in the area. When the Red Sea was opened to American shipping in 1941, the 1938 record level of US exports was doubled within a year and outstripped British exports to the area.[111] Thus, to control the tempo of US trade and to codetermine the use of Lend Lease, the British government strove to incorporate US agencies into the existing British supply centre, languishing as an inert offshoot of the Ministry of War Transport. With American representatives on the Supply Centre, 'almost complete control over American commercial and Lend Lease exports to the Middle East for civilian use' was achieved.[112]

Once Vichy control of French West Africa had been ended effectively in December 1942, the American State Department sought to subordinate the area economically to American controls, over French North Africa, which were exercised by the North African Economic Board (NAED).[113] Lord Swinton, the British war cabinet representative in West Africa, did his utmost to keep the French West Africa separate from the North, to extend the influence of British West Africa into the French area and fend off growing American influence. The State Department wanted the British West Africa Supply *Centre* of Achimota, which uneasily centralised supply and import controls for the Gambia, Gold Coast, Nigeria and Sierra Leone, converted into an Anglo-American Supply *Council* for the whole of west and equatorial Africa. However, the British insisted on retaining the Achimota centre and forming an umbrella Anglo-American Supply Council. French- and Belgian-dominated supply centres at Dakar (for West Africa, Brazzaribe (for equatorial Africa) and Leopoldville (for the Belgian Congo) would, along with Achimota, be subordinate to the West African Supply Council (WASC), which in turn would be subject to the authority of the combined boards in London and Washington.[114]

The appointment of Admiral Glassford as Roosevelt's personal representative in West Africa was delayed for 6 months in early 1943 while political and economic conflict raged between American and British authorities. In London the Colonial Office was split from the Foreign Office and the production, supply and transport ministries over the question of Anglo-American collaboration. The Colonial Office wanted to subject Glassford to Swinton's personal influence on the grounds that 'we do not need or desire any American in Accra to teach us how to do our own job in our own territories'.[115] Glassford, it was assumed, would be taught the realities of British colonial policy by Swinton. Furthermore, if Americans were allowed into the Achimota Centre, 'It would appear logical that Anglo-American supply centres should be set up in East Africa and in other parts of the British colonial Empire'.[116] Not only would the Americans bring the French with them but they would also provide the occasion for South African intervention north of the Zambezi, 'despite the dangers which, on the long range view, this may entail to British colonial interests'.[117] Smuts, it was reported, regarded the French and Belgian Congo as southern African economies; if the US was to be part of a supply council encompassing equatorial Africa, then South Africa should equally have a voice in production, supply and trade decisions. For the Colonial Office, the British Empire in Africa was being squeezed between competing American, French and South African pressures. But, for the Foreign Office and the supply ministries, the British cabinet could not stand apart from American intervention in West Africa.

United States economic missions poured into West and Central Africa during 1942–3. For instance, during March 1942 US representatives to the combined board in London agreed to hold off from purchasing rubber but, in fact, American firms, the US Board of Economic Warfare and the Rubber Reserve Corporation, all with apparent State Department approval or oblivion, pressed the Free French agencies to sell at prices above those agreed by the combined board in London. The same happened to industrial supplies purchased from American firms,[118] and this was in spite of reports that the Free French were 'extremely sensitive' about any attempt at 'foreign' (US) control over Arican colonies and their attempt to use the sanction of withholding rubber as a means of extracting political recognition from the Roosevelt administration.[119] Swinton banned trade between British and French West Africa to attempt to force the French administration in Dakar from holding up the oilseed supply to Britain in favour of supplying North Africa, and by extension metropolitan France, when the US cut down exports of fats to Britain in late 1942. But US agencies refused to comply with the British ban and by March 1943, in the face of increased American supply, Swinton was forced to resume trade with French West Africa.[120] From Washington, Lord Halifax (the British Ambassador) reported that Britain had to cooperate with US agencies to stop them buying separately French West African oilseeds in return for American supplies. The US administration was reluctant to see its supply of raw materials and equipment supporting 'the UK commercial interests of the West African Produce Board': 'Do not forget that whilst we are accustomed to use our established trading organisation [firms such as Cadburys and the United African Company] as part of government procurement, the whole New Deal philosophy machinery... is strongly against any such practices.'[121]

In the Belgian Congo the American Board of Economic Warfare (BEW) acted independently of the US agencies, particularly the State

Department, and competed with the Lend Lease agency, OLLA, to procure rubber, copper and cobalt through linking Congo finance to dollars and supplying textiles and tyres at the expense of British and South African suppliers.[122] It was the fragmentation of agencies comprising the thrust of US state intervention overseas which struck fear into British government departments outside the Colonial Office.

It was hoped that US involvement in the Supply Centres as part of a super Anglo-American Council would provide the 'orderly development of American participation in the war effort in Africa':[123]

> The choice therefore was not between formal collaboration and no contact with them, but between formal collaboration on a regular and controllable basis and unorganised and possibly very harmful incursion by more or less irresponsible Missions organised by the Board of Economic Warfare.[124]

To provide this objective, American anglophiles were sought out and supported against anglophobes, such as Murphy, the President's representative in Algiers; the Near East division of the State Department was pitted against the European division, which sought West African subjection to North Africa.[125] The fragmentation of the US state overseas served to protect specific British colonial interests while the total thrust of American imperial intervention was supported to counter French pressures on the Empire. Thus, an Anglo-American-South African Council was imposed, with the threat of trade sanctions, upon the French Supply Centre in Madagascar, a Free French colony, at the same time that the British Colonial Office vainly held out against a direct American presence on the British West African Supply Centre.[126]

Supply councils were given two objectives by London. The first was to coordinate the distribution of scarce imports and regulate the use of shipping space, and the second was to create a framework for regional industrialisation in view of the shortage of shipping and the employment of import controls to control exports from Britain and other centres of supply, such as India, which were directed at the war effort. We have mentioned that shipping was the most significant supply constraint facing Anglo-American combined production, particularly from mid-1942 to the end of 1943 during the period in which supply councils were firmly established. The cumulative and combined production of ships did not exceed the cumulative tonnage of merchant sinkings until autumn 1943.[127] Even if sinkings were concentrated in the Atlantic, merchant shipping space across other safer oceans, such as the Indian

Ocean, was reduced to make up for losses in the Atlantic. the Middle East Supply Centre reduced the use of merchant shipping space by four-fifths within a year by exercising the right to screen import increases on a regional basis and overriding territorial controls which were subject to local trading and capitalist interests.[128] MESC redirected external trade for the region as a whole and promoted, on a regional basis, import substituting industrialisation according to the direct precepts of war and the war-imposed necessity to satisfy civilian demand and therefore 'accommodate as far as possible the sensibilities of an area swimming in nationalism and constantly stirred up by enemy propaganda'.[129]

In both West and East Africa industrialisation was promoted through the regional supply councils. The exemplary case was the East African Industrial Management Board, established in 1942, to produce chemicals and building materials, after the imported supply of these commodities had been cut by combined boards. Manufacturing plants were established by State enterprise, with the Kenya government pledged to hand over the plants to private enterprise after the war.[130] East African Industries, now a Unilever subsidiary, was thus formed as a result of a regional attempt to promote import-substituting industrialisation. The Colonial Office, long held by colonial governments to be antipathetic towards colonial industrialisation on the grounds of Board of Trade intervention to protect British exports and employment, was forced to reappraise colonial industrial policy. In September 1942, in response to a request by the Governor of Kenya (and as Secretary of the East Africa Governor's Conference, head of the supply council) for a statement on industrial policy, the Colonial Secretary declared that he could only approve projects which 'on balance' saved shipping space and or eased the combined manufacturing constraint. No positions could be taken on the appraisal of projects that involved post-war assumptions.[131] 'In view of acute shortage of supplies of machinery and of labour of all kinds, it is no longer possible to embark upon projects which are not required in the interests of the war efffort, however desirable they may be on purely long-term considerations'.[132] Projects using local materials on a regional basis, as in the Kenya case within East Africa, did not require approval, but projects using imported materials and equipment would be unlikely to be approved.[133] The fact that industrialisation, through the usage of second-hand machinery and low level technology,[134] did proceed outside Colonial Office controls was a cause of concern for the Board of Trade, which was forced equally to reappraise policy.

In mid-1943 the Board of Trade reappraised its pre-war assumption that industrialisation in the empire would reduce employment in Britain: 'Discouragement of UK participation in industrialisation overseas may well prove, in the long run, to diminish rather than to increase employment here.'[135] The Treasury was divided on this question. It was pointed out that a distinction should be made between capital and consumer goods, industries and exports. Consumer-good-producing firms had objected to industrialisation but capital good exports could be promoted by consumer good production in the Empire on the grounds that textiles, for instance, 'are bound to lose ground in the face of the world wide tendency to industrialisation . . . It is no use trying to swim against the tide'.[136] On the other hand, and harking back to the sterling balance problem, Henderson doubted whether British industrial capacity would be sufficient to meet both domestic and Empire demand for capital goods.[137] In any case, there was no institutional focus through which industrial firms might be involved in imperial industrialisation to serve national policy, which was expressed through the British state. This, like so much else and including aspects of planned trade, explains why regionalism, however well established as a cardinal principle of colonial policy by 1945, was developed specifically within the framework of war experience.

Regional ventures of the post-war period, such as the Central African and Malayan Federations or the East African High Commission, drew much from war experience but were inflected by local contingency rather than drawn out by the principle of supra-territorial control over production and trade. Firstly, to keep the advantage of total war, the British government pushed strongly for the perpetuation of the Middle East Supply Centre after 1945 and Bevin, as Foreign Secretary, frequently returned to an Anglo-American regional venture for the Middle East during the post-war period.[138] Unlike 1942, British enthusiasm was met by American antipathy in 1944–5. As early as May 1943 Cordell Hull had insisted that the US should return to, and extend, independent economic policy in the area. Conflict, over oil, civil aviation and other national interests, between Britain and the US developed after 1944. In August 1945 the State Department objected to the continuation of production and trade controls and called for the dissolution of the Centre.[139] Without US participation, the Supply Centre was doomed, as was the case also in West Africa.

Secondly, the arguments about post-war British imperial industrial policy centred on the forum in which the policy could be implemented. In 1943 it was appreciated that the post-war momentum for industrialisation would be initiated on national grounds. A Treasury official stated that industrialisation was 'designed to benefit the national economy and earn its protection that way'. It followed that no intra-imperial arrangement to plan industrial investment was possible.[140] The Board of Trade concurred, since it would be 'unwise' to assume 'any large-scale and detailed inter-governmental planning of industrial development throughout the Empire. . . . This may presuppose a higher degree of Government control over private enterprise than would be practicable'. Furthermore, Empire governments would not delay their own reconstruction plans until 'major international policy questions' were settled.[141] This was fair enough for the dominions but where did it leave colonial governments? The regional experience of state-sponsored industrialisation did not auger well for the Colonial Office. In appreciating that regional planning meant regional control independent of London, the Colonial Office called for the establishment of central instruments of control. A 'central organisation' in the form of a standing committee under the aegis of the Ministry of Production in Britain should plan production. 'Hitherto, for reasons of organisation, the initiative rests normally with the Colonial Governments themselves, who are clearly unable to put forward proposals in the light of full knowledge of the supply – shipping situation'.[142] But when the rationale for combined production fell, when the US withdrew the regional machinery of total war, then colonial governments' 'organisation' would no longer be constrained. The constraint could only be perpetuated by a British central system of planned production, a system rejected by Keynes, in 1945, as 'starvation corner' and thus, according to him and others (including Caine of the Colonial Office), entailing the 'sacrifice' of any colonial development programme.[143]

Thirdly, above all, the British desire to preserve the colonial territory as the form of administration, as opposed to the regional authority as the venue for trusteeship and coordinating agency for production and control, served to emphasise the local coordinates of industrial regulation. Administration regulated conditions for the reproduction of labour power and the effects of industrialisation upon wage employment. Regional councils and industrial boards sponsored industrial production as part of war experience. Local colonial governments faced the consequences of war experience, in which post-war industrial policy of local governments was rooted. Before the Africa-wide spate of labour strikes in 1945 and the immediate post-war period, the Colonial Office had a premonition of things to come. In 1943 Dawe (of the Office) insisted that the post-war problem for colonies would be jobs for workers in industries created during war-time, industries which, it was reported from Nigeria, had created 'a body of African craftsmen' who had become accustomed to 'new skills and new types of employment'. For the first time probably the Colonial Office in London recognised the growth of an industrial proletariat in Africa. In doing so, the Office faced the warning and threat of another premonition for the post-war period. The Ministries of Production, Food and the Board of Trade insisted that industrial development would draw labour away from the 'most important' colonial supply of raw materials. It was also 'undesirable' to give any long-term guarantees for the protection of industries that used British imports and competed with British exports.[144]

CONCLUSION

Lee and Petter, for instance, give the impression that 'certain parallels clearly existed between the central administration of wartime controls and the new initiative for a centrally inspired development policy'.[145] This impression is misleading. War-time central administration was based upon the principles of total war and expressed in the terms of equal sacrifice and no net national advantage. The conflict between these two principles was worked through by the experience of war. This experience put Britain at a distinct disadvantage with respect to the United States. In the US, although war production increased from 2 to 40 per cent of total industrial output between 1939 and 1943, private consumption increased by 12 per cent for the war as a whole. In 1944 the US produced nearly 50 per cent of world manufacturing output, 40 per cent of world armaments and 60 per cent of Allied war materials. In Britain industrial capacity was converted to war use rather than transformed by the scale of increase that was achieved in the US, where the volume of manufacturing output increased by 300 per cent over the war as a whole. Thus, in Britain private consumption fell by 22 per cent between 1939 and 1945 and export production was reduced by two-thirds.[146] By 1945 the experience of war had forced the Labour Government to subject external economic policy to the terms of control which could be exercised by the US through the application of its $3.75 billion loan. The implication of this subjection became clear during the convertibility crisis of 1947, but one response to this crisis was a fervent ideological attempt, by the Labour Cabinet, to make Britain independent of US economic controls.[147] This drive for British national economic independence was the corner stone of colonial economic development between 1947 and 1950, when central direction in development policy was most obvious. However, development policy was centralised on quite a different basis from that of war-time imperial policy.

Early import-substituting industrialisation was part of colonial war experience and it was accompanied by a severe reduction in consumption. With 1939 as a base of 100, official cost of living price indices for wage-workers' consumption increased to 130 in the US and 135 in Britain but 220 in India and 176 in Nigeria.[148] Wage rates for industrial workers in India fell to 67 (1939 = 100).[149] This underemphasises the extent of relative disadvantage for colonial workers, whose wartime experience in the military had created an upward shift in socially necessary means of subsistence and made veterans accustomed to a higher standard of living.[150] Average real wage rates in Britain increased to 105 in 1943 and 114 in 1945 (1939 = 100)[151] and the reduction in private consumption was, through taxation, to be made up by the post-war increase in social, welfare-based consumption. Colonial development policy after 1945, and until 1947, was a resumption of the welfarist approach, which had been developed pre-war but now became more acute, as a result of falling consumption, during the immediate post-war period.

The irruption of 1947 shifted the direction of development policy to fulfil British as much as colonial needs. Though phrased in terms of mutuality between British and Colonial need, the Labour cabinet idea was to incorporate the post-war colonial hinterland, now predominantly African, as a source of food and raw materials to replace imports from dollar sources. This central design looked as if it replicated the 1940 experience of the phoney war, when colonial governments were urged to save dollars before Lend Lease reduced the necessity to do so. It may have appeared to extend the regional forms of supply which developed after 1941 and led to state-sponsored industrialisation. However, state-sponsored enterprise was, as part of the 1947 design, now directed from Britain and not, initially at any rate by conception, mediated by regional organisation. The fundamental point is that colonial production and trade were now to be subject to direct British state intervention at points of production and not confined to the coordinates of money payments, sterling, as the framework of control over trade and markets and thus production. Only the colonial territories, of sterling balance holders, provided a potentially secure source of sterling imports. When independent sterling holders, now including India and the Middle East states as well as small European states such as Eire and Denmark, drew on their sterling balances, the use of the balances was subject to negotiation between the holders and the British government.

Unlike the colonies, these countries could negotiate a claim to the supply of scarce British capital goods in return for the sterling earnings. The colonies, on the other hand, had no such negotiating power and could be left to wait longer for the supply of scarce imports from Britain. The Colonial Development Corporation (CDC) was created as the central British vehicle to establish schemes and projects which were to expand the production of food and raw materials to meet British need. In the drive to meet British need, production became a direct object of policy; finance and trade was expected to change as a result of the intervention of state enterprise, compensating for the deficiency of private enterprise in expanding colonial production.

The same principle applied to control over colonial commodity trade. The controls and bulk purchase arrangements that were introduced during the war to make supplies available for the war effort under the combined production and exchange system were continued but now to support the construction of a British national economy. Colonial governments, and the Colonial Office, which had acquiesced in war-time controls for the combined war effort, now began to protest against the constraints post-war controls imposed upon colonial trade and returns from commodity production. While colonial producers were denied direct access to US markets, British government bulk purchase prices were held below US prices to subsidise British consumers.

The 1947 irruption was short-lived, lasting only to 1950, because it was immediately apparent that large-scale agrarian schemes under CDC (and Overseas Food Corporation) management were proven to be unproductive. After 1950, CDC became less an instrument to intervene directly in production and more an agency of state-sponsored international banking capital. During the 1950s and after, when schemes proved to be productive and, at least, earned financial surpluses on their current operating account, they were based, in the agrarian sphere at any rate, on the superintending of small-scale household production by local colonial administrations. Unlike the principles of total war and war experience, British state intervention in production was limited by the degree to which intra-imperial trade was denationalised during the immediate post-war period. This owed much to the form in which supply controls during the war were organised around the persons and institutions of British merchant companies. It also owed much to United States pressure, now made naked without the countervailing presence of US government agencies on combined boards and regional authorities. And in the transition to colonial political independence the 1947 design of British state intervention came up against the increasingly antagonistic social force, however unevenly developed, of an indigenous bourgeoisie in particular colonies. In this grander sense there were parallels with the war: the construction of a British national economy was squeezed between pressure from the US and from the Empire itself.

NOTES

1. J. Bowden, 'Development and Control in British Colonial Policy, with reference to Nigeria and the Gold Coast: 1935–1948' (PhD thesis, University of Birmingham, 1980), p. 246 (Churchill to Eden, Foreign Secretary, 31 December 1944, PREM 4/31/3).
2. Churchill (Prime Minister) to Beaverbrook (Lord Privy Seal), 7 May 1944, PREM 4/49/2.
3. J. M. Lee and M. Petter, *The Colonial Office, War, and Development Policy* (London, Maurice Temple Smith, 1982), p. 75.
4. See, for instance, Bowden, '*Development and Control*'; D. J. Morgan, *The Official History of Colonial Development,* Vol. 1. (London, Macmillan, 1980), chs 1–6.
5. See M. Cowen, 'Capital and Household Production: the Case of Wattle in Kenya's Central Province' (PhD thesis, University of Cambridge, 1979), chs 3 and 4.
6. See A Phillips, 'The Makeshift Settlement: Colonial Policy in British West Africa' (PhD thesis, City University, 1982).
7. H. Radice, '*The National Economy: a Keynesian myth?', Capital and Class*, 22 (1984), p. 124.
8. See P. Bareau, 'The Sterling Area', in R. S. Sayers, *Banking in the British Commonwealth* (Oxford, OUP, 1952); P. W. Bell, *The Sterling Area in the Postwar World* (Oxford, OUP, 1956), Intro., ch.1; S. Strange, *Sterling and British Policy* (Oxford, OUP, 1971), ch.2; F. Hirsch, *The Pound Sterling, a polemic* (London, Gollancz, 1965).
9. In a different connection see B. Anderson, *Imagined Communities* (London, NLB, 1983); in the same connection, M. McKinnon, '"Equality of Sacrifice": Anglo-New Zealand Relations and the War Economy, 1939–45', *J. of Imperial and Commonwealth History*. 12 (1) (1984).
10. *Annual Statement of the trade of the United Kingdom*, 1945 (Vol. 1) (London HMSO, 1947), p. 266.
11. R. Clarke, Anglo-American Economic Collaboration in War and Peace 1942–49 (Oxford, OUP, 1982), p. 27; also see D. F. McCurragh 'Britain's Dollar Problems 1939–45', *Economic Journal*, 58 (3) (1948).
12. See Table 1 below.
13. Clarke, *Anglo-American Economic Collaboration*, p. 25.
14. R. Law (FO), memo, 'Mr Richard Law's Visit to the United States' (WP (42) 492), 21 September 1942, CAB/123/239.
15. See A. R. Prest, *War Economics in Primary Producing Countries* (Cambridge, CUP, 1948).
16. See P. Addison, *The Road to 1945* (London, Cape, 1975).

17. R. S. Sayers, *Financial Policy 1939–45* (London, HMSO, 1956), p. 21.
18. A. S. Milward, *War, Economy and Society 1939–45* (London, Allan Lane, 1977), p. 9.
19. Milward, *War, Economy and Society*, pp.21–2.
20. Cranborne, memo, 'African Defence Situation', in Cranborne to Churchill, 28 September 1940, PREM 3/99/1.
21. Churchill to Cranborne, 21 October 1940, PREM 3/99/1.
22. A(42) 2nd meeting, 16 September 1942, CAB 95/10.
23. Earl Winterton, 'The Mobilisation of the British Commonwealth', *Quarterly Review*, 276 (548) (1941), p. 157.
24. Winterton, pp. 159–60.
25. Churchill to General Ismay (Secretary of State for War), 5 July and 19 August 1940, PREM 3/293/3.
26. War Office memo, 'Memorandum on the possibilities of offensive action in East Africa', 5 July 1940, PREM 3/293/3.
27. Eden (Foreign Secretary) to Churchill, 13 June 1940. PREM 3/293/3.
28. Japanese battle navy:

	Battleships	*Carriers*	*Cruisers*	*Destroyers*	*Submarines*
All (actual), Dec. 41	10	10	38	112	65
Indian Ocean (Est.) March 42	3	3/4	12/13	30	25

H. P. Willmott, *Empires in the Balance: Japanese and Allied Pacific Strategies in April 1942* (London, Orbis, 1982), p. 116; Joint Intelligence Sub-committee, memo, 'Scales of Attack – Indian Ocean Area', (JIC(42)85), 12 March 1942, CAB 81/4.

29. Ad hoc sub-committee, War Cabinet, memo, 'Defence Plans for bases in West Africa' (D10(42)63), 21 March 1942, CAB 81/4.
30. Milward, *War, Economy and Society*, pp. 24–6, 31–6; Willmott, *Empires in the Balance*, pp. 69, 72–3, 87, 161.
31. CO, memo, 'Estimated Colonial Production of main Strategic Commodities in relation to world production', 1947, CO537/2974.
32. *Annual Statement of Trade*.
33. R. Kindersley, 'British Overseas Investments in 1935 and 1936', *Economic J.* 47(4) 1937.
34. W. K. Hancock and M. M. Gowing, *British War Economy* (London, HMSO, 1949).
35. J. M. Keynes, memo, 'Overseas Financial Policy in Stage III' (WP(45)301). 15 May 1945 CO 537/1378, reproduced in D. Moggeridge (ed.), *Collected Writings of John Maynard Keynes*, vol. 24 (London, Macmillan, 1979), p. 265.
36. Keynes, *Overseas Financial Policy*, p. 256.
37. Keynes, *Overseas Financial Policy*, p. 258.
38. See Addison, *The Road to 1945*; Sayers, *Financial Policy*, pp. 44–5.
39. Keynes, *Overseas Financial Policy*, p. 258.
40. See S. Pollard, *The Development of the British Economy 1914–1980*, Third Edition (London, Arnold), pp. 216–7.
41. D. A. Low and A. Smith, *History of East Africa*, Vol. 3 (Oxford, OUP,

1976), p. 590; G. K. Helleiner, *Peasant Agriculture, Government and Economic Growth in Nigeria* (Illinois, 1966), p. 500; also calculated from Cmd. 7224.

42. *Annual Statements of Trade.*
43. L. Amery (Secretary of State for India) to Waley (Treasury), 10 August 1942; PREM 4/49/2; D. Moggeridge, 'From War to Peace – the Sterling Balances', *The Banker*, 122 (1972), p. 1033.
44. Moggeridge 'From War to Peace', p. 1033.
45. Amery, memo, 'Report of Committee on Indian Financial Questions' (WP(44)398), 19 July 1944, PREM 4/49/2.
46. Calculated from Table 2.4 above and from Keynes, *Overseas Financial Policy*, p. 265.
47. Ismay to Churchill, 'Forces in India – August 1943', 20 August 1943, PREM 3/147/9; Brooke (Chief of Imperial General Staff) to Churchill, 13 March 1943, PREM 3/293/3.
48. H. A. Shannon, 'The Sterling Balances of the Sterling Area 1939–49', *Economic J.* 50(3) 1950, pp. 540–1; Sayers, *Financial Policy*, p. 253.
49. WP(44)398; Prest, *War Economics*, p. 36.
50. Prest, *War Economics*, p. 38.
51. Churchill to Kingsley Wood (Chancellor of Exchequer) 23 July 1942, PREM 4/49/2. D. Moggeridge, 'Economic Policy in the Second World War', in M. Keynes (ed.), *Essays on John Maynard Keynes* (Cambridge, CUP, 1975), p. 186.
52. WM(43)106 conclusions, 27 July 1943, PREM 4/49/2.
53. WM(44)102 conclusions, 4 August 1944, PREM 4/49/2.
54. See, for instance, W. R. Louis, *Imperialism at Bay The United States and the decolonization of the British Empire 1941–1945*. (Oxford, OUP, 1977); Lee and Petter, *Colonial Office*.
55. Law (FO) to Eden (Foreign Secretary), 4 January 1943, FO 371/35310. (FO)
56. Attlee (Deputy PM) and others, memo, 'Colonial Policy' (WP(42)544), 5 December 1942, CAB/123/239.
57. R. J. Moore, *Churchill, Cripps, and India, 1939–1945* (Oxford, OUP, 1979), p. 51.
58. WM(42)428 concl., 1 August 1942, PREM 4/49/2.
59. Linlithgow (Viceroy) to Amery, 20 September 1942, PREM 4/49/2.
60. WM(43)106 concl., 27 July 1943, PREM 4/49/2.
61. Catto (Financial adviser, Treasury), memo, 'India's Sterling Balances', 9 August 1943, T236/148.
62. Rowe Dutton (T) to Eady (T), 12 November 1943, T236/149.
63. Catto, 'India's Sterling Balances', 9 August 1943, T236/148.
64. McCurragh, 'Britain's US Dollar Problem', pp. 357–60.
65. Catto, note, 'Gold and Dollar reserves of British Empire: use to prevent increase in sterling liability', March 1943, T160/1238.
66. Treasury (Keynes), memo, 'The overseas assets and liabilities of the UK', 5 August 1943, T236/148.
67. See, for instance, K. M. Wright, 'Dollar pooling in the Sterling Area, 1939–52' *American Economic Review*, 44(3) (1954).
68. C. F. Cobbold (Bank of England) to Eady, 26 October 1943, T236/149.

69. Catto, memos, 'India', 28 October and 5 November 1943, T236/148.
70. Treasury, 'Overseas Assets', 5 August 1943, T236/148.
71. A. Sen, *Poverty and Famines* (Oxford, OUP, 1981), pp. 63–78; Prest, *War Economics*, pp. 40–55.
72. Moggeridge, 'Economic Policy in the Second World War', p. 187.
73. WP(44)398.
74. See, for instance, R. N. Gardner, *Sterling – Dollar Diplomacy: Anglo-American Collaboration in the Reconstruction of Multilateral Trade* (Oxford, OUP, 1956); A. Van Dormael, *Bretton Woods* (London, Macmillan, 1978).
75. Moggeridge, 'From War to Peace', pp. 1034–5.
76. Keynes, memo, 'The problem of India's Sterling balances', 10 August 1943, T236/148.
77. Moggeridge, 'From War to Peace', p. 1034.
78. Moggeridge, 'From War to Peace', p. 1035.
79. J. Hurstfield, *The Control of Raw Materials* (London, HMSO, 1953), pp. 66–80, 137–97.
80. Hancock and Gowing, *British War Economy*, p. 241; K. M. Stahl, *Metropolitan Organisation of British Colonial Trade* (London, 1951), p. 26.
81. A supply section was set up within the CO to deal with the problem of supplies for thc colonies, and its files, in CO 852, illustrate the problems; Lee and Petter, *Colonial Office*, pp. 78, 84. For a case study of Tanganyika, see chapter 5 by N. J. Westcott in this volume.
82. Se CO 852/346/10–12 and CO 852/347/1–5 (18856 files); F. V. Meyer, memo, 'British Colonial Exports, 1939–1945', August 1946, CO 852/650/14.
83. See CO 852/346/12 and CO 852/445/1; Meyer, 'British Colonial Exports'; *Report on Cocoa Control in West Africa 1939–43*, Cmd. 6554, 1944; C. Leubuscher, *Bulk Buying from the Colonies* (London, RIIA, 1956), pp. 20–3; P. T. Bauer, *West African Trade* (Cambridge, CUP, 1954), pp. 257–8.
84. See CO 852/311/10 and CO 852/431 11.
85. Lee and Petter, *Colonial Office*, pp. 77, 112.
86. Cranborne to all African Governors, 21 and 24 March 1942, CO 822/111/46705 and TNA (Tanzania National Archives) 30157/55.
87. H. D. Hall and C. C. Wrigley, *Studies in Overseas Supply* (London, HMSO, 1956), pp. 205–61.
88. Hall and Wrigley, *Overseas Supply*, pp. 312–56; Lee and Petter, *Colonial Office*, pp. 86, 112; see Table 4 above and Central Statistical Office, *Statistical Digest of the War* (London, HMSO, 1951), Tables 145, 146.
89. Hall and Wrigley, *Overseas Supply*, p. 282; Hancock and Gowing, *British War Economy*, p. 376.
90. Hurstfield, *Control of Raw materials*, pp. 169, 171.
91. See C. C. Wrigley, 'Kenya: patterns of economic life, 1902–45', in V. Harlow and E. M. Chilver (eds), *History of East Africa*, Vol. 2 (Oxford, OUP, 1965); P. Moseley, *The Settler Economies: Studies in the economic history of Kenya and Southern Rhodesia 1900–63* (Cambridge, CUP, 1983).
92. Moyne to all Colonial Governors, 5 June 1941, CO 859/81/12905/4 (reproduced in CO, *Colonial Policy in War Time* (Cmd 6299), 1941).

93. See N. J. Westcott, 'Stabilising Commodity prices: state control of colonial commodity trade during and after the Second World War', *Third World Economic History and Development Group Conference*, Leicester, 1984.
94. Bauer, *West African Trade*, pp. 247–59; Lee and Petter, *Colonial Office*, 87–8; see CO 852/430/18000.
95. Leubuscher, *Bulk Buying*, pp. 9–29; Westcott, 'Stabilising Commodity prices', p. 6.
96. Clay (EA) to Carstairs (CO), 3 February 1943, CO 852/525/13; also, TNA 34953/I–II.
97. C. Ehrlich, *The Marketing of Cotton in Uganda, 1900–50* (PhD thesis, University of London, 1958), p. 288.
98. Leubuscher, *Bulk Buying*, 29–41; see Meyer, 'British Colonial Exports', p. 14; Kenya and Tanganyika, *Agricultural Reports*, 1942–5.
99. N. J. Westcott, 'The East African Sisal Industry, 1929–1949: The marketing of a colonial commodity during depression and war', *J. of African History*. 25, 4 (1984).
100. W. Freund, *Capital and Labour in the Nigerian Tin Mines* (London, Longmans, 1981), ch. 5; I. Henderson, 'Economic origins of decolonisation in Zambia, 1940–45, *Rhodesian History*, 5 (1974), p. 5; Meyer, 'British Colonial Exports', pp. 9–10.
101. Clauson (CO), minute, 22 June 1943, CO 852/503/19.
102. Stanley (Colonial Secretary) minute, 1943, CO 583/270/29; Clarke (T), note, 21 December 1945, T236/56; see correspondence in T236/57 .
103. Caine, minute, 27 November 1946, CO 852/650/14.
104. See Morgan, *The Official History of Colonial Development*, Vol. 1, pp. 157–9.
105. Law to Eden, 4 January 1943, FO 371/35310.
106. W. R. Louis, *Imperialism at Bay 1941–1945*, p. 127 (Eastwood to Martin (PS, Prime Minister), 1 September 1941, PREM 4/42/9).
107. *Parliamentary Debates*, House of Commons, 391, 13 July 1943, column 142.
108. C(45)4th meeting, 15 November 1945, CAB 134/52.
109. Lee and Petter, *The Colonial Office*, p. 89.
110. M. W. Wilmington, *The Middle East Supply Centre* (London, University of London Press, 1971), p. 30.
111. Wilmington, *Middle East supply Centre*, pp. 73,5.
112. Wilmington, *Middle East Supply Centre*, p. 74.
113. Halifax (British Ambassador, Washington) to FO, 15 Aptil 1943, CO 852/509/3; also see J. Giblin, 'A Colonial State in Crisis: Vichy Administration in French West Africa'. Paper given to the conference on 'Africa and the Second World War', SOAS, University of London, May 1984.
114. Melville (CO) to Creasey (CO), 27 January 1943, CO 852/509/3.
115. Swinton (WA) to Stanley (Colonial Secretary), 31 May 1943, CO 852/509/3.
116. Creasy, note on meeting at Ministry of War Transport, 4 January 1943, CO 852/509/3.
117. Creasy, note, 20 January 1943; Dawe (CO), note 21 January 1943; Price (DO) to Benson (War Cabinet Offices), 12 January 1943, CO 852/509/3.
118. Africa Committee minute, (A(42)4), 21 August 1942, CAB 95/10.

119. Africa Committee meeting, (A(42)1st), 25 August 1942, CAB 95/10.
120. Allied African Economic Affairs Committee meetings (AEA(C)43, 1st–6th), 13 March–2 April 1943, CAB 95/13.
121. Halifax to FO, 15 April 1943, CO 852/509/3.
122. Acting British Consul, Leopoldville, to FO, 19 June 1943; Halifax to FO, 28 June 1943, CO 852/509/3.
123. Africa Committee, (A(42)4), CO and FO note, 'American Paticipation in the War Effort in Africa', August 1942, CAB 95/10. Also see R. W. Graham, 'American Imperial Interests in West Africa During the Second World War'. Paper given to conference on 'Africa and the Second World war', SOAS, University of London, May 1984.
124. CO meeting, 30 December 1942, CO 852/509/3.
125. Halifax to Foreign Office, 4 June 1943, CO 853/509/3.
126. Allied African Economic meetings (AEA(C)43, 12th, 13th), 7, 12 May 1943, CAB 95/13.
127. Clarke, *Anglo-American Economic Collaboration*, p. 14.
128. Wilmington, *Middle East Supply Centre*, Ch. 7.
129. Wilmington, *Middle East Supply Centre*, p. 35.
130. N. Swainson, *The Development of Corporate Capitalism in Kenya 1918–77* (London, Heinemann, 1980), ch. 4; see material on EA Industrial Research and Development Board in TNA 30525.
131. Cranborne (Colonial Secretary) to Governor, Kenya, 19 October 1942, CAB 95/10.
132. CO, memo, 'Policy regarding Industrial Production in Africa' (A(42)7), 12 September 1942, CAB 95/10.
133. Cranborne to Governor, Kenya, 19 October 1942, CAB 95/10.
134. Swainson, *Development of Corporate Capitalism*, Ch. 4.
135. BoT, memo, 'UK participation in Empire Secondary Industries', July 1943, T236/173.
136. Proctor (T) to Playfair (T), 3 August 1943, T236/173.
137. Henderson (T) to Playfair, 29 July 1943, T236/173.
138. M. Cowen, 'The British State and Agrarian Accumulation in Kenya', in M. Fransman (ed.) *Industry and Accummulation in Africa* (London, Heinemann, 1982), p. 148.
139. Wilmington, *Middle East Supply Centre*, pp. 164–6.
140. Playfair to Rowe Dutton, 27 July 1943, T236/173.
141. BoT, memo, July 1943, t236/173. A(42)7, 12 September 1942, CAB 95/10.
142. Caine (CO) to Hall (Colonial Secretary) 9 June 1945, CO 537/1378.
143. A(43) 1st meeting, 19 February 1943; CO, memo, 'Secondary Industries in West Africa', 12 February 1943, CAB 95/10.
144. A(43) 1st meeting, 19 February 1943, CAB 95/10.
145. Lee and Petter, *Colonial Office*, p. 76.
146. Milward, *War, Economy and Society*, pp. 64–71; Clarke, *Anglo-American Economic Collaboration*, p. 15.
147. See Cowen, 'British State and Agrarian Accumulation'; M. Cowen, 'The British State, State enterprise and an Indigenous Bourgeoisie in Kenya after 1945', in P. Lubeck (ed.), *African Bourgeoisie* (forthcoming); M. Cowen, 'Early years of the Colonial Development Corporation: British State enterprise overseas during late colonialism', *African Affairs*, 83, 330

(Jan 1984); N. J. Westcott, 'Sterling and Empire: the British Imperial Economy, 1939–51', ICS seminar paper, London (D/82/5), 1983.
148. Prest, *War Economics*, p. 5.
149. B. Warren, *Inflation and wages in underdeveloped countries* (London, Cass, 1977), p. 59.
150. M. Cowen and J. Newman, 'Real wages in Central Kenya', 1924–1974', *mimeo*.
151. *Statistical Digest of the War*, Table 190.

3 Labour Mobilisation in British Colonial Africa for the War Effort, 1939–46

DAVID KILLINGRAY

Soldiers fight battles but civilian labour is required to supply the war machine and sustain an army in the field.[1] Nineteenth-century military campaigns in tropical Africa relied on large numbers of porters and labourers to carry munitions and food to the front line.[2] During the First World War well over 1 million carriers were employed in various theatres, particularly in East Africa, where conscription was widely used and conditions were harsh and mortality high.[3] The Second World War introduced the concept of 'total war', with every part of the economy increasingly mobilised to support the war effort. From the outbreak of war in 1939 governments assumed extensive powers, especially over the mobilisation and direction of labour for military and war production purposes. In Britain the efficient 'system of manpower budgeting became a very powerful instrument' to balance the whole war economy.[4]

Britain extensively exploited her colonial African resources of men and raw materials for war purposes in the First World War. The process was repeated in a more systematic and efficient way in the Second World War. Metropolitan controls regulated trade in primary products and steadily integrated the colonial economies into the imperial war economy. Labour was mobilised on a large scale for both military and civilian purposes. The small local colonial armies, the King's African Rifles and the Royal West African Frontier Force in East and West Africa, and the Sudan Defence Force, rapidly expanded by voluntary recruitment and conscription, were used throughout the war campaigns in Africa, the Middle East, and south-east Asia. A large part of this new African army consisted of non-combatants recruited specifically to serve as general military labour, or pioneers. Civilian labour was also mobilised for war production, but increased war-time demands led to labour and food shortages, particularly after 1942, and certain colonies resorted to conscription in order to secure an adequate supply of workers for agriculture and mining.[5] Forced labour was widely practised throughout colonial Africa, although in British colonies by 1939 the prevelant form was customary or communal labour. As a signatory of the League of Nations Convention on Forced Labour, 1930, Britain had agreed to suppress compulsory labour except where it was required in an emergency.[6] Until the late 1930s the Colonial Office in London barely had a coherent colonial labour policy, each colony establishing its own employment policies and practices within a generally accepted framework of principles. Industrial unrest on the Copperbelt in 1935 and riots in the Caribbean in 1937 demonstrated the need for governments to supervise labour administration and welfare, and led to the establishment of labour departments in individual colonies.[7]

The first pieces of emergency legislation were passed in British colonies on the outbreak of war. Under defence regulations governments had power to conscript Europeans for military service and, strictly speaking, also Africans. However, substantial sections of the domestic economies of colonies continued to be run on free market lines. Labour was not in short supply, as it had been before the Depression, and government departments and the army competed with each other for manpower. The army required substantial supplies of labour to construct military installations, especially in East Africa to support the campaign against Italy in 1940–1, and for the African Line of Communications. In West Africa labour was needed to build airfields for the US-directed air supply route to the Middle East, and for the vital naval base and harbour at Freetown. In order to prosecute the war, colonies built new roads and government buildings, constructed harbours and military plant of all kinds. Much of this official work was undertaken by Public Works Departments and military labour battalions.

A more systematic study would be required to calculate the total volume of labour employed for war purposes throughout British colonial Africa. Well over 10 000 men were employed in building the bases for the United States air-ferry service on the Takoradi–Kano–Khartoum route in 1941–2,[8] while the construction and maintenance of a new road and rail system to bring vital bauxite supplies from Mt Ejuanema in southern Gold Coast employed a labour force which reached 13 000 in October 1943.[9] In the Sudan in 1942 well over 50 000 man-days per month were being devoted to the stretch of road from Bor to Jebelein and Sudanese labour companies continued to work the North-South road until the North African campaign ended in 1943.[10] Wage labour forces increased in size as a result of this accelerated demand for labour. The Nigerian Public Works Department, placed on a 'care and maintenance' basis in 1940 when its labour force numbered 10 000, was rapidly expanded and reached 55 000 in 1942; wage labour in Freetown numbered 10 000 in 1939 but peaked at 45 000 in 1943.[11] Labour was not only attracted to urban centres by work and wages but also forced out of smaller trading centres and towns and the rural areas into the wage labour market by war-time inflation and acute shortages of goods.[12]

As labour shortages increased, governments abandoned laissez-faire ideas for interventionist policies. Labour demands varied from colony to colony, depending on local war-time conditions. For example, Kenya's pre-war labour surplus was eliminated by late 1940, but continentally, the decisive date was early 1942 when the Far Eastern colonies were lost to the Japanese, with the result that increased demand was placed upon Africa to supply vital raw materials. The answer to local acute shortages of labour and output, especially of foodstuffs, in specific regions and industries was the introduction of conscription. Strong apprehension existed in the Colonial Office about practices, even emergency ones, that could be interpreted as forced labour but in the colonies themselves officials, and specially settlers and those engaged in the business of war production, took a far less cautious and more immediate view. In non-British colonies sensitivities about using forced labour appear to have been far less pronounced. Italy already widely used forced labour, indeed announced it as a positive virtue; war-time exigencies increased its use.[13] Similar increases occurred in the French colonies, under both Vichy and Gaullist regimes, and in Belgian and Portuguese territories. Compared to the British, the French evinced less concern for native welfare and whether forced labour was employed by private plantations and business.[14]

Although the military and civilian authorities sometimes competed with each other for scarce labour resources, we can, for practical purposes, treat them separately. The army was under imperial direction and its demands often over-rode those of local colonial administrations. Unlike civilian labour, military recruits enlisted for several years, received a uniform and some training, came within a reasonably well organised social welfare system, and were liable to serve overseas. War-time military organisation totally transformed the old structures of the African colonial forces. By contrast, civilian labour recruited for war production was more likely to work under traditional employment practices on plantations or in mines. There were few outcries against the employment of conscripted non-combatants in the army but frequent denunciations of abuses suffered by conscript labour in civilian employ.

MILITARY LABOUR

The British recruited well over half a million soldiers from their African colonies during the Second World War. The vast majority of these men were recruited specifically as non-combatants (auxiliaries or pioneers), labourers in uniform, although the exigencies of war meant that a good number of them also received some training in arms and assumed combatant roles. Military labour came from every colonial territory. In 1940 the Military Labour Corps, formed in East Africa, was used in the campaign against the Italians. For the Middle East operations, from 1941 onwards, military labour was primarily organised in the East African Military Labour Service, the African Auxiliary Pioneer Corps, and the West African Military Labour Corps. Unlike the 1914–18 war, the British cautiously avoided recruiting a uniformed military labour force in Egypt,[15] although by 1942 200 000 Egyptians were employed directly by the Allied armies as general labour on construction work; by 1944 War Department workshops and other service roles required in the region of 60 000 men.[16] South African, and to a lesser extent Southern Rhodesian, hostility to arming Africans meant that most non-Europeans enlisted for the war effort in the Union served in non-combatant roles.[17]

In January 1940 Malcolm MacDonald, the Secretary of State for the Colonies, in a report on colonial manpower to the Cabinet, argued that there was inadequate equipment to form combatant units in Africa and that the first call should be upon local defence and then for pioneer units. The Cabinet rejected this idea of enlisting military labour but policy changed with Italy's entry into the war and the start of the East Africa campaign.[18] Labour was recruited in the East African territories and the Sudan for the operations in Ethiopia and Somaliland. The next call for labour was for the North African campaign. EAMLS troops were drafted to the Middle East theatre in 1941 and recruiting was extended in late June of that year to the High Commission Territories.[19] As the North African campaign intensified, Middle East Command demanded more African labour, the line and communication and ancillary manpower requirements being put at 135 000 in April 1942. The East

African Governor's Conference offered up to 20 000 men (100 000 were already serving with East Africa Command) while the civil authorities in West Africa thought the four colonies could contribute 100 000. Manpower surveys carried out in West Africa in February–April 1941 suggested that the area might provide 150 000 men. At that date the Gold Coast already had 30 000 people directly engaged in war work, while Nigeria estimated that a further 100 000 combatants and non-combatants might be recruited mainly from the south-east province and Cameroons.[20] The East African territories were reluctant to divert labour away from industrial and agricultural work and offered around 30 000 men.[21]

These consultations of labour requirements were carried further at two manpower conferences, in Cairo in mid-August, and in Nairobi during September and October 1942, which discussed the numbers, organisation, and technical aspects.[22] Further conferences were held in Nairobi and London in May 1943 but the end of the North African campaign and the surrender of Italy altered the immediate urgent demand for labour. By then the East African Governors' Conference stated that Kenya, Northern Rhodesia, and Nyasaland were 'virtually dry' of men and that 'the time has come to call a halt to this Middle East drain on East African manpower'.[23] Sir Henry Moore, the Governor of Kenya, urged on London a serious review of the recruiting situation in light of the need for increased agricultural production in East Africa, and he suggested that the burden should now fall on the West African colonies, which had 'not been anything like so heavily recruited'.[24] Although East Africa continued to supply a steady flow of military labour to North Africa, the main source of supply now switched increasingly to West Africa, which area also provided the bulk of the military labour required for the Asian theatre. Late in 1942 Wavell, the C-in-C India, asked the War Office to consider using West African troops in Burma, where their porter and jungle capacity would be invaluable. The first Auxiliary Groups with the 81st(WA) Division went to India in September–October 1943, and the groups with 82nd(WA) Division followed in May 1944.

Non-combatant military recruits enlisted under terms similar to combatants. In East and West Africa recruits were often allocated to combatant or non combatant units according to immediate manpower needs and on the basis of the physical appearance of individual recruits. Pioneer work, especially carrier labour in West Africa, was despised, and men sometimes deserted in order to rejoin the army but in a combatant unit. Non-combatants had to serve for the duration, or until such time as their services were no longer required. As soldiers they received a uniform and food and the few facilities offered by the welfare services, which only very slowly became part of the African colonial forces. Rates of pay varied. East Africans received a basic rate of sixpence a day with fourpence remitted; soldiers from the HCT had ninepence plus ninepence remitted, while West Africans were paid one shilling a day with expatriate allowance if overseas. Differing pay levels led to inter-unit unrest, although the most serious grievance among African military labourers, especially in North Africa, was the lack of home leave. At the start of the war medical rejection rates for both combatants and non-combatants were high. However, as the demands for labour increased, medical inspections became more perfunctory and army feeding and exercise was expected to build up recruits to a satisfactory physical standard within three months. Even as early as January 1941 the men of the 1st Company Mauritius Pioneers and Artisans were reported as 'of very poor standard, many with bad teeth and quite a number suffering from endemic venereal disease, malaria and dysentery'.[25]

The imperial authorities in 1939–40 did not envisage African troops being used other than in Africa. As the war progressed, pragmatic needs amended traditional ideas and prejudices. Non-combatant labour was used widely throughout North Africa, especially in Egypt, Libya and Tunis, and in Malta and the Levant. During the Mediterranean conflict, in April 1943, nearly 600 Basuto pioneers, along with Mauritian and Palestinian labourers, lost their lives in the sinking of the *Erinpura* en route from Alexandria to Malta, a tragedy that rivalled the large number of deaths suffered by the South African Native Labour Corps in the loss of the *Mendi* during the First World War. A small number of African troops also served in Italy in 1943–5, as medical orderlies and in charge of mules carrying artillery. West African carriers played a vital role in the forest campaigns in Burma; East and West African troops performed general labouring duties in India and Ceylon.

Military operations required all manner of general labour work plus a vast range of trade skills. African military labour assumed important routine roles comprising manual labour and garrison duties, thus relieving European troops for other roles. African non-combatants served as labourers on docks, in stone quarries, building fortifications, and for general construction work; semi-skilled men and tradesmen were employed as signallers, in printing maps, as fire-fighters, and lorry drivers. In Haifa Basuto labourers worked under factory conditions, dismantling old vehicles for spares and making petrol cans.[27] Unfortunately there are few personal accounts by Africans describing non-combatant duties, an important gap that needs to be filled by oral research.[28] It is clear, however, that interspersed with periods of idleness were times of intensely hard work. West Africans pioneers, it was reported in 1943, 'are being worked so hard', while Charles Arden-Clarke, visiting Basuto troops said:

> I came across instances of companies which appeared to me to have been kept too long at heavy labour under hard conditions without change or respite to the detriment of their morale and discipline.[29]

Non-combatants took on combatant roles, substituting for European troops on garrison duty and as guards on stores and prisoners. One quarter of the Swazi contingent trained with light machine guns, and in mid–1944 certain porters in Burma received rifles and sten guns. In North Africa detachments of non-combatants were diluted with European combatant units and served as artillerymen there and in Italy. By the end of the war the distinction between combatant and non-combatant roles had become somewhat blurred, a comment as much on the changed attitudes to African military worth as to the acute need for military manpower.

In the early months of the war non-combatant labour in East Africa was drawn from the traditional military recruiting grounds, from the so-called 'martial races', and from those areas that had been the main sources of supply of migrant labour. Thus many of the first Kenyan recruits for the EAMLS came from Nyanza province,[30] and in Uganda they were drawn from West Nile province, an area which had a long tradition of supplying the heavy labour for industries such as sugar cane and sisal cutting and the handling of timber.[31] Tanganyikan recruits came initially from Kigoma and Mbeya, but as the war continued, recruiting was extended to other regions.[32] In mid-1941, when the C-in-C Middle East requested African manpower, he suggested that below latitude 22 degrees south might be found Africans who were accustomed to the cold and who might therefore be suitable for service in the Mediterranean area. When recruiting of pioneers began in Bechuanaland, the chief of the Batwana, whose people lived north of 22 degrees south, rejected the suggestion that his men should form a company under the South African Defence Force to serve in the Caprivi Strip.[33] The first recruiting campaign in the HCT began in late June 1941, the second in early 1942. During 1941 artisans also came from Mauritius and the Seychelles. In West Africa the majority of non-combatants came from Nigeria and Sierra Leone.

Official, and semi-official, accounts of African war-time service in the army, by Moyse-Bartlett, Haywood and Clarke,[34] Gray, and Bent, refer to enlistment as largely voluntary. This was far from so. Certainly some men did volunteer, attracted by the prospect of regular food, an opportunity to learn a skill and to earn money. In East Africa, and even in the Seychelles, the depredations of carrier recruitment in the First Word War had left strong memories and a widespread antipathy to military labour. At the start of the war supplies of migrant labour from Ruanda-Urundi into Uganda dried up as labourers were fearful of being rounded up as porters.[35] Officials in Tanganyika had great difficulty in meeting the quotas for each district. This is clearly shown in the Provincial Commissioners' Reports for 1939 and 1940:

> 1939. Southern Highland Province: At first the call for recruits was undoubtedly most unwelcome. Men were wanted quickly and there was no time for preliminary groundwork designed to counteract memories of the carrier corps of the last war . . .
>
> Western Province. As was to be expected conscription for the EAMLS proved too sudden an innovation for the . . . Waha of Kigoma District who took alarm despite all measures taken to assure them that they were not required for combatant service. The repercussions spread northwards to the Kibondo Division . . . To continue would inevitably have resulted in a mass exodus of the people to the bush . . . whilst the most violent reaction to conscription came from the Waha, the Wafipa were not unalarmed . . . and many took to the bush or vanished across the border.[36]

Voluntary labour was equally difficult to obtain in Northern Rhodesia; officials estimated in April 1942 that only 3000 volunteers would be forthcoming although conscription might produce 9000. In Nyasaland officials suggested that attempts should be made to recruit military labour on the Rand, where there were 30 000 migrant Nyasas. Compulsion would be difficult in the colony because of the nearness of the frontiers, and there was already a shortage of labour, with up to 75 000 men absent in Southern Rhodesia.[37] In Southern Rhodesia labour was conscripted in 1940–1 to build airfields required for the Empire Air Training Scheme. Native Commissioners called on chiefs and headmen to supply men. In a country where contract and forced labour were widespread this new form of *chibaro* was strongly resisted. The work was unpopular, especially during the ploughing season, and the wages offered were lower than those received by poorly-paid farm labourers. Some men also feared that they would be conscripted for work outside the country. As a result, at the approach of government messengers and recruiters, men took to the bush and to the hills. When conscription began in the Bulawayo district, hundreds of men fled across the border into Bechuanaland. There is also evidence that some European farmers, anxious to retain their labour force, assisted Africans to avoid conscription. From early 1940 onwards several thousand Africans were employed to build eleven airfields throughout Southern Rhodesia.[38]

Many of those recruited by the military were conscripted or impressed by arbitrary means. Describing an auxiliary group, without uniform, being sent from Nigeria to Gambia and Freetown, the official war historian of Southern Rhodesia stated that embarkation at Lagos was not an orderly affair:

> In fact there appeared to be men who strongly resented being put aboard and who had to be roughly handled before they accepted the situation . . . it was not until Freetown was reached that it was discovered that several of the 'troops' were in reality Lagos dock hands. They eventually turned out quite good soldiers.[39]

Conscription of non-combatant labour occurred in every British African territory. Before Compulsory Service Regulations were introduced – for example, in Tanganyika in July 1940 and Kenya in October 1940 – quotas of recruits had been imposed on areas and operated by District Commissioners through the Native Authorities. When formal conscription began in Tanganyika, 'most of the male population of Bagamoyo took to the bush' and 'were afraid they would be impressed if they came near the town', while in Dar es Salaam tax defaulters were conscripted.[40] In Southern Tanganyika in 1943 the DC reported on the resistance of the Makonde to conscription:

> Conscription has had to develop into a cunning procedure on the part of both the hunter and the hunted. A date is fixed with the Liwalis and any signs of the impending action, such as the ordering of lorries for the transport of the recruits to Lindi and preparation of notices of selection, must be kept secret. The Liwalis give the Jumbes the shortest notice possible so that stray words or demeanour may not cause suspicion. Then in the night preceding the fatal day a swoop is made and a few of the weak, meek, and slow are gathered. Relatives and friends have previously been warned or are 'missed'. On the other

hand, the hunted, after a certain period, begin to feel it is time attention was paid to them and so, in order to baffle the Jumbes at night they go to sleep in the huts of the persons who are not likely to be bothered on account of conscription (widows, old people) or make themselves scarce until the danger is past. It is useless to be shocked at such procedures. It is this or nothing. The Wamakonde in fact accept the procedure as natural.[41]

Within the framework of customary social and political order many Africans obeyed the instructions of chiefs to join the army. In the HCT some chiefs took a leading part in recruiting for the AAPC. Men did not volunteer but were often prodded and threatened by chiefs in Bechuanaland.[42] The discussions about recruiting at a secret session of the Basutoland Council in October 1943 give a picture of the true nature of enlistment practices. Senior chiefs generally favoured recruiting, for, as the late Paramount Chief Seciso said, 'when the chief goes to war he does not go alone. He goes wearing his blanket and the blanket is his people'. Maama Lechese argued in Council that voluntary recruitment had not worked as thirty men 'refused to enlist when they were told to join voluntarily' and they only agreed when ordered to do so by the Paramount Chief. In March 1942 chiefs and headmen in the Teyateyaneng district opposed recruiting and 'hid their people . . . The orders I had received', said Lyon Mahoa, 'were to send out chiefs and ask them to call their men together and then pick out a number of young men . . . That was a good way of recruiting but the chiefs and sub-chiefs were against it because they did not like their men to join up'. Opponents of recruiting burnt huts and 'many people joined up for the mines in order to evade the army'.[43] Summing up the discussion Charles Arden-Clarke, the Resident Commissioner, reported: 'The debate makes abundantly clear the attitude of every Masutho towards so-called "voluntary recruiting" for the Army. There is no such thing – it is and always has been compulsion, naked and unashamed'.[44]

Compulsory Service Regulations were imposed in West Africa in 1941, principally as a reserve power if districts failed to produce quotas of recruits. Conscription was more limited than in East Africa, and it was not until July 1942 that the WAMLC was formed.[45] Ten thousand conscripts were soon raised, including the press-ganging of several hundred men sleeping out in the streets of Bathurst in November 1942.[46] Compulsion was used to enlist lorry drivers and craftsmen, mostly from southern regions of the West Africa colonies, many of whom were literate and invariably very reluctant recruits. In the Gold Coast many artisans refused to register as required in late 1941 and early 1942, although lorry drivers could more easily be controlled through driving licences. The high figures for desertion from the armed forces in November 1943 – 42 per cent of all Ashantis and 20 per cent of men from the colony – gives some idea of the unpopularity of military service and conscription.[47]

Popular resistance of one form or another to military labour recruitment occurred in every British colonial territory. Men took to the bush or crossed borders to escape chiefs and recruiters. In Buha, Tanganyika, opposition was so intense that conscription was suspended for two years.[48] New recruits found themselves marshalled to railway stations and, in some cases, confined to barbed-wire compounds under armed guards. In Basutoland the *Lekhotla la Bafo* (Commoners' League), led by Josiel Lefala, opposed the British presence in the country and recruiting for the AAPC. As a result of his militant resistance to labour recruiting, Lefala was arrested and detained for the duration.[49]

Official attitudes towards military labour demands were often caught between the desire to aid the war effort and the equal interest to protect the long-term economy of the colony. There was also the need to find the balance of economic and political interests in the competition for labour from the military and the domestic market. Private commercial interests sometimes overrode patriotic principles, as, for example, in Swaziland, where Europeans opposed Swazis joining the army:

> Natives were threatened by farmers that if they joined up their kraals would be destroyed and their people driven off the land, and they were threatened by mine recruiters that their cattle would be seized for the repayment of advances; all kinds of lies were spread about conditions of war service and what was likely to happen to them. . . .[50]

In Southern and Central Africa politico-economic relations with South Africa fashioned official thinking about recruitment. Tshekedi Khama, anxious to prevent Bechuanaland's incorporation into South Africa, in February 1941 rejected the Resident Commissioner's suggestion that the Bamangwato join the South African Native Military Corps; he insisted that his people serve under the British flag. The Bechuanaland administration was concerned not to antagonise South Africa and also to maintain a flow of labour to the Rand and thus ensure the mines as a continued source of the protectorate's revenue.[51]

However, the major complication arising from military demands for labour was the threat that it posed to the domestic labour market and the urgent need to maintain agricultural production and provide adequate men for the mines, dock installations, and other essential services. The great increase of war-time labour came largely from those areas that traditionally supplied migrant labour. At the same time as areas lost manpower, the colonial state increase the demand for agricultural output. The army consumed large quantities of foodstuffs and the metropole urged increased production of primary exports for the war effort. By late 1943 Bechuanaland had up to 40 per cent of its male labour force absent from the country, either serving in the AAPC or working in South Africa. Nyasaland was in a similar position, while Northern Rhodesia reported in 1943 that only 30 per cent of able-bodied males were left in villages for food production. Drought in many regions of East, Central, West and Southern Africa in 1942 and 1943 resulted in cumulative low crop yields; lack of manpower led to acute food shortages. Military recruiting further exacerbated this to the extent that it was suspended in Central Province, Tanganyika, from February to April 1943. In the Southern Province it was reported that conscription had caused 'disruption and disorganisation'. By the middle of the war Northern Rhodesia was not only short of manpower but had to import 40 per cent of its food requirements.[52] In 1942 Southern Rhodesia experienced drought, and this, combined with an absence of labour, led to 'an acute food shortage as far as the native population is concerned', another reason why the authorities were reluctant to impose conscription.[53] And so serious was famine in certain districts of Uganda in 1944 that the authorities refused to allow men needed for emergency food planting to leave the area.[54]

Labour demands for agricultural export crops rivalled military recruiting. The bumper sugar crop in Mauritius restricted recruiting for the Auxiliary Corps in 1941. In Kenya in July 1943 the governor secured a reduction in military recruiting 'in face of the increasing demand for production of rubber, pyrethrum, sisal, maize, wheat, tea, sugar, copper, oil seeds . . .', made more acceptable because the colony had exceeded its allocated recruiting target for the Middle East.[55] The authorities in Nigeria, with the support of Lord Swinton, the Resident Minister, succeeded in reducing the number of pioneers demanded for the Middle East in 1943 so that labour could be concentrated on producing palm kernels demanded by the British Ministry of Food.[56] At times troops were organised to grow crops on army farms and they were also used in public works' schemes and anti-locust campaigns.

Military recruiting in Central and Southern Africa competed directly with traditional mine-labour recruiting. Nyasaland had an agreement with the Witwatersrand Native Labour Association (WNLA) to supply the Rand with 8500 migrant workers annually. Recruiting was suspended in 1940 to help recruiting for the King's African Rifles, and resumed in 1941. In February 1942 WNLA asked for the quota to be raised to 15 000 men annually, but the authorities replied that military demands must first be met. By agreement WNLA recruiting was closed down but the Governor accused the Association of hindering 'military recruitment by connivance at illegal deportation of natives from Nyasaland . . .' The colony also attempted to restrict migration of Nyasa workers to Southern Rhodesia until military targets had been reached. This action brought strong protests from the Governor of Southern Rhodesia and the Colonial Office responded by instructing Nyasaland to ensure labour continued to move into Southern Rhodesia 'for their war industries'.[57]

The revenues of the HCT relied heavily upon the earnings of migrant workers in South Africa but the authorities were faced with the demand for military labour which could only be met if mine recruiting was suspended. Smuts, the South African prime minister, wanted the labour supply from the HCT maintained; he feared white working-class unrest if mine production was disrupted. Nevertheless it was agreed to suspend recruiting for 6 months as from 1 July 1942, the British representative suggesting that South Africa look for alternative labour from Portuguese East Africa.[58]

In West Africa conscripted civil labour was used in the Jos tin mines of Nigeria; and the authorities in Sierra Leone sought to maintain adequate labour for both military and naval installations in Freetown and the local iron ore mines. Mines were a source of skilled labour. The gold mines of the Gold Coast had a labour force of 34,000, of whom 3,000 were artisans. Throughout 1941 and 1942 closure of the gold mines was discussed in order to release skilled labour for the army and other war production. Arguments against closure stressed the possible problems of unemployment and the value of gold to the colony's economy and also as a source of foreign exchange under the Lend Lease agreements. In November 1942 'severe reduction' was agreed, and although this released skilled labour, it is unclear to what extent the military or other sectors of the economy benefited.[59]

Freetown was a vital base for naval and mercantile marine operations in the South Atlantic. From mid-1940 to late 1942 it was seen as vulnerable to Vichy threats. The working population of the town increased in the early years of the war, placing additional strains on accommodation and food supplies. A large part of the labour force was employed in the port, bunkering and discharging ships. The productivity of these port workers fell far short of official approval. Workers, it was reported, refused to work after dark and turned up only when it suited them, while sudden strikes contributed to growing congestion in the port. In May and June 1941 the Royal Navy and the Ministry of War Transport suggested that additional workers be imported and that all harbour labour 'be treated as a whole body'.[60] The means to do this already existed and were further strengthened by the Defence (Compulsory Services) Amendment regulations, December 1941, which scheduled certain establishments as 'essential services' and gave the colonial state the power to conscript manpower for the war effort. Such regulations were not always easy to implement and enforce when privately owned companies pursued their own policies of wage levels and dismissals. As a solution to the problems in the port, the C-in-C South Atlantic argued for a centralised labour force, with unskilled workers organised into a West African Military Labour Corps. This was agreed in June 1942 and both Nigeria and the Gold Coast supplied artisan companies, which were dispatched to Freetown.[61]

The Colonial Office was cautious about extensive compulsory enlistment of labour under military command in Freetown, although such schemes had been adopted in East Africa and the policy was recommended by the chief labour adviser in West Africa. Governor Stevenson strongly urged conscription of port labour. He wrote:

> I am appalled at the standard of labour in Freetown at present. I have watched a number of gangs engaged in different work and all were moving and working so slowly that it was obvious that they were deliberately making an effort to do as little work as possible . . . The remedy for this shocking state of affairs is adequate supervision . . . things have got to such a state that conscription into Army Labour Corps Companies will, as far as I can see, provide the only remedy which can be effected within a reasonable time . . .[62]

It was a solution he reiterated in April 1942, when, he reported, the 'labour is daily becoming more out of hand and . . . output is now approximately thirty per cent of that of pre-war'.[63]

Although these difficulties, and the inter-service competition for manpower, were in part resolved to official satisfaction by additional emergency legislation in May 1942 and the appointment of an army officer as Director of Service Works to control the allocation of labour, the productivity of port labour remained low. Conscription began in

Freetown in November 1942, but a year later Lord Swinton, the Resident Minister, wrote of continued slacking by labour and the need for drastic supervision and reform. He reported Admiral Rawlings' description of port labour at Freetown as 'a study of African still life'.[64] Matters were not improved by the severe shortage of rice throughout late 1942 and 1943, which 'resulted in the labourer being in a state of malnutrition and it is physically impossible for him to make a sustained effort over a long day'.[65] By April 1943 conscription had put 9540 men into various branches of the army, and this system continued for the duration.

African reactions to military service are largely unrecorded. Desertion rates, which might be high in the territory of recruitment, rose dramatically when troops were due to be shipped overseas but naturally fell to a low level in a strange country. Politics appear to have impinged little on African auxiliaries, who for the most part were illiterate. Strikes and riots occurred but these were invariably occasioned by unit rivalries, boredom, lack of women, poor social and welfare facilities, and the slow process of demobilisation once the war was over.[66] Demobilisation was indeed slow, held up by shipping shortages, and military labour was not fully repatriated until early 1947.

In the immediate post-war years the British government looked to colonial Africa for a continued supply of military labour for the Middle East. Recruits came from the HCT and Mauritius and were employed mainly in pioneer roles and occasional garrison duties in North Africa. Palestine was excluded from their area of operations, as the Dominions Office, sensitive to South African white opinion, was anxious to avoid any confrontation between black troops and European Jews. Recruiting in the HCT began in July 1946, soldiers being enlisted to serve for two years. Protests came from the nationalist press in South Africa and in London from Dr Harold Moody, that veteran watchdog of African interests, this time wearing the hat of the London Missionary Society.[67] Mauritian troops served in Egypt and Cyrenaica until 1951, and none too happily in the last two years.[68] Altogether 3000 men from the HCT and 3000 Mauritius Pioneers were employed with Middle East Land Forces in the years following the war.

CIVILIAN LABOUR

Conscription for military labour was an accepted practice in war-time. Compelling labour to work during emergencies was a common and accepted practice in British colonies, but large-scale conscription for civil production in war-time, especially for private enterprise, was a new departure in policy. Compulsory Service regulations in each colony empowered government to impress labour, but this was only used to any extent in Kenya, Tanganyika, Northern and Southern Rhodesia and Nyasaland, principally for agricultural production, and in Nigeria in the tin mines. Civil conscription was first used in East Africa in 1940–1, thus establishing a precedent in raising labour for essential services that could be followed by other colonies as labour shortages increased after late 1941. In East and Central Africa compulsion of labour for certain agricultural production continued after the war had ended.

Several recent studies have examined forced labour in the war-time economies of Kenya, Tanganyika, Northern Rhodesia and the Nigerian tin-mining industry.[69] The Colonial Office in London disliked forced labour for moral reasons. Many officials also believed, often quite correctly, that impressed labour was inefficient labour. Conscription was costly to implement and involved government in transporting, housing and providing medical facilities for labour; and often the system benefited inefficient producers and bad employers and helped to keep wages down when war-time inflation was rapidly eroding purchasing power. This was, for example, the case with forced labour used in the Tanganyika sisal industry.[70] Officials in London expected that the war-time emergency would require the use of conscripted labour for essential services within the colonies, but they often found it difficult to accept the idea that European-owned farms and plantations should be included in such schemes.

During the 1930s the Colonial Office, spurred by growing industrial unrest in the colonies, had increased its welfare concern for colonial labour. Forced labour, even in war-time, was viewed as a regressive step only to be taken as a short-term emergency measure. Decisions on large-scale forced labour were taken at War Cabinet level; consent was usually given for impressment for a limited period of time but invariably war demands meant that the period was extended, often for the duration. Imperial decisions to allow forced labour in East Africa were severely criticised in the Commons in March 1942, principally because African labour was being employed on private estates owned by Europeans.[71] Such criticisms continued to come from within Parliament but also from officials in the Colonial Office.[72] A Cabinet statement of 20 September 1943, and a further memorandum by the Secretary of State for the Colonies, Oliver Stanley, on 29 October, authorised the continuation of forced labour and proposed a full investigation into the system in the colonies. Sir Julian Foley for the Ministry of Supply, and Major Orde Browne for the Colonial Office, both reported on East African forced labour, in December 1944 and June 1945 respectively. Their reports pointed out certain abuses but they concluded that private enterprise had not unduly benefited from forced labour and that, given the circumstances of the war economy, labourers had received adequate protection. Such reassurances never completely stilled Colonial Office apprehensions, which were revived with the continuation of forced labour into 1946.

East Africa was the source of vital food supplies for the army in the Middle East. The region's agricultural export crops, such as rubber, sisal, cotton, pyrethrum, coffee and tea, were also required for the imperial war effort. During the 1930s, as a result of the Depression, the old labour shortage had disappeared. However, this situation was changed in Kenya by late 1940, and throughout the whole of East Africa by early 1942, when new demands were placed on the economies of the three territories. With a growing labour shortage, European farmers demanded government action to conscript labour for agricultural production.[73] Conscription was most extensive in Kenya and Tanganyika, although forced labour was used as a short-term emergency measure in Uganda – for example, in Busoga – in 1943.[74]

Imperial approval was given in October 1941 for the conscription of agricultural labour in Kenya. The Government announced a special labour census and appointed a committee under Walter Harrigan, Director of Man Power, to consider conscription. The Harrigan Committee report, of February 1942, stated that agriculture was short of labour by 10 per cent and that this gap should be met by conscription. The result was the introduction of the Defence (African Labour for Essential Undertakings) regulations, which established an Essential Undertakings Board with power to decide which industries were eligible for forced labour.[75] Under this system conscript labour was used for the whole war period, and on into September 1946, in industries such as sisal, sugar, lime-burning, rubber, and flax production, Nearly 3000 conscripts worked on the railways and others were employed in service works such as irrigation schemes.[76] Sisal was the largest single industry employing forced labour, in November 1944 taking 10 265 workers, over half the total conscripts.[77] The majority of conscripted labourers were in private employ – about 12 000 as against 2000 in Government service in March 1944.

To improve labour supply in Kenya, conscript camps were established in February 1944. Recruiting denuded whole districts of able-bodied males and reduced food production, thus placing heavy burdens of agricultural work on women and children. In Nyanza, Meru, and Nyeri men left home and took shelter in the bush to avoid recruiters; the hard work on sisal estates was specially hated. Desertion was the most common form of resistance. The Kitui District Annual Report, 1943, stated: 'The unpopularity of conscript labor is so evident that some deserters have been arrested two or three times without in any way dampening their intention to desert a fourth time.'[78]

By mid-1944 the Tanganyika wage-labour force had grown in size, and 35 000, or 11 per cent, of the total consisted of conscripted workers. Conscription began on a large scale in early 1942 and increased steadily in 1943–4. Labour was used primarily for the production of foodstuffs and agricultural export crops, mainly sisal, rubber, and pyrethrum.[79] Harsh penal sanctions imposed under the compulsory labour regulations punished those who resisted recruitment or who deserted.

Between 1939 and 1941 the older industries of sisal-growing and gold-mining, the former already hit by the Depression of the 1930s, were subject to Government restrictions. Wages on the European-owned sisal and rubber estates were low and labour supply consequently slack; Africans could earn more money in the new demand industries of maize-growing, cattle, sugar and diamonds.[80] With the loss of the South East Asian sisal and rubber supplies in late 1941, urgent attempts were made to revive Tanganyikan rubber production and to expand the output of sisal. Faced with the need to increase production, and a labour shortage on the rubber plantations, the government introduced conscription in November 1942, initially impressing 2800 Gogo from the Central Province. These conscripts, men unfit for military service, were forced to work for a period of 12 months on the rubber plantations at wages fixed at a basic level of 12 shillings per month. By July 1944 a total of 9650 men had been recruited from the Central Province, and 6 months later a further 3873 conscripts had been secured to replace those repatriated. This process continued well into 1946. In August 1943 local labour was also conscripted, plus 500 men from Arusha and 1138 Haya. By 1945 the labour force on the rubber plantations had risen to 21 235, of whom 7428 had been conscripted.[81]

Desertion was the most common form of resistance by forced labourers. To prevent this, the Tanganyika authorities created guarded compounds for the workers and corporal punishment was used to induce men to turn out for work. The government required increased plantation labour to meet war-time demands for rubber but it also urged peasants to produce larger food surpluses to feed the military and the enlarged labour force. Conscription removed men from household cultivation and placed much of the burden of food production on women. Famine conditions, caused by poor and excessive rains in Tanga Province in 1940–3, were exacerbated by conscription. In the Handeni District the peasantry called the harsh exaction 'the time of rubber'.[82]

Tanganyika became a major supplier of sisal after 1941; its importance to the war economy was such that military recruiting was restricted in sisal-growing areas while large numbers of conscript workers were rounded up in other regions to help expand production. At the end of 1941 the combined effects of drought, food shortages and a reduction in food rations to labourers on sisal plantations had brought about a drastic fall in the number of workers in the industry. Estate owners urged on government the need for conscription and this was begun in late 1942, but, following a War Cabinet decision, greatly increased in September 1943. Conditions on the estates were hard, the work harsh and living accommodation of a very poor standard or barely existent. Sisal work was unpopular, but by the end of 1945 about 24 000 Africans had been impressed on the estates. The 'free' labour also increased, and included a substantial number of women and children.[83] To meet the growing demand for foodstuffs, the Tanganyika Government attempted to make the colony self-sufficient in food crops. The drought of 1942–3 reduced output, and in order to maximise planting for the next season, all labour and military recruiting was suspended in Kenya and Tanganyika at the start of the growing season, from February to April 1943.[84] Later that year conscription was resumed and forced labour was employed in growing wheat, maize, sugar, beans, and coffee. Essential foodstuffs and pyrethrum employed 6500 conscripts in 1943–4, 6000 in 1944–5, and a larger number in 1945–6. By the end of the war a total of 84 500 Africans had been conscripted for work on the estates.

The strategic significance of Mauritius increased with Madagascar's adherence to Vichy in mid-1940, and further with Japan's military victories in the eastern Indian Ocean region. Labour was required for three priorities: to increase the output of sugar, to feed the island itself, and for defence works principally for the Royal Navy. Sugar and food production utilised a reserved labour force of 58 000, which included women and children. After January 1944 defence works shed labour. The casual traditional labour practices of Mauritius were regarded by officials as a serious barrier to increased war-time productivity. Various incentive schemes produced little improvement, nor did an attempt to organise a voluntary civil labour corps 'without disciplinary sanctions'.

The authorities therefore deemed 'it . . . necessary to introduce compulsory labour. Men who are called up are recruited into the Mauritius Labour Corps under officers of the Mauritius Government who are responsible for their administration, discipline and non-technical supervision to ensure that there is no wastage of labour'.[85]

Labour conscription in Northern Rhodesia was introduced in February 1942 for food production, largely at the behest of European settler farmers. The imperial priority was to maximise the output of the Copperbelt. As a result the labour force in the mining area doubled in size between 1939 and 1944. This placed an increasing and heavy demand on the food-producing areas of the colony, already suffering from drought and poor harvests, which they were unable to meet. Maize consumption on the Copperbelt rose from 320 000 bags in 1939 to 500 000 bags in 1943 and meat consumption increased to 55 000 head of cattle a year. Local food supplies were inadequate and by 1942 mine companies introduced food-rationing for mine workers and maize was being imported from Argentina by the imperial authorities.[86] In an attempt to increase maize production, the Colonial Office agreed to compulsory labour being used to prepare land for a two-month period starting in mid-February 1942. The Labour Commissioner had power, through District Officers, to conscript up to 730 Africans aged 16–45 years. Conscription was extended for a further 3 months and thereafter made permanent in a standing Native Labour Corps, which remained throughout the war, and well after it had ended, providing certain European farmers with a regular supply of farm labour and expanded maize cultivation.[87]

The Colonial Office was unhappy about the use of forced labour on privately owned European farms, but it was reluctant to add the antagonism of white farmers to the existing hostility of white mine-workers. Commenting on the situation in Northern Rhodesia, Sir Harold Tempany voiced London's apprehension:

> I am thoroughly distrustful of the whole of this . . . It seems to me that advantage is being taken of this emergency to expand the cultivation of maize on European farms and to enable the farmers to if necessary use compulsion to secure the necessary labour to increase their cultivation, while at the same time as far as I can see nothing is to be done to enable the native growers to expand maize cultivation also . . . I have an uncomfortable feeling that the present position may have been to an extent engineered.[88]

The main concern of the Colonial Office was not compulsion for agriculture – that practice was well established in East Africa – but that forced labour might provide increased private profits to white farmers settled on the railway belt. The War Cabinet, in agreeing to an increase in the number of agricultural conscripts in October 1943, emphasised the great importance attached 'to the limitation of profit where the use of conscripted labour is allowed for private employment'.[89] Nevertheless white farmers came to depend on conscripted labour and by July 1945 the governor could argue that, although he and his officials disliked the system, 'if I stop conscription at once there is not a shadow of doubt that our food requirements will not be met'.[90] Gore-Browne, the legislative council member representing African interests, commented that 'the problem here is semi-compulsory labour for European farmers on the Railway line . . . The solution of the food trouble lies in the organization plus better conditions for human labour on the farms'.[91] The several thousand impressed labourers employed throughout the war helped to increase maize production, but conscription also helped perpetuate inefficient methods of agriculture and harsh employment practices to the short-term financial benefit of white farmers.

In Southern Rhodesia, where thousands of men had been conscripted to build air installations in 1940–1, the government hoped to avoid further conscription. It feared that such a policy 'might frighten the voluntary labour from Nyasaland, Northern Rhodesia and Portuguese East Africa – labour on which we are almost entirely dependent. If the alien labour took fright and went home we should have to close down almost everything in the colony'.[92] A combination of food shortages, caused partly by the drought of 1941–2 and demands by white farmers for labour, brought about a new government labour conscription scheme in Southern Rhodesia in 1942. The Compulsory Native Labour Act, described in the Legislative Assembly as vital 'if we are to make our maximum war effort',[93] provided an increased number of low paid labourers for many white farmers and also for employment in sectors of the economy labelled as 'essential services'. In Belingwe District, for example, the Native Commissioner put pressure on chiefs to send young men to the mines and other areas of the economy experiencng labour shortages. Recruiting continued in the District after the end of the war, when the Native Commissioner reported that 'compulsory labour is extremely unpopular . . . whether in the Reserves or elswhere', and as a result young men had been encouraged to migrate to South Africa.[94] The official figure for conscripts in the period 1943–5 was 33 145, most of whom were enlisted for farm work.[95]

A small amount of forced labour was used on the Northern Rhodesia Copperbelt, but the largest, and most scandalous, use of forced labour for mining was in the opencast tin mines on the Jos Plateau of Nigeria between April 1942 and April 1944. Two recent studies have examined in some detail this war-time exploitation of Northern Nigerian peasants.[96]

After the loss of Malaya and the Dutch East Indies in early 1942, Nigeria became the main source of tin supplies to Britain. The whole output and stock had been bought by the Ministry of Supply in December 1941 and an increase in output was urgently demanded. It was not possible to import capital equipment for the mines; increased production would need to come from an increased labour force. Mine wages remained at a fixed level and the Nigerian authorities used indirect administrative pressures and moral suasion via the Native Authorities in an attempt to enlarge the number of migrant labourers at Jos. When this clearly failed to achieve the desired results, conscription was agreed to in early 1942. The intention was to raise tin output to a target of 20 000 tons per year.

Conscription began in April 1942 and lasted for 2 years. In that time over 100 000 peasants were conscripted, mainly from the provinces of Northern Nigeria.[97] Forced labour was introduced suddenly and early in the farming season. Peasants clung to their land, resisting recruiters and the efforts of compliant chiefs who acted for the Nigerian Government. On the Jos Plateau, a region with an inhospitable climate for people from the warmer savanna areas, inadequate preparations had been made to receive additional labourers and their families. Welfare and medical services were grossly inadequate, housing was poor, and food in short supply. The whole scheme was ill-prepared and badly timed. The death rate from disease, particularly among the Tiv migrants working on the Tente Dam, reached 10 per cent in 1943, caused deep concern in the Colonial Office and resulted in demands in the House of Commons for an end to forced labour in the tin mines.[98] Labourers deserted in large numbers, as many as 60 per cent being absent in the period April – June 1942. Peasants unfamiliar with such labour worked reluctantly and slowly. Their poor health and unbalanced diet meant that output per man was extremely low. Although the labour force increased by 40 per cent, reaching a monthly average of 71 000 men in 1943, production only rose by 6 per cent to a maximum output of 17 463 tons, a figure well below the production target set for 1943. Conscription proved a brutal failure, an example of peasant welfare being sacrificed to the interests of maximising tin output for the imperial war effort.

The British Government resisted demands to end forced labour in the

Nigerian tin mines and attempted to improve working and welfare conditions for miners. Eventually it was the economic and moral lessons of the system that persuaded them to abandon forced labour. Conscription not only failed to increase the output of tin but it had also diverted labour from other production, especially essential food supplies and groundnuts. The brutal operation of the system appalled officials in the Colonial Office, and it was largely their demands that brought forced labour to an end in April 1944.[99]

CONCLUSION

Recent studies of twentieth-century war and society, mainly in a European context, have given due weight to the civilian role in the war effort. The ratio of combatants to non-combatants widened by the Second World War; more factory and farm workers were required to keep one soldier in the field by 1940 than in 1914. In Africa the same was probably true. Although African Colonial Forces relied more upon muscle than machinery, by 1942–3 they had been expanded and organised on modern military lines in terms of feeding and clothing and, to a certain extent, also equipment. Africa's combatant contribution was significant in sub-Saharan theatres and in Burma; its greatest contribution was in the steady supply of military labour that substituted for European and American troops in the Middle East and North African campaigns.

Equally African civilian labour made an important contribution to Allied war production, particularly in the British colonies where economies were brought increasingly under imperial direction and control. Forced labour represented only a small proportion of the total labour force mobilised in Africa for the war effort. Elements of force undoubtedly were used to secure labour for war-related work and to meet labour shortages in most colonies. Groups of urban workers, such as dockers and railwaymen, who gained industrial power during the war, who stuck for improved conditions and formed trade unions, and were recognised by the new labour departments and trade union advisers, have been examined by historians. The mass of workers caught up in war production, peasants on farms and plantations and construction sites, are more difficult to study. They are also more numerous and thus important to the war effort. Unlike many of the organised urban workers, they ended the war with few material advantages to show for their labours. Indeed, they may have been economically poorer as a result of inflation. They should not be forgotten.

NOTES

1. The classic account is M. van Creveld, *Supplying War: Logistics from Wallenstein to Patton* (Cambridge, CUP, 1977).
2. Howard Bailes, 'Technology and imperialism: a case study of the Victorian army in Africa', *Victorian Studies*, No. 24, 1 (1980), for an account of supply in the Zulu campaign 1879–80 and in Egypt in 1882. W. Nasson, 'Moving Lord Kitchener: Black Military and Supply Work in the South African War, 1899–1902; *J. Southern African Studies*, 11, 1 (1984).
3. D.C. Savage and J. Forbes Munro, 'Carrier recruitment in the British East African Protectorate, 1914–18', *J. of African History*, VII, 2 (1966); G. W. T. Hodges, 'African manpower statistics in East Africa, 1914–18;, *J. of African History,* XIX, 1 (1978); David Killingray and James Matthews, '"Beasts of burden": British West African carriers in the First World War', *Canadian J. of African Studies*, 13, 1–2 (1979). On the over 300 000 Egyptians labourers recruited by the British in the First World War see Peter Caddy, 'British policy and Egyptian unrest, 1914–1920' (unpub. PhD thesis, Univ. of London, 1982). Surprisingly, very little has been written about the vast army of labourers, several million strong and drawn from all parts of the globe, which supported the Allied Western Front in Europe.
4. Margaret Gowing, 'The organization of manpower in Britain during the Second World War', *J. of Contemporary History*, 7, 1–2, Jan.–April 1972, p. 166.
5. In 1940–1 it was suggested that unskilled West African labour be brought to the United Kingdom for work in war industries. The Colonial Office rejected the idea mainly on climatic and health grounds; see CO 968/40/4.
6. League of Nations, Fourteenth Session, 1930. See also G. St. J. Orde Browne, *The African Labourer* (London, 1933), ch. VII and Part II.
7. David Souter, 'The introduction of modern labour administration in British Colonial Africa, 1937–1946: the case of Nigeria', unpub. paper presented to African History Seminar, SOAS, Univ. of London, 21 Jan. 1981.
8. Deborah W. Ray, 'Pan American Airways and the Trans-African Air Base Program of World War II' (unpub. PhD thesis, New York Univ., 1973), p. 108.
9. Sir John Shuckburgh, 'Colonial Civil History of the War' (unpub. typescript, Colonial Office), 4 vols (1949), vol. I, p. 261. CO 554/139/33764, 'Report by Maj. Orde Browne on Visit to West Africa, November 1943–March 1944, Gold Coast', Conf.
10. Robert O. Collins, *Shadows in the Grass. Britain and the Southern Sudan 1918–1956* (New Haven, 1983), pp. 400–402.
11. N.A. George-Cox, *Finance and Development in West Africa* (London, 1959) p. 223; A. R. Prest, *The War Economics of Primary Producing Countries* (Cambridge, 1948), p. 241.
12. John Iliffe, 'A history of the Dockworkers of Dar es Salaam', *Tanzania Notes and Records*, No. 71 (1970), p. 128.
13. Margery Perham, *The Government of Ethiopia* (London, 1948), p. 233.
14. Jean Suret-Canale, 'La fin de la Chefferie en Guinee', *J. of African History*, VII, 3 (1966), pp. 474–5; and his *French colonialism in Tropical Africa* (London, C. Hurst, 1971). See also James L. Giblin, 'The Vichy years in French Africa' (unpub. MA thesis McGill Univ., 1978), pp. 104 and

134–44. Brian Weinstein, *Eboué*, London, OUP, 1972), pp. 300–1; Richard A. Joseph, *Radical nationalism in Cameroun. Social origins of the U.P.C. rebellion* (Oxford, Clarendon Press, 1977) pp. 50–1.

15. FO 371/23372/4639, 23 Nov. 1939.
16. Prest, *War Economies*, pp. 126–7.
17. See ch. 7 below by Grundlingh; M. Roth, '"If you give us rights we will fight". Black involvement in the Second World War', *South African Historical J.*, 15 Nov. 1983; Kenneth N. Grundy, *Soldiers without politics. Blacks in the South African Armed Forces* (Berkeley, 1983).
18. Shuckburgh, 'Colonial Civil History', vol. I, pp. 40–1. Public Record Office, Kew, WO 253/1 and WO 253/7 on African labour for the Middle East.
19. On the military service of the High Commission Teritories see R. A. R. Bent, *Ten Thousand Men of Africa* (London, 1952) on the Bechuanaland Protectorate, and B. Gray, *Basuto Soldiers in Hitler's War* (Maseru, 1953). Also D. Kiyaga-Mulindwa, 'Bechuanaland and the Second World War', *J. of Imperial and Commonwealth History*, XIII, 3 (1984). PRO. WO 253/1 'Middle East Labour'.
20. PRO. CO 968/75/14504/45A Part I, 'Manpower: Requirements of GHQ Middle East, 1942', Brig. A. J. K. Pigott to Lord Lloyd, Colonial Office, 15 April 1942, secret.
21. Ibid. Replies by N. Rhodesia, Nyasaland, and S. Rhodesia, April and May 1942, secret.
22. Ibid. Part II, African Manpower Conference, Cairo, Aug 18–21 1942; and CO 968/131/6, Manpower Conference, Nairobi, 30 Sept.–1 Oct., 1942, secret.
23. PRO. CO 968/3/13. 'East African Manpower Requirements of Army in Middle East, 1943', secret, East African Govs. to Sec. of State at Col. Office, cypher tel. No. 562, 12 June 1943.
24. Ibid. Moore to Sec. State at CO, cypher tel. 27 July 1943.
25. Ibid. Manpower Requirements, Mauritius. Note by Maj. D. G. Pirie, 1 Jan. 1944. The army failed to provide adequate facilities in the Middle East for African labour in 1941: see PRO. WO 253/1 Col. H. G. L. Prynne to Col. F. J. Scott, June 1945.
27. Gray, *Basuto Soldiers*, pp. 72–84; Bent, *Ten Thousand Men*. PRO. DO 35/4071, 'Swazi Regiments of the African Pioneer Corps in the War 1941–45'. Record by Maj. F. P. van Oudtshoorn.
28. Bildad Kaggia, *Roots of freedom 1921–1963: autobiography* (East African Publ. House, Nairobi, 1977). See also 'The Swazi Pioneers, Sept. 1941–March 1945', a 55 pp. roneod history of the Pioneers compiled by three Maswati members of the Corps, which includes accounts of journeys to Egypt, in North Africa, and to Italy. Copy in DO 35/1183/Y. 1069/32. In Tripoli the Pioneers produced a newspaper, *The Swazi Gazette*.
29. PRO. DO 35/1183Y.1065/1/1. 'African Auxiliary Pioneer Corps in Middle East. Report of meeting . . . to consider education . . .', 28 June 1943; and 'Report of visit of the Resident Commissioner of Basutoland to HCT serving in the Middle East, 27 May 1943', by Charles Arden Clarke.
30. Anthony Clayton and Donald C. Savage, *Government and labour in Kenya 1895–1963* (London, Frank Cass, 1974), p. 232.

31. P. G. Powesland, *Economic policy and labour*, ed. E. E. Elkan (Kampala, EASIR, 1957), p. 70.
32. Walter Rodney, *World War II and the Tanzanian economy* (African Studies Research Center, Cornell Univ., No. 3, 1976), pp. 13–14; N. J. Westcott, 'The impact of the Second World War on Tanganyika, 1939–1949' (unpub. PhD thesis, Univ. of Cambridge, 1982), p. 44.
33. Kinyaga-Mulindwa, 'Bechuanaland Protectorate'.
34. H. Moyse-Bartlett, *The King's African Rifles. A study of the military history of East and Central Africa* (Aldershot, Gale & Polden, 1956); A. Haywood and F. A. S. Clarke, *The History of the Royal West African Frontier Force* (Aldershot, Gale & Polden, 1964).
35. Powesland, *Economic policy and labour*, p. 67.
36. R. R. Kuczynski, *Demographic survey of the British Colonial Empire* vol. II (London, 1949), pp. 345–6.
37. PRO. CO 968/75/14504/45A Pt. I, 'Manpower requirements of GHQ Middle East 1942', Nyasaland 27 April 1942.
38. P. McLaughlin, 'Collaborators, mercenaries or patriots? The "problem" of African troops, in Southern Rhodesia during the First and Second World Wars' (unpub. seminar paper, Univ. of Rhodesia, 1979), p. 11. Kenneth P. Vickery, 'Wars and Rumours of Wars. Southern Rhodesian Africans and the Second World War', paper given to conf. on 'African and the Second World War', SOAS, Univ. of London, May 1984, pp. 9–11.
39. J. F. MacDonald, *The War History of Southern Rhodesia*, vol. II (Salisbury, 1950), p. 507.
40. John Iliffe, *A modern history of Tanganyika* (Cambridge, CUP, 1979), p. 370.
41. J. Gus Liebenow, *Colonial rule and political development in Tanzania. The case of the Makonde* Nairobi, (East African Publ. House, 1971), pp. 161–2.
42. Kinyaga-Mulindwa, 'Bechuanaland Protectorate'.
43. PRO. DO 35/1183/Y.1069/1/1. Minutes of secret session of the Basutoland Council, 26 October 1943, Recruiting for AAPC.
44. Ibid. Arden-Clarke to Lord Harlech, 20 November 1943, secret.
45. PRO. CO 554/133/33829 Part II, Resmin, West African War Council Mins, 1942–3, secret, 22 July 1942.
46. Shuckburgh, 'Colonial civil history', vol. 1, p. 43. Rhodes House Library, Oxford. Mss. Afr. s. 1743 (168) RWAFF Papers: Hamilton pp. 6–7.
47. David Killingray, 'Military and labour recruitment in the Gold Coast during the Second World War', *J. of African History*, 23, 1 (1982), pp. 90–4.
48. Westcott, 'Impact of Second World War on Tanganyika', p. 47.
49. Jack Halpern, *South Africa's hostages. Basutoland, Bechuanaland and Swaziland* (Harmondsworth, 1965), pp. 169–71.
50. J. S. M. Matsebula, *A history of Swaziland*, 2nd ed. (Cape Town, 1976), p. 176, quoting an army officer.
51. Kinyaga-Mulindwa, 'Bechuanaland Protectorate'. The South African Native Military Corps, established June 1940, had a cumulative strength of 122 254 by February 1943. In addition, 45 000 men served in the Cape Corps, established May 1940.
52. PRO. CO 968/13/6. 'Manpower East Africa'. African Manpower conference, Nairobi, 7 May 1943, secret; CO 968/3/13. East African Manpower

Requirements for Army in East Africa, 1943, secret. WO 106/2913. The East African Govs. Conference to Sec. of state for Cols, Most secret cypher tel., 23 November 1943, stated that East African (which included N. Rhodesia and Nyasaland) forces totalled 240,000 and that the percentage of able-bodied males away from home in wage-earning or the forces was Kenya 65 per cent, Tanganyika 45 per cent, Uganda 34 per cent, and Nyasaland 58 per cent.

53. PRO. CO 968/75/14504/45A Pt I, secret, Manpower Requirements GHQ Middle East, 1942.
54. Powesland, *Economic policy and labour* pp. 71–2.
55. PRO. CO 968/3/13. Moore to Under Sec of State at CO, cypher tel, 24 July 1943.
56. PRO. WO 106/2913. Labour Companies West Africa to Middle East, 1942–5, Resmin to Sec. of State for Cols, most secret cypher tel, 31 May 1943; and 'Note on Labour Companies East and West Africa', top secret, April 1944. CO 968/5/13018/36, 'West Africa. Manpower Requirements for the Army . . .', secret. Poynton to Maj. Gen. Galloway, WO, 4 June 1943, most secret.
57. PRO. CO 968/75/14504/45A Pt II. Richards to Sec. of State for Cols, secret cypher tel., 14 October 1942, and related correspondence. Richards, Governor of Nyasaland, had asked for authority to inform the S. Rhodesian Government that the order of priority for his colony was Middle East labour, essential local food production, local industries, Southern Rhodesian requirements, and the Rand mines 'in that order'. *Ibid* Meeting in Salisbury to discuss East African Manpower, 29 May 1942.
58. Ibid. Pt. I. High Comm to DO, secret, 15 May 1942, and related correspondence.
59. Killingray, 'Military and labour recruitment', pp. 86–7.
60. PRO. MT 63/281. West Africa: Freetown. Representatives' reports 1941.
61. PRO. CO 968/132/1. C-in-C S. Atlantic to CO, 4 January 1942; Bourdillon, the Governor of Nigeria, said that 'conscription would be resorted to if necessary to complete personnel required', while Burns, the Governor of the Gold Coast, wrote that the 'only satisfactory method to obtain these [artisans] is under Compulsory Services Ordinance. Registration was in progress and calling-up will start towards the end of January'.
62. Ibid. Stevenson to Dawe, 1 February 1942.
63. PRO. CO 267/682/32306/2. Stevenson to Sec of State for Cols, cypher tel., 7 April 1942; and Stevenson to Dawe, private, 4 April 1942.
64. PRO. CO 968/94/1. Swinton to Oliver, secret and personal, 20 December 1943. CO 554/139/33764, Report by Maj. G. St. J. Orde Browne on visit to W. Africa, Nov. 1943–March 1944, conf.
65. PRO. MT 63/284. Report of Works Development Cte . . . chaired by Brig. R. Briggs, 24 November 1943.
66. W. R. Shirley, *A history of the Nigerian Police* (Lagos, Government Printer, 1950), pp. 66–8 on Pioneer riots at Aba and Calabar in October 1943; also PRO. DO 35/1183/Y.1069/1/1 Pt II, for Basuto unrest in the Middle East in 1945–6.
67. PRO. DO 35/1184/Y.1069/2/3; and DO 35/1184/Y.1069/2/4; *Die Burger* 14 and 24 August 1946.

68. PRO. CO 170/364. Mauritius Legislative Council. Sessional Paper No. 12, 1951 'Mauritius troops in Egypt and Cyrenaica'. 'Pioneers in the M.E.L.F.', *The Royal Pioneer*, 10, March 1947; 'R.P.C. Depot M.E.L.F'. ibid. 2, 11, June 1947.
69. Clayton and Savage, *Government and labour in Kenya*; J. N. Westcott, 'Impact of Second World War on Tanganyika'; W. Freund, *Capital and labour in the Nigerian tin mines* (London, 1981); David Souter, 'Colonial labour policy and labour conditions in Nigeria, 1939–1945' (unpub. DPhil thesis, Oxford Univ., 1981); and a forthcoming London PhD thesis by Mandy Banton on labour in Northern Rhodesia.
70. Westcott, 'Impact of the Second World War on Tanganyika', p. 92.
71. H.C. Debs. 26 March 1942. On War Cabinet policy, see the summary provided by Shuckburgh, 'Colonial civil history', vol. 11, pp. 82–5.
72. E.g. CO 691/184/42374, Dawe mins. 17 and 31 July 1943, quoted by Westcott, 'Impact of the war on Tanganyika', p. 157.
73. Clayton and Savage, *Government and labour in Kenya*, p. 238.
74. J. J. Jørgensen, *Uganda. A modern history* (London, 1981), p. 121.
75. Clayton and Savage, *Government and labour in Kenya*, pp. 239–41. PRO. CO 882/2. 'Conscription of labour for non-military service in Kenya', Papers for Labour Advisory Committee, Sept. 1942.
76. Shuckburgh, 'Colonial civil history', vol. 1, pp. 80–1.
77. Clayton and Savage, *Government and labour in Kenya*, p. 257, Appendix III, table 2. Shuckburgh, 'Colonial civil history', p. 80 provides lower figures.
78. Clayton and Savage, *Government and labour in Kenya*, p. 243.
79. Shuckburgh, 'Colonial civil history', vol. 1, pp. 81–2.
80. Westcott, 'Impact of the war on Tanganyika', p. 151; see also Westcott, 'The East African Sisal Industry, 1929–1949: The Marketing of a Colonial Commodity During Depression and War', *J. of African History*, 25, 4, 1984.
81. Westcott, 'Impact of the War on Tanganyika', pp. 84–6.
82. Jim Giblin, '"The Rubber Time": Handeni District, Tanzania, during the Second World War', unpub. paper given to conf. on 'Africa and the Second World War', SOAS, Univ. of London, May 1984.
83. Ibid. pp. 90–2. John Iliffe, *A modern history of Tanganyika* (Cambridge, 1979), pp. 371–2.
84. Westcott, 'Impact of war on Tanganyika', p. 136; Clayton and Savage, *Government and labour in Kenya*, p. 241.
85. PRO. CO 968/131/12. 'Man Power: Mauritius. Notes of discussion at Col. Office, 4 August 1943', by Dir. of Labour, Mauritius.
86. Robin Palmer, 'Land alienation and agricultural conflict in colonial Zambia', in Robert I. Rotberg (ed.), *Imperialism, colonialism and hunger: East and Central Africa* (Lexington, Mass., 1983), p. 103.
87. Shuckburgh, 'Colonial civil history', vol. 1, pp. 78–9.
88. PRO. CO 795/123/4510912, min. of 13 February 1942, quoted by Palmer, in Rotberg, *Imperialism, colonialism and hunger*, p. 103; see also the min. by Orde Browne on p. 104.
89. Shuckburgh, 'Colonial civil history', vol. 1, p. 79.
90. Ibid. p. 79, quoting Waddington to Col. Office, 27 July 1945, CO 795/128/45109/12. See also Maud Shinwaayi Muntemba, 'Rural underdevelopment in Zambia. Kabwe rural district 1850–1970' (unpub. PhD thesis, Univ. of

California, Los Angeles, 1977), pp. 214–15.
91. PRO. CO795/128/45109/12, Gore Brown to Creech Jones, 1945. See also HC. Debs. 14 November 1945.
92. CO 968/75/14504/45a Pt. I, 'Manpower requirements', Southern Rhodesia to DO, 1 May 1942.
93. Southern Rhodesia Leg. Ass. Debs., vol. 22, 9 June 1942, col. 1449.
94. Per Zachresson, *An African area of change. Belingwe 1894–1946* (Gothenburg, 1978), p. 163.
95. Vickery, 'Wars and Rumours of Wars', pp. 12–15.
96. Freund, *Capital and labour*, ch. 5; Souter, 'Colonial labour policy', ch. 5.
97. Ibid. p. 174 and table on p. 185; Freund, *Capital and labour*, p. 143, table 5.1. Tukur Bello Ingawa, 'Rural labour in southern Katsina Emirate during the colonial period c.1900–1939', seminar paper SOAS/ICS, Univ. of London, Nov. 1983, pp. 9–10.
98. Souter, 'Colonial labour policy', pp. 192ff. and p. 200; Freund, *Capital and labour*, p. 147, table 5.3. HC. Debs. 24 June 1942 and 4 August 1942. Harold Macmillan, *Blasts of War 1939–1945* (London, Macmillan, 1967), pp. 169–71.
99. PRO. CO 554/139/33764. Report by Maj. Orde Browne on visit to West Africa, November 1943–March 1944, conf., Nigeria.

4 The Depression and the Second World War in the Transformation of Kenya

JOHN LONSDALE

ARGUMENT

In the course of depression and war Kenya underwent a double transformation of its state and society. The colony matured, but partially, from a segmentary into a centralised state and thereby became ungovernable. Its peoples faced unprecedented divisions, so that many of the weak felt that the strong had gone out of control.

This unsteady revolution in the high politics of the state and the deep politics of society unfolded in three stages. The adversities of the 1930s demanded the centralisation of public power. The state acted to save itself first, its dominant supporters, the white settlers, only second. Political patrons, white and black, were glad to be its clients, so as to preserve the social order. The opportunities of the war then converted the state into the settlers' instrument, but only briefly and imperfectly in fact and never in law. Political leaders strengthened their constituencies. The powerful, again, both white and black, did so in order to break with past social constraints, the weak in order to try to restore them. So the conflicts of the post-war reconstruction, in which the metropolitan government, the settlers, African elites and the African poor were all joined in a battle for incompatible futures, converted the state into an unruly political arena. It ceased to be a broker; its government became, instead, the prize.

In all this Kenya was rather different from most of the other territories of British tropical Africa. Elsewhere the discontents of the depression had likewise stimulated official dreams of purposive state action to

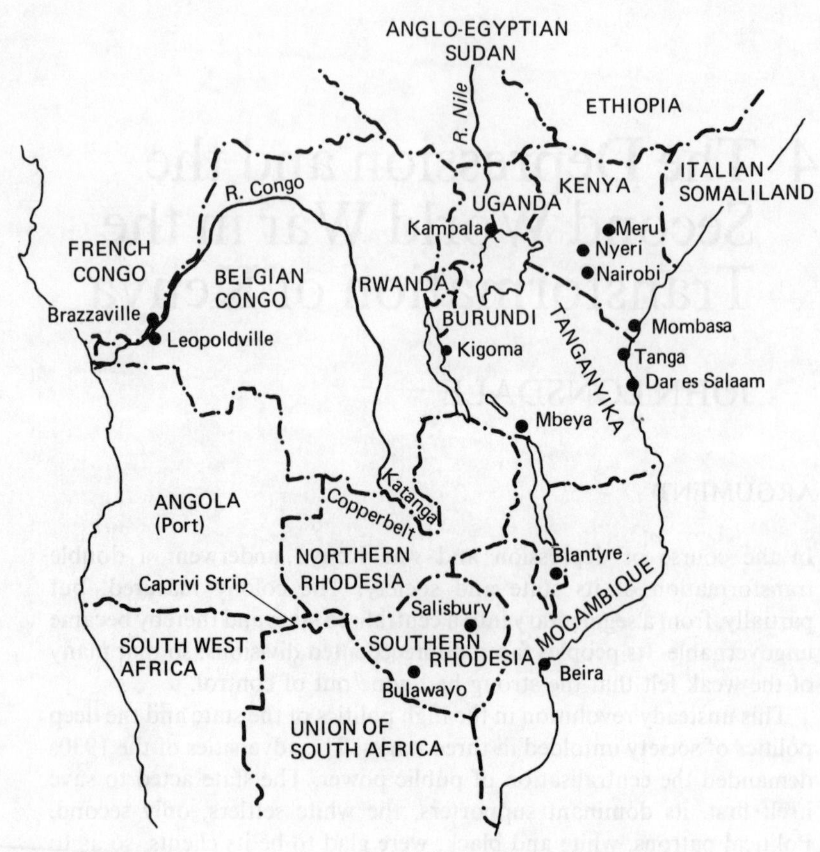

MAP 1 *Central and Eastern Africa*

foster welfare and production. But it took the rapaciousness of war to jerk such plans into action. Most colonies had survived the years of blight with a miserly retrenchment; they become not more governed, but less. Kenya's white settlers, however, were too well organised and too much aware of their dependence on the state to allow that. Moreover, unlike African cultivators, they were propertied capitalists. Their salvation required that the state become capital's guarantor, almost a collective farm manager. But precisely because the state in Kenya had to engineer a response to the depression rather than merely endure it, so Kenya's post-war conflicts were all the more unmanageable. The state was able to maintain most, not all, of the settlers in the depression only because it first saved itself on the foundation of taxable African production; and as African production enlarged, so African divisions widened. Post-war African nationalism was inflamed as much by internal African conflict as by racial subordination. Equally, the ebullient settler nationalism of the day could never have existed had not white farmers survived the world slump to take advantage of the global struggle. It took the 1950s and Mau Mau to show the full contradiction between the costs of depression and the rewards of war.

THE SEGMENTARY STATE

The colonial state had never been an honest broker. It could not be. Its very existence required the conscription of African resources in the service of immigrant employers and traders. These, or so it was officially imagined, would repay the large public debt that imperial Britain had imposed on her East African colony by building that lunatic line, the Uganda Railway. This primitive accumulation of African land, labour and livestock, first by conquest and then by taxation, stamped the indelible mark of partisanship on the state. But it was not its only inheritance; for the official imaginings remained largely unfulfilled fantasies until the late 1920s, just before they were doomed by depression. It was the British taxpayer who eventually paid for the original railway line, and it was African agriculture which dominated Kenya's domestic food markets; as late as 1913 about three-quarters of export earnings also came from African sources. It needed the stimulus of the First World War to establish most white farms and plantations,[1] and they were vulnerable to setbacks thereafter. Africans therefore paid both their direct taxes and their duties on imported consumer goods as much by selling their wives' domestic produce as by wage employment for whites. The state had to come to terms with the big men of African rural society, both those it found and those it created in the initial politics of conquest, as much for its fiscal health as for its political stability. The state's relations with Kenya's African peoples remained complex and uncertain. Officials had to organise their collective expropriation while they encouraged their individual accumulation. The state's coercions rested on the divisive politics of collaboration through which – it is an over-simplification – the sons of poorer families went out to work for whites, while wealthier families sold their surplus vegetables and grain in order to send their sons to school.[2]

If Africans were devious subjects, white settlers were but factious allies in colonial development. Because they were capitalists whom metropolitan capital distrusted, they could do little to help the state themselves while demanding much of it in return. They were supposed to produce for export, but their credit shrivelled under any attempt to dictate the conditions of their land tenure. Their big men made their pile by holding land empty in speculation on a brighter future rather than by putting it under the plough, and their political rows were a constant threat to the state. Their demands for more African labour made the politics of collaboration still more divisive within and caused righteous indignation among the liberal establishment at home. Their outcries against Indians, whose trade in African produce undercut them in domestic markets and raised the price of African labour, upset the diplomacies of an Empire of which the corner stone still stood across the Indian Ocean.[3]

In the 1920s Kenya had a harshly unequal economy but a ramshackle polity. At the core of the state, it is true, the political administration was staffed by men of common background and like mind, the new gentlemen of Britain's managerial middle class. They shared a philosophy of enlightened command, alert to the reciprocities which African obedience expected of white power, but confident enough of their mission to slap down protest when the politics of co-optation failed.[4] But the government of this machine – the Colonial Office, successive governors and their chief official advisers – had no clear vision of the purpose to which it should be addressed. Even in the prosperous late 1920s white settlement was too burdened with debt to shape its own future; the management of extraction from and collaboration with Africans was a standing contradiction; and the Viceroy over the water held a veto, twice exercised within the decade, over any prospective hurt to Indian interests.

All these perplexities were soothed, but scarcely solved, by the segmentation of the state, in both its institutions and its political conventions. Much of this segmentation was deliberate policy, but the potential political estates which might otherwise have been so destructively opposed were in any case internally divided. The conjuring trick of rule was both to play upon these factional divisions and to convert the contestants' clamour against each other into claims upon different levels of the state. By the early twentieth century the British imperial mind instinctively saw all politics as racial politics; its settled opinion held that race relations could only be bad. If mutual harmony was too much to hope for, then the peace of separation was to be preferred. No colonial official ever seriously pressed for the desegregation of racial access to land until the 1950s. There were periodic dreams of buying the settlers out – the Second World War induced one such fancy in Harold Macmillan[5] – but that was quite a different matter and reinforces the point. The state's mediation of racial economic contradiction can best be seen where it could not be avoided, in the central relation between white employer and black worker. The state did all it could with its own coercions to prevent settlers going out to recruit their own labour, and if workers then deserted, as they frequently did before the 1930s, the state pre-empted employer reprisal by the severe but simple device of making such breaches of private contract a cause of criminal prosecution rather than civil suit.[6]

Settlers were represented at the centre of the state in the Legislative Council (LegCo). African representation was at first confined to personal dealings between chiefs and district commissioners. Local Native Councils were conceded as district-level forums in the 1920s, but only so as to divert African attention from the centre. Indians, awkward as always, could not be fitted into this segregation of political levels. With Europeans, they had to be consulted on municipal affairs, but on LegCo they were refused the common electoral roll with whites they had demanded. When they then boycotted the council in protest against the communal franchise, the government did not too officiously strive to persuade them back to their seats. At the first sign of organised inter-racial alliances in the 1920s, when settlers and Indians each called on Africans to accept their protection against the other, the government declared their game to be out of bounds and reserved it for the state, under the magic codename of Trusteeship.

Trusteeship was the spell under which government claimed the right to hold the unequal ring between the races. The material and authoritative resources of the state helped to redefine their separate internal divisions. These same divisions in society worked upon the state. The equivocations can be seen in its relations with all three communities. Among the white settlers, 'small man' farmers were often at odds with their self-appointed leaders, the concessionaire speculators. Government paid heed to these big men in LegCo. It also aligned its own interest in public economy with theirs in the private capital market by refusing to force down land prices with state-assisted settlement schemes. The future of white settlement was thus mortgaged to its first arrivals, and the premiums they demanded were suicidally high.[7] But this self-inflicted wound at the heart of settlerdom created a fiscal weakness in the state. By the late 1920s therefore the state had a distinctly ambiguous relation with the settler leadership; for the specialised crop committees, through which it then tried to increase farm production, steered the smaller working farmers away from their leaders' political associations. Indians were split too, but by religion, sect and caste, and by the vigorous competition of their trades. Their most important field of access to the state's resources lay in education. And here their sectional charity was welcomed at the elementary level, while their sectional sensitivities were as often bruised at the higher levels of schooling, where increased state funding demanded economies of cultural and linguistic scale. African cultivators and herdsmen exploited parochial ecologies. These became encased in the decentralised bases of the state. Administrative districts started as levels of state extraction. They then became arenas of African competition for the resources levied by their councils. Mission societies invested years of ideological labour in giving these political localities a vernacular literature, a Bible, of their own. Chain-migration then took their young men off, with the protection of their kinsmen, to colonise the towns. Once there, workers exploited their employers' stereotypes of tribal aptitudes as a counter in wage-bargaining. In all these ways administrative conveniences were being appropriated as African assets. Tribes were being imaginatively born.

In the 1920s, then, and for all its unified structure of inequality, Kenya was a maze of patronage and faction. Dominance seemed to be exercised, whether by white over black or between one African and another, by personal suasion and violence rather than through the impersonalities of property and the law. Because the only accepted political categories were those of race and tribe, they were separated and subdivided by the state rather than given any joint focus for negotiation and mobilisation by recognition in the central governing institutions. This segmentary political culture survived to mould the conflicts of later years. But the framework of competition changed and the options of coalition enlarged, especially among Africans. The framework was changed mainly by the actions of the state. The options were enlarged more by the creative explorations of men, as they tried to find the language in which to translate the narrow complexities of material interest into the broader morality of new communities.

DEPRESSION AND CENTRALISATION

The political segmentation of the 1920s rested on twin economic divisions. The first, a continuing primitive accumulation, was designed to create white capitalists and black workers. Forced African savings were converted into a reckless rate of capital formation by external borrowing at high, fixed rates of interest secured upon the public revenues. Africans' taxes supported settlers' services. Taxation was deeply regressive. Nobody could put a figure on it, but most officials and observers thought it a scandal. On one calculation, an average African family – and it is a misperception to imagine that agrarian society was an egalitarian bundle of such amorphous peasants – would have paid about 30 per cent of its money income in tax in 1926, a settler family only half that rate.[8] But the investment in expansion could continue merrily enough so long as markets were buoyant and ordinary government revenues with them. By 1929 Kenya's public income was three times as high as in 1913.[9]

The second division split the produce markets, for primitive accumulation had never been as decisive as the settlers hoped. They had aimed to capture the local market as a base for breaking into markets overseas. So they got the state to reinforce administrative segregation with barriers against African competition. The state had already alienated African land, and now went on to place the African cattle trade under frequent quarantines and to ban African coffee-planting. The settlers wangled protective tariffs for local foodstuffs, reinforced by lopsided railway rates by which settler maize could be carried below cost while African imports, cottons especially, were overcharged.[10] Yet despite all this official philanthropy, white farmers were only partially successful. From the export market, it is true, they managed to exclude virtually every item of African origin save hides and skins. But in the domestic market whites managed to cling only to the meagre pickings of the quality trade with their fellow white consumers. They surrendered to African producers most of the growing trade in maize, which was both the staple cereal and the standby of smaller farmers. Africans also supplied the towns with most of their meat and vegetables.

There were four reasons for this partial settler failure. First and fundamentally, the state could never be entirely extricated from its early politics of African collaboration; for some Africans, at least, colonial rule had to be seen to pay. Next, white capital was divided between the consumers and producers of maize. The big coffee and sisal planters preferred to buy their workers' rations cheap from African growers, rather than pay their fellow white farmers a subsidy for racial solidarity. Thirdly, settler agriculture as a whole was weak, farming over-priced land on insufficient capital, growing temperate crops with tropical pests for distant markets that never entirely recovered from the First World War. Small farmers survived lean years by crossing the racial boundaries which their leaders had got the state to impose. Almost all whites made a good half of their farms available to African cultivation and grazing, in return for family labour; and many whites traded in African produce or let out pasture to African cattle dealers, for the final factor was the competitive energy of peasant economy. In the 1920s most Africans still went out to work in order to invest in a wife and land. Rising standards of subsistence and honour, which included imported clothes and children in school, were financed as much by expanded cultivation as by wage employment. The best quantifiable evidence for this extension of African market production is the doubling of African farm wages in real terms during the 1920s.[11] Settlers had to compete with their workers' alternative opportunities as peasants. This contradiction between capital and labour in the produce markets was also supportable so long as farm profits continued to rise.

Both props of this divided structure gave way in the early 1930s. Export prices fell below the settlers' costs of production, especially, and crucially, in maize.[12] The slump in market values was deepened by nature's attack on marketed volume, as drought scorched what locusts spared. Kenya's export earnings fell from £3.4m in 1930 to £1.9m in 1934.[13] General economic activity, for which petrol imports are perhaps the best measure, collapsed in 1933 to less than one-third of the level of 1929.[14] Banks and exporting houses declined to advance crop finance against uncertain rainfall and sliding markets. One in five white farmers left the land, Karen Blixen most famous among them. Many weathered the storm by panning for the alluvial gold providentially found at Kakamega, in the African province of Nyanza. But departures exceeded arrivals at Mombasa. Maize acreages halved in 5 years. In the 1920s £30m of private capital may have been invested in the Highlands. In the 1930s perhaps £20m was written off.[15]

The state's finances were in almost equal disarray. Its revenues shrank, particularly the duties on wines and spirits. What turned fiscal crisis into near catastrophe was the burden of past capital formation, which had to be paid for at 5 per cent, the highest interest charges in British Africa. London's loan charges had accounted for nearly one-fifth of revenue in 1928; at their greediest, in 1932, they swallowed up just over one-third.[16] Most of the debt was in the railway, and its operating losses soared. The demand for high-rated imports fell, but farmers strove to maintain their export deliveries of cereals, which were carried at sub-economic rates.[17] The only source of revenue that political power could prevent from sagging was the African Hut and Poll Tax. Capitalist farmers were being crushed by the burden of past debt and current recession. African peasants could be forced to carry it.

The divisive solutions with which the state had contrived to juggle a tolerable stability in the 1920s had collapsed into a single problem, how to increase marketed production on borrowed money that was not available, except to the state, which was practically bankrupt. Past capital formation had become public debt and private ruin. Only the domestic market promised any profit, and then only because its price levels could be politically manipulated above export parity. There was nothing the government could do about the export market, in which Kenya's producers were such puny performers. It did try all it could to promote maize exports, both by subsidy and the suspension of some handling charges. The consequences were instructively disastrous. The effort itself was feeble, amounting to less than £300,000; it helped a bit, but for one season only; and yet it virtually emptied the colony's tiny treasury. For Kenya had almost no minerals, unlike South Africa or Southern Rhodesia, which could be tapped as a fount of subsidy, to bear the costs of agricultural protection and economic diversification. In Kenya that burden would have to be carried, if at all, by the pygmy state. The collapse of the private land market forced it to shoulder the responsibility, if the unthinkable were to be avoided and white settlement saved. In the more prosperous years private lenders and commercial banks had opposed the floating of a state Land Bank. Funded against future public revenue and lending to farmers on soft terms, the bank would have depressed capital values. But now, in the slump, the new bank had the delightful effect of rescuing them, by transferring private liabilities to the state. But Kenya was again reminded that small is weak, for the bank's capital was exhausted in buying out the settlers' private mortgages, so as to keep them on the land. Scarcely any funds remained for the bank's intended purpose, which was to finance the conversion of cereal monoculture, 'maize-mining' as it was known, to mixed, dairy farming. Mixed farming – something which had been forced on the arable areas of England in the great agricultural depression of the late nineteenth century – was doubly desirable, ecologically sound and safer from African competition. But it was also something for the future, a dream for warding off future depressions rather than a means for waking out of the nightmare of the present one.[18] To do that, the settlers needed higher prices for what they currently produced, on existing markets. This was a controversial exercise even for the established minority of wheat and dairy farmers. Their cooperative societies were given the statutory power to coerce all producers into joint marketing pools; these were protected against import competition by raised tariffs or railway rates. Thus supported, the artificial domestic price enabled farmers to carry their export losses. The only losers were the few efficient producers and the wealthier urban consumers, Indian and European.[19]

Maize was a different matter. Any manipulation of its domestic market could only be at the expense of the European plantation industries and the myriads of African growers. But the planters' export earnings were holding up scarcely better than the farmers'; they were contributing a larger share of the colony's trade; and their labour costs were critical. As for African taxpayers, they were keeping everybody else afloat. The Director of Agriculture, of all officials the one most friendly to the white farmers, had to admit in 1931 that African cultivators, unencumbered as they were by debt, were 'the large, stable, productive element in the country'.[20]

If the economics of survival was difficult, therefore, its politics were infinitely more so. Something would have to give. Not all interests could have equal claims. No general solution was possible within an unchanged political economy. No political institution existed, other than the state's administration, which could propose or mobilise a generalised solution; and the state had neither the resources, nor the will, nor the goad of a united political constituency, to attempt a heroic exercise in standing still. The major political estates, white and black, were in any case already in turmoil. The settler leadership was infuriated by the way in which the metropolitan government had bluntly confiscated its previous vision of the future. 'Self-government' may never have convinced many, even among its chief protagonists, as a practical objective, but it was a powerful symbol to invoke in daily bargaining against the 'trusteeship' of the state. In the early 1930s both the Labour Government and its National successor, even its Tory Secretary of State, had firmly declared that no self-government was possible in Kenya if it did not include Indians and Africans in its executive.[21]

The settlers then lost their official trumpeter, Sir Edward Grigg. He had been succeeded as governor by Sir Joseph Byrne, who treated them as if he were still head of the Royal Irish Constabulary and they republicans. He soon showed how he would tackle the crisis; he would assert the authority of the state against the politics of settler agreement. He refused to attend the settlers' Convention of Associations, denying its established status as a governing institution. He replaced the settler chairman of the Board of Agriculture with his official departmental director. The settlers protested, but not for long. They had now learnt for themselves what the Colonial Office had long resented in them, that their own political claims inevitably raised questions that were much better left unasked, about how their present power might in future be shared with Indians and Africans.[22] Moreover, the settlers needed the authority of the state as never before, to manage their relations with their markets and their creditors.

African politics were as excited at the time, and as weak. The Kikuyu Central Association, more and more the party of the small traders, had won a great victory over its rivals the chiefs and its patrons the missionaries in its defence of the practice of female circumcision. But the dispute had served only to reveal the dreadful struggle at the heart of Kikuyu society, as increased market production provoked men to claim unprecedented control over their women's labour.[23] The KCA, moreover, remained in a state of clientship upon district commissioners when pressing its commercial interests.[24] Similar divisions and the same dependence can be seen in the other great centre of agricultural population, among the Luyia and Luo peoples of the Nyanza Province in western Kenya. The Luyia were disturbed by the settlers' gold rush in their midst, but divided on the means of protest. The Luo leadership was also bedevilled by conflicts between chiefs and traders, scarcely distinguishable from each other save in the differentiation of their official backing.[25] Only among the Kikuyu were there signs of the adaptation of popular culture to opposition politics. Elsewhere those Africans who could no longer afford to withdraw from the market in dumb insolence had yet to discover a political means of expression more ample than the deputation to the district office.

It was not entirely without some hope of tacit acquiescence therefore that Kenya's government set the state to work on managing the crisis. The measures were ad hoc and borrowed from elsewhere, from New Zealand and Australia, from Great Britain and, from nearer at hand, Uganda and Tanganyika. With its gold South Africa could be no more than an unattainable mirage. But a strategy was discernible, and traces of a political philosophy. The strategy was 'organised marketing', the philosophy something akin to corporatism, the attempt to coopt into state institutions the representatives of organised sectional interests which cut across the gross divisions of race and, if it should ever come to that, of class. This tendency, like perhaps all political doctrines, began as no more than an elementary political caution; for it began to look very much as if the previous buttress of order, the segregation of racial interests, could not possibly hold out against the even sterner oppositions which the depression had revealed between the different factors of production – markets and capital, land and labour.

The unity of the problem and its solution was clear to government, and recognised, reluctantly, by the settlers too. What Kenya needed above all was more production, and by black as much as white. Only a combined rather than a racially protected export sector could give Kenya some weight in overseas markets and with the shipping lines; only higher African incomes could offer settlers the prospect of a mass market for anything more sophisticated than maize; and only a greater flow of commodities could put the under-employed capital of the railway to efficient use. There were two other central elements for survival. Any increased production would have to be compatible with sustained fertility rather than dependent upon soil exhaustion, and the government would have to create a new political base for economic revolution, by depriving the previously self-evident racial political estates of their legitimacy and rallying power. New forms of the state would have to foster the centralisation of economic interest instead. Otherwise the conflicts between old and new producers, which would reflect the disparities between the costs of settler capital and the more easily hidden costs of peasant labour, could only too easily be translated into racial confrontation. The settlers also had to accept that the state could do nothing for them collectively, once it had emptied the exchequer in maize subsidies. They would have to organise their own salvation in division, crop by crop – or 'industry by industry' in the contemporary usage – with no public resource save that of statutory regulation. Africans, on the other hand, had to be organised by the state for its own salvation. Hitherto their ethnic and social differences had been conveniently exacerbated by oscillating migrant labour and the factional politics of collaboration. But their produce was needed now, more than their labour. Their potential for wider political organisation appeared to be all the more threatening; for the administered prices of organised marketing would hit the pockets of those who most seemed able to mobilise them, their traders.

Organised marketing rested on the tripod of producer cooperation, guarantees for merchant capital, and state supervision of their market relations. Not unnaturally, settlers and officials were deeply suspicious of a capitalism that had let them down. They shared the physiocratic belief that land was the source of all value. They thought that production was best increased by investing the surplus retained by farmers and the state rather than through the redistributed profits of trade. The export market provided the widest scope for the multiracial combination of producers, merchant capital and the state, but in new crops rather than in those currently dominating the plantation sector. A model of such cooperation already existed in the Nyanza sugar industry, where the white-owned mills were supplied by dependent outgrowers, both Indian smallholders and larger British farmers. But such combination was not extended to Africans until the 1950s. Sisal was never considered in such terms. It was externally controlled, it needed too much starting capital, and its market recovered from the depression the soonest. The international tea agreement precluded any thought of adding African smallholder to British plantation production. But even left to themselves the planters looked for the independent authority of the state; not trusting the position to one of their own number, they asked the local District Commissioner to chair their growers' association.[26] The state sponsored a coffee board, and while it could not coerce the dealers into agreement with the planters, it could force the latter to accept the first, very small, experiments in African coffee-growing in 1933 – a departure of first-rate symbolic importance.[27] But the important expansions of African production occurred either in crops in which settlers had already come to grief, like cotton and cashew nuts, or in those in which they had only a minor interest, like wattle,[28] tobacco and various soft fruits.

In each case merchant capital was enticed into making or extending an investment in processing, ginning, shelling, drying, canning and so on. There was a package offer of incentives, state pressure on the chiefs to organise production, state inspection of marketed qualities, and an exclusive buying licence to keep out competitors. There was one qualification: that the state must be satisfied that growers' prices were fair. From 1928 to 1935 the number of white veterinary and agricultural officers in the African areas increased in number from thirteen to thirty-two,[29] or from under 12 to 26 per cent of the departmental staff. These officials were as much concerned with policing markets as with animal and crop husbandry. Their authority came from the Marketing of Native Produce Ordinance of 1935, which consolidated earlier regulations on centralised markets, trader licensing, and produce inspection. The state now had the power to decide who could trade in African crops and livestock, and used it to encourage a corporatist hierarchy of commerce, making it easier for African traders at local markets by confining Indian dealers to more central ones. This pleased nobody.

Indians thought, with justice, that the power was aimed against them, but African traders complained similarly, and European farmers remonstrated almost loudest of all.[30] It was certainly with the products in which white farmers and Africans shared an interest that the corporatist strategy met its most interesting failures.

Beef and maize were the problem products. They were both essential to settler farming, but Africans sold far more of either and more cheaply, if also at lower qualities. But the domestic market was not all that fussy. In the mid-1930s Africans supplied an estimated three-quarters of the slaughter-stock and maize sold on the internal market.[31] In addition, the barter market, which was almost certainly larger, was entirely in African hands. The settler strategy of damming up African supply had thus failed completely in the local market, while its very success overseas had left the frail little settler exports stranded. The trick needed now was some control that could release but restrain the tide of African supply, so that it floated settler production rather than swamped it.

Of the two failures, that in beef was the more obviously dramatic, culminating in the march of over 3000 Kamba men and women on Nairobi in July 1938. They walked 40 miles and camped on the city's racecourse for more than three weeks. They were protesting at the compulsory culling of what Europeans saw as their surplus cattle, to be sold off cheap to Liebigs' packing plant. Government had spent years coaxing this new investment into Kenya, in the expectation that a large throughput of African cattle for canning would enable Liebigs to chill European beef for export, a bargain basement supporting more costly quality.[32] The Kamba people lived nearest to the packing plant, and their land was notoriously overgrazed. If multiracial corporatism in the livestock industry was ever to succeed in relieving the pressure on African pastures while floating settler beef on to the market, it had to succeed with them. But it failed. The state called an end to compulsion. Too many middle-aged Kamba men were just beginning to invest in cattle. Too many of these were clerks from Nairobi, or else in the colony's police force. The discontent that the first stirred up it looked as if the latter might be reluctant to suppress.[33] Africans had armed themselves with the same strengths as the settlers, a populist cause and a purchase on the state machine.

The story of maize in the depression was dramatic too, but in its irony. The settler maize farmers, who portrayed themselves as the white community's backbone, were desperate to obtain a statutorily controlled domestic market. This would allow them to force African maize, bought cheap at controlled markets and sold dear at controlled outlets, into sharing the settlers' loss on exports. The white producers' cooperative, the Kenya Farmers' Association (KFA), could then raise its pay-out to its members. The state did not oppose this scheme. Officials came to be persuaded that African growers would not lose and might even benefit; for the subsidy which they would be forced to pay white growers might be less than the Indian traders' margins on the free market. The decisive opposition came from the planters, and the state had no power to resolve this conflict between two branches of capital. Corporatism was not designed to bridge so wide a gap. The KFA did not get its monopoly. It decided to make use of the new convenience of centralised markets in the African reserves, in order to try to corner the African maize supply instead. It almost succeeded; and therein lay its failure.

By 1941 the KFA was handling around 60 per cent of the marketed African crop, but only because of its successful price competition with Indian and African traders. Under the spur of the KFA's entry into the local market, the Nyanza grower's price jumped from the pittance of less than 2 shillings per bag in 1935 to between 5 and 7 shillings for the last 3 years of the decade. The price responsiveness of peasants is notoriously hard to calculate, owing to the overriding influence of the weather on their surplus. But some fairly reliable, if rough, indication of their response to, and growing dependence upon, the market can be seen if one looks at the Nyanza province's maize sales in successive years of market slump only. In all intervening years, sales rose considerably higher. All figures are in thousands of tons:

1927:	6.5	1943:	29.8
1930:	8.75	1948:	39.8
1934:	20.75	1953:	50.0
1936:	20.25		

Market expansion drew African rural capitalism in its wake. All the main agricultural districts had increasingly active trader organizations, which tried to break into the politics of organised marketing. In 1936, a lean year agriculturally, importers in Nyanza sold at least three times as many ploughs, ghee separators and millstones for water-powered maize mills (often owned by chiefs) as in the conventionally more prosperous late 1920s. African land values soared while white farm prices slumped. The most dramatic African land rush occurred in the Kimilili area of northern Nyanza, where Christian villages broke up into ploughing syndicates from which, in turn, emerged large farmers. Their farmers' association developed close market links with the KFA. Indeed, the KFA competed so keenly with Indian traders that its members were unable to compete with African farmers. The tide of Nyanza African maize supply rose three-fold in volume in the 1930s, not floating but swamping settler production, which sank by two-thirds in the same years. Those poorer settlers who did not leave the country contrived to scrape by either on the KFA's trading profits or in the short-lived Kakamega goldfields, or by 'kaffir farming', that is, by renting out land to their squatters rather than by employing their labour. Their district councils tried to usurp the role of the Public Works Department in building roads in the African reserves. Such off-farm incomes had been a common means of getting a farming stake in the early years of primitive accumulation. For many they were now no more than a means of primitive survival.[34]

The more fundamental factors of production, land, finance and labour, constituted another set of problems which cut across the corporatist solutions that were beginning, at the smaller settlers' expense, to be cobbled together in the markets. The great issue of the day was no longer racial land apportionment but the productive usage and conservation of the land on both sides of its boundary.[35] Thanks to the collapse of cash subsidies in the early 1930s and their replacement by state-funded credit in the Land Bank, the state found itself committed to what it had hitherto managed to evade, a self-interested responsibility for the preservation of settler land values. In the depression, more than ever, that depended on increased production. But the mixed farming, which was pressed on all sides as the Highlands' salvation, raised in particularly acute form the problem of African farm labour.

Labour tenancy had been an efficient means of acquiring a workforce for undercapitalised farmers trying out new crops in unfamiliar conditions for unproven markets. Squatter family cultivation spread the risks of innovation, their livestock cleaned up pastures, their rents could substitute for farm earnings, the labour of women and children was easily to hand in seasonal emergencies. Squatters became a problem – the settlers called it a 'menace' – only with change, and the 1930s were the worse for causing change in two dimensions. The slump forced many white farmers to revert to being landlords, living off squatter rents or taking their cut from their squatters' produce sales. Barely acceptable behaviour in the early 1920s, this was anathema now to a leadership whose only political resource was the symbolic indispensability of the improving white farmer. Kaffir-farming gave too easy a handle to critics, who contrasted the Highlands' idle acres with the teeming African reserves. It also made conceivable the impossible, the establishment of African claims on white farmland through what in English law would have been squatters' rights. These changed realities were all the more threatening when set against the change that was planned, for an essential element of mixed farming would be high-grade dairy cattle, too delicate to coexist with hardy squatter stock. The discrepancy between fact and dream not only increased the rage of the farmer against the squatter but of settlers against each other. Dairymen and maize-farmers felt betrayed by ranchers and planters. Ranchers used squatter herds as their foundation stock, planters bought squatter maize. But dairymen also loathed the squatter cattle their maize-farming neighbours were happy to accommodate.

So the Resident Labourers' Ordinance of 1937, which increased farmworkers' labour obligations and virtually eliminated their grazing rights, both essential preconditions for mixed farming, turned out to be an immensely complex measure. But no intricacy could have been sinuous enough for it to conform with the evolving corporatist strategy of evading all clashes of interest in the economics of reform. The Act itself, and the circumstances of its introduction, embodied three ominous contradictions. First, it ranged capital against labour by setting farmers against their peasant workers. But, next, it withdrew the state from any supervision of this conflict in the relations of production, in direct contrast to the position in the markets; for the quarrels between settlers over the squatter menace were altogether too contentious for the state to resolve. It therefore left the implementation of the new law to 'local option', area by area, as neighbouring farmers agreed among themselves. This was to prove a fatal abdication of state power in face of the disorganisation of capital. Finally, the Colonial Office insisted that the law's introduction must be delayed until land was found for squatters who refused to accept the demotion from tenant to labourer. Settlement areas would have to be found for them in those intermediate areas designated neither as white nor as African reserves. The Kenya government failed to satisfy London on this point until after the outbreak of war. It was very difficult to find suitable land. Later tragedies – the mass evictions from the Olenguruone settlement in 1950 and, three years later, the dreadful massacre at Lari – would suggest that it had been impossible.

The delay confirmed the apparent seriousness of the demographic and ecological crisis facing the colony, and stiffened the settlers' resolve not to allow peasant cultivation on their White Highlands to be part of its solution; for it was not possible for surplus or recalcitrant squatters, with their large flocks and herds, to be received back into the reserves from which some of them had departed a generation or more ago. No matter whether they had been pulled out on to the settler estates by a frontier ambition, or pushed by a patron who wanted his land not under clients but the plough, the land rights of most of them had meanwhile been extinguished. There had been too much population growth in the past decade. More importantly, there had been too much concentration of land ownership, as unequal agrarian societies became still more unequal in their hold on market and educational opportunities.[36]

Trusteeship for the 'paramountcy of African interests' had been the password for unfettered colonial control over the segmentary state in the 1920s. Now 'soil conservation' gave ideological cover for the transition to the centralising state of the 1930s. The earlier codeword had justified a watching brief, the new one demanded managerial action. It applied the principle of state trusteeship to the land. Like all powerful symbols, it meant all things to all men. It was astonishing how rapid was the 'greening' of high political discourse in a Kenya that found it impossible to agree on anything else. Concern over soil erosion, declining yields and overgrazing had been expressed since the mid-1920s, in an era of increasing aridity.[37] But by the late 1930s there was talk of little else in official and farming circles. It legalised the Land Bank's supervision of white land husbandry, to turn it away from 'maize-mining'. The spectre of erosion summed up settler fears for their children's future; it gave them another stone to throw at the scapegoat squatters, who were so much better than the settlers at mining the fragile fertility of the Highlands. In the reserves, the need for soil conservation justified the paramountcy of coercion in the African's interest. It was the excuse for the compulsory purchase of the Kamba cattle, to pack them off to Liebigs. It was the drum which called out compulsory labour, once a week in some areas, to dig contour ditches or fence-in afforestation plots.

By the end of the 1930s the cry of the land in peril was also beginning to be voiced by those who had been scared by the huge increase in marketed African production. These included settler maize-farmers, naturally, but there were senior administrative officers, too, who became alarmed by the way in which their patronage relations with African society were subverted by the rise of ambitious and wealthy men, landowners and lorry-owners, big men who owed too little to the district commissioner and who snapped their fingers at or, worse still, lined the pockets of his chiefs. District Commissioners began to talk darkly of 'soul erosion', selfish individualism. But soil conservation split the official mind. The old school thought in terms of heroic state action, to defend peasant traditionalism with compulsory labour and compulsory livestock sales. The new school, with agricultural officers prominent among them, thought in terms of state encouragement for peasant innovation. They looked forward to the grant of individual title to planned smallholdings for the progressive few, who would manure and contour their land, and rotate their crops, because it made them a profit rather than because it saved them a fine. Official opinion was to be distracted by this dilemma for nigh on 20 years. Nobody disputed that African land tenure would have to change; Africans, after all, were changing it. The sensitive issue was the degree and direction of state intervention in the process. Most of those who called for compulsory direction of conservation labour or forced cattle sales quailed at the thought of the wholesale dictation of new land law. Nobody who advocated individual holdings considered that they should be free of some form of state or communal supervision of their husbandry. The ambiguity was nicely put in the Governor's statement to LegCo in 1936, that policy would encourage 'small holdings organised within the native system of land tenure . . .'[38]

Such ambiguity best characterises the politics of the depression as a whole. There is no doubt that the government's strategy of survival had a coherent, corporatist intention. The precedents, both in political thinking and in administrative arrangements, were quite widespread in Britain at the time.[39] And, shortly after his retirement as governor, Sir Edward Grigg set out their advantages with admirable frankness. He confessed himself attracted by Mussolini's 'functional system of organisation'. Translated to Kenya, its executive would be responsible not to a legislature full of 'political busybodies' who were bound to play up racial divisions, but to corporations of agricultural, business and professional interests conducted by 'men of capacity' drawn from all races, who would not have to abandon their ordinary livelihoods to become 'professional politicians'.[40] The Colonial Office, equally, welcomed the prospect that the functional specialisation of white politics in the hands of the 'non-political farmer' would silence 'the usual gang of more or less professional politicians'.[41] Government departments developed their own clienteles; and the network of special-interest boards was capped with a Standing Board of Economic Development which worked out market-sharing or price-fixing agreements between interested parties in private.[42] The most striking success of the strategy came in 1936, when the government seized the opportunity provided by the Italian conquest of Ethiopia to disband the settlers' 'commando', the Kenya Defence

Force. This had organised whites sectionally, to defend themselves against blacks. It was replaced by the Kenya Regiment, an officer-training unit that fitted whites for hierarchy. In any future emergency the King's African Rifles, East Africa's regular army, would be able to expand with a cadre of local white officers; settlers would then be leading black troops against the Empire's enemies, and under imperial command.[43] It was the corporate dream, in khaki. This official coup provoked the settler leadership to walk out of the governor's executive council. Up country, the floundering maize-farmers were also threatening civil disobedience in protest against their hard times and, still more, their exclusion from the corporate decisions of those whose interests spoke louder than theirs. But the excitement soon subsided; most whites were only too glad to clutch at the hem of state authority. Their leaders even dared to hope, with Sir Edward Grigg, that this corporate clientage might raise the whole issue of the settler future to the status of an economic necessity, far above the uncertain political arena.[44] But the Rift Valley would have to be turned into bustling white farmland first.

In the end, these settler hopes were dashed. Corporatism failed to disguise their dominance. This was mainly because, with respect to Africans, it was scarcely even tried. In its western European home, fascist corporatism was designed to reconcile the class divisions of a common citizenry. But Kenya was a society of estates. Even whites and Indians were unequal citizens, and Africans were unenfranchised subjects. There were four corollaries, which variously blunted or overturned the corporatist hopes of harmony.

First, although African agriculture was a major beneficiary, it did not become organised in support of the state. Producer cooperatives got little further than talk; the protections they might have offered were superseded by the bargains struck between the monopsonist crop-processors and local officials who took the part of their peasants. Peasant wives were scarcely functional specialists. Large African farmers were a minority with too few friends. Secondly, these big men of rural society were affronted by the manner in which the new economic centralisation authorised the state's technical departments, in agriculture, education, health and animal husbandry, to trample on the developing self-esteem of Local Native Council autonomy. For Africans this clash between the new centralising and the old segmentary states hurt as much as did, for settlers, the government's suppression of their Defence Force. District Commissioners seemed not to have heard the corporatist message at all; they had more than enough factional conflict to cope with already, without conceding the demands of African traders and big farmers for special council representation. Thirdly, when, as began to happen just before the war, prominent African subjects were coopted across the line of citizenship on to local government committees and central government's advisory boards, they could not carry any self-interested followings with them. Indeed, they were cut off from them. In order to remain working farmers or traders therefore, and in a complete reversal of corporatist hopes, such notables had no option but to become 'professional politicians', repairing their social relations in societies without the institutional networks of farmers' associations, newspapers and clubs that exposed settler spokesmen to constant accountability. But, finally, Africans were facing a deeper problem than this. They had to consider the immorality of their own class formation, in a colonial situation which permitted to class advantage almost no political responsibility.

As agricultural production expanded on rising land values, so rural accumulators, social climbers who began to find that they had to exclude their juniors if they were to get on themselves, tried to recreate, in wider forms than previously known, fields of competition in which inequality had a legitimate existence. While they became more clannish themselves and disowned their tenants, they also helped to create wider reciprocities by sponsoring the cultural invention of tribes and shouldering the responsibilities of racial emancipation. A functional corporatism of their special interests was the very last thing that might meet their moral dilemma. Moreover, their attempts to join material interest and moral plausibility were frustrated at both the 'tribal' and the 'national' level by the way in which their colonial rulers were free to propose quite contrary remedies for the social ill of class. District Commissioners tried, with degrees of uncertainty that varied with their capacity for wishful thinking, to recreate what had never existed, traditional tribes pleasing to the metropolitan imagination, organic communities innocent of internal conflict. Both sides made claims to defend the peasantry from the other. In these ambiguities between white and black middle classes, incumbent and aspirant, there was perhaps only one clear point of agreement. Nobody of standing saw a need for the corporate recognition of labour.

Despite its lack of congruence with the cutting edge of African ambition, the government's strategy appeared in the middle 1930s to achieve a perhaps surprising degree of social order. But when markets picked up towards the end of the decade, there were signs that it might only have been a strategy for coping with depression, not for underwriting recovery; for as conditions eased, three excluded groups – African workers, African traders and white farmers – began to stir.

The rise in African land values in the 1930s had begun to harden the inequalities of Kenya's agrarian societies into stratification, among the Kikuyu especially. Poorer families no longer had a sufficiency of land for survival. Proletarianisation occurred in the countryside. Its effects were first politically visible in the towns. The Mombasa strikes of 1939 signalled this gathering transition from short-term migrant labour to a lifetime of urban work, just as soil erosion marked the approaching end of the long fallow in African agriculture. The state's reaction revealed the poverty of the corporatist imagination in a colonial context. Government at last created the separate Labour Department for which the Colonial Office had long pressed, but the state did not oblige employers to recognise African trade unions. It was not until the 1950s that the Department came to act as the creative broker of the corporate interests of capital and labour, above and below the citizenship line.[45] Meanwhile, the segmentations of race and state were too deeply ingrained. Workers were left to their own devices.

African traders, too, began to organise themselves to match the state's centralisation of trade. They began to claim that they, not the state in its surveillance of the exclusive crop-buyers, were the best defenders of peasant interests. As yet their funds were pitifully small. They nevertheless turned out some vernacular manifestoes, even, in Kikuyuland, a journal, *Mwigwithania*, 'The Reconciler', which mixed improving homilies and political education, and had Kenyatta for a time as its editor. Traders in different parts of the country not only helped thus in the cultural elaboration of tribes, they also turned their minds to the question of linking their interests together on the same territorial scale as the settlers' KFA. At almost its last meeting before the outbreak of war enabled the state to ban it as a seditious organisation, the Kikuyu Central Association discussed with its counterparts from Nyanza, 200 miles away, how they might jointly market maize.[46]

The final excluded group, and those most capable of disturbing the peace, were the smaller settlers. Almost everything the state had contrived during the depression had been intended to buttress the conditions for their survival. The forces of the market had proved stronger, threatening an altogether unintended revolution in the political economy. The settler backbone, the maize-farmers, had almost snapped under the weight of African production. Kenya was well on the way to becoming not a settler's but a planter's country, more like Tanganyika, in which the transient managers of metropolitan capital would look on African production as a gratifyingly cheap input for rather than a baleful competitor with their own. That was not at all the future to which the settler leaders looked nor, more importantly, the end to which the state's credit had been tied up, through the Land Bank, in white farmland. For the first time in Kenya's history the settler big men and the state shared a pressing interest in appropriating fresh public resources in a scheme to tempt new white immigrants to gamble their private funds on the future capital value of the Highlands as a whole.[47] More investment in settling more farmers on the rising market seemed to be the only way to meet the bill for keeping so many of their predecessors from going under in the slump.

If prosperity should make a lasting return, all these intimations of conflict could only grow. African social differentiation would widen. Expelled from rural patronage, African workers would have to look to their collective defences. African farmers and traders would have more resources to devote to politics. They would have to invest especially in the recovery of responsibility, if they were to smother the independent efforts of those whom they had expelled. The revival of settler farming would be the end of the squatter. All these possibilities moved closer, if not immediately, as East Africa entered the war.

WAR AND COMPETITION

Kenya entered the Second World War in three stages. Each had very different effects. The first two magnified the weaknesses of the old Kenya; the third made the colony new, by making farming pay. Prospects of profit stirred dreams of power. Domestic production was at least as important as experience of overseas destruction in transforming men's conception of possible futures. African squatters and farmers did relatively as well out of the war as white farmers, possibly better, since they had less debt to pay off. Educated and skilled Africans did well in employment. But at the bottom of the heap the poorer peasants and labourers barely hung on to what capital they had in land and had to pay increasingly inflated prices for citizenship, whether measured in terms of material consumption or in educational, that is, cultural, investment. War-time prosperity reunited whites but divided blacks more bitterly, not just against whites but against each other. The language of politics, now that there was the cash with which to shout it, became fused into one opposed whole. 'The land in danger' was its central evocative image, with its claims on the past sanctifying bids for the future. 'Soil conservation' was the language of retentive white control, the closure of options. The cry for the 'stolen lands' was its contradiction, a demand that the future be reopened, and in terms that held an equal, because indeterminate, appeal to all Africans, landless and land-grabber alike.

The first nine months of conflict with Germany were, as in Western Europe, a phoney war. It did no more than enlarge the market for migrant labour. African volunteers overwhelmed the army recruiting centres; nor did settlers wait to be conscripted. Otherwise the war merely rubbed salt in the half-healed wound of the depression. The fighting, when it came, was a continent away. Shipping space was allocated to the wrong ocean, the Atlantic, and Britain's bulk suppliers were either the dominions or the dollar legatees of the old informal empire of free trade. All this was made bleakly plain to Major Cavendish-Bentinck ('C-B'), the settlers' new leader and a duke-presumptive, when he took the manager of the KFA on a sales trip to London. There they found that the Ministry of Supply was interested only in Kenya's sisal and tea, neither of them farmers' crops. The Ministry of Food begrudged paying over the odds for 10 000 tons of East African maize. It was contractually bound to take Argentina's 10 *million*, and the Foreign Office wanted to outbid Hitler for the cereals of the Danube basin. Indeed, the Colonial Office rather sneered at the settlers' proffered 'small parcels' and repeated the homily of the 1930s, that the inclusion of African produce would make Kenya's export package a size worth greater consideration.[48]

Mussolini's entry into the war in June 1940 looked altogether more promising. The already expanding King's African Rifles, with its settler officers drafted from the Kenya Regiment, was joined by two infantry brigades from West Africa and a full South African division with a supporting air arm, in all about 75 000 men. The overseas food market was a mirage no longer; here it was, coming in with every troopship at Mombasa and every lorry convoy from the south, up Tanganyika's Great North Road. In late 1941 this domestic export market doubled again, with an influx of tens of thousands of Italian prisoners and assorted displaced persons. Farm production began to grow, under the management of settlers' wives. So settler agriculture, with its men away earning a new form of off-farm income, shared, briefly, in one of the standing problems of African cultivation. The campaign up in the Ethiopian highlands, similarly, gave every tribe its hero: Sergeant-Major Kirotho of the Kikuyu, Sapper Ogongo of the Luo, and Sergeant Leakey, VC, of the Europeans, probably the only man to have attacked a tank not only bare-handed but also stark naked.[49]

But it was the third phase of the war, from late 1941, which transformed Kenya. With the end of the Ethiopian campaign Kenya had ceased to be a frontline state; it now became a strategic base. Two battles changed the picture, the battle of the Atlantic and the Japanese attack on Pearl Harbor. The first caused the British resident minister in Cairo to call on Kenya to 'produce to the utmost and save our ships'.[50] All the food that Kenya could provide would be bought in the Middle Eastern theatre of war. The German U-boat had saved the farmer. It was the Japanese Zero that saved the planter, a week or so later. The Japanese took over the fibre plantations of the East Indies and sent the world demand for East Africa's sisal soaring. But the farmer benefited too, since Kenya's pyrethrum daisies were the basis of the insecticides needed for Far Eastern tropical warfare. Between them these two crops earned more than twice as much as the military sales of Kenya's foodstuffs. By 1943 Kenya's earnings from military and civil supply stood at £5.7 million, no less than three times her total domestic exports at the bottom of the depression in 1934.[51] The depression had finally lifted.[52] Pearl Harbor had inaugurated the long commodity boom. Before it faded in the mid-1950s, this put Kenya's settler agriculture at last on to a firmly capitalist footing and accelerated African social stratification, both with fatal results.

At the time men had more immediate problems. In January 1942 white maize-farmers threatened to hold up their harvest; other settlers refused to put more land under the plough. Patriotism was all very well, but for a community still floundering in debt it had to show a profit. The state was calling for increased agricultural investment; then the state must accept the increased liability for crop failure and guarantee a return on the capital employed. The poorer maize-farmers had imitated the Gold Coast cocoa farmers, in despair. Their wealthy leaders copied earlier metropolitan examples, in hope. As British farmers had done in the First World War, they accepted that their production should be conscripted, with the assurance that the state, not the farmer, should carry the attendant risks. The Increased Production of Crops Ordinance of 1942 accordingly provided grants for breaking new land for essential crops, in which maize was included; it also guaranteed a minimum return in the event of the failure of any harvest, which would otherwise be bought at a guaranteed price.[53]

The ordinance cast an entirely new light on the maize-farmers' continuing call for a statutory marketing pool, for the government now had the interest of the state to protect, not just that of one section of farmers. The state's credit was now to be laid out in maize cultivation. The state was now to guarantee prices, to growers and buyers. But the government was not pledged to all growers, only the expensive ones. It had to guard them, because that now meant the state, against being undercut in the market. It quite literally could not afford to encourage increased settler maize cultivation unles it also prohibited its customers from buying direct from the cheaper, African, suppliers. The state faced the old problem of floating settler production without swamping it, but with the unwelcome new predicament of finding itself in the same boat. The government duly instituted Maize Control in July 1942. Secure in its statutory monopoly, Control was able to command a consumer price high enough to guarantee the settlers' rate of return. African growers were paid only between 55 and 65 per cent of the settlers' price, a margin which was to narrow in later years. Government explained away this price discrimination by the fact that Control's agents performed for peasants what white farmers had to do for themselves – bag their maize, cart it to railhead, and put aside a fund for farm improvements. It is a matter for unresolved historiographical dispute whether these administrative charges for market services and producers' savings also included a disguised cross-subsidy from black peasants to white farmers.[54] Beyond any dispute is the fact that the real losers from maize control were African urban workers. Their staple food costs rose to the new protected price. It did not matter whether they bought from controlled outlets or on the black market; this simply flourished in the protected price gap between producer and consumer. Workers' wages barely followed suit.

The demands of war had finally established what settler propagandists had been claiming since the 1930s, that maize was an 'essential industry'. Before the war their cause had been weakened by their calls for subsidy and refuted by the planters. Now extraordinary measures were justified by the imperial crisis. Settlers spotted the danger there; they were quick to shift to a firmer ideological footing when poor harvests and increasing military demand coincided in a severe food shortage, in some areas even famine, early in 1943. The subsequent enquiry heard conflicting evidence on whether the controlled price regime had exacerbated the shortage. Some said that the settlers had received their price encouragement too late, others that African grower prices had dropped too low. The settler view carried the day (as it had failed to do in the food shortage of 1929), helped by the conventional wisdom on soil conservation. Commercial farmers, it seemed obvious, were more reliable suppliers in adverse conditions than peasant families, who would sell only when, and if, they first had enough to eat. With Africans scraping away ever more of their soil fertility, their own subsistence was bound to take an ever greater priority over the market. In this way the White Highlands became accepted in the official mind as East Africa's famine reserve; and famines were more certain a hazard than war.[55]

The 1930s were being put sharply into reverse; Kenya was becoming a white farmer's country as never before. Nor were the farmers mere clients, grateful for government hand-outs. Settlers had become, in effect, public sector managers, exercising the powers of the state through delegated authority. The corporatist structure of boards and committees with which the state had repressed any concerted settler pressure was now turned on its head. It became the channel for settler action. This was partly because the official establishment of the state was depleted by war service, partly because the organisation of war production demanded a managerial competence to which the state had never pretended, but mostly because the state had no political base strong enough to permit it to discriminate between all the various private interests clamouring to take advantage of the patriotic opportunity. Nobody other than the farmers and businessmen themselves had the authority to ration their access to credit or machinery. The settlers themselves created, and thereby captured, the whole overlapping framework of production and supply committees which organised farm management and improvised ingenious measures to secure fertiliser and machinery, as well as the transport and tractor pool which followed the planting and harvest seasons around the Highlands.[56] Settlers began to earn an unwonted reputation for productive efficiency. However much the British War Office might suspect them of offloading on to the army all manner of hidden subsidies, it had to admit that its East African supplies were almost without exception cheaper than those it bought not only in the Middle East and Ceylon but also in South Africa.[57] The Agricultural Production and Settlement Board at the centre of the committee network could now quite truthfully be described by Cavendish-Bentinck, its chairman, as 'practical farmers sitting round a table', the corporatist planner's heaven.[58] Settlers were no longer in imagination, as few of them had ever been in truth, a set of aristocratic playboys giving in to altitude, alcohol and adultery. Happy Valley had been given its symbolic quietus with the murder of Lord Erroll in January 1941, hours before the start of the Abyssinian campaign.

Settlers were becoming respectable. More important, they were becoming united. The large employers were soon reconciled to the costs of Maize Control. During the 1943 food shortage they had had to send many of their workers home. Imported maize prices rose sharply, and the necessary shipping space was almost unobtainable. Local settler reliability was worth paying for. Until 1952, indeed, the world commodity boom was such that Control was able to square the circle, both paying prices profitable to the farmer and selling to consumers at prices well below import parities.[59] During the war, then, urban and plantation employers did not have to pay over the odds for reliability of supply; they got it on the cheap. The internal reciprocities of settlerdom went further than that. Sisal and pyrethrum were both important dollar earners. So Kenya did unusually well in its allocations of Lend-Lease farm equipment. So, too, did the Nairobi importers of American vehicles and machinery. By the end of the war the settler leadership was shared between the two LegCo members for Nairobi, C-B and Sir Alfred Vincent. The latter was the war-time Director of Road Transport and Controller of Petroleum Products, by virtue of his ownership of the import agency for General Motors.[60] Since the 1930s government had deliberately consulted business opinion in order to break the farmer dominance of white politics. Now that many farms were well capitalised, farmers and businessmen were becoming harder to tell apart.

The settlers had not come any closer to the assumption of political responsibility, in strictly constitutional terms. But the war had fulfilled their hopes of the 1930s, that the very solidity of their existence would become the one fact all policy would have to take for granted. They had gained, in other words, a hegemonic position. By the end of the war they were no more in debt than any other capitalist farming community. Their share of Kenya's tax revenue was no longer a scandal. African direct taxation remained stable at around £540 000 through the war years, declining therefore in real terms. Total direct taxation more than doubled, from £707 000 in 1938 to an estimated £1.9 million in 1948, thanks entirely to the growth in settler and Indian personal taxes; the rich were beginning to bear a more 'national' burden.[61] They had not only achieved what has aptly been termed 'agricultural self-government',[62] their supply and production boards were governing institutions which by convention handled large amounts of annual crop finance on the state's behalf and effectively removed a major area of economic policy from government hands. Where their own self-government trenched most painfully on the other political conventions of the state lay in their relations with their squatters. The 1937 Ordinance had allowed them, under 'local option', full discretion as to when they would in each district throw off the old social constraints, terminating former tenancies and imposing new, very much more restrictive, ones. The war had greatly increased the capitalisation of almost all the white farming districts; in 1944 they began to move, with the wealthier farmers dragging the more marginal settlers after them, against the vast, tentacular, peasant economy which had grown up under their noses and which, like them, had prospered greatly during the war. It was a chilling reminder that, for all the managerial modernities on the surface of the settler economy, there remained, beneath, much of the racially divisive business of primitive accumulation still to be done.

Africans themselves, and in marked contrast to the white community, became still more divided as a result of the war. The differentiations were both regional and social; the politics of division was as much tribal as class in its language. Politics had as much to do with the search for African constituencies as with protest against settler dominance and colonial rule.[63] Racial protest was, in part, a means with which to establish the right to speak for a particular African interest, even a means to establish that here was an interest for which no other Africans could legitimately speak. Such claims could rest only on the basis of political investment, in time, in hospitality, in the press, in transport to meetings. The war had brought more division because it had brought more money. Money brought more politics.[64] Africans had grown increasingly bitter. A few of them had also become rich.

The fundamental African division was regional, between the agricultural and pastoral regions and peoples. The war accelerated the hitherto slow devaluation of Kenya's livestock economies against its cultivating communities. The precolonial free market exchanges between them had already been irrevocably upset by the rapid growth of cereal demand for the wage-labour force, by the emergence of education to rival livestock as a channel of investment, and by the greater reliability of wage labour over herding as a rewarding form of male employment.[65]

War-time price controls enhanced this 'scissor' effect. Maize prices to African growers – even the official ones – doubled during the war; the prices for potatoes and beans, which were particularly important to Kikuyu growers, doubled in the first three years alone.[66] In the northern Kikuyu district, Nyeri, and in Embu, the army paid for factories to dry the vegetable produce of no less than 11 000 smallholding families, whose seeds were issued and rotations planned by the Agricultural Department.[67] The scheme was at once the apotheosis of official hopes in the 1930s for the productive linkages between peasant smallholders, capitalist monosony and state supervision, and the forerunner of a large element in Kenya's 'agricultural revolution' of the 1950s. Among the most prosperous of Kenya's peasantries were the most vulnerable, the squatters on the white farms. In 1947 a survey showed that in the most fertile areas the average squatter family earned nearly twice as much as a skilled African mechanic or clerk in Nairobi, not from the head of the household's wages, which were those of an unskilled worker and only 10 per cent of his family's income, but from produce sales. The extraordinarily high rate of polygyny among squatters, 1.8 wives each among the married squatters sampled in Naivasha, confirmed that the White Highlands were a frontier of colonising opportunity for a flourishing black peasantry.[68]

Livestock prices, on the other hand, were rigorously repressed throughout the war, and a free (that is, 'black') market escape was much more difficult; stock routes could be policed in a way in which women with head-loads could not. Such was the extreme complexity of the African livestock market, with a wide and fluctuating price differential between districts, that it is difficult to give more than impressionistic evidence. The political administration felt that requisitioning cattle for the army was 'probably one of the hardest of the many unpleasant tasks' it had to perform.[69] To take just one province, Nyanza, the controlled price for slaughter bulls in 1945 was barely half what they had fetched in 1936 and just about the same as the first price to be recorded, in 1907 – a tremendous drop, therefore, in real terms.[70]

The buying policies of the Maize and Livestock Controls have been much criticised on the score of their racial discrimination in pricing. A wider reflection suggests that some part of this criticism is misplaced. A proportion of the price differential was taken up by what was called a cess or levy or, more plainly, an administrative profit. Similar levies were made on Uganda cotton-growers, and on the cocoa- and palm-growers of West Africa, where they were known as marketing board surpluses. The main motive, as in Uganda, was anti-inflationary, at a time of severe shortage of consumer goods. In Kenya two other official preoccupations were important, one open, the other latent. On the one hand, a levy would both reduce some of the price incentive to exhaust soil fertility and fund post-war conservation schemes; on the other, it was widely felt that too much cash was bad for the native's character and worse still for his discipline.[71] Nevertheless, the Colonial Office's sensitivity on the issue of Kenya's racial inequalities set a firm limit to the forced savings which might be levied on its peasantry; moreover, the maize cess, which seems never to have risen above 30 per cent of the grower price, was, like the profits of the Livestock Control, credited to the local councils of the producer districts, not to the state. The marketing board surpluses from the peasant colonies took a higher percentage of the grower price; they rested for longer in London as forced loans to the metropolis, and when eventually spent they went largely on infrastructural and industrial investments of doubtful advantage to the primary producer.[72] There were, it appears, some benefits to being an African peasant in a settler colony, after all; local colonialism was too exposed ideologically to be as exploitative in this respect as metropolitan imperialism.

But if Kenyan cultivators and herders were not exploited to quite the same extent as their West African counterparts, there was nonetheless an important variation in their ability to enjoy the 'post-war credit' held up for them by the marketing Controls.[73] The maize-exporting districts of Nyanza soon started to spend their accumulated Betterment Funds, as they were called, on conservation schemes that did little to limit agricultural incomes but much to increase local employment. Reconditioning in the pastoral areas was slower to implement and, whilst it may have fended off further land degradation, could by itself do nothing to raise pastoral incomes.[74] By the end of the war there was a division, marked as never before, between the agricultural, relatively rich, politically active districts and the pastoral, relatively impoverished districts where political activity took forms that rarely reached the notice of the readers of the African press in the towns.

Social divisions were as marked within each region, and in the countryside as much as in the towns. In both the main agricultural areas, but in Kikuyuland more than in Nyanza, rural social and productive relations were continuing their painful revolution. Before colonial rule, wealth and power rested in clients who had to be supported by delegated rights in land. But as markets, population and power expanded under colonial rule, so the value of land rose while the worth of clients declined. Land law was forced to be made, ousting the law in persons and ousting persons from the land. Complex bundles of rights in land were cut through by men with money and influence and appropriated for their own. Labour was got by marriage, as before, but also, and increasingly, by paying workers rather than by protecting dependants.[75] What settlers were determining to force on their squatters, Africans had been doing to each other, more slowly, more piecemeal, since the 1920s. What look to be class attitudes began to appear, and from above they may even have been unconscious. When the state legalised the compulsion of black labour for 'essential' white agriculture during the war – a provision scarcely used save in sisal – the wealthiest of Nyanza's African farmers colluded with the state to get their own workers exempted from conscription.[76] In Kikuyuland, influential councillors outraged the mass of their constituents by calling for the registration of individual title to land. It was also in Kikuyuland, in the closing years of the war, that soil conservation work first showed its socially discriminatory character.

The wealthier tended to have land that was flat, which needed no contour terracing. The poor not only had to labour to terrace their own, often steeply sloping land, but also to work on projects of 'communal benefit' such as roads, under the supervisory eye of the wealthy and often to their unearned benefit, too.

But local government budgets were perhaps the main generators of differentiation. While the state's direct tax burden on Africans stabilised, local native council revenue expanded three-fold in the war, to £350 000 in 1945. The local rate varied from district to district, but in each district a flat rate was levied on all. Local taxes were therefore even more regressive than in the colony as a whole. The money went on education, health, agricultural and veterinary improvements, and roads. All these heads of expenditure benefited only those who could pay for the service, who were salaried by the council, or who had surplus crops to send to market.[77] Inequality between Africans was becoming more deeply institutionalised, and increasingly banal.

In the labour market, differentiation between Africans both reflected the emerging agrarian hierarchy, as the wealthy invested in education, and reinforced it, as the well paid were able to invest in land.[78] The range of skill, responsibility and reward opened up enormously during the war. Kenya's war effort depended as much on coopting African skills as Indian or European. The army provided the widest avenue of advance. By the end of the war 97 000 Africans had served in the forces. The army had trained 600 of its own teachers and no less than 15 000 drivers. About 70 per cent of demobilised soldiers were reckoned to be literate, a huge addition to the ranks of those with vulnerable expectations, as the colonial government was nervously aware.[79] Settlers too were alarmed to find how dependent they were on African expertise even on their farms. The government's soil conservation service employed teams of skilled Africans in the Highlands, surveyors who knew their algebra and trigonometry, bulldozer drivers, and so on, under the supervision of African Assistant Soil Conservation Officers who enjoyed an income and an authority that white farmers found intolerably subversive of proper labour relations, that is, between master and servant.[80]

Kenya's towns were transformed. Mombasa's African population virtually doubled in the war, from 55 000 to 100 000; Nairobi's went up by over half, to about 66 000. At an early stage in the war non-agricultural employment outstripped agricultural employment, never to be overtaken again. The occupational structure of the employed male workforce shifted quite noticeably up the gradient of skill and pay, with many of the more educated or adept thus earning increments which enabled them to keep pace with the soaring cost of urban living. But there was also, and still more so in the years immediately after the war, a large influx of unskilled young men who rarely found a day's pay. All, from skilled and long-term employees down to those who scoured unsuccessfully for an honest living, faced increasingly intolerable housing conditions. The unskilled labourers and unemployed must also have been increasingly bitter against those – largely their fellow Africans – from whom they hired a lodging or bought their food.[81]

In all these corners of African society men and women faced questions of authority and obligation still more intense than in the 1930s. They were moral questions before they were political ones, and were posed from within what people imagined a community ought to be. There were all sorts of resentments to be seen. Resentment of the young against the old was perhaps the most prevalent, some returning soldiers even going to the lengths of founding among themselves an Anti-dowry Association, to prevent their gratuities from being appropriated by their elders.[82] That the association collapsed almost the moment the men got home is perhaps just one indication of the way in which increased competition for resources can as much strengthen personal dependence as stimulate new, and therefore subversive, ties of association. The later 1940s are generally regarded as the age of Kenya's militant trade unionism. It would be just as true to see them as the age of militant ethnic welfare associations. The bewilderments of class formation, tribe formation and racial consciousness were in part an indication of the difficulties men and women had in imagining new communities for themselves.[83] But they also reflected the difficulties encountered by their rulers in imagining what new political forms might best secure their subjects' consent and control.

During the war Kenya was torn by two quite contrary constitutional tendencies – between planned reform of African local government and expedient concession to African opinion at the centre – very much like British West Africa at the same time.[84] There was, first, the tradition of the 1930s, of enlarging the powers and scope of local government. In Kenya this tradition had little to do with the ghosts of indirect rule,[85] since no official was deluded into thinking that his chiefs had any consensual authority. The modernisation of local government had much more to do with the politics of collaboration, constantly shifting as new claimants for administrative attention and local government funding came forward: first, mission teachers, then traders and farmers, and, by the end of the war, Makerere-trained executive assistants in the agricultural and veterinary departments. Provincial Commissioners were constantly asking themselves how the ambitions of the young could be kept in constitutional paths, and as frequently finding the answer in modifying the Local Native Councils, tinkering with electoral procedures one year, with sub-committees the next and, in the war, the beginnings of informal meetings of members from neighbouring districts. There was talk of some Central Native Council, which might in future serve as an electoral college for African members of LegCo; and grafted on to this hierarchy of civic training it was easy to envisage the cooptation of Africans, men of weight, wealth and loyalty, on to the quasi-corporatist network of advisory boards. By the end of the war Africans were full members of the boards which dealt with African education, with labour and wages, and they were the majority on the board which advised on African local government finance.[86] These two channels of access to state power seemed to provide a convenient balance between the decentralisation of African political competition and the centralisation of their specialised advice. The enlargement of local power and patronage brought in 'the younger and more progressive elements'.[87] The cooptation of chiefs and, after the war, junior African officials, on to the advisory boards defended the prestige of collaborators. Both forms of accommodation went to build up what were widely called 'district establishments', big men in their little worlds but, it was intended, still beholden to official patronage for any wider connexions.

But the war introduced quite a different prospect, too – bodies of African opinion which, if they were not yet called national, were certainly very far from being local. It has long been questioned whether demobilised soldiers were as important as once was thought for the raising of post-war political consciousness in Africa. Such doubts are proper but neglect the equally important question of how their rulers anticipated their return. In early 1944 Governor Sir Henry Moore was much exercised at the prospect, and the memoirs of Bildad Kaggia and Waruhiu Itote, both of them to become leaders of Mau Mau, show that he had some reason.[88] But Moore was anxious to appease not only the guessed-at opinions of the young men who had gone overseas but also the known wishes of their elders and betters who had stayed at home. The district establishments were beginning to get around, mostly because the state needed them to, whether they were chiefs travelling up to Nairobi on advisory board business, or schoolmasters, postal clerks or veterinary assistants posted to another district. But they had their private interests too, which demanded their active investment in widening social circles, so that by the end of the war it is proper to talk of a national elite. It became more difficult to distinguish between the officials and unofficials in their aspirations for change. By 1943 it was commonly agreed in the local councils of the main agricultural districts that there ought soon to be an African member of LegCo; and African army warrant officers, whose loyalty was unquestioned, were determined to hold executive responsibility when they returned to civil life.[89]

Meanwhile an unofficial, very well educated elite nationalism was taking shape on the tennis courts of the Alliance High School, the black Eton of Kenya.[90] Young Peter Mbiyu Koinange, recently returned from America and Britain, the first black graduate, combined both official and unofficial strands of elite nationalism in himself. His father had been a senior chief, his family was the most powerful in southern Kikuyuland; but he himself ran the teacher training college at Githunguri, the apex of Kikuyu efforts to provide their own Western education. Late in 1943, with the aid of Jimmy Jeremiah, a man from the coast, he canvassed the support of dozens of chiefs, councillors, priests and traders in his petition to be nominated to LegCo by the governor. It was only the third national political campaign organised by Africans in Kenya's history. The first two, in the early 1920s and late 1930s, had ended in bannings and detentions. This time it was politically impossible for the state to do other than meet the petitioners' wishes without, so far as possible, giving them the credit.[91]

AFTERMATH

Eliud Mathu, another schoolmaster from southern Kikuyu and the only other African graduate (Fort Hare and Balliol), was nominated to LegCo in October 1944. He was chosen in part, at least, to show Koinange that constituency-building would not pay. Two months later came the arrival of a new governor, Sir Philip Mitchell, a man known in the past for his dislike of settlers, and now armed with a brief from the Colonial Office to bring them gently to heel.[92] Even before the war was over, therefore, Kenya was rent by competition to capture the future by control of the state. Those with power, the settlers and the government, threw against each other the ideological resources of the 1930s, the one striving to keep a hold on the corporatist framework of war-time production, the other to wrest it back from them in order to reassert the authority of the state. Those without power, Africans of many different constituencies, tried to convert the profits they had made out of the war into the contemporary political idiom of freedom, only to find that settler nationalism had got its claims in first.

It was this combined and contradictory political geology of the 1930s and 1940s, together with the growing crisis of settler capitalisation and African class formation, which shaped the post-war crisis of Kenya's state and society. There were, at the least, four distinct levels of political and social disorder.

First, the government had no way of recapturing the commanding heights of the state except by coopting on to the government benches as Member for (virtually Minister of) Agriculture the quietly determined Pooh Bah of the settler war effort, Cavendish-Bentinck. But he was not the representative of a corporation, the coffee industry as it might be, or mixed farming. He was the political head of a new community, whose nationalism had been fired and funded by war in just the same way as had African nationalism. The old conjuring trick of pre-war rule was played out. All three races were now represented at the centre, twice over, both in the legislature and in the structure of specialised boards; their inequalities of representation and power were doubly visible.

It was, secondly, not just war but capitalist accumulation that had created new communities. The capitalisation of settler agriculture on expanding markets at last appeared to make possible the dream image of Kenya's promotional literature in the 1930s, a White Highlands of the Home Counties, with trout streams added but scarcely an African to be seen.[93] Such was the dominance of the language of soil conservation that, despite its misgivings, the Colonial Office had no convincing alternative to offer when the pre-war white settlement scheme was pulled off the shelf and dusted over. Its prospectus claimed that more intensive white farming would provide more for Africans in employment than the old extensive methods of the past could promise them by squatting.[94] The Labour Commissioner warned that the extinction of squatter rights would be 'the rock on which good relations between Black and White will split'.[95] But there was nothing the state could do to persuade the settlers to accept the full logic of the class consciousness which they were so determinedly provoking; it had given the necessary powers away to their district councils in the 1937 Act. Settlers refused to accept the existence of peasant communities on their farms any longer. But they also refused to consider the alternative, carving out free labourers' villages between farm boundaries; these too would admit the inadmissible, a right of African residence on the Highlands that was not conditional upon an employer's contract. The largely Kikuyu squatters, about one quarter of the Kikuyu population, were first stripped of the rights of personal dependants and then denied those of a class. It is scarcely surprising that they reacted to the restriction orders, which began to be served on them in 1944, with a 'gathering storm of despondency'.[96] It was a fitting historical irony that the first oaths of resistance to the new terms of employment were sworn at Soysambu, the home of white settlement's founding hero, the late Lord Delamere.

Thirdly, where the politics of soil conservation in the 1930s had been ambiguous, in the mid-1940s they were single-minded. Before the war, coercion had been limited and, when faced with African resistance as among the Kamba, it was soon abandoned in favour of its contradictory alternative, individual incentive. These ambiguities continued during the war. When asked to suggest ways of absorbing demobilised soldiers, officials thought equally of enrolling them in a 'Land Army' of land conservers and of encouraging them to be progressive smallholders. Likewise, the Director of Agriculture envisaged a variety of ways forward in African land tenure, from individual to communal farming, according to local ecology and population density; he refused to see his department as a soil conservation service alone.[97] But that is what it very largely became for a few, crucial years after the war. The reasons were many and complex, because soil conservation, as already explained, was only partially about conserving the soil. It was about authority, accountability for right husbandry, and ideal images of social relations. Until 1947 there was little internal argument among officials that what was needed for the African lands was regimentation, communal control of land husbandry by whatever indigenous authorities could be dug up from under the layer of executive chiefs, and a distinct slowing of the tendency to cash-cropping, which destroyed both soil fertility and social harmony.

The underlying reason, discussed below, was the uneasy official awareness, difficult to pin down, that African society was separating out into antagonistic strata which would shortly make support for one's collaborators incompatible with the consent of the population as a whole. But this would be a cause for caution, not for the energy with which the programme of soil conservation was in fact pursued. One has to account for political will rather than sociological doubt. Four reasons suggest themselves. First, two pilot examples of supervised individual smallholdings had collapsed soon after the war, leaving heroic communal action without a convincing competitor. The dehydrated vegetable scheme, focused on the factory at Karatina, had had to be abandoned when military demand ended and the world market seemed destined to be taken over by North American freeze-dryers. The former squatters settled at Olenguruone, under the conditions for Colonial Office assent to the 1937 Resident Labourers Ordinance, refused to the point of collective eviction to allow any kind of state direction over how they farmed their (in any case totally unsuitable) land. Second, it was difficult to be confident about incentives for improved husbandry in face of the post-war slump which, all experience taught, must surely come. Third, over-population seemed to be the chief cause of poverty in many African reserves and any clarification of land rights would be bound to convert mass misery into the despair of mass landlessness. But, finally, these negative reasons for defensive soil conservation were converted into an angry forward drive by Cavendish-Bentinck's takeover of agricultural responsibility. His settler constituents felt that their own future had been betrayed by the government's unwillingness to govern; his colleague Sir Alfred Vincent felt 'natives shd [sic] be compelled by law to do things for own good'.[98] Government's weakness, as they saw it, stiffened the settlers' resolve not to allow any part of their Highlands to act, however temporarily, as a leasehold safety valve for African populations while their Reserves were rehabilitated.

So strong was settler determination, so powerful the example of their wartime increases in well managed productivity, that Governor Mitchell himself, like so many of his predecessors, became their most effective advocate. In order to retain their confidence, without which their farm investment must falter, and African employment with it, his government showed a firm 'refusal to be "rattled"' by African opposition.[99] But this very ideology of retentive control, under settler political direction, made almost any land policy impossible to carry through. African cultivators felt increasingly under threat. It was not just, as their leaders increasingly reminded them, that the white farmlands had been stolen from them in the past. The settlers' state was stealing control over African lands, and thus implicit property rights in them, even now.[100] The government was paying an unsustainable price for its recapture of state power.

The final, and fundamental, level of social disorder afflicted African agrarian society as a whole. The main agricultural peoples were undergoing the increasingly acute ordeal of class formation. The war's end brought a frantic scramble, particularly in Kikuyuland, for such scraps of property and security as one could deny one's neighbour. Of the vast sums spent on litigation, much, pathetically, was spent by the poor against the poor, who thereby invested in their own impoverishment. Old authority became new oppression, and that was a problem for the colonial state and its African claimants alike. District Commissioners found it increasingly difficult to find popularly acceptable levers of action. Their obvious allies and agents were no longer the 'influentials' or 'progressives' of the past but men who were palpably different from and in their interest opposed to the mass of the people. Chiefs were no different in this respect from their main opponents, the traders. So the nationalist leaders found themselves in much the same predicament at the state. They were hard put to persuade their listeners that their separate interests were the same, and the state found it impossible to allow the politicians the patronage that might have been a substitute for leadership. The accumulated geology of decentralised administrative power was firm against the invasion of its private access to central government authority by anything that smacked of a more representative legitimacy.

Nationalist leaders were obliged to make ever more radical claims if they were to capture the imagination of men whose fathers their own fathers had very probably dispossessed of their rights in land. By the time the constitutional leaders shrank back from the enthusiasms they had aroused, the dispossessed had acquired a sterner leadership of their own. Kenya's post-war crisis was in part a crisis of the state, with segmentary and centralised, corporatist and elective institutions of power and representation in discordant conflict. Kenya did not again become governable, and on a new political base, without the direct application of metropolitan force in the Mau Mau emergency. But it was also a crisis of class, when the strong became ungoverned and the weak tried to defend themselves. White capitalist farmers struggled to release themselves from their peasant workers' grasp; and Mau Mau was in part the squatters' counter-revolution. Settlers also struggled to keep the state out of the hands of their rivals, the emerging rural African bourgeoisie; and the teachers and traders conjured up the image of a nation. The nationalists struggled for responsibility; their followers were desperate to turn back class formation and regain the land.

CONCLUSION

Colonialism was a social process that decolonisation continued. Depression and war transformed Kenya independently of any metropolitan 'forward thinking', or of the restructuring of metropolitan capital. While the colonial state was ostensibly designed to promote the settler interest, it could not avoid raising their competitors, the big men of African agrarian society. In part their very existence was an ineluctable corollary of the state; for power had to be delegated and, with that, the burdens and benefits of rule were made divisible. But big men began to become capitalists as their production was summoned up to keep the state afloat, to carry the settlers through the depression; and their property was entrenched, at other Africans' expense, by the opportunities of war. The social conflicts of this gathering capitalist transition disorganised the state. But it remained a blocked transition. All the conflicting relations of subordination and domination, the rights of peasants and squatters no less than the claims of district commissioners and landlords, had been strengthened by the enormous joint enterprise of war. It needed the crisis of Mau Mau to force open, in part, this impacted political economy. All the same, the peoples of Kenya had scarcely been immobile. What I have tried to show is how, in a very literal sense, Kenya became a single, because bitterly divided, social formation.

ACKNOWLEDGEMENTS

This essay incorporates the accumulated deposit of several years of working on and talking about Kenya with many colleagues. Among those who will recognise some of my ideas as theirs, more widely than can be indicated in footnotes, are David Anderson, E. S. Atieno-Odhiambo, Bruce Berman, Fred Cooper, Mike Cowen, Tabitha Kanogo, Greet Kershaw, Ben Kipkorir, Gavin Kitching, Godfrey Muriuki, Mike Redley, John Spencer, David Throup and Richard Waller. Additionally, David Anderson, Greet Kershaw, John Iliffe, Mike Redley and Richard Waller made valuable comments on the first draft. They are not responsible for the shortcomings which remain.

NOTES

1. As shown in the important revisionist work of John Overton, 'Spatial Differentiation in the Colonial Economy of Kenya: Africans, Settlers and the State 1900–1920' (PhD thesis, Cambridge, 1983).
2. John Lonsdale and Bruce Berman, 'Coping with the contradictions: the development of the colonial state in Kenya, 1895–1914', *J. African History* 20, 4 (1979), pp. 487–505.
3. All this, and much subsequent observation on the settlers between the wars, is based on another important revision, by M. G. Redley, 'The Politics of a Predicament: The White Community in Kenya 1918–32' (PhD thesis, Cambridge, 1976).
4. Bruce Berman, *Control and Crisis in the Colonial State: The British Domination of Kenya, 1895–1963* (Philadelphia, 1986), ch. 3.
5. Macmillan, minute of 15 August 1942. PRO: CO967/57/42.
6. Anthony Clayton and Donald C. Savage, *Government and Labour in Kenya*

1895–1963 (London, 1974), ch. 4; B. J. Berman and J. M. Lonsdale, 'Crisis of Accumulation, Coercion and the Colonial State: The Development of the Labor Control System in Kenya, 1919–1929', *Canadian J. African Studies*, 14, 1 (1980), pp. 55–81.

7. Redley, 'Predicament', *passim*; Paul Mosley, *The Settler Economies: Studies in the economic history of Kenya and Southern Rhodesia 1900–1963* (Cambridge, 1983), Table 2.3, p. 17.
8. Max Salvadori, *La Colonisation Européenne au Kenya* (Paris, 1938), 206; on the question of capital formation, R. L. West, 'Sources of Aggregative Fluctuations in the Market Sector of an Underdeveloped Economy, a case study: Kenya Colony and Protectorate, 1923–1939' (Ph.D) thesis, Yale, 1956), pp. 98–114.
9. S. H. Frankel, *Capital Investment in Africa: Its Course and Effects* (Oxford, 1938), Table 38, pp. 184 f.
10. E. A. Brett, *Colonialism and Underdevelopment in East Africa: ThePolitics of Economic Change, 1919–39* (London, 1973), pp. 92 ff; but see Mosley, *Settler Economies*, pp. 30–39, which modifies this picture of discrimination, especially over time.
11. Mosley, *Settler Economies*, Table 4.2, p. 116; for the same general point, Gavin Kitching, *Class and Economic Change in Kenya: the making of an African Petite-Bourgeoisie* (New Haven and London, 1980), chs 3 and 9; Sharon Stichter, *Migrant Labour in Kenya: Capitalism and African Response 1895–1975* (Harlow, 1982), ch. 3.
12. 'Production costs' were more of a political than economic concept, given the wide range of settler farming efficiency; for which, Mosley, *Settler Economies*, pp. 172–8.
13. Frankel, *Capital Investment*, Table 43, facing p. 192.
14. *Index of Motor Spirit Imports into Kenya 1928–1945 (1929 = 100)*

1928	52	34	49	1940	214
29	100	1935	86	41	438
1930	82	36	62	42	400
31	61	37	82	43	330
32	58	38	132	44	326
33	27	39	133	1945	324

Calculated from Conference of East African Governors, *Report on a Fiscal Survey of Kenya, Uganda and Tanganyika by Sir Wilfred Woods* (Nairobi, 1946), Appendix 2, p. 161. The idea is from John Iliffe, *A Modern History of Tanganyika* (Cambridge, 1979), p. 288.

15. Salvadori, *Colonisation*, pp. 120, 108, 217.
16. Frankel, *Capital Investment*, pp. 178, 182.
17. Alun Smith, 'Financial Restraint, Technological Innovation and Administrative Initiative: Transport and Communications in Kenya 1929 to 1952', paper for Cambridge Conference on the Political Economy of Kenya (1975), p. 4.
18. For the settlers in the Depression, see ibid.; Redley, *Predicament* , chs. 10 and 11; C. C. Wrigley, 'Kenya: The Patterns of Economic Life, 1902–1945', ch. 5 in V. Harlow and E. M. Chilver (eds), *History of East Africa, ii* (Oxford, 1965), pp. 247–60.

19. The fullest analysis is in Vincent Liversage (who was the government's agricultural economist), 'Official Economic Management in Kenya 1930–1945' (typescript, 1945; Rhodes House: Mss. Afr. s. 510), chs 3 and 4.
20. *Annual Report of Department of Agriculture 1931* (Nairobi, 1932), p. 97.
21. Note by Sir Samuel Wilson on discussion between the Secretary of State and Lord Francis Scott, 2 Aug 1933. PRO: CO 533/436/3198.
22. Scott to Wilson, 12 April 1933. PRO: CO 533/436/3198/2.
23. I owe this suggestion to Shula Marks. For the conflict over women's work, see Greet Kershaw, 'The Changing Roles of Men and Women in the Kikuyu Family by Socio-Economic Strata', *Rural Africana*, 29 (1975–6); Kitching, *Class and Economic Change*, pp. 121–30; and, for a feminist perspective, Renée Saurel, 'L'enterrée vive: charcutage et safari au pied du Mont Kenya', *Les Temps Modernes*, 34, 392 (1979), pp. 1352–72.
24. Correspondence in Kenya National Archives (KNA): PC/CP.8/5/3.
25. J. M. Lonsdale, 'Political Associations in Western Kenya', pp. 589–638 in R. I. Rotberg and Ali A. Mazrui (eds), *Protest and Power in Black Africa* (New York, 1970).
26. Kenya Tea Growers Association to Chief Secretary, 13 August 1938. KNA: PC/NZA.3/1931.
27. Carolyn Barnes, 'An Experiment with African Coffee Growing in Kenya: The Gusii, 1933–1950' (PhD thesis, Michigan State University, 1976).
28. M. Cowen, 'Capital and Household Production: the case of Wattle in Kenya's Central Province, 1903–1964' (PhD thesis, Cambridge University, 1979).
29. Bruce Berman, 'Administration and Politics in colonial Kenya' (PhD thesis, Yale University, 1974), p. 72.
30. Legislative Council, *Debates*, (1935), 2–3 July, 8–9 July, 3 August.
31. Robert L. Tignor, *The Colonial Transformation of Kenya: The Kamba, Kikuyu and Maasai from 1900 to 1939* (Princeton, 1976), p. 328; Liversage, 'Official Economic Management', p. 84.
32. *Kenya Land Commission Evidence iii* (Nairobi, 1934), p. 3346, evidence of R. J. Stordy, formerly Chief Veterinary Officer. For precisely the same idea in coffee, T. S. Jervis, 'The Marketing of Coffee', *East African Agricultural Journal* 2, 6 (1937), pp. 459–64.
33. J. R. Newman, *The Ukamba Members Association* (Nairobi, 1974); J. Forbes Munro, *Colonial Rule and the Kamba: Social Change in the Kenya Highlands 1889–1939* (Oxford, 1975) ch. 11; Tignor, *Colonial Transformation*, ch. 15.
34. Liversage, 'Official Economic Management', ch. 5; Elspeth Huxley, *No Easy Way: A History of the Kenya Farmers' Association and Unga Ltd.* (Nairobi, 1947), pp. 108–16, 124; W. H. Munro, 'An Economic Study of Maize Marketing in Kenya, 1952–1966' (PhD thesis, Michigan University, 1973), p. 29; Mosley, *Settler Economies*, pp. 47–50; Paul Vermouth, 'The Beginning of Maize Cash-Cropping in Kimilili, 1908–1935' (Nairobi University, History Seminar Paper, 1978); Director of Public Works to W. M. Ross, 13 February 1932, Rhodes House: Mss. Afr. s. 1178.
35. *Report of the Kenya Land Commission* (Cmd. 4556, 1934) is conventionally thought of as settling land apportionment, the old problem; so it did, but it had more to say on the new problem, land usage.

36. Frank Furedi, 'The Social Composition of the Mau Mau Movement in the White Highlands', *J. Peasant Studies*, I, 4 (1974), pp. 486–505; R. Van Zwanenberg, *Colonial Capitalism and Labour in Kenya 1919–1939* (Nairobi, 1975), ch. 8; R. M. Wambaa and Kenneth King, 'The Political Economy of the Rift Valley: A Squatter perspective', ch. 9 in B. A. Ogot (ed.), *Hadith 5: Economic and Social History of East Africa* (Nairobi, 1975); Tabitha Kanogo, 'The Historical Process of Kikuyu Movement into the Nakuru District of the Kenya Highlands, 1900–1963' (PhD thesis, Nairobi, 1980).
37. For evidence: C. E. P. Brooks, 'The Fluctuations of Lake Victoria', *J. of East Africa and Uganda Natural History Society*, 22 (1925), pp. 47–55; B. W. Thompson and H. W. Sansom, 'Climate', ch. 3 in W. T. W. Morgan (ed.), *Nairobi: City and Region* (Nairobi, 1967), Figs 11a and 11b, pp. 30 f.
38. C. K. Meek, *Land Law and Custom in the Colonies* 2nd edn (London, 1949), p. 99, for the governor's statement. More generally, V. Liversage, 'Tenure of Native Land in East Africa: The Economic Aspect', *East Afrn. Agric. J.*, I, 5 (1936), pp. 372–83; Colin Maher, 'Land Utilization as a National Problem: With Special Reference to Kenya Colony', ibid., 2, 2 (1936) pp. 130–44; I. D. Talbott, 'Agricultural Innovation and Policy Changes in Kenya in the 1930s' (PhD thesis, West Virginia University, 1976); David Anderson, 'Depression, Dust Bowl Demography and Drought: The Colonial State and Soil Conservation in East Africa during the 1930s', *African Affairs*, 83, 332 (1984), pp. 321–344.
39. L. P. Carpenter, 'Corporatism in Britain 1930–45', *J. Contemporary Hist.*, 11, 1 (1976), pp. 3–25.
40. Sir Edward Grigg, *The Constitutional Problem in Kenya* (Nottingham, 1933), pp. 24–8.
41. Secretary of State, draft despatch to the Governor of Kenya, 27 May 1937. PRO: CO.533/479/38077.
42. Cowen, 'Wattle', ch. 5.
43. Information from Major General Sir Alec Bishop (attached to C.O., 1937–9), 11 May 1976.
44. It was symptomatic that settlers accepted that they could have no more seats in the public forum of LegCo and that while they were given a greater role in government planning on the Executive Council, they had to share it with an Indian and a (white) representative of African interests: E. S. Atieno-Odhiambo, 'The History of the Kenya Executive Council, 1907–1939' (PhD thesis, Nairobi, 1973), pp. 311–30.
45. Clayton and Savage, *Government and Labour*, pp. 222–5.
46. Director of Civil Intelligence to PC Nyanza, 22 December 1939. KNA: PC/NZA.2/554.
47. Colony and Protectorate of Kenya, *Land Settlement Committee Report* (Nairobi, 1939).
48. Editorial, *East African Standard*, 8 December 1939; Report of Delegation from the East African Territories, and minutes thereon by Melville, Caine and Stockdale, June 1940. PRO: CO 533/518/38103/2B.
49. E. M. Salmon, *Beyond the Call of Duty: African Deeds of Bravery in Wartime* (London, 1952); L. S. B. Leakey, *By the Evidence: Memoirs 1932–1951* (New York and London, 1974), pp. 144 ff; information from

my near neighbour Fergus Wilson, onetime agricultural officer on Zanzibar and at Kakamega, and first Professor of Agriculture at Makerere, whose friend John Howard was probably the last man to see Leakey alive.

50. Quoted in *Food Shortage Commission of Enquiry Report 1943* (Nairobi, 1944), p. 12.
51. Atkin (War Office) to Seel, 24 April 1944. PRO: CO 533/535/3846.
52. The insight is from Wrigley 'Kenya: patterns of economic life', p. 264; see also N. J. Westcott, 'The Impact of the Second World War on Tanganyika, 1939–1949' (PhD thesis, Cambridge University, 1982), ch. 4.
53. Michael Redley, 'White maize and the colonial state in Kenya, to 1943', typescript (1979); for the precedent, Edith Whetham, *The Agrarian History of England and Wales, viii: 1914–1939* (Cambridge, 1978), chs. 7 and 8.
54. M. P. Miracle, 'An Economic Appraisal of Kenya's Maize Control', *East Afrn. Ec. Review*, 6 (1959), pp. 117–25; Ian Spencer, 'Settler dominance, agricultural production and the Second World War in Kenya', *JAH*, 21, 4 (1980), pp. 497–514; and Mosley, *Settler Economies*, pp. 51 ff, all take a critical view; W. H. Munro, 'Maize Marketing', pp. 177–181, takes a more lenient one.
55. The first sustained critique of the official wisdom is in the *East Africa Royal Commission 1953–1955 Report* (Cmd. 9475, 1955), ch. 7. The criticism was firmly rejected in the *Despatch from the Governor of Kenya commenting on the East Africa Royal Commission 1953–55 Report* (London, 1956).
56. J. F. Lipscomb, *We Built a Country* (London, 1956). ch. 6, gives a firsthand account.
57. Atkin to Seel, as in note 51.
58. In Legislative Council *Debates*, 4 February 1944, col. 38.
59. Munro, 'Maize Marketing', pp. 45–60. This period of below-market prices tends to be ignored by critics of Control.
60. Negley Farson, *Last Chance in Africa* (New York, 1950), pp. 46–9.
61. *Report on a Fiscal Survey ... by Sir Wilfred Woods*, p. 93. There were, however, sharply rising levels of African local government income, the implications of which are considered below.
62. Michael McWilliam, 'Economic Policy and the Kenya Settlers, 1945–1948', pp. 171–92 in K. Robinson and F. Madden (eds) *Essays in Imperial Government presented to Margery Perham* (Oxford, 1963).
63. John Spencer, *KAU: 'The Kenya African Union* (London, 1985).
64. cf. Richard Rathbone, 'Businessmen in Politics: Party Struggle in Ghana, 1949–57', *J. Development Studies*, 9, 3 (1973), pp. 391–401. For the press: Fay Gadsden, 'The African Press in Kenya, 1945–1952', *J. African History*, 21, 4 (1980), pp. 515–35.
65. Kitching, *Class and Change*, ch. 8.
66. Liversage to Financial Secretary, 14 October 1942; KNA: Agr. 1/718. For longer term increases in agricultural sales, Mosley, *Settler Economies*, 86.
67. Correspondence in PRO: CO 533/535/38516.
68. J. H. Martin, 'Economic Survey of Resident labour in Kenya' (mimeo 1947), pp. 4, 7. Furedi's research shows that the wealthiest squatter areas were the main bases of Mau Mau organisation in the Rift Valley.
69. *Report on Native Affairs 1939–45* (Nairobi, 1946), p. 42.

70. Nyanza Province Annual Reports, selected years, For Maasai stock prices, Mosley, *Settler Economies*, p. 102.
71. If 'politics' is the antithesis to 'discipline', then the officials were right.
72. D. K. Fieldhouse, 'Labour Governments and the Empire–Commonwealth, 1945–51', in R. Ovendale (ed.), *The Foreign Policy of the British Labour Governments, 1945–1951* (London, 1984).
73. The term comes from C. C. Wrigley, *Crops and Wealth in Uganda* (Kampala, 1959), p. 70.
74. Kenya Ministry of Agriculture, *African Land Development in Kenya* (Nairobi, 1962), especially introduction and ch. 6. It appears that the Kikuyu had to pay no cess at all on their vegetable produce, presumably owing to the impossibility of its collection.
75. Greet Kershaw, 'The Land is the People: A Study of Social Organization in Historical Perspective' (PhD thesis, University of Chicago, 1972); Michael Cowen, 'Differentiation in a Kenya Location' (University of East Africa Social Science Annual Conference, Nairobi, 1972).
76. Hunter (DC. North Kavirondo) to Fazan (PC. Nyanza), 11 March 1942; KNA: PC/NZA.3/1932.
77. I am indebted to discussions with Professor Greet Kershaw on these points; but see also David Throup's important 'The Governorship of Sir Philip Mitchell in Kenya, 1944–1952' (PhD thesis, Cambridge University, (1983) chs 3 and 4. For LNC revenue: *Report on Native Affairs 1939–45*, Appendix B.
78. This seems to have been the main dynamic of class formation in Kenya, as argued by M. Jean Hay, 'Economic change in Luoland: Kowe, 1890–1945' (PhD thesis, University of Wisconsin, 1972); Cowen, 'Differentiation' and a number of subsequent papers; and generalised from them in Kitching, *Class and Change*.
79. David L. Easterbrook, 'Kenyan Askari in World War II and their Demobilization, with Special Reference to Machakos District', pp. 27–58 in *Three Aspects of Crisis in Colonial Kenya* (Syracuse University, 1975).
80. Correspondence between Rongai Valley Association, Colin Maher and Director of Agriculture, February–April 1942; KNA: Agr. 1/718.
81. Clayton and Savage, *Government and Labour*, ch. 8; Stichter, *Migrant Labour*, pp. 109–23.
82. Bildad Kaggia, *Roots of Freedom* (Nairobi, 1975), pp. 57 ff.
83. Benedict Anderson's *Imagined Communities; reflections on the Origin and Spread of Nationalism* (London, 1983) seems to me to be marvellously illuminating.
84. John Hargreaves, *The End of Colonial Rule in West Africa* (London, 1979), ch. 2; R. D. Pearce, *The Turning Point in Africa: British Colonial Policy 1938–1948* (London, 1982), chs 3 and 4; John Flint, 'The Failure of planned decolonization in British Africa', *African Affairs*, 82, 328 (1983), pp. 389–411; Robert Pearce, 'The Colonial Office and planned decolonization in Africa, ibid., 83, 330 (1984), pp. 77–93.
85. Here I disagree with M. P. K. Sorrenson, *Land Reform in the Kikuyu Country* (Nairobi, 1967), p. 58.
86. Chief Secretary, confidential circular 'Native Political Development and

the Representation of Native Opinion', 9 December 1941, copy seen in KNA: PC/Coast 2/286; W. S. Marchant, confidential memo 'Establishment of Provincial Local Councils', n.d. enclosure in Governor Moore to Secretary of State, 21 March 1944; PRO: CO 533/532/38032/4.

87. Moore to Cranborne, 19 June 1942; CO 533/526/38144.
88. Kaggia, *Roots*, chs 3–5; Waruhiu Itote, *'Mau Mau' General* (Nairobi, 1967), pp. 9–15 and ch. 3.
89. Interview with Isaac Okwirry, 29–30 August 1980, on the night train from Nairobi to Kisumu. Okwirry was a warrant officer in the KAR in both the Abyssinia and Burma campaigns. He was one of the first to be appointed an Administrative Assistant, and the first African to be nominated to the official benches of LegCo, 1952.
90. B. E. Kipkorir, 'Carey Francis at the Alliance High School, Kikuyu, 1940–62', 143, in idem. (ed.) *Biographical Essays on Imperialism and Collaboration in Colonial Kenya* (Nairobi, 1980).
91. Koinange's petition and official correspondence on it in CO 533/532/38032/4.
92. Throup, 'Mitchell', chs. 1 and 2.
93. Photographs in *Kenya, Britain's Most Attractive Colony*, rev. ed. (Nairobi, 1936).
94. Colony and Protectorate of Kenya, *Report of the Settlement Schemes Committee, 1944* (Nairobi, 1944).
95. P. Wyn Harris to Chief Native Commissioner, 11 October 1945; KNA: Lab.9/1040.
96. Kanogo, 'Kikuyu Movement', p. 313.
97. Correspondence in KNA: PC/NZA. 2/1935 'Post-War Employment Committee'; Director of Agriculture, circular AGRIC.16/273, 'Development Plans', 5 September 1944, KNA: Agr.1/268.
98. Andrew Cohen, notes on meeting between Arthur Creech Jones and European Elected Members, n.d. (1946). PRO: CO 822/114/46523/1.
99. Despatch of 2 June 1950 to Secretary of State, printed in Colony and Protectorate of Kenya, *Agricultural Policy in African Areas in Kenya* (Nairobi, 1951), p. 15.
100. Again, I owe this Kikuyu perspective to Greet Kershaw.

5 The Impact of the Second World War on Tanganyika, 1939–49

NICHOLAS WESTCOTT

'War', says Tristan Tzara in Tom Stoppard's play *Travesties*, 'is capitalism with the gloves off'. During the Second World War Tanganyika experienced colonialism with the gloves off.[1] A sleepy imperial backwater, acquired late and held somewhat ambiguously under a Mandate, was transformed into an indispensible economic asset to Britain's war effort. For Africans it was a reminder of their subordination to a distant ruler and distant events. 'It is a fact that Imperialism has brought Africans face to face with the European war of Nationalism', declared the Swahili newspaper *Kwetu*.[2] Many Africans in Tanganyika, remembering their past, were ready and willing to fight against the Germans; but they did not miss the point, as they were so often told, that they were fighting not just for the King but for 'freedom'. The economic hardship and government intervention that accompanied the war effort precipitated a change in African attitudes towards colonial rule that brought its end within immediate view.

This paper is a thematic summary of the war's impact on Tanganyika. It over-simplifies and omits a great deal, but is intended to provide a framework for analysing the effects of the war in one territory which may be used for comparison with other parts of Africa. This is not a chronological account, but it is essential to remember that in war, even more than at other times, it was the conjuncture of particular, often unforeseen circumstances that produced effects which then became the historical basis for all that followed. Often, in commodity marketing or in food supply, for example, circumstances and planning leapfrogged each other: planning to deal with unexpected events being overtaken by other events, temporary expedients becoming established policies and being rationalised as the intended solution. The traditional turning point of 1945, although valid, has become so entrenched that it has damaged our understanding of the period.[3] Tanganyika's experience suggests that the continuities straddling 1945 are stronger than the differences: the 'post-war commodity boom', for example, can be said to have begun in 1942 when the allies became desperate for raw material supplies; but in practice it did not begin for many until 1948–9 when artificial controls over trade began to be lifted. Although in terms of political development 1945 remains the fulcrum, from the economic point of view 1942 and 1948 are more valid turning points; and, it will be argued, it is the economic impact of the war that is most significant.

I

Despite fears in 1942 that Japanese warships would any day appear off the East African coast, Tanganyika remained untouched by fighting during the Second World War. The crucial impact of the war was economic and most other significant changes stemmed directly or indirectly from this. Some might argue that the war was a temporary period of economic distortion, an aberration that did not influence the long-term development of the economy; or that it merely accentuated elements already inherent in the economic structure. On the other hand, the war did transform the world economy from one of excess commodity supply to one of raw material shortage; and it transformed the role of government in mediating the market and organising production – giving rise to an argument that has continued ever since between politicians, administrators and economists about the effects of government economic management. In market terms, Tanganyika – like Argentina – should have had the chance to develop more rapidly than ever before. In fact that development was blocked by the imperial connection and Tanganyika was left chasing its tail in a downward spiral of enforcement and inflation, trying to increase production with an ever-diminishing supply of imports.[4]

Tanganyika's economic subjection to imperial command was felt essentially in the control of her external trade. As soon as war broke out, the imperial government imposed controls to protect the sterling area against a drain on its dollar and gold reserves by restricting all imports from non-sterling countries, and sought to rationalise shipping. Both had an immediately adverse effect on the territory: 'Tanganyika', noted the Financial Secretary, 'has been largely dependent on non-sterling sources for many of its principal imports and restriction on these imports will mean shortage of many articles'.[5] Other than food, Tanganyika imported almost all its capital and consumer goods from overseas and was in no position to build up import substitution industries. A system of import licensing was introduced and as imports declined the government introduced rationing for essential fuels (petrol and whisky). Those imports that were permitted went largely to the settlers and sisal-growers for essential war production. Cotton piece goods were in such short supply that the more distant areas of Tanganyika reverted to bark cloth to cover their nakedness.[6] The volume of imports fell to half their pre-war level by 1942–3, though inflation meant that their value remained the same. The volume reached its pre-war level again in 1946, but this was now nowhere near enough to meet the increased demand. Import controls remained in force for non-sterling goods until the 1950s because of the continued pressure on sterling, and supply only began to satisfy demand after 1948. Until 1947 Tanganyika ran a substantial balance of payments surplus, swelling her sterling balances in London and helping to prop up sterling by earning more dollars than she spent. The cost was that Tanganyika was starved of the imports she needed to develop at a time when cash and market opportunities were there.[7]

The first two years of war were characterised by the collapse of Tanganyika's traditional export markets. Sisal, coffee, groundnuts and other crops that had been sold to continental Europe found their markets destroyed as German tanks rolled to the Atlantic and Mediterranean coasts. Coffee prices fell dramatically until, in 1941, a frost hit the Brazilian crop; and the Bombay cotton market went haywire, opening and closing in random conjunction with the fluctuating fortunes of war and of Indian domestic politics. There was strong pressure on governments to assist colonial producers in these adverse circumstances. In Tanganyika's case the government stepped in from fear of the economic and political consequences of allowing export industries to collapse. The British Government was persuaded to purchase the sisal crop, and the Tanganyika administration agreed to guarantee purchase of the cotton crop. But governments, unused to taking commercial risks, were even more cautious than businessmen in protecting themselves against loss by fixing producer prices low and profit margins high. The sisal crop was either used in Britain or sold to the USA on a 'no profit no loss' basis, so only the consumers gained. For cotton, however, the Tanganyika administration was able to sell the crop, through agents, on the Bombay market at what a smug Director of Agriculture called 'a handsome profit'.[8]

Then, in 1942 the world market (or what was left of it) changed dramatically. With the loss of the Far East and the entry of America into the war, an unlimited demand was created for sisal, rubber, pyrethrum, tin and a host of minor exports, including food. Every possible means had to be found to supply the allied war effort. Government control over commodity marketing was quickly extended. Britain took control of both cotton and coffee crops, not to support the producers but to secure supplies and to ensure that every available resource was directed to the most appropriate, and nearest, end. In Tanganyika, as elsewhere, the government was in no position to undertake the physical marketing of commodities itself, and it therefore formed existing trading companies into exporters' 'pools' operating under a government control board. As long as supplies were secured, prices were secondary. Nevertheless for most bulk-purchased commodities they were fixed below any free market equivalent, partly because the government argued there was no free market, partly to prevent inflation in import-starved colonies. In Tanganyika the effect varied. Cotton production stagnated or declined as other crops became more profitable. The same applied to coffee and copra, while the groundnut trade was killed off completely. Crops with uncontrolled prices, like tea and tobacco, or with generous prices to encourage production, like pyrethrum, expanded rapidly. The government had begun, in a haphazard fashion, to manipulate production through price.[9]

The Tanganyika administration also sought to increase production in other ways. There was pressure from London to maximise the production of rubber and sisal, and pressure from the local settlers for help in producing 'essential foodstuffs' for military and domestic needs. Through great effort and cost the government revived production on some derelict and overgrown old German rubber estates, but only by conscripting the poor and harmless Wagogo as rubber tappers.[10] The sisal growers and settlers demanded two things of the government: agricultural machinery and labour.

Machinery could only be obtained from America, for dollars, and was therefore strictly licensed. But so important was East African production to the Americans (who sent their own envoy there) and so effective was the lobbying of the settlers that they eventually received most of the machinery they needed. So while Africans, who had no hands on the political levers of power, went without iron hoes, the sisal growers got their locomotives and the settlers their tractors.[11]

Labour was available locally but could not be so easily directed by government. During the first year of war the government had taken legal powers to conscript all inhabitants for essential war needs and used them, to fulfil the military quotas, which grew as the war progressed. By 1945, 86 740 of the fittest young Tanganyikan Africans had served with the military. This left fewer men in Tanganyika to work on their own farms or estates. By 1943 settlers and sisal-growers were both insisting the government conscript labour for them. The governor was prepared to do so and Colonial Office opposition was overridden by Churchill, who told the Cabinet that if British people were subject to civil conscription, there was no reason why the colonies should be exempt.[12] By the end of the war therefore a further 84 501 Africans had been conscripted for the estates. The wage-labour force had grown from 240 000 before the war to 340 000, and during 1943 it was estimated that 45 per cent of African men were absent from their homes. Those in the army waxed fat and returned healthy; those on the estates grew thin and went home debilitated by disease. Officials tried to enforce welfare provisions but they were too few and had too many other preoccupations to have much success until they began penalising bad employers in 1945. The cost of this labour extraction was felt not only by the hapless conscripts; it also exacerbated Tanganyika's war-time food problems.[13]

The changes in Tanganyika's external economy had a profound effect on the domestic economy. In food production the two overlapped. In late 1941 the Middle East desperately needed food and East Africa was ordered to increase production by every possible means. It was decided to fix the prices and guarantee a market for all foodstuffs and offer settlers additional financial incentives. An Increased Production of Crops Ordinance provided generous loans and guaranteed minimum returns for estate production, and the government promised African producers that it would buy at the published official prices all produce brought for sale to the official native authority markets. The government would thus secure all available surplus foodstuffs for export. But it proved more complicated than that and the new arrangements brought as much chaos as control to food marketing. The settlers did well enough, for the fixed prices for maize and wheat were more than generous. But for African produce, the government either set a price too low, as for rice, most of which was sold illicitly on a fast-growing black market, or they were unable to fulfil their promise to buy everything produced, as with groundnuts: thousands of sacks rotted in up-country godowns, producers went unpaid and groundnut production for export virtually died.[14]

The problems were just beginning to manifest themselves when the

1942 and 1943 rains failed. The Central Province, worst hit as usual, suffered prolonged drought and famine. Suddenly it became a question not of getting more to export but of finding enough to live on. The administration was panic-stricken. It had to guarantee food supplies to the workforce on estates to ensure that production was maintained, and to the towns to prevent urban unrest, but under war-time conditions it was impossible to import food to cover the shortfall. In this situation the government was forced to intervene ever more substantially in the production and marketing of food.[15]

The support for settlers was made even more generous to encourage bigger acreages of maize where cultivation had previously been uneconomic. The further rise in maize and wheat prices also stimulated African production of these crops, which increased significantly despite the administration's attempt to discriminate against African farmers through a two-tier pricing system. To increase African production, the government generally preferred to use a stick rather than a carrot: native authorities and agricultural officers were instructed to enforce minimum acreages of 'famine crops' such as cassava and sweet potato, and encourage soil conservation techniques, such as tie-ridging, which had become the fashion during the 1930s. Both were unpopular and implemented with very variable success by a growing army of agricultural instructors (described by one provincial commissioner as little better than 'ill-informed policemen').[16] It is hard to generalise about food production where regional variations were so great, but there appears to have been a widespread increase in monocropping among Africans of maize for the market and cassava for subsistence, the one more risky but profitable, the other easier and more dependable but less nutritious.

A measure of the government's desperation was that, under the influence of the enthusiastic but erratic Director of Agriculture (R. W. R. Miller), it entered into food production itself. The ill-fated Northern Province Wheat Scheme was an ambitious project to convert wide stretches of Masai pastureland into a giant mechanised wheat farm. The land was commandeered and tractors ordered in 1942, but delays prevented production until 1944, when the worst food shortages were over. With one or two exceptions, crop yields were poor, costs of production were high and the whole scheme uneconomic. It was wound up in 1947 with a loss to the government of £170 000 and the sad lesson that 'the Northern province cannot be treated in the same way as a Canadian prairie'.[17]

Finally, the government tried to alleviate the food problems by controlling distribution. In 1943 a Produce Control was established with powers to buy all food put up for sale in official markets at the official price, and to sell it wherever it was most needed. The idea was to create a national market for food and allow the government to use local surplusses from one area to meet shortages in another. Although a good idea, it did not work in practice; officials lacked the necessary resources to enforce it, and as one confessed, 'as produce controllers we are just laughable'.[18] Farmers and traders both turned to the black market where prices were substantially higher. When the rains failed again in 1946, this dual food market became even more exaggerated and probably exacerbated the effects of the shortage. But the government persevered and when a third famine struck in 1949, it reconstructed the Produce Control into a Grain Storage Department with a similar but more effective role. Although the tale of government intervention in the food market during the 1940s is a sorry one, it is true that each time the rains failed the system worked slightly better and fewer people starved. But it is not clear that the government's efforts helped African cultivators secure their own subsistence. Rather it was taking the burden on itself.

Shortages of food and labour were not the only problems besetting Tanganyika's domestic economy during the war. The increased incomes from crop exports and soldiers' remittances were not matched by increasing imports. More money chasing fewer goods resulted in inflation. Roughly speaking, prices doubled during the war and trebled between 1939 and 1949, which does not account for some goods becoming altogether unobtainable. Again the government took remedial action, but again with very mixed results. The rich were more heavily taxed, both income and excess profit taxes being introduced soon after war began; but the incomes of sisal-growers, settlers and businessmen seem to have grown faster than inflation or tax restricted them and European and Asian government employees received generous cost-of-living allowances. Africans, on the other hand, found their incomes restricted by the control of produce prices and wages, and the salaried clerks received allowances that nowhere covered the real increase in their cost of living. Wherever possible, employers offered rations rather than cash increases, but these were often unpalatable and very unpopular with Africans. The government tried to control the retail price of food and consumer goods, but without much success. The more elaborate the system devised by the all pervading Economic Control Board (that 'great octopus of control', as one DO called it), the more ingenious the methods of evading it. In Mwanza it was discovered in 1945 that the town's entire allocation of bicycles and most hoes and piece-goods were distributed on the black market to selected customers at greatly inflated prices. It was how shopkeepers survived.[19]

The war accentuated differentiation within Tanganyikan society, encouraged the use of cash and the development of a national economy. Besides the sisal-growers and settlers (especially some of the Greeks who made fortunes in tobacco), it was the Asian traders who profited most from the war. Among Africans the war profited those with something to sell which was not strictly controlled – cattle, maize, beeswax, vegetables, for example. For the Chagga, for instance, the war was a time of great prosperity. But the burden of war fell mostly on those without economic or political leverage, on the poorer African peasants and on those in towns or on estates who worked for wages. What is clear is that, whatever the intention, government intervention in the economy did not bring greater equality (though it may have prevented even greater inequality), but generally it worked to the benefit of those who possessed political and economic muscle.[20]

II

The war brought managerial government to Tanganyika. The path had been laid down during the 1930s when, in the face of the depression, colonial officials began contemplating more active economic intervention in the interests of faster development. But they planned nothing on the scale of war-time economic management: the almost complete takeover of export marketing and the attempted control of domestic prices and distribution. Some of the controls were effective, but others caused more distortion than development. Once on the slippery slope to market control, the government found it almost impossible to get off, even had it wanted to.[21]

War-time intervention had been partly offensive, to increase production and support sterling in the interests of the imperial war effort, and partly defensive, to protect the territory's producers and consumers and maintain the solvency and stability of the colonial state. After the war the administration continued the controls for the same reason unless there were positive reasons, whether political or economic, to abandon them.

In sisal there was a powerful reason to abandon control: the sisal growers wanted to run the marketing themselves, and what the sisal growers wanted, the government usually gave. The matter was complicated by the fact that the industry itself was split; locally-based producers, led by the irascible Eldred Hitchcock, wanted a centralised marketing system run by the growers themselves, while the merchants and their clients wanted to return to a free market. The latter were eventually able to block the centralised scheme, and sisal reverted to a more or less free market, which, at the time, provided growers with extremely good prices.[22]

Coffee marketing, however, remained under government control, mainly because of the continued imperial interest of earning and saving dollars, which made East African coffee – as a substitute for Brazilian – especially valuable to the sterling area. The government took advantage of its control to reorganise coffee marketing in Bukoba, ostensibly to improve quality though in practice the government control board yielded a substantial revenue for local development projects. Control also continued for cotton, which the government continued to sell for ever more handsome profits on the Bombay market. Only when the government helped organise producer cooperatives to undertake marketing in Bukoba and Sukumaland in the 1950s did the post-war commodity boom really reach African peasants there.[23]

As long as food and import supplies remained erratic, the government also remained involved in food and retail marketing. It tried to ensure an equitable distribution, and prevent shortages, particularly of food in the towns, provoking political unrest. But it seems likely that the system of rationing and the attempts at price control directed as much criticism towards government as it deflected from it. The government persevered, but was undoubtedly relieved when improved supplies of both food and consumer goods in the 1950s enabled it to withdraw from so exposed a position.[24]

Conscription had been the most traumatic intervention, both for the Africans and the administration itself. In Buha it nearly provoked a revolt, and the ill-feeling it engendered is reflected in the massive desertion of conscripts from the estates. Despite the settlers' pleas for its continuation, the new Labour government ordered that conscription end as soon as possible, and by 1946 no conscripts remained on the estates. The war had forced the administration out of its previous laissez-faire approach to labour welfare, and although it afterwards abandoned the obligation to supply labour, it did not abandon the duty to enforce good labour conditions, even if improvement was slow. For the employers, government intervention had at least enabled them to keep wages low in a period when they might have been greatly inflated.[25]

The government also abandoned its direct concern with production. The rubber estates and the Wheat Scheme were closed down and Creech Jones' proposal that the electricity company be nationalised was rejected by the Governor on the grounds that the government could not cope. The

Groundnut Scheme was an aberration – the greatest white elephant the African bush had ever seen. Once again it was discovered that there was a difference between East Africa and the North American plains, which required more than machines and will-power to overcome.[26]

The burden of work created by the government's attempts at economic management fell on fewer and older shoulders. Those officials who could escape to the Forces did so. Those left behind, few of whom had any qualifications in economics or management, found themselves swamped by paper from Dar es Salaam requiring them to control this, collect that and distribute the other. District officers had to rely more heavily on the Native Authorities to collect quotas of conscripts and enforce minimum acreages, which, being unpopular measures, put many chiefs in a quandary. Those most concerned to keep their salaries complied; others prevaricated and were dismissed. The DOs' previous painstaking attention to the niceties of tribal succession evaporated. What was needed was an efficient administrative machine, and tribal legitimacy had to be subordinated to this. The extent of this change should not be exaggerated, but where the façade of indirect rule was already cracking, as in Upare, the cracks widened to the extent of making the whole structure unstable. As the hand of colonial rule became heavier, it became harder to find collaborators who could retain the full confidence of their subjects.

Among European officials morale sank as the workload increased. District annual reports of the mid-1940s reflect a resignation and cynicism not heard before. In Tanganyika the 'second colonial occupation' after 1945 was merely plugging holes made by the war, The Groundnut Scheme apart, Tanganyika's era of development only really began in 1949. But, however short-staffed the administration, no Africans were appointed as administrative officers until the end of the decade. There were, the government claimed, simply no Africans capable of doing the job yet, and African advancement should in any case be through the development of Native Authorities. But this was becoming a matter of high colonial policy to be decided in London.[27]

III

The war changed the balance of power not only within Tanganyika but between Tanganyika and London. In political as in economic policy the key decisions were now made by the imperial goverment, often, but not always, in the Colonial Office. The study of colonial policy in the 1940s is a well worn path,[28] but Tanganyika's experience illuminates some and contradicts others of the themes already outlined by the pioneers.

The war had forced the three East African governments to cooperate on a wide range of economic and military matters. This coincided with a revival of settler ambitions to create a new dominion in East Africa and produced a crisis over proposals to promote 'closer union' between the territories. The crisis was defused and produced only a very watered-down East African High Commission in 1948, designed merely to coordinate economic services such as transport, customs and research. Although during the war the Mandate became a legal fiction, Tanganyika was again placed under international supervision as a United Nations Trusteeship Territory afterwards. The British settlers were furious, the Africans delighted; but neither had any influence on the decisions, made by a British government eager to cooperate with the USA and the fledgling UN.[29]

On this local and metropolitan authorities agreed. On the speed of political development they did not. A couple of chiefs were appointed to the Legislative Council in 1945, as much to strengthen the authority of the chiefs as a whole as to represent Africans, but the administration remained wedded to indirect rule and a timetable for self-government that stretched over the horizon. In London that end was already in view and the CO began at first to persuade and then, with Twining's appointment as governor in 1949, to bludgeon a reluctant Tanganyika into speeding up its local government reforms. Another difference emerged over white settlement. The local administration wanted to realienate all the ex-German farms around Kilimanjaro and Meru, whereas the CO wanted a large portion of them returned to the Chagga, because, as Cohen argued, 'From the long term point of view . . . relations with the Chagga are far more important than relations with the European settlers'. A compromise was reached, but though it satisfied the Chagga, it aroused the Meru to a protest that gravely embarrassed the government when taken to the UN.[30] Despite the CO's activities, however, the educated Africans, the aspiring politicians, were still left out in the cold and no new generation of collaborators emerged.

The other product of the war years was a more vigorous policy of colonial development. This policy was neither as simple nor as important as many have suggested. The development plans themselves reflect mainly the political forces acting on those who drew them up and were, in Tanganyika's case at least, largely irrelevant during the 1940s. The Groundnut Scheme, for instance, appeared in no development plan and served mainly to distort those that did exist by diverting resources to a futile end. What mattered was not the plans but the economic reality of an imperial economy that dictated trade and marketing patterns, and the small-scale efforts of individual officials in the districts.

Tanganyika's first development plan of 1940 was the product of a committee dominated by settlers: it advocated more white settlement. The CO did not approve, having more than enough trouble with Kenya. Tanganyika, they advised, should give more emphasis to African development. The war and the Colonial Development and Welfare Act also favoured an increased provision for welfare schemes, and the revised plan of 1944 faithfully reflected this. But CO attitudes had changed: development should now concentrate on an economic investment in production to increase the colonies' own resources. This was at least partially reflected in the 1946 Ten Year Development Plan, but this in turn was criticised by Cohen for neglecting education, so necessary if an educated class was to be prepared for the transfer of power, and Tanganyika was duly told to expand education. By the end of 1949 Tanganyika had spent only £3 million on its development plans, barely half its allocation and one-tenth of the money spent on the Groundnut Scheme. This was primarily due to the import restraints and reflects the fact that during the 1940s the imperial government was looking for immediate gain from Tanganyika, not long-term investment in it. This was the most immediate legacy of the war; but in the longer term, power over colonial policy had been transferred to London, which was paving the way to transfer it to the Africans.[31]

IV

Only a small minority of Tanganyikans participated directly in the Second World War, fighting with the King's African Rifles in Ethiopia, North Africa, Madagascar and Burma. Back home, service in the armed forces gave them status, health and money, which in many cases was rapidly dissipated on wine, women and cattle.

Only those Africans who had been politically aware *before* they were recruited seem to have picked up new ideas in the course of their service. Some returned convinced that 'Education and Health are the two most important things the Africans fail to get'; others established small (and often short-lived) associations, such as the 'Musoma New Living Boys', as a symbol of their modernity. But most returned to their *shambas*, spent their money and continued as before.[32]

The real revolution took place at home. It was stimulated by a combination of British propaganda, which brought even the most backward areas in touch with the war through the free, official newsheet *Habari za Vita*, and deteriorating living conditions caused by the economic impasse already described. One thing conscription had shown was the abysmal level of health among Africans. The war and the short commons that went with it did little to improve that, but at least it was recognised as something to be remedied. Conscription, both civil and military, also forced many people to move from their home areas for the first time. The known world grew wider. Migration to the towns increased, if only as an escape from the growing oppression in rural areas. Not that life in towns was much easier: it was expensive and overcrowded and wages were low. Some women sought their fortune in prostitution;[33] men sought it anywhere. But even those with money had problems, for 'What is the use of money if there is no food to buy?', as *Kwetu* complained.[34] Not only food but all the staples of daily life – clothes, kerosene, cooking-pots, soap and accommodation – were hard to find and exorbitantly expensive.

Those who suffered most heavily in relative terms were the clerks, the salaried elite. During the war their real standard of living fell dramatically, making it increasingly difficult to maintain the standard of wealth and status they had prized before the war. Complaints multiplied, disillusion spread and associations were reactivated to pursue their grievances. The growth of African political activity during the 1940s in Tanganyika has been described elsewhere.[35] Here there is space only to look at how the war contributed to the change in African political thought, from loyal support to outright criticism of the British administration, and how this and political activity in some rural areas indicate that the collaboration on which the British depended was breaking down.

One point in Britain's war-time propaganda sank home, that this was 'a war for freedom'.[36] Writing to their employers in 1943 to complain about their working conditions, Dar es Salaam dockers declared:

> . . . from day to day we are being kicked and beaten just not like human beings . . . the treatment we receive from the African Wharfage is equal to the Nazi German, but we are being told that we are at war with the Nazi German because the Nazi want to enslave the world, how is it that an English is making us a slave in the face of the capital of this country? You are also aware that our brethren are fighting up North and in other parts of the world all for freedom . . .

The more educated drew a more directly political conclusion:

> India is to have her HOME RULE as a reward for her sacrifices . . . The African has done his duty in a war that only indirectly concerned him, will the victory be the old fable to him or is he going to be allowed a share of it this time . . . ?
>
> *Kwetu* has only one conclusion to come to: 'The orange that is squeezed too hard yields bitter juice' . . . WE ASK FOR GOOD DEMOCRATIC GOVERNMENT.[38]

But far from becoming more democratic, the government seemed to take less notice of African opinion. The more it tried to manage the economy, the more it was criticised and the more Africans began to feel it was not acting in their own best interests. There was an increasingly acute feeling that Africans as a racial group were suffering and this encouraged them to make common cause. Horizontal linkages began to be made between African groups seeking redress from government. As conditions worsened, unrest increased, culminating in the 1947 general strike. For the first time clerks joined dockers in protest and a strike starting in Dar es Salaam spread to other towns throughout the territory, affecting even the government teachers at Tabora Girls School.[39] Things had changed. War had sharpened the focus of colonialism and the soothing rhetoric of civilisation had given way to talk of freedom and development. Educated Africans had become disaffected and were beginning to look for ways to change the government and make it more responsive to their needs.

Disillusion affected the rural areas too, mainly where an emerging peasantry wished to challenge Native Authorities, which were becoming more authoritarian. The Chagga were handled with kid gloves and their political energies channelled into the campaign for a Paramount chief. But in Upare in 1944 and Usambara after the war there were major political disturbances directed at the native authorities and through them at the colonial government. Local political dissidents in these two areas were also, through the African Association, beginning to link their local campaigns to national political activity. The culmination of this process came with the Meru Land Case, which brought together many of the strands of post-war political change: government policies of economic development and white settlement, settler political pressure, disillusion with and the failure of the Native Authorities, the connection between local and national political activity, and the international implications of colonial policy. It signalled a turning point in rural politics as the 1947 strike had in urban politics, although the two strands were not to be drawn together until 1954 with the founding of TANU.[40]

V

The war stimulated the growth of managerial government in Tanganyika but at the same time began a process that steadily diminished the autonomy of the colonial administration there. Increasingly it was subject to political control from above and political pressure from below, more and more decisions being taken on orders from London or as a result of pressure from local groups, whether black or white. Ultimately the administration could only watch as the transfer of power was negotiated between British politicians in Westminster and African nationalists in Tanganyika. This was the end result of a historical process in which the war had been a decisive moment. But at the time, Tanganyika had played its allotted role in the imperial scheme of things. It had given essential support to the war effort and to Britain's self-preservation, at a cost to itself which was not only great at the time but which had a lasting effect on the territory's economy.

Throughout the war Tanganyikan Africans had remained remarkably loyal to Britain in the struggle against Germany. They had borne a heavy burden: their resources and manpower had been used to the full. The Second World War had brought great difficulties to Tanganyika but they had been suffered stoically. After the war, however, the sacrifices continued but were now seen as exploitation. In using the Empire as a crutch during the 1940s, the British put more strain on it than it could bear and inevitably it began to break apart.

NOTES

1. Tom Stoppard, *Travesties* (London, 1975), p. 39; a point already noted (as so many others) by Professor J. Gallagher, *The Decline, Revival and Fall of the British Empire* (Cambridge, 1982), p. 145. J. Iliffe, *A Modern History of Tanganyika* (Cambridge, 1979).
2. *Kwetu* (Dar es Salaam), July 1942.
3. Iliffe associates the war with the depression as a continuous crisis, whereas my own view, at least for Tanganyika, is that the impact of the two was fundamentally different. See Iliffe, *Tanganyika*, ch. 11.
4. The mechanism of this imperial economic system is discussed in chapter 2 of this book.

5. Minute by Sandford, 1 Dec. 1939, TNA 27592 (Tanzania National Archives).
6. Southern Province Annual Report (PAR), 1944.
7. Tanganyika, *Trade Reports*, 1939–1948. J. F.R. Hill and J. P. Moffett, *Tanganyika: A review of its resources and their development* (Dar es Salaam, 1955), pp. 739–43. (The picture is distorted by massive imports after 1947 for the Groundnut Scheme.)
8. Killick to Chief Secretary, 30 Oct. 1940, TNA 28259/5. For sisal see the 18002 files in CO 852/311, 431 and 432 (Colonial Office records, PRO).
9. Information gathered from Tanganyika files in CO 852 and Tanganyika, *Annual Reports of the Agricultural Department*, 1939–45.
10. See TNA 31573 and TNA 31275.
11. Colonial Supply Mission and sisal files in CO 852.
12. Details in CO 691/184/42374.
13. Tanganyika, *Annual Reports of the Labour Department*, 1940–6. TNA 30178 and CO 691/191/42374.
14. Information from TNA 30157 and subsequent files, and from various District Annual Reports in TNA. Full references to this and other subjects discussed are in N. J. Westcott, 'The Impact of the Second World War on Tanganyika 1939–1949' (PhD thesis, Cambridge University, 1982).
15. This and the following paragraph are based on TNA 30626 and sub-files; for the Lake Province, see TNA 215/694/IV.
16. The Gogo sang (and, I am told, still sing) a song about it:

    'Let us show the chiefs the *shamba* has been planted.
    Plant in rows to keep the *bwana* happy.'

    (I am grateful to Graham Thiele who recorded the song in Dodoma). A good example of the campaign in the Lake Province is in TNA 215/694/III.
17. Nobody, it seems, has told the Canadians, who have been trying to run a similar scheme in the same area since 1974 (*The Guardian*, 2 Dec. 1983). TNA 30349/I–IV, and Hill and Moffett, *Tanganyika*, p. 385.
18. Kigoma District Annual Report (DAR), 1943, TNA 967:821.1. TNA 31301 and 31886.
19. Mwanza DAR, 1945, TNA 41/128/20, and other DARs and PARs; for an African perspective, see *Kwetu*, 1942–5.
20. The only comparative study is still A. R. Prest, *The War Economics of Primary Producing Countries* (Cambridge, 1948), which illustrates the contrast with the Middle East. Whether the increase in wage labour contributed to a process of class formation would need more extended discussion.
21. The analogy is with C. Baker, 'Colonial Rule and the Internal Economy in Twentieth Century Madras', *Modern Asian Studies*, 15:3 (1981), pp. 575–602.
22. This is discussed at length in N. J. Westcott, 'The East African Sisal Industry, 1929–49: The marketing of a colonial commodity during depression and war', *J. of African History*, 25. 4 (1984).
23. Coffee: TNA 37200/I–II. Cotton: TNA 34953/III; Tanganyika, *The Cotton Industry*, 1939–53 (1953).
24. See, e.g. TNA 31555/1 (food), TNA 33161/I–II (piece goods) and TNA 36127 (ECB). Also *Kwetu*, 1946–9.

25. G. St. J. Orde Brown, *Labour Conditions in East Africa*, Colonial No. 193 (London 1946). Correspondence in CO 822/117/46748. For events in Buha, see J. J. Tawney's Diaries for Oct.–Dec. 1940 (Rhodes House, Oxford).
26. A number of unsatisfactory accounts exist; the most readable is still A. Wood, *The Groundnut Affair* (London, 1950), but the most interesting material is in MAF 83/1746 on, and CO 852/603 and 912.
27. These paragraphs are based on the impression given by many DARs and PARs of the 1940s. On African administrative officers, see TNA 16245/5 and CO 691/197/42259/5.
28. So much so that it is almost worn out. Among others the path has been trodden by (in chronological order) Lee, Robinson, Gupta, Louis, Lee Hargreaves, Cell, Pearce, Morgan, Lee and Petter. I have even trespassed on this territory myself in the article cited below.
29. N.J. Westcott, 'Closer Union and the future of East Africa, 1939–1948', *J. of Imperial and Commonwealth History*, X:1 (1981), pp. 67–88. For trusteeship, see CO 968/160–3 and CO 537/1444–58.
30. Minute by Cohen, 13 Oct. 1948, CO 691/200/42498. Also TNA 16528/I–VI.
31. The 1940, 1944 and 1946 development plans were all published by the Tanganyika Government. Colonial Office comment is in the 42303 files in CO 691.
32. Sgt. Rutenganio, quoted in Oldaker to Sandford, 5 May 1945, TNA 31642/27. Report by D. C. Musoma, 14 Sept. 1946, TNA 215/1603/A/217.
33. There are no statistics, but prostitution seems to have increased in proportion to the number of soldiers and sailors passing through Tanganyika (which increased ten- or twenty-fold). By 1944 Tanga was said to have 'nineteen streets in which practically every house is of doubtful repute'. (Medical Officer, Tanga, 1 Dec. 1944, TNA 20887/II/19a.) Fortunes were certainly made, if complaints from African clerks about inflated rents paid by prostitutes are to be believed. Like other war-time changes, the spread of prostitution did not abate but continued after the war.
34. *Kwetu*, 8 March 1943.
35. Iliffe, *Tanganyika*, ch. 13 and (ed.) *Modern Tanzanians* (Nairobi, 1973), ch. 12.
36. 'Utenzi wa Vita vya Uhuru' is the title of Shaaban Robert's epic poem about the war (Nairobi, 1967), though it consists largely of versified Swahili translations of Churchill's greatest speeches.
37. Labourers of the African Wharfage Co. to the General Manager, Smith Mackenzie, 1 Jan. 1943, TNA 10849/879.
38. *Kwetu*, 11 June and 1 Aug. 1941.
39. Material in TNA 27271, Eastern and other PARs for 1947, and *Tanganyika Standard*, September 1947. Generally, see correspondence in Suleiman papers, TNA 571, and TNA 19325/II on the African Association, and TNA 63/L/1/4/2.
40. I. N. Kimambo, *Mbiru, Popular protest in colonial Tanzania* (Historical Association of Tanzania, 1971). Korogwe and Lushoto DARs, 1946–50. Japhet papers in TNA, and 'Reports on the Meru Land Problem' by M. J. Davies and H. Mason, and by B. George in Rhodes House, Oxford.

6 The Impact of the Second World War: the Case of Kweneng in the then Bechuanaland Protectorate, 1939–1950

BRIAN MOKOPAKGOSI III

The impact of the Second World War on African communities has remained a neglected theme in the colonial history of the continent. In studies published in recent years a good deal of attention has tended to focus on the political, social and economic impact of the war on the continent as a whole,[1] on particular regions[2] or individual colonies.[3] Where in-depth studies have been made, they have focused on such themes as the impact of the war on returned soldiers,[4] and its consequences for the development of nationalism.[5] Few studies have yet been made of the impact of the war on a particular community, where both oral and archival data can be used to illuminate the consequences of the war on farmers, traders and women and children left behind by the soldiers, at the grassroots level.

Kweneng, in what was then Bechuanaland Protectorate, affords a particularly good case-study of the impact of the Second World War on one particular African community. In the first place, though the Bechuanaland Protectorate was one of the smallest of Britain's colonial territories in Africa in terms of its population, a mere 276 000 in 1940, it supplied over 10 000 men for war service between 1941 and 1945, that is 16 per cent of its eligible adult male population. In the second place, the majority of the soldiers who survived the war returned to their homes in Kweneng rather than settle outside their original homeland, and it has

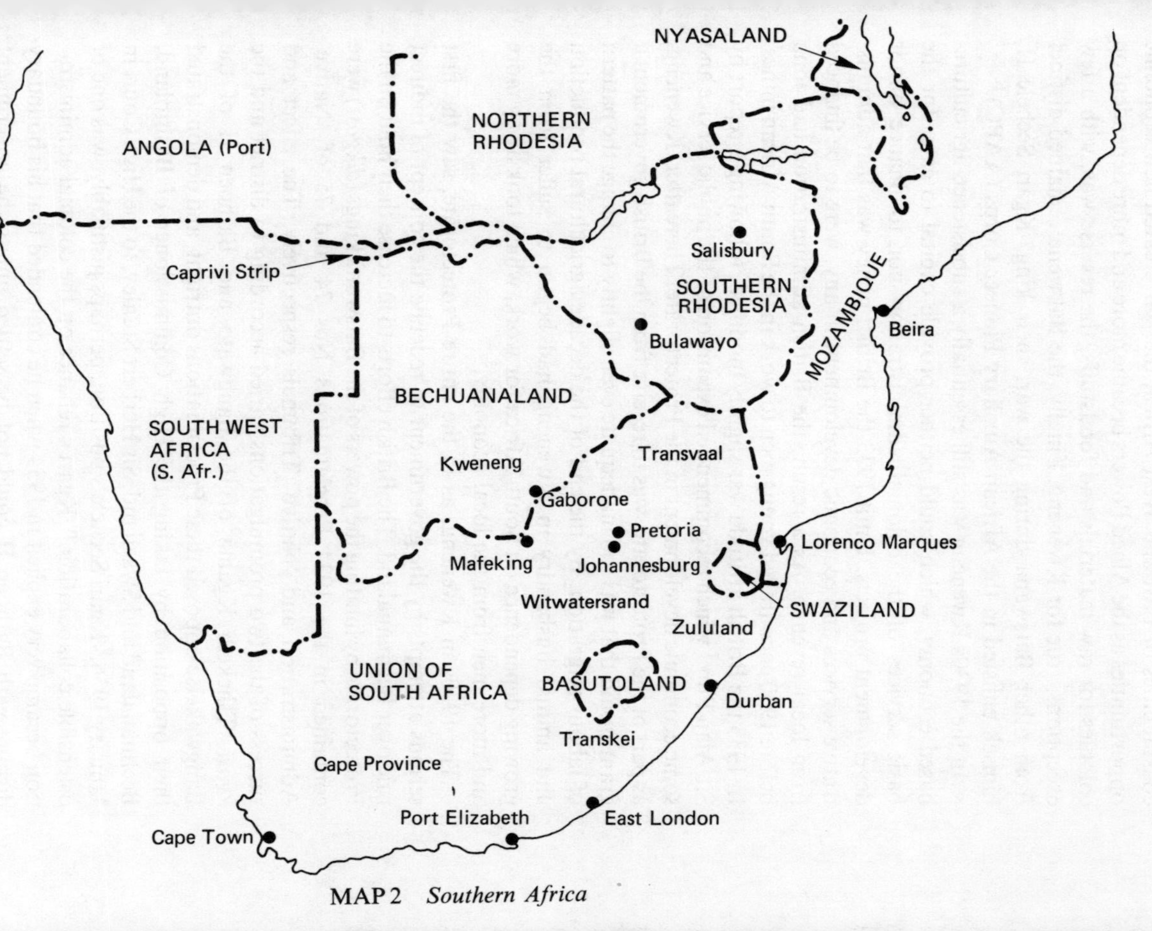

MAP 2 *Southern Africa*

been possible over the period 1980–4 to interview a large number of survivors. Third, Kweneng is a relatively small Tswana state in area and population, so that intensive fieldwork leading to valid generalisation has been possible. Fourth, while in other parts of Africa, especially the coastal cities of East and West Africa, the war created new economic opportunities as the Allied Powers became more and more dependent on colonies for raw materials and foodstuffs, the reverse was, with a few exceptions, true for Kweneng. Finally, the Bakwena remained distinct from other Batswana during the war; their king, Kgari Sechele II, himself enlisted in the African Auxiliary Pioneer Corps (AAPC).[6]

In the 1930s Kweneng was still essentially a subsistence-agriculture-based economy, which could neither provide capital to cater for the basic services of the colonial administration nor to finance minor development projects. Until 1933 the British policy was that administrative services and economic development, if any, were to be financed from local revenue. As a result, the British administration had long before 1930 encouraged young men to work in the South African mines. In 1933 the British attitude was slightly modified, following a report by Sir Alan Pim,[7] which recommended expansion of the public service and some economic development in the Protectorate. Thereafter, Kweneng, as part of the Protectorate, was to receive from the British government a grant-in-aid that was too inadequate even slightly to change the pattern of labour migration. By the end of the decade agricultural production and animal husbandry in Kweneng had begun to suffer from the growing dependence on South Africa for work, which took away more and more men from the local economy.[8]

The 1930s in Kweneng, as in the entire Protectorate, saw the first serious attempts by the government to redefine the concept of indirect rule over Bechuanaland. The British efforts to increase their hold on the Protectorate by limiting the powers of the Batswana kings (*dikgosi*) were contained in the 1934 Proclamations Nos 74 and 75 of 'Native' Administration and 'Native' Tribunals respectively. The effect and success of the two promulgations varied according to district and the *kgosi*. Tshekedi Kgama of the Bangwato and Bathoen II of the Bangwaketse opposed these Proclamations outright, and demonstrated their opposition by taking the High Commissioner of Basutoland, Bechuanaland and Swaziland, Sir Herbert Stanley, to the High Court in January 1936.[9] Kgari Sechele's position, perhaps justifiably, was one of ostensible collaboration.[10] Kgari's reliance on the colonial administration became very explicit in 1934 when he contended that his boundary dispute with Bathoen II could not be settled unless the government intervened. Kgari's position becomes clear and understandable if viewed in the larger context of his battle to establish his legitimacy by shifting his power base from the British to his nation.

Kgosi Kgari Sechele II was installed as the Kwena *kgosi* in June 1931, following the deposition and subsequent deportation to Gantsi of his brother Sebele II.[11] Kgari was not the next in line of succession, but his popularity with the colonial administration helped him to emerge as the preferred candidate. Lacking legitimacy and the support of his people, Kgari was to depend entirely on the government until 1939, when Sebele died. Thereafter, a few people began to see him as their *kgosi*, someone more than a mere functionary of the government. Researchers have misunderstood Kgari's uneasy position with regard to collaboration,[12] while the colonial government mistook it for obedience. The view of the colonial government is confirmed by Cardross Grant, Assistant District Commissioner of Molepolole, in a confidential report on the *Kgosi*:

> Kgari is most loyal and always ready to support the government in any scheme put up for the advancement of his people. He is inclined to rely too much on the administration, this partly due to his laziness and partly to the fact that he is a creature of the administration, and it is natural that he should look to government for support.[13]

Overlooked is the latent effort by the *kgosi* to win the support and confidence of the Bakwena. Already by 1939 all the councillors who Kgari chose when he assumed power had been replaced by men who supported him. To the administration, it was an act of folly, because he was getting rid of people whose experience he needed.[14] In 1941, for the first time in his 10 years as *kgosi*, he threatened the government with resignation, following a dispute over his use of 'tribal' officers to run errands, a privilege he claimed on the basis of Tswana custom.[15] To Kgari, therefore, the Second World War provided a powerful opportunity to demonstrate his capacity as a leader, a practice in accord with Tswana custom. However, as will become clear later, in his effort to prove his capability Kgari failed to evaluate the Bakwena's willingness to fight in the war.

After the war broke out in 1939, the Resident Commissioner (RC), Charles Arden-Clarke, called all the *dikgosi* to Mafeking to explain to them 'about the war and get a vote of loyalty from them'.[16] The *dikgosi*, aware or unaware of the expectations of the government, immediately expressed their continued loyalty to the Crown and 'offered' to assist – an offer that was turned down. They were instead advised to enlist their men in the Native Military Corps (NMC) of South Africa, which they refused.[17] The Tswana *dikgosi* wanted the identity of the Protectorate soldiers to be maintained, because only in doing so could they make political capital out of assisting Britain. According to colonial records, the officials regarded the 'offer' as merely an expression of loyalty to their protector.[18] The 'offer' viewed in the light of British rule in Bechuanaland has a much deeper significance than the colonial records lead us to believe. The 'willingness' of the *dikgosi* to supply men to the British war effort appears to have been rooted in the old fears that the Protectorate might be incorporated into the Union of South Africa as well as the implications of a possible victory of the Axis powers.

In 1895 Kgama, Sebele and Bathoen had travelled to London to protest against the possible incorporation of their territories into the lands administered by Rhodes' British South Africa Company (BSAC), and the fear of incorporation, particularly into the Union of South Africa, had continued upto the 1930s.[19] Britain, more interested in being relieved of the expense of administering the Protectorate, welcomed the idea of incorporation into the BSAC. For a number of reasons, however, including the fact that, contrary to Rhodes' belief, there was no gold in Bechuanaland and his playing an embarrassing role in the Jameson Raid, the question of incorporation was dropped.[20] The 1909 Act of South African Union also expressed South African interest to incorporate all adjacent territories, including Bechuanaland. Although Anthony Sillery argues that the failure of incorporation was primarily due to the reluctance of the Boers to promise the franchise to the Africans, the failure to incorporate the Protectorate appears to have been due mainly to British efforts to combat Boer expansionism, missionary protests in London, and the world wars, especially the participation of the Batswana on the side of the British Crown.[21] When the Second World War broke out, the *dikgosi* strongly believed that possible German–Boer cooperation (including the pro-Nazi elements in the former German colony of South West Africa) would, in the event of a British defeat, result in the absorption of Bechuanaland into South Africa. To prevent a victory of the Axis powers, the *dikgosi* 'offered' to assist Britain. For two years, nevertheless, the British government showed no interest in the *dikgosi*'s offer.

In 1941, however, when manpower deficiencies hit the North African and Middle East Campaigns, the *dikgosi*'s offer suddenly became important. The British finally turned to Bechuanaland, Basutoland and Swaziland for 'the supply of non-European labour units'. Britain believed that in North Africa, and possibly also in South East Europe, climatic conditions were unfavourable for East Africans, who otherwise could have been used to meet manpower requirements.[22] People in the British territories south of 22° latitude were thought capable of withstanding such conditions. The Batswana AAPC men were recruited primarily as labour units – to dig trenches, construct bridges and aerodromes, and load and unload arms and munitions – an arrangement consistent with the interests of the South African racist authorities.[23] As the war intensified and Britain required more and more combatant soldiers, Batswana units began to assume such roles. This is confirmed by some of the Bakwena exservicemen, who maintain that when the war ended in 1945, they were fighting in Yugoslavia as part of the Fifth Army.[24] The status of the AAPC also changed. In June 1942 the AAPC was approved as a corps of the British Army and in June 1944, in recognition of its 'fine service', its title was changed to the African Pioneer Corps (APC).[25]

Although the decision to recruit for war in the Protectorate grew partly out of the initiative of the Protectorate *dikgosi*, the units of the AAPC were formed in the midst of widespread popular resistance and indifference. Bakwena were, not surprisingly, reluctant to fight in a war that appeared to have little or no obvious relevance to themselves. In fact, most Bakwena recruited into the AAPC claim either to have been deceived or forced into joining for service. They did not share the willingness of *Kgosi* Kgari Sechele II to assist the British Crown from the outbreak of war. The number of 'volunteers' fell far short of the required quotas, and it is obvious that they joined for reasons other than those expressed or understood by their *Kgosi*.

Those Bakwena who 'volunteered' to join the AAPC did so to please *Kgosi* Kgari and not to express their loyalty to the British Crown, as colonial records might have us believe. Archival as well as oral data make no mention of people who might have joined the AAPC to get a salary or even to avoid problems at home. According to contemporary informants, *Kgosi* Kgari Sechele capitalised more on the Bakwena loyalty to their *Kgosi* than explaining clearly the broader issues relating to their service in the war. Some 'volunteered' in order to win Kgari's recognition after the war. Kgari convinced others that the war was global and that their participation was in reality the defence of Kweneng.[26] Such tactics of the *Kgosi* failed, nevertheless, to produce enough recruits, and soon Kgari began to use force in recruitment. Forced recruitment went on, with the colonial government's reluctant agreement, and it appears to have been the dominant method of recruitment in Kweneng, particularly for the later AAPC companies.

Recruitment for the AAPC in Kweneng was met with instances of outright defiance of the *Kgosi*'s authority. The Gabane people, for instance, at one stage refused to be enlisted in the AAPC under the Bakwena.[27] Gabane resistance resulted in a serious act of violence against Bakwena recruiting representatives, requiring intervention by the colonial administration. One man, Raletsatsi, was hospitalised.[28] The Gabane people, of Balete origin, had never been happy at being under the Bakwena, in whose territory they had settled, and their resistance may have been stimulated by a desire to demonstrate their independence.

Other acts of defiance of Kgari's authority took place at Lentsweletau. Motswakhumo Kgosidintsi, the headman, responded to Kgari's call by sending only four men to enlist in Molepolole, arguing that a foreign war was not going to be given priority over local agricultural production.[29] Some Kwena regiments were sent out to Lentsweletau to capture men for recruitment, but even that failed to change Motswakhumo's mind.[30] Individual acts of defiance were numerous throughout Kweneng. Some people hid themselves in caves, *disigo* (grain stores), forests and *diphikwa* (bush-stacks) in order to avoid going to war.[31] Some men avoided the draft by looking after Bakwena herds, especially in the remote areas of Kweneng. Such examples indicate that people were generally reluctant to be recruited.

Recruitment appears to have been carried out across all levels of Kwena society. Although in general social status and political rank do not appear to have determined who was recruited into the AAPC, teachers and tribal and government clerks were under-represented. Women, children, the elderly, the *Bakgalagadi*,[32] and the disabled were also exempted. All able-bodied men were drafted into the AAPC. There were doctors in Molepolole and Lobatse to check the fitness of the recruits before leaving for service overseas.

Although the majority of the Bakwena were reluctant to fight in a war not of their own choosing, available sources reveal that a significant number of men participated. However, it is impossible to determine precisely how many Bakwena went to war. What is certain is that the Bakwena belonged to four companies, the first of which left for the Middle East in 1941. Table 6.1 shows the composition of the companies:[33]

Other Bakwena also enlisted in the NMC, for which statistics are not available. Altogether between 1000 and 1200 able-bodied Bakwena participated in the Second World War as members of the AAPC and NMC.[34]

TABLE 6.1 *Bakwena companies in AAPC*

AAPC company	*Bakwena*
No. 1973	356
No. 1980	375
No. 1984	358 (with Barolong)
No. 1969	374 (with Batswana)
Total	1463

The manpower drain in Kweneng became serious in the 1940s when recruitment to the South African mines was intensified. Some Bakwena chose mine work to avoid being drafted into the AAPC, or because it was better paid. The Bechuanaland Government wanted to maintain the flow of labour to the South African mines in order to generate needed capital. Even when recruitment for the AAPC intensified, men continued to go to the mines and some to parts of the Transvaal as farm labourers.[35] Although in 1942 the operations of the Native Recruiting Corporation (NRC) were suspended for 6 months (from July to December) in order to allow the recruitment of No. 1984 company to be completed, a minimum of 1020 men went to the mines that year. Table 6.2 shows the number of the Bakwena who went to the mines from 1940 to 1945.[36]

It appears therefore that about 35 per cent of the male population was outside Kweneng in 1945, a level sufficient to retard economic development.[37]

The absence of so many able-bodied men had serious implications for agricultural production and general economic development in Kwen-

TABLE 6.2 *Bakwena mine recruits, 1940–5*

Year	*9-months contract*	*Assisted Voluntary Service (AVS)*	*Total*
1940	2278	—	2278
1941	1352	—	1352
1942	1020	—	1020
1943	1548	395	1943
1944	871	397	1268
1945	1206	841	2047
Total	8275	1633	9908

eng. The responsibility for food production was delegated to the elderly, women, AAPC medical rejects, and the 'draft resisters', popularly known as *Masiapitse*.[38] In addition, part of their labour was forced into agricultural production for the war effort. With no extra hands to look after their cattle or plough their fields during the absence of their able-bodied folk, the Bakwena who remained at home were worst affected by the war.

Thus, with a large part of the productive manpower away at the mines and the war, the process of economic development in Kweneng was slowed down considerably. During the war the development projects that were undertaken exploited the Bakwena rather than improved their lives. The already over-burdened Bakwena frequently had to level the Molepolole/Gaborone road for use by the colonial administration and the NRC. The administration also had the Bakwena build six granaries in Molepolole and one each in Gabane and Thamaga for storage of 'warlands' grain,[39] also to 'assist the Empire in war effort'.[40] ('Warlands' were fields specially cultivated during war-time). Traditionally, the Bakwena regiments did public works, but with men at the mines and the war, these tasks were either not done at all or fell to women, children and the disabled. Consequently the Bakwena at home had to concentrate on the struggle to survive, which left little time or effort for development projects. The Second World War affected Kweneng in other ways than economic.

Because *Kgosi* Kgari had enlisted in the AAPC, his absence from Kweneng resulted in a number of problems, particularly the extent of British control over Kweneng chieftaincy, which Kgari had already begun to check. When Kgari left for the war in 1942, a regency of three councillors approved by the government was appointed to lead the Bakwena. Letlamma Sechele, Kgari's brother, became the head of judicial affairs; Jacob Sechele was in charge of schools; and Martinus Seboni took care of agriculture and veterinary affairs. The regents are said to have worked harmoniously until 1943, when Letlamma took to heavy drinking and in the process neglected his duties.[41] As a result, many court cases were postponed indefinitely,[42] or so it would appear, while some cases that could have been tried by the Kgotla were tried by the District Commissioner. The number of cases tried by the DC's court rose from 58 in 1942 to 94 in 1943, and dropped to 62 after Kgari's return from the war in 1944.[43]

The Bakwena assisted the colonial government in a variety of ways during the war. In 1939 the Bakwena and other Batswana started a war fund to which each male was expected to contribute. No precise figures are available to indicate the Bakwena's total contributions. It is, however, clear that the Bakwena contributed £1422 of the £10 000 that was donated to Britain towards the purchase of two Spitfire aircraft.[44] In some villages outside Molepolole, including Thamaga, contributions are said to have been levied at a beast per person, because they were told by Kgari that by so doing they were clearing themselves from possible draft into the AAPC.[45] The war fund was used by Britain to pay allotments to soldiers' wives and dependents, to assist the crippled and other war victims, or for social welfare payments. Although money was flowing in and out of Kweneng, economic development in general was not boosted.

The colonial administration's utilisation of the 'warlands' is another example of the exploitation of the Bakwena during the war. In a bid to increase agricultural production the colonial government made Bakwena plough the 'warlands', the harvest of which was used to raise money to help meet war expenses. This use of the 'warlands' was in fact an abuse of a traditional system. The government called them 'tribal lands' to give the impression that it was following the traditional custom of common production during wars.[46] The Bakwena understood this to mean the traditional custom of ploughing *masotla* for the *kgosi*.[47] Ironically, informants do not remember having ploughed 'warlands', but colonial government records contain statistics showing production from the fields. In 1941 and 1942, 100 and 113 bags of sorghum respectively were harvested from the Kweneng 'warlands'.[48] The Annual *Agricultural Reports* for Kweneng show that the 1949–5 period was characterised by frequent late rains, resulting in very low yields. Nevertheless, the overburdened Bakwena were expected to provide labour to plough the 'warlands'. The 'progressive farmers'[49] appear to have limited themselves to copying new farming methods and getting the very scarce advice of the Agricultural Demonstrator.[50]

As in agriculture, the colonial administration's efforts in animal husbandry in Kweneng only served the colonial interests and those of the 'progressive farmers', who tended to associate with the Europeans to exploit the poor peasant farmers. In 1931 a Bull Camp was started at Ditshukudu by the administration for improvement of Bakwena's cattle. The Bakwena provided the initial capital for the project, and 120 cattle were selected arbitrarily from the people's herds and were bought at £2 each, irrespective of the difference in their quality.[51] The camp was not put to use until 1939 because the Bakwena did not take their cows there, but when the war broke out, the project was revived under the new name of the Cattle Improvement Centre. Small stock was added to the service. A veterinary officer was employed to encourage Bakwena to adopt new animal husbandry methods. In practice, the Bakwena here meant the few successful farmers who could afford to take their cattle there as well as buy young bulls from the Centre. Just as the Bull Camp before it, the Cattle Improvement Centre apparently was also unpopular among the Bakwena and in 1947 the government recommended its closure. Some cattle were sent to the South African abattoirs and the rest sold to colonial officers and Bakwena at prices beyond the means of the poor peasant farmers.

Although the colonial government claimed that the Cattle Improvement Centre and agriculture projects were intended to improve the lives of the Bakwena, their timing suggests otherwise. The encouragement to increase food production and the revival of the Cattle Improvement Centre during the war shows that they were meant to benefit the war effort, as the abandonment of the latter immediately after the war indicates. During the war an Agricultural Demonstrator (AD) was stationed in Kweneng to advise the Bakwena in the ploughing of 'warlands' but not in cultivating their own lands. The Bakwena were expected to apply experience gained from the 'warlands' to their lands. The Bakwena, who opposed the 'warlands' idea, simply rejected the ADs along with the system they represented. Furthermore, the 'warlands' too were not productive enough to demonstrate the effectiveness of modern farming methods. It was only a very small group of Bakwena 'progressive farmers' who benefited.

The progressive farmers, whose strength had increased largely as a result of the commercialisation of the cattle industry, which was very lucrative during the war, and agriculture, benefited significantly from modern farming techniques introduced in the 'warlands'. Most, having received some missionary or Western education and in some cases because of their closeness to the *kgosi*, were in a better position than the ordinary poor peasant farmers to understand colonialism and turn it to their own advantage. Modern farming required not only labour and careful observation but capital investment. It included the purchase of suitable seeds and machinery, as well as chemical fertilisers (though cattle manure could be used as a substitute). The progressive farmers, financially better off than most and producing primarily for commercial purposes, were able to accept the cost of modern methods and reap economic and in some cases political benefits. As a result, some of those educated and successful farmers, such as Martinus Seboni, rose to positions of political prominence.[52] The poor peasant farmers, including the emerging agrarian labourers, who went to the mines and the war in great numbers to support the war effort, could not benefit from these

TABLE 6.3 *Annual turnover of twelve Kweneng stores, 1942–6*

Year	*Total turnover (£)*	*% Growth*
1942	66 568.7.1	–
1943	83 265.4.0	25
1944	141 666.3.6	70
1945	144 267.11.4	2
1946	135 089.16.10	−6.4

policies and became the primary victims of intensified agricultural crisis.

The Second World War should not be seen simply as an event that revealed the extent of colonial exploitation in Kweneng, but also as a complex situation whereby different social classes were affected in different ways. For the Kweneng traders, for instance, the war was a welcome opportunity to rise to affluence. Lack of accurate statistical records kept by the Kweneng traders, as well as their unwillingness to give interviews, makes it very difficult to assess their war-time profits. However, available evidence suggests that the traders made fortunes, especially with the expansion of the local market through incoming remittances from the mines, as well as allotments for the dependents of the AAPC soldiers, which are said to have been used essentially for purchase of foodstuffs. The figures in Table 6.3 of the annual turnover of the twelve trading stores in Kweneng at the time show that some significant changes in the volume of trade occurred during the war period.[53] These figures cannot be used to calculate profit, but the percentages certainly demonstrate that there was growth during the war.

Furthermore, an evaluation of the colonial records and oral sources shows that the rising affluence of the traders was largely attributable to the unfair trading relations that existed between them and the local people. The records indicate that the cattle business was booming during the war, a condition that does not appear to have affected the purchase price of cattle from the Bakwena.[54] From 1939 until after the war there were numerous complaints of profiteering by shopowners throughout the Bechuanaland Protectorate. Reports by colonial officers during the war reveal that traders determined the prices of goods by the capacity of the 'Natives' to pay.[55] Towards the end of the war profiteering had got out of control and few regulations were issued to control the prices of such commodities as sugar and paraffin. However, the traders had learnt ways of evading such measures. The Molepolole District Commissioner, Mr Sullivan, confirmed in 1944 that when traders were warned not to charge high prices, it was clear that:

> Prices will not increase but quantity of, say, sugar sold for one shilling will be reduced imperceptibly. If this pernicious custom is aided by barter, the very purchase price, which is seldom coin . . . is subjected to fluctuations at the will of the shopowners.[56]

There are claims by wives of former soldiers, that traders used to charge them higher prices for scarce commodities because they knew they had money. At this stage two conclusions can be made: that the money in circulation in Kweneng during the war did not benefit the Kwena economy, and that Kweneng was sandwiched between two exploitative forces, the rising rural petty bourgeoisie and international capitalism.

While the Bakwena at home had to contend with economic and social problems created by the demands of a foreign war, the Bakwena at the war-front suffered from official sanctioned isolation. Although ex-servicemen proudly recall their casual association with a wide cross-section of the people at the war, such as Indians, Americans, Arabs, French and Italians, and other Africans, they also argue that chances to work with them were limited.[57] Bent paints a different picture, although his constant reference to the Pioneers as tribal units at the war-front seems to confirm the forced isolation that former AAPC recruits still remember. Bakwena, like other Batswana, maintained their company identity even when in leave camps. Kgari's presence in the AAPC also might have been responsible for the limited interaction. Apart from his authority over the Bakwena, he was also a Regimental Sergeant-Major, a position which entitled him to visit all Kwena companies and to punish offenders.[58] His position also appears to have assisted him in establishing control over the Kwena Pioneers. The work of the Bakwena, even as divisions of the British army, contributed further to their isolation.[59]

As the Bakwena Pioneers returned to Kweneng, the homecoming, apart from rejoining their families, was not entirely a pleasant one. Only two Bakwena were killed in action, which means that the majority returned home.[60] Conditions of life in Kweneng were very unpleasant at the time, mainly due to the frequent late rains that affected the area between 1940 and 1945 and resulted in poor harvests. Late rains could also not be utilised successfully, owing to the absence of productive manpower. Inter-regional and local self-sufficiency, which existed before capitalist penetration, had been destroyed completely, and shops had become the primary sources of food.[61] It appears that a significant number of Bakwena Pioneers returned home with venereal diseases, and some with tuberculosis. In 1946, for instance, more males than ever before were treated for gonorrhea and even more approached the medical officer for B + B63 tablets.[62] More heartbreaking problems awaited them in their homes. Many ex-servicemen found their wives with illegitimate children, and a number of court cases resulted, some of which are said to have ended with the break-up of families. The government's failure to keep its promises also made the Pioneers' homecoming very unsatisfactory. After several years of loyal service, the Pioneers claims to have received only what they had saved in the form of deferred pay, ranging from £30 to £100. Only a few, who had either security or Kgari's backing, were given loans from the Bechuanaland Soldiers Benefit Fund, to 're-establish themselves in business'.[63] According to that arrangement, it was once again the poor peasant farmers who remained at home, and the majority in the AAPC who did not benefit. The Pioneers therefore had returned to innumerable problems, which took a long time to remedy.

From the end of the war, and right into the 1960s, the Bakwena tried unsuccessfully to revive their economy from the ruins of war. The colonial administration, though the principal contributor to such an economic crisis, failed to assist the Bakwena in their struggle to reconstruct their economy. Colonial measures, represented in the Colonial Development and Welfare Act of 1945,[64] were inadequate to change the lives of the Bakwena in general. The funds were too small and grants varied from district to district. Until 1955, when a new Colonial Development and Welfare Fund Act was promulgated, Kweneng as part of the Protectorate was forced to operate on a tight budget that provided for no expansion of welfare services and development.[65] Quill Hermans rightly concludes that:

> Nothing occurred between 1885 and 1955 which contributed significantly to Botswana's economic and financial development. Bechuanaland's economy and the domestic fiscal resources available to its administration were inadequate for the purposes of achieving social and economic advancement . . . The policies pursued by the British Government, moreover, did not recognise political and economic development as an objective.[66]

The only development projects that appear to have occurred in post-war Kweneng before 1955 were the drilling of a few boreholes and the building of a few primary schools, including Neil Sechele and Kealeboga Primary Schools. In Letlhakeng no school was built until after independence.[67] It is of interest to note that it was not until 1950 that the British government repaid the load of £5169 14s 6d that it had received from Kweneng free of interest during the war.[68]

Post-war migrant labour statistics reveal that Kweneng was hit by acute unemployment. During the war the colonial government had directed all its economic and financial resources towards the war effort and did nothing to support or start local industries, which in turn could have generated capital for economic development and created jobs to absorb the returning soldiers. Many informants say that after the war some ex-servicemen went back to farming, but most went to South Africa to look for jobs in the mines. The statistics also show a rise in the number of mine-workers after 1946,[69] from 1961 then to 3472 in 1949. The stage had been set for the Protectorate's dependence on South Africa for employment right into the 1960s.

CONCLUSION

The Second World War has been credited with releasing forces that championed the struggles for independence in areas under colonial rule, but the Kweneng experience does not fit this pattern for several reasons. The unfortunate isolation of the Bakwena AAPC companies at the war provided very little opportunity for interaction with Batswana from other parts of the Protectorate, let alone with other colonial peoples. Ethnic organisation characterised the British military and colonial policy.[70] After the war, returning Bakwena ex-servicemen lost touch with one another because of lack of employment in the territory. No programmes were undertaken to benefit the returning Pioneers, so that it was impossible for them to organise as a group. The Bakwena ex-servicemen could not organise themselves even to petition the administration. In Kweneng therefore the ex-servicemen failed to produce protest movements that the nationalists could have exploited to speed up the struggle for independence. Developments in post-war Kweneng support Stevens' attribution of later nationalist protest to lack of a homogeneous population.[71] The Second World War in Kweneng therefore not only failed to assist nationalism but weakened the political position of the Bakwena.

The war and the long absence of the Pioneers together worked to the detriment of Bakwena's society. Kgari's absence from his capital allowed the colonial administration to interfere even more in Kweneng affairs. After the war, Kweneng had quite a number of broken families, something that was uncommon in the pre-war period. In addition to social problems the Bakwena were forced to contend with the grave problems of underdevelopment and dependence.

During the war, more than ever before, the Bakwena economy

became vulnerable to British exploitation. Colonial policies were undoubtedly directed towards aiding the powerful and exploiting the weaker sections of society. Kweneng's human and other resources fell to the disposal of the colonial administration in the effort to finance a European war. When the war broke out, the Bakwena had to contribute to the war fund and plough the 'warlands'. They were also encouraged to go to the mines. Throughout the war and immediately after it ended the Bakwena assisted Britain with free interest loans,[72] which were financed essentially from the Cattle Export Levy Fund, reactivated in 1942.[73] A situation was created whereby the Bakwena contributed to the restoration of a capitalist economy that survived by exploiting them.

The Pioneers returned with high expectations for material gains, and when these did not materialise, they blamed *Kgosi* Kgari for failing to ask the administration to reward them. When the loan scheme was discontinued after a very limited number of the Bakwena ex-servicemen had received loans, Kgari was blamed for ensuring that only his friends benefited.

The Second World War in Kweneng revealed the nature of British colonial exploitation, which had sharpened class division and allowed greater inter-class exploitation, favouring the administration, traders and the 'progressive farmers'. The war also intensified the existing patterns of emigration, which had serious implications for Kweneng's agriculturally based economy. Although the question of political incorporation into the Union of South Africa was less of an issue after the war ended, economically the war situation greatly contributed to the Protectorate's informal incorporation into the South African economy.[74]

NOTES

1. M. Crowder, 'The Second World War: Prelude to Decolonisation in Africa', in M. Crowder (ed.), *Cambridge History of Africa*, Vol. VIII (Cambridge, 1984).
2. J. F. A. Ajayi and M. Crowder, *History of West Africa*, Vol. 2 (London, Longman, 1974); A. J. Knoff, 'East Africa and the Returning Asakari: The Effect of their War Service', *Quarterly Review*, 285 (1981), p. 571.
3. In this category of studies is included R. A. R. Bent, *Ten Thousand Men of Africa: A Study of the Bechuanaland Pioneers and Gunners: 1941–1946* (London, 1952), but the problem with this study is that Bent adopted a very paternalistic perspective; D. Killingray, 'Military and Labour Recruitment in the Gold Coast during the Second World War', *J. of African History*, 23,1 (1982); D. Kiyaga-Mulindwa, 'Bechuanaland Protectorate and the Second

World War', *J. of Imperial and Commonwealth History*, XII, 3 May 1984.
4. G. O. Olusanya, *The Second World War and Politics in Nigeria, 1939–1953* (Ibadan, 1973).
5. Ibid.
6. Botswana National Archives (henceforth BNA), S.397/8, 'Chief Kgari Sechele II of the Bakwena – Release for Military Service', D. C. Molepolole to Government Secretary, Mafeking, 1942. It is of interest to observe that unlike his friend, the deposed Kgosi Molefi Pilane of the Bakgatla, who was pressured by the colonial government to go to war, Kgosi Kgari requested the administration to release him for military service.
7. A. Pim, *Financial and Economic Position of the Bechuanaland Protectorate* (London, 1933).
8. M. Leepile, 'The Impact of Migrant Labour on the Economy of Kweneng: 1940–1980' (History Seminar Paper, University College of Botswana, 1981), p. 4.
9. 'Bechuanaland Protectorate: High Commissioner's Proclamations and the More Important Government Notices from 1st January–31st December 1934', Vol. XIX (1934).
10. BNA, S.359, 'Native Administration and Tribunal Proclamations: 74 and 75 of 1934: Bakwena Experiment', Resident Commissioner to High Commissioner, 2 Oct. 1935.
11. K. Molotsi, 'The Impact of Colonialism on the Institution of Chieftainship: The Kweneng Case – 1885–1961' (History Seminar Paper, University College of Botswana, 1981), p. 21.
12. In 1981 a number of research papers were presented to the History Department of the University of Botswana by final year (BA) students and there was a general agreement that Kgari was nothing less than a functionary of the colonial government. Outstanding on the subject were E. Tafa, 'The Rise of Conservative Bourgeois Nationalism: Politics in Kweneg'; and K. Molotsi, 'The Impact of Colonialism on the Institution of Chieftainship: The Kweneng Case – 1885–1961'.
13. BNA, S.433/9, 'Confidential Report of Kgari Sechele II: 1935–1940', Assistant D. C. Molepolole to Resident Commissioner, Mafeking, 2 Feb. 1938.
14. Ibid., Resident Magistrate, S. Towne, Molepolole, to Resident Commissioner, Mafeking, 1 June, 1935.
15. BNA, S.397/7/1, Chief Kgari Sechele II – Confidential', Kgosi Kgari Sechele II to D. C., Molepolole, 8 Feb. 1941.
16. BNA, S. 134/1 'War with Germany – 1939 Onwards: Natives; Expressions of Loyalty and Cooperation', Proceedings of a meeting between the Batswana *dikgosi* and the Resident Commissioner, Mafeking, 5 September 1939.
17. D. Kiyaga-Mulindwa, 'Bechuanaland Protectorate and the Second World War', p. 35.
18. BNA, S. 135/7, 'War with Germany: Chief Tshekedi's proposals for the formation of the Native Corps', DC Serowe to Government Secretary, Mafeking, 26 February 1941. The DC reported 'The point which the Chief desires to stress is that he and his tribe wish to place their services at the disposal of the British Govermnent, and do so at no cost to Government.

Whatever happens the Chief and his tribe wish to have their sympathies and desires placed on record and brought to the notice of His Majesty's Government'.

19. A. Sillery, *Botswana: A Short Political History* (London, 1979), p. 106.
20. D. Denoon, *Southern Africa Since 1800* (London, 1972), p. 83; R. P. Stevens, 'Establishment of the Bechuanaland Protectorate', in D. L. Cohen and J. Parsons (eds), *Politics and Society in Botswana* (Gaborone, University College of Botswana, 1976), p. 37.
21. M. Perham and L. Curtis, *The Protectorates of South Africa* (London, Oxford University Press, 1935), pp. 51–66.
22. Kiyaga-Mulindwa, 'Bechuanaland Protectorate', p. 2.
23. That the South African Government did not want the Batswana and other Southern African blacks to be used as combatants is well known. Most contemporary informants claim that when the war ended, they were allowed to retain their guns, which were subsequently confiscated when they reached Durban: Interviews with Mosotho Molefe, Molefe Ward, Molepolole, 3 March 1984; and Marlance Bodigelo, Kodisa Ward, Molepolole, 2 March 1984.
24. BNA, S. 140/3, 'War with Germany – 1939 Onwards: The History of the War in Bechuanaland Protectorate', Resident Commissioner to High Commissioner.
25. Interviews with Mosotho Molefe, Molefe Ward, Molepolole, 3 March 1984; Marlance Bodigelo, Kodisa Ward, Molepolole, 2 March 1984; Return Motsewakgosi, Masilwana Ward, Molepolole, 6 August 1980.
26. Interviews with Petrus Ngwanaang, Suna Ward, Molepolole, 8 August 1980; Koosenye Segakisa, Difetlhamolelo Ward, Molepolole, 3 March 1984; Majaasula Moeng, Ntloedibe Ward, Molepolole, 1984.
27. BNA, S. 136/7, 'War with Germany – 1939 Onwards', an extract from *Inkululeko*, 20 November 1942.
28. BNA, S. 137/3, 'War with Germany – 1939 Onwards', DC, Molepolole to Government Secretary, Mafeking. 9 November 1942.
29. Interview with Motswasele Ositilwe, Kgosing Ward, Lentsweletau, 7 August 1980.
30. Ibid.
31. Like other Batswana, Bakwena cultivators usually cut trees in the fields and left them to dry before burning them. During the war men are said to have dug under these branches and made hiding places. The story told by Bakwena today appears rather exaggerated, but it endorses the fact that men were avoiding recruitment.
32. The Bakgalagadi, apart from the few who were in Molepolole, were exempted. The Bakgalagadi were regarded as culturally inferior people who could be used by the superior Bakwena as a source of labour. Allowing them to go to the war would have been equivalent to giving them independence and subsequent loss of free labour by the Bakwena. This is confirmed by G. Y. Okihiro, 'Hunters, Herders, Cultivators and Traders', p. 123.
33. BNA, S. 136/7, 'War with Germany – 1939 Onwards', 1939. The official records of the colonial administration during the war indicate that company No. 1984 was composed of Bakwena and other Batswana and No. 1969 of Bakwena and Bangwaketse. The composition listed by Bent, that No. 1984

was Bakwena and Barolong and No. 1969 Bakwena and Batawana, may be more accurate, because he served in the war with Batswana Pioneers.

34. All that we have is that 700 Batswana were enlisted in the NMC.
35. Statistics of those who went to work in the South African farms has not been located. Informants are therefore the only source on the subject. In other places close to the railway line, such as Ramotswa, the figure of those who skipped to South Africa could be estimated by the number of rail tickets purchased at the Ramotswa station. See Kiyaga-Mulindwa, 'Bechuanaland Protectorate', p. 5.
36. BNA, S. 264/6, 'Annual Reports – Kweneng – 1940–45', DC, Molepolole to Government Secretary, Mafeking.
37. The total number of males at the mines and the war was used against the 1946 male population figure to arrive at 35 per cent. That was based on two assumptions, that 50 per cent of the male population were under 15 years and that from 1945 to 1946 there were no significant population changes. The population statistics as shown in the table below are adopted from the 'Report on Census of the Bechuanaland Protectorate', 1964.

Year	*Males*	*Females*	*Total*
1936	12 895	13 755	26 650
1946	19 914	20 212	40 126
1964	34 896	38 192	73 088

38. *Masiapitse* are those men who avoided recruitment into the AAPC by hiding. They must have spent more time running from recruiting agents than engaging in productive activities.
39. The 'warlands' were fields introduced by the colonial government during the war. All the Bakwena were required to participate in ploughing them, scaring birds, and harvesting the crop. The produce from the 'warlands' was sold and the proceeds given to Britain to help in the war effort.
40. BNA, S. 263/6, 'Annual Reports – Kweneng: 1940–45'.
41. BNA, S. 397/8, 'Chief Kgari Sechele II of the Bakwena – Release for Military Service'.
42. Ibid.
43. BNA, S. 264/6.
44. BNA, S. 140/3, 'War with Germany – 1939 Onwards'.
45. Interview with Simakoko Otukile, Tau Ward, Thamaga, 13 August 1980.
46. BNA, S. 298/4/1, 'Produce of Bechuanaland Protectorate – Efforts to Increase Native Production – 1939: Notes of the Meeting of the Sub-Committee on Increased Production and Storage of Grain', 25 April 1941. See also Hoyini H. K. Bhila, 'The Impact of the Second World War on the development of peasant agriculture in Botswana 1939–1956: *Botswana Notes and Records*, 16 (1984), pp. 63–71.
47. *Masotla* were fields ploughed collectively by the people for the *Kgosi*, who distributed or sold its produce to them in times of strife, at low prices.

48. BNA, S. 264/6, 'Annual Reports – Kweneng: 1940–45'.
49. C. Bundy, *The Rise and Fall of the South African Peasantry* (London, 1979), p. 92. Bundy defines 'progressive farmers' as a class of 'small-scale commercial farmers', comparatively wealthier, owners of large units of land who produce primarily for cash, and who have broken with traditional ways.
50. It is also important to note that there was only one Agriculture Demonstrator in the whole District.
51. BNA, S. 298/4/5, 'Produce of Bechuanaland Protectorate: Report of the 9th meeting of the Tribal Agriculture Production Committee', Director of Livestock Services, Mahalapye to Government Secretary, Mafeking, 1942.
52. Martinus Seboni, perhaps because of his education, was very popular with the government. Seboni was a councillor to *Kgosi* Kgari and during the war he served as one of the regents. Although from the 1950s he spent his life in South Africa, his family became very active politically with the emergence of nationalist parties in the early 1960s.
53. BNA, S. 246/6, 'Annual Reports – Kweneng: 1940'; DC, Molepolole to Government Secretary, Mafeking.
54. Ibid.; BNA, S. 140/3, interview with Koosenye Segakisa. Segakisa was employed by Brink (a prominent cattle dealer) to buy cattle for him from Bakwena, for which he paid him a commission of 5 shillings. He claims that he later bought his own licence and did well. He admits that as a successful farmer he benefited from the Cattle Improvement Centre. He claims to have bought twenty-six cattle from the Centre when it closed in 1947. Segakisa was one of the first cooperators, in a highly selective scheme which was financed from the Colonial Development and Welfare Fund of 1954. On the cooperator system, see C. O. Molebatsi, 'Agriculture Transformation and the Rise of the Kulak Farmers in Kweneng – 1939–1966' (History Seminar Paper, University College of Botswana, 1981).
55. BNA, S. 135/2, 'War with Germany – 1939 Onwards: On the Question of Profiteering and Price Control'. DC Molepolole to Government Secretary, Mafeking, 1944.
56. Ibid., DC Sullivan, Molepolole to Government Secretary, Mafeking, 1944.
57. This is supported by all exservicemen who have been interviewed.
58. Bent, *Ten Thousand Men of Africa,* p. 66.
59. Ibid., *passim.*
60. Ibid., p. 107.
61. Interviews with Basono Phuthegelo, Mogotsi Ward, Molepolole, 5 August 1980; Rantshobotho Moitlamo, Kodisa Ward, Molepolole, 29 July 1980.
62. BNA, S. 329/5/2, 'Annual Reports for the Scottish Livingstone Hospital', Medical Superintendent to DC, Molepolole, 1946. B + B63 tablets were at the time considered best in treating cases of venereal disease.
63. BNA, S. 139/4/5, 'King George's Fund for Soldiers' Warfund', 1943.
64. BNA, S. 140/3; BNA, S. 264/6; also referred to in the A. C. B. Symon, 'Economic and Financial Report on the High Commission Territories' of 1954.
65. Quill Hermans, 'Towards Budgetary Independence: A Review of Botswana's Financial History', *Botswana Notes and Records*, Vol. 6 (1974), *passim.*

66. Ibid, p. 108.
67. Interview with E. G. Reokwaeng (MP), Letlhakeng, 11 August 1981.
68. BNA, S. 139/3, 'War with Germany – 1939 Onwards: History of the War in the BP', Principal Auditor, Mafeking to Government Secretary, Mafeking, 1 March 1950.
69. BNA, S. 500/9, 'Annual Report – Kweneng, 1949', DC, Molepolole to Government Secretary, Mafikeng, December 1949.
70. W. F. Gutteridge, 'Military and Police Forces in Africa', in P. Duignan and L. H. Gann (eds), *Colonialism in Africa: 1870–1960*, Vol. II (Cambridge, 1970), p. 289. Gutteridge argues that until independence the Royal West African Frontier Force (RWAFF) was organised on a strong territorial structure in order to inhibit any feeling of belonging together.
71. R. P. Stevens, *Lesotho, Botswana and Swaziland* (London, 1967), p. 114.
72. BNA, S. 140/6, 'War with Germany – 1939 Onwards: Loans, Free of Interest to the United Kingdom Government for the Duration of War', Minutes of the Meeting of the African Advisory Council of 18 April 1942.
73. Hermans, 'Towards Budgetary Independence', p. 98.
74. O. Selolwane, 'Colonialism by Concession: Capitalist Expansion in Bechuanaland Protectorate: 1885–1950', *Pula. Botswana Journal of African Studies*, II, 2 (1980), p. 102.

7 The Recruitment of South African Blacks* for Participation in the Second World War

LOUIS GRUNDLINGH

Although the history of South Africa and the Second World War has received considerable attention (especially the military aspects), nothing substantial has yet been written on the participation of South African blacks in the war. Capt. J. C. Knoetze and Lt. M. Hallack respectively completed factual reports on the Non-European Army Services (NEAS) outside South Africa[1] and a record of the NEAS[2] shortly after the war. H. J. Martin and N. Orpen dismissed black participation in a few lines,[3] while E. Roux[4] and recently K. W. Grundy[5] each touched on the topic in passing. In an article in the *South African Historical Journal*, M. Roth also cursorily dealt with the subject of South African blacks in the Second World War.[6]

Traditional government policy in South African was that only whites should serve in combatant roles in the armed forces. The spectre of blacks trained to use firearms roused white fears about the security of the racially organised state. Coloureds and Asians, and particularly the black majority, were largely restricted to non-combatant roles in the Defence Force. However, the exigencies of war meant that non-whites might be placed in combatant units. After an initial reluctance to utilise blacks for the South African war effort, the Government eventually decided in June 1940 to establish the NEAS. This organisation consisted of three sections, the Cape Coloured Corps, the Indian and Malay Corps

* The terms African 'Blacks' and 'Africans' are used as synonyms.

and the Native Military Corps (NMC). Whereas recruitment for the first two Corps was undertaken by the Director of Recruitment, recruitment for the NMC came under the Native Affairs Department.

There are two main themes to this essay: the methods used by the Native Affairs Department to induce blacks to enlist, and the various factors that influenced black recruitment.

The methods of recruitment used before 1942, according to the Director of the NEAS, were 'on a rather hit-and-miss basis'.[7] The dire need for manpower, aggravated by the defeat of the Allies at Tobruk, pressed the Director of the NEAS to organise the recruiting effort on a more efficient basis.

Recruiting was reorganised with new methods. Use was made of an improved and expanding communication media, and a special emphasis was placed on the personal approach of recruitment tours undertaken by specially selected recruiting staff. Both methods corroborated the official view that blacks were particularly impressed by ostentatiousness and therefore special attempts were made in this direction.

This attitude was clearly expressed by Lt. J. B. Bruce in his report on recruiting propaganda amongst the blacks. He argued on racial lines that 'colour' appeals to the natives:

> While a blaze of colour might offend the susceptibilities of Europeans . . . almost any colourful reproduction will appeal to natives . . . a 'motion' picture of doubtful educational value would be better than a large number of 'still' pictures of proved educational value for Europeans . . . Nothing takes the place of 'personal contact' with the natives. Consequently all forms of propaganda media must be supplementary to personal contacts. This is, of course, not true of Europeans, who resent the persistency of salesmen and other personal mediums of advertising.[8]

Films and mobile film units were ideally suited for this purpose, as Lt. Bruce noted in flowery language: 'Such films, depicting the native being transformed from an insignificant atom of a native territory to a swash-buckling brave of the NMC, have an enormous valuc'.[9] Col. Stubbs agreed and commissioned 'the preparation of a film, or series of films, depicting the building up of a Native soldier from civilian life to that of a finished soldier'.[10]

Definite requirements were laid down for these recruiting films. Lt. Bruce's suggestions were closely heeded; in order to create enthusiasm and a strong desire to enlist it had to present the NMC in as favourable a light as possible. These films were clearly designed with propaganda value in mind and had to be simple and direct so that even the 'unsophisticated and often illiterate audiences'[11] could comprehend them. The writers of the different scenarios stressed in particular that blacks should be regarded as 'genuine' soldiers – but 'genuine' as perceived from a white perspective. Hence the anachronistic depiction of black soldiers wearing modern uniforms but armed with assegais was considered as a happy combination between the warriors of the nineteenth century and the changed conditions of the twentieth century. The scenario writers clearly thought the blacks' loyalty would be aroused by such a portrayal, which also referred to their nineteenth-century mode of warfare: 'Now this is a soldier of today. See how differently but how well he is dressed . . . You will notice that he still carries an assegai'.[12] Clearly, for the authorities, blacks lived in a timeless void; customs of the nineteenth century also applied to the twentieth century.

These films, which were shown in townships, hospitals, beer halls and reserves, attracted much attention and were well attended. Although this was officially interpreted as proof of success,[13] it is a moot point whether the blacks attended the shows because of their content or because of their sheer novelty value. In all likelihood, however, the entertainment value was the main drawcard.

Besides the use of films, recruiting posters in the vernacular were drawn up and displayed at Magistrates' offices, Native Commissioners' offices, police posts, beer halls, railway stations, cinemas, clubs, schools, and in buses, trams, and trains. The posters accentuated the danger of a German victory and the need for recruits. In a fairly dramatic poster, reminiscent of the famous First World War poster 'Your country needs you', the blacks were called upon to rally to the flag in the face of the possible devastation inherent in a Nazi victory.[14] Later it was realised that this approach was too general and vague to appeal to blacks and the poster was superseded by one with a more direct and immediate message – the pay offered by a recruiting sergeant.[15] In addition, loudspeakers were used to inform Africans in townships about the recruiting campaign and special radio broadcasts were also considered. However, this was turned down, apparently to avoid offending the susceptibilities of a section of the white population.[16]

Apart from the weekly *War News Bulletin* of the Department of Native Affairs, arrangements were also made with B. G. Paver,

Managing Director of the *Bantu Press*, that articles dealing with life in the army be published. A sum of £500 was paid for advertisements in the black newspapers circulating throughout the Union. It was believed that these advertisements and the two weekly columns in the newspapers, 'Soldiers Gossip Column' (concerning the personal activities of the soldiers who had joined up) and the 'Soldiers Friend Column' (where general enquiries pertaining to the NMC were discussed) would encourage recruiting.[17] Reports on black response to these newspapers and the news bulletins are contradictory. From Rustenburg it was reported that the Government *News Bulletins* were eagerly anticipated and read throughout the district.[18] However, it was also remarked that the bulletins were hopelessly out of date and failed to keep the blacks in touch with the war effort. Moreover, very few blacks read newspapers at all.[19] The recruiting officials also believed that the publication of letters, speeches and circulars by various chiefs to their followers would contribute substantially to the recruiting effort.[20] These appeals, however, assumed that blacks owed a loyalty to South Africa and the British Government, proclaiming in obviously hollow rhetoric that if they joined the NMC, they would 'assist the forces that stand for freedom and liberty' and, ultimately, that they would then be recognised by other nations of the world.[21]

With the objective of generating local interest in the war and promoting recruitment, a number of military training camps and depots were established in African territories like Zululand and Transkei. Despite this extensive undertaking, the training camps evidently did not meet official expectations; the Director of Non-European Army Services concluded that: '. . . until recruiting results reveal that the principle of establishing . . . additional camps are justified, I do not see my way clear to consider additional camps'.[22] The fact that only two or three blacks actually attested at Eshowe in Zululand per month[23] emphasised the failure of this attempt to make the military more visible and alive to African communities. This method was complemented by sending black soldiers into African communities to enlist their kinsmen. For instance, those on leave were exhorted to use their influence among their own people in persuading them to enlist, and it was suggested that they might receive a pecuniary award for every recruit they brought in.[24] The urgent need for more recruits in early 1942 led the authorities to order selected blacks to return from the Middle East to assist in recruiting.[25] However, this method was not wholly successful, as is evident from a letter written by Lance-Corporal M. Mqali. While he was on leave he tried to persuade his friends to enlist:

I met them, they took no notice about this which when I spoke the thing you sent us to people that we should ask them to join in when we have gone for leave they answered in the form of a question as this how can you join because when you have joined the children are troubled. Others asked me why I have not ploughed and yet I have joined for the Government . . .[26]

Other soldiers, perhaps regretting their decision to enlist, actually discouraged prospective recruits from enrolling by informing them of the hardships of army life.[27]

Perhaps the most important method of recruiting was employing chiefs and headmen as recruiting agents among their people. The authorities thought these leaders had considerable influence and that their people might therefore more readily respond to their appeal than that of Native Commissioners, who were not always popular amongst the blacks and were sometimes viewed with suspicion.[28] It was argued that 'tribal instincts are still strong amongst the Natives and if chiefs could be made to feel that they, rather than Native Commissioners, were regarded as being responsible for producing recruits, such an increase in interest would possibly result'.[29]

Furthermore, the authorities believed that they erred by asking for volunteers. They would have been able to obtain more recruits if they adhered to the custom whereby the chiefs themselves took the lead and joined the army and had the power to conscript their followers. The official view was that 'it was an acceptable tradition with the Bantus that when a chief sits on his "arm chair" and commands his warriors to go out to meet the enemy, he is not serious about it until he takes to the arms himself and set the example of what must be done'.[30] By adopting this attitude the authorities could, of course, waive their formal policy of only enlisting volunteers and simultaneously proclaim that they were piously respecting tribal traditions.

The authorities undoubtedly though the chiefs and even the councillors of the Natives Representative Council wielded considerable power, because they made special arrangements for selected chiefs and councillors to visit the soldiers in various training units where the chiefs were generously treated. D. L. Smit, the Secretary for Native Affairs, was a strong supporter of this idea: 'We want to make a bit of a fuss of the Native members of this Council because they exercise a lot of influence among the educated Natives throughout the country. If we have them on our side in the recruiting it will be all to the good'.[31]

The chiefs, however, were by no means unanimous in their desire to help the Government with the recruitment campaign. Some of them were openly hostile and did not hesitate to oppose recruiting. Their lukewarm and unenthusiastic attitude was one of the reasons for the poor results.[32] Some chiefs objected to the fact that they were not consulted beforehand as to conditions of enlistment before recruitment was opened. Chief David Dalindyebo (Chief of the Tembus) and Chief Victor Poto (Chief of Western Pondoland) apparently viewed this in such a serious light that they boycotted recruitment meetings. The Chief Magistrate of the Transkeian Territories, R. Fyfe King, considered this action utterly presumptuous and noted 'that they have in fact placed the dignity of their positions before the needs of the country'.[33] A similar incident took place at Ndwedwe the following year when the Ndwedwe chiefs neglected to turn up for a meeting to discuss ways and means for obtaining recruits. The Chief Native Commissioner for Natal at that stage, H. C. Lugg, regarded their attitude as most reprehensible and contemplated depriving them of their stipends for 12 months.[34] This action can also be construed as proof that some of the chiefs and influential leaders were not prepared to act as Government collaborators.

On the other hand, there were also those who willingly assisted the authorities, though they might not have represented the wishes of their kinsmen and followers. Chief Kaka from the Matatiele district, a staunch supporter of the war effort, dearly experienced this when he lost his chieftainship in an election to headman Beyman. W. H. Seymour, Native Commissioner Matatiele, explained this from his own perspective: 'His [Kaka's] sentiments about getting natives into the army were far in advance of the people amongst whom he was living and like all men of advanced ideas, he suffered for them'.[35] That his followers might have had 'advanced ideas' themselves by not traditionally following the Government line apparently did not occur to him. However, after the war, the Department of Native Affairs did not regard the chiefs' contribution as particularly noteworthy.[36] In the northern areas of the country, for example, the chiefs were only responsible for 16 per cent of the recruits.[37]

In keeping with the whites' somewhat stereotyped conception of what might appeal to the blacks, recruitment marches were held in large centres as well as ostentatious military displays of bands playing loudly and with great gusto. In addition, it was considered that 'Musical Chairs' with vehicles and other skilful driving, squad drill, physical training displays, fire drill and first-aid demonstrations would also capture the imagination of the blacks.[38] It certainly succeeded in drawing the crowds; however, as was the case with the films, the majority of blacks enjoyed the spectacle but remained unmoved by its message.

On most of these occasions it was particularly noticeable that only women, children and elderly men were present, Senator E. H. Brookes and W. H. Seymour explained that the absence of young men could be ascribed to the custom among the blacks that only the older men attended these meetings.[39] However, as only young men were enlisted and the recruitment drive was specifically geared to net the young men, their absence must seriously have militated against the success of the recruitment meetings. Those young men who did attend were certainly not interested in enlisting. Some of them asked the officials pointed questions, such as 'What had the Government done for them?' 'Would they be armed?' 'Where is the land you promised us? You do not tell us the truth. The Europeans are cheating us.'[40] This prompted officials to report that the blacks were 'hostile' and 'insolent'.[41] Other youths were simply scared: 'A large number of young natives who would have made likely recruits, appeared to be afraid to enter the hall and no amount of coaxing would induce them to do so'.[42] Eventually fewer and fewer demonstrations were held, partly because of their limited yield but also because white opinion baulked at such brazen displays of military 'power' to impress Africans.

As in most war-time recruitment campaigns in Africa, 'sweet persuasion' was not the only method used. Officially the Government disapproved of any form of coercive action to increase the number of recruits. This was clearly stated by the Secretary for Native Affairs:

> If the intention is that they should be allowed to compel members of their tribes to enlist in the Native Military Corps I must state quite emphatically that this Department cannot countenance any such action. The principle underlying the creation of military forces in the Union is one of voluntary enlistment and the Government cannot be expected to acquiesce in any departure from such principle.[43]

Nevertheless there is evidence that some chiefs ordered their men to enlist. From the Zoutpansberg area in the Northern Transvaal Africans complained that recruiting officers with the help of the chiefs rounded up men without giving them any explanation why they should join up, forcing them to choose between enlisting or paying a fine in cattle and goats. Furthermore they graphically described the hardships caused by such methods:

> It is not taken into consideration that a man's brothers may be in the Army and he may be the sole support of his family . . . In fact it actually hinders the War effort because it interrupts the people's production and undermines the confidence of the people in the Government.[44]

The view that forced recruitment was quite acceptable was also expressed, it being said that it was not an African custom to ask for volunteers to go to war; the chiefs should merely have ordered their men to comply.[45] This appeal to former customs was of course a convenient pretext to mask the racist assumption that blacks had no right of choice in these matters. This was bluntly expressed by one of the recruiting officers, the Magistrate of Vryheid: 'It is useless to ask a native whether he will kindly join the Forces, he should be compelled to do so by his Paramount Chief in the interest of their Country and not by the Government'.[46] Likewise, W. O. H. Menge, an Assistant Native Commissioner for Marico, argued that, 'If we go along and say recruits are wanted on a purely European basis [i.e. voluntarily], this is not appreciated by the Natives'.[47] Officially therefore the authorities did not condone coercion. Unofficially, however, a fair degree of force was used so that the recruits obtained in this way could not be described as genuine volunteers but rather as 'conscripted volunteers'.[48]

Turning to the ideological content of the recruiting campaign, the refrain to fight for and to defend their so-called 'freedom' was repeated without regard for the actual position of the oppressed majority; if the South African blacks supported the Allies' war effort, their so-called 'liberty' would be secured because 'they are fighting together with the three greatest liberty-loving nations of the world – Britain, Soviet Union, America'.[49] It was, at best, a crude attempt to ignore the divisions of class and race in South Africa, and although such an appeal might have had some relevance to whites, it was entirely inappropriate when directed at prospective black recruits.

Of course the recruiting drive was also adversely affected by certain practical difficulties, such as a lack of sufficient staff, insensitive and ill-informed recruiters, problems in devising ways and means to make a widespread and direct appeal to a largely illiterate people and making the war issue a live one to them.[50] Moreover, the divided ideological milieu and structural context in which recruiting took place was highly inimical and detrimental to a successful recruiting campaign – irrespective of how well it was organised.

Particularly disappointing to the authorities was the poor response from the Zulu. In keeping with colonial thinking in the rest of Africa, the

Zulu was regarded as an outstanding 'martial race'.[51] A. Kirk-Greene has recently provided a comprehensive exposition on the history of this myth in colonial Africa. He points out:

> For the first, it seems that, while all military qualities were desirable, in the final analysis reliability, loyalty and discipline had precedence over valour, fearlessness and fighting skills in the determination of who was the 'good' soldier. As for a martial race, there is some support for the argument that one of the criteria was to have fought against the British – perhaps a reformulation of the British tradition of admiring a plucky loser as much as a clear winner.[52]

On the other hand, so-called 'non-martial races' frequently also manifested the above conditions for military prowess.[53] J. 'Bayo Adekson indeed noted that this cliché is an unworkable concept as it fails to explain why these 'martial races', in spite of being considered so warlike, contributed far less to the colonial forces than the 'less martial races'.[54] The validity of this popular notion seems therefore utterly suspect, because judgments about martial worth, loyalty and disloyalty, the amenability of one group of people rather than another to military discipline were often subjective and superficial. However, these nineteenth-century myths spilled over in the twentieth century and persisted in many military minds.

As far as South Africa was concerned, the 'martial' qualities of the Zulu were often based on the subjective observance 'that the average raw Zulu . . . is full of martial ardour and takes naturally to soldiering, as anyone can testify who has witnessed tribal rights or attended large war dances in the Reserves'.[55] History was conveniently invoked (but out of context) to substantiate this claim: 'This district [Nongoma] bred many of the old Zulu warriors who, years ago, overran a great portion of South Africa, subduing other Native tribes and making a brave stand against the Europeans in the country',[56] a view which echoes Kirk-Greene's comments on British admiration for former enemies.

In a futile and almost absurd ironic fashion, the myth of the 'martial race' was brought home to the Magistrate of Richmond, who reported after persistent endeavours to enlist Zulus that only 'two very old boys of between 65 and 70 said they would like to go to wash dishes'.[57] The martial ideal was indeed in the minds of the European recruiters rather than in the innate quality of the men they recruited. Some of the authorities realised that the prevailing policy of not arming the blacks with firearms seriously militated against a warlike spirit amongst the blacks whom they considered as 'martial races': 'How was it possible to work up the spirit of the offensive among natives if the only training given them was that of watchdogs, patrolling a fence with assegais and at the sign of danger being ordered to withdraw? If the natives were given arms and trained as soldiers a different story would be told'.[58]

The structural constraints of South African society loom large in an evaluation of the reasons why blacks refused to enlist. Under these circumstances blacks saw no reason to show their allegiance to 'democracy'. A leading article in a black Natal newspaper explained:

> What is needed it not mere drugging of the non-European with assurances that this is his war. He would not need to be told twice if he believed it to be really so . . . The exhortations and assurances are sounding very hollow . . . when what he knows immediately is that in the Union's version of Democracy eight million Bantu are denied the citizen's duty to work in the manufacture of war equipment for his country's fighting forces for no reason other than that he has a dark skin.[59]

For some blacks the real and immediate war was not in Europe or in North Africa, but much closer to home in South Africa. Many blacks argued along the lines that as far as their own position and struggle were concerned, there has never been 'any peace';[60] they had to wage a continuous war to alleviate their hardship and improve their circumstances. In a large measure therefore the structural positions of Africans was responsible for their apathetic attitude towards the war effort. Recruiting officials consistently complained that blacks were 'not interested', 'lukewarm', 'complacent' and 'lacking in enthusiasm'.[61] As it was clearly a 'white man's war', they could not see why they should assist where the ultimate result would not be to their advantage.[62] In particular they were not prepared to defend the white man's interest in a country where 'everything worthwhile is a privilege of the white man'.[63] Hence the simple but important question was asked: 'What have we to fight for?'[64] Moreover, when news was received of Allied setbacks in 1942, certain blacks did not see why they should fight, as it appeared that the Germans in any case would be victorious. Some, it would seem, were actually prepared to welcome a German victory – to them any change, of whatever nature, was an improvement on the *status quo.*[65] For other blacks the war was simply too far removed to be of any real concern. 'This is a war', an elderly man of Peddie told M. Ballinger, 'for people thousands of miles away on the other side of the world. It has nothing to do with us, and already it is making life harder for us.'[66]

In some instances this apathetic attitude changed into overt resistance. Various reports stated that 'individuals had forestalled the recruiting effort' and 'the youth of 20 to 30 years loafing in the kraal is not only not interested but is obstructive'.[67] The Non-European United Front of the Transvaal issued a pamphlet publicly exhorting the blacks not to enlist unless their grievances had been redressed.[68]

A myriad of other factors also deterred Africans from enlisting. For one, inequality in black and white service conditions was a consideration. Probably the biggest rebuff the blacks received when their service conditions were laid down was the instruction (strictly adhered to) that they would only be armed with assegais and knobkerries. Many blacks were estranged by this decision. They felt that as they were not fully trusted, there was no sense in joining the army. Furthermore, the hazardous duty of guarding military property with primitive and outdated 'weapons' was considered sheer folly. By following this policy the blacks found themselves at a loss, as one explained the dilemma: 'The officer has told us that natives should not have arms but should have assegais. I cannot use a rifle, thanks to master, but I cannot use an assegai either, thanks to master'.[69]

Inequalty with regard to the rates of pay was also an impediment for prospective recruits. The basic pay was 2s 3d per diem for recruits without dependents and 2s 6d for recruits with dependents. Recruits in the Cape Coloured Corps and the Indian and Malay Corps received 2s 6d per diem while the remuneration of the whites was 5 shillings a day.[70] The idea that blacks would enlist because of patriotic motives was a pipe-dream; they wanted substantial financial inducement. 'If you can pay me £8.10s. in the military service I will join. But there is always a cloud before me – three pounds seven shillings six pence for month – I fint [sic] it a very meagre subsidy to a man with a family. This worries my mind every time but I wish to defend our country and our things – this I find as my bounden duty.'[71] A sense of duty did not, however, override the pecuniary considerations. The success or failure of recruiting hinged on economics, especially as many blacks did not want to jeopardise the welfare of their families by inadequate remuneration.

Not only were the financial benefits too meagre to induce enlistment, but the discriminatory practices in the army also had an effect. According to Dr A. B. Xuma, President of the African National Congress,

> It is the consensus of opinion among African people of all classes in the Union, both urban and rural, that the condition of service for the African soldiers and the pin-pricks and humiliation he is subjected to at times, apparently to put an inferiority complex in him, tend to

> discourage the African people from joining the Native Military Corps and cognate units . . . We cannot maintain these peacetime discriminations in the army and expect the victims of such discriminations or their friends and relatives to rush in their thousands to the army to defend them.[72]

Furthermore, the practice of discrimination in the South African society was also reflected in the administrative bureaucracy responsible for recruiting. This contributed to the reluctance of blacks to enlist. They were afraid that they would be arrested for tax arrears if they presented themselves for enlistment. Blacks without passes who wished to enlist were also not accepted but ordered to return to their homes to obtain the relevant document. In most cases they were penniless and had no train fare to return home. This treatment had far-reaching ramifications: blacks felt that the Government did not really need them, so their already meagre trust in the Government dwindled further. Of course they did not return but spread word of their humiliating experience.[73]

In addition prevailing labour conditions also influenced the recruitment campaign in various ways. Some felt it would be disloyal and therefore impossible to leave their employment in the absence of their white employers who had left for Active Service. Others had no choice – they lived on white farms and were therefore not free to enlist because of their tenancy obligations. They were afraid of being evicted if they did not honour their contracts.[74] Farmers also spread rumours among their labourers that many blacks were killed in North Africa.[75]

Moreover, adverse farming conditions brought about by a serious drought in the summer rainfall area and unusually heavy rains resulting in floods in the winter rainfall area[76] had a dual effect on recruitment. On the one hand, because of crop failures, the blacks considered joining the army; but on the other hand, the women discouraged them as they were afraid they might be left without support.[77]

Fear and apprehension also played a part in their disinclination to enlist. The blacks still retained vivid memories of the sinking of the SS *Mendi* during the First World War, when 615 people (including a large contingent of South African blacks) lost their lives. Consequently, when told that they would be required to travel by sea, many refused to enlist. This fear was aggravated by descriptions of torture if blacks fell in to enemy hands.[78] Their fear was dramatically justified after the fall of Tobruk, when many South Africans were captured or lost their lives and when the *Nova Scotia* sank off the Natal coast and nearly 300 badly mutilated bodies were washed ashore, reminding the blacks of the *Mendi* disaster. These events had a very bad effect on recruiting.[79] In addition, some blacks who might have considered enlistment feared possible harassment and reprisals from that section of the white population who did not support the war effort.[80]

The authorities advanced so-called 'subversive' propaganda as another reason why the blacks did not enlist. They were inclined to regard anything not in keeping with their policy as 'subversive' propaganda. Examples of this were remarks by blacks that 'it was a white man's war and did not concern them',[81] German propaganda exhorting blacks not to enlist,[82] evidence of pro-Japanese propaganda among blacks on the grounds of so-called colour kinship,[83] threats that the names of those blacks who had enlisted would be given to the Germans when they invaded South Africa,[84] and a strong anti-war feeling among literate blacks.[85] Captain George Sutter, Adjutant of the 21st Field Regiment South African Artillery, thought that 'questions, which in the opinions of those closely and intimately acquainted with the Zulus over many years could never emanate from the native mind'[86] were asked everywhere were sure proof of 'subversive' activities. Such a remark bore out the gross underestimation by the authorities of blacks' ability and desire to be well informed before enlisting, and clearly indicated how nebulous the term 'subversive' had become.

The Government's obsession with subversion among Africans reflected to some degree the tensions in South African society. In a country where arbitrary and harsh white rule touched non-whites at every stage blacks often distrusted whites – an important underlying reason for problems encountered in the recruitment campaign. For instance, the treatment meted out in the past by officials of the Department of Native Affairs and other Government officials, especially the police, created a sense of suspicion, reluctance and hostility when these very officials exhorted them to enlist.[87] The following incident also illustrates the distrust among the blacks. When the Native Affairs Department tried to introduce fertiliser cheaply in the Bulwer district, the blacks intimated that they would not avail themselves of the offer 'as the Government had failed to get them to join up and were now going to poison their crops with this fertiliser'.[88]

On the whole, it indeed seems that because white interests persistently dictated the nature of the recruiting campaign, it effectively also inhibited the campaign, as B. G. Paver aptly remarked: 'Recruiting has been undertaken with one eye on the political field and another on the mining and farming interests'.[89]

However, if there were so many adverse conditions inhibiting blacks to enlist, the question arises why 80 000 eventually attested. It appears unequivocally clear that the foremost reason for this phenomenon was the economic factor. It seems appropriate, therefore, to examine the participation of blacks in the Union Defence Force in terms of economic 'push–pull' factors – not dissimilar to those pertaining to migratory labour. In this respect Kenneth W. Grundy noted: 'A decision to enlist is always a product of a highly personal perception of one's overall career and social prospects in the context of a particular set of situational determinants. Black recruitment is a two-way process involving the absence of opportunity in civil society and the attraction of the armed forces'.[90] This becomes clear in considering the position of those blacks in the Transvaal who enlisted – they constituted more than half of the total number of recruits. Particularly in the Northern Transvaal, where the mealie crop production was extremely poor, owing to a severe infestation of 'streak disease' and a plague of so-called 'army-worms', there were few escape routes for blacks. In addition to these adverse agricultural conditions, the northern part of the country was stricken by a devastating drought during 1941–43, which resulted in large-scale crop failures. This effectively deprived many blacks of a livelihood, so that many families suffered extreme privation and famine.[91] A further consequence of the drought was that many farmers summarily dismissed their black employees, adding to the number of unemployed.[92] No wonder that Lt-Col. R. Fyfe King, callously remarked that 'the best recruiting districts both for the Army and the Mines, are those which reap little'.[93] These harsh economic conditions were exacerbated by the higher prices of the strictest necessities of life, mainly brought about by the war.[94] The upshot was that many blacks were forced to join the army in order to escape destitution – a classic example of economic 'push–pull' factors determining a choice of employment.

Although on an inadequate scale, the army at least provided regular pay,[95] free food, clothing, housing, medical care and allotments to soldiers' dependants. It was a question of relative poverty and improvement.

Furthermore, although evidence in this regard is scant, it appears that some blacks joined in the hope of learning a trade and others regarded it as an educative and prestigious experience. Thus B. W. Mcanyangwa applied to enlist as late as January 1945 so that he 'would be the only African teacher that has joined up in Aliwal North out of African male teachers'.[96]

In addition, it seems as if some blacks were motivated by their loyalty and patriotism to South Africa, the King and the British Empire to enlist.[97] But this was not an unqualified expression of loyalty, as J.

Sephiphi remarked, 'We wanted to go and fight for the country thinking that maybe we'd get a better life when we came back'.[98]

The authorities attempted to appeal for recruits from specific areas and groups. They hoped to enlist blacks from the urban areas, with training and experience, who were thought likely to make good non-commissioned officers. The official view was that blacks from the urban areas should have been the ideal recruits, because they were generally more literate than the rural blacks and more experienced in handling tools and machinery, which would have facilitated their military training.[99] But the poor pay offered by the army, and the official policy to avoid prejudicing white employers of labour, in most cases effectively drew a line between the literate urban black and the illiterate rural blacks.[100] D. D. T. Jabavu and Z. K. Matthews realised the effect remuneration had on the type of man recruited: 'While pay is by no means attractive even for the "mine-boy" type of recruit it is positively discouraging to the "superior" type of recruit'.[101] The result was that about 80 per cent of the blacks recruited came from the rural areas, where, as indicated above, their conditions were generally inferior to those offered by the army. This meant that the majority were illiterate farm labourers or peasants.

It was also a noteworthy feature of recruiting that there was a lack of response from those between 20 and 30 years of age. These men preferred to work in the mines – the main rival for labour with which the army had to contend. The result was that while the blacks employed on the mines reached record figures in 1941,[102] the army had to be content with older men as recruits.[103]

However, there were also literates and semi-literates who enlisted, especially teachers, ministers of religion, clerks and interpreters, who regarded it as their duty.[104] They were more the exception than the rule, as an anti-war feeling amongst the literates was rife. However, a number of blacks who were well educated and held responsible positions in civil life enlisted. One was Sgt Doyle Modiagotla, who was not only a professional builder but was also an ex-serviceman from the First World War and politically active during the interwar years.[105] The frequently harsh treatment meted out to the Native Labour Contingent during the First World War apparently did not prevent a few of its members from re-enlisting. Stanford Wauchope, the son of Rev I. Wauchope who was drowned in the *Mendi* disaster, also enlisted, although he was the headmaster of an Anglican School in Germiston prior to enlistment.[106] The son of the renowned Sol Plaatje, Halley Plaatje, who boasted a number of credentials to his name, including holding a teaching certificate, ex-General Secretary to the ANC, former General Secretary to the South African Bantu Rugby Football Board, and a 'licensed driver without a blemish' also offered his services.[107]

A number of reasons thus account for African participation in a white man's war. Contrary to white expectations and rhetoric, these were mainly, although not exclusively, unrelated to notions of patriotism and loyalty. Those blacks who did enlist were more concerned about survival in a hostile world than 'lofty' considerations; to them military life, even with its attendant dangers and hardships, provided a temporary shelter.

It seems therefore that the recruiting methods did not effectively induce blacks to enlist. The inequality of black and white service conditions, the rebuffs blacks frequently received from the administrative bureaucracy, mistrust, fear and apprehension were additional impediments. But because of economic realities 80 000 blacks, constituting a quarter of the manpower in the Union Defence Force during the Second World War, eventually decided to enlist.

NOTES

1. South African Defence Force Documentation Centre, Pretoria (SADFDC), Native Military Corps Files (NMC NAS) B 3 Box 66, J. C. Knoetze, 'Historical Survey of the Non-European Army Services outside the Union of South Africa, 1945'.
2. SADFDC, Union War History (UWH) Box 159, Narratives and Reports Units and Formations (Narep Unfo) 13, Lt M. Hallack, 'Record of Non-European Army Services, 1939–1945', 1946.
3. H. J. Martin and N. Orpen, *South Africa at War. Military and Industrial Organization and Operations in connection with the conduct of War, 1939–1945*, Vol. VII (Cape Town, Johannesburg and London, 1979) pp. 150–1.
4. E. Roux, *Time Longer than Rope. The Black Man's Struggle for Freedom in South Africa* (Wisconsin, 1978) pp. 302–16.
5. K. W. Grundy, *Soldiers with Politics. Blacks in the South African Armed Forces* (Berkeley, Los Angeles and London, 1983), pp. 63–89.
6. M. Roth, ' "If you give us rights we will fight": Black Involvement in the Second World War', *South African Historical J.* xv (1983), pp. 85–104.
7. NMC NAS 3/4/1 B 4 Box 2, Col. E. T. Stubbs, Director of Non-European Army Services (DNEAS) to Adjutant-General (AG) (3), 1 July 1942.
8. NMC NAS 3/4/1 B 5 Box 1, Note on Native Recruiting Propaganda by 2/Lt J. B. Bruce, undated.
9. Ibid.
10. NMC NAS 3/21 A 4 Box 12, DNEAS to Deputy-Adjutant-General (DAG), 27 Dec. 1941.
11. NMC NAS 3/21 A 5 Box 15, Notes on draft synopsis of a film, 31 Dec. 1941.

12. NMC NAS 3/21 A 5 Box 12, K. Maxwell to T. Gutsche (Film Adviser), 7 May 1942. See also NMC NAS 3/21 A 5 Box 12, Report by Lt Hall on a film, 'A five cup matter', issued by the Tea Market Expansion Board. (Accompanying letter, DNEAS to Deputy Director Military Intelligence (DDMI), 5 March 1942.)
13. SADFDC, Director of Non-European Army Services Files (DNEAS-NAS) 8/21 Box 34, DNEAS to recruiting officer, NEAS, 13 Feb. 1943; Central Archives, Pretoria (CAP), Department of Native Affairs Files (NTS) Box 9127, File 68/363/18, Additional Native Commissioner Bushbuckridge to Secretary for Native Affairs, 9 July 1941; DNEAS NAS 3/4/13 Box 6, Officer Commanding (OC) NMC Recruiting Transvaal (Maj. T. E. Liefeldt) to DNEAS, 19 Nov. 1942; DNEAS NAS 3/4/13 Box 6, Report by Lt S. Horwitz on a recruiting tour, 26 Nov. 1942; NMC NAS 3/4/20/1 B 9 Box 5, S/Sgt M. H. du Plessis to DNEAS, 21 Dec. 1942.
14. NMC NAS 3/21 (A) A 4 Box 14 and NMC NAS 3/21 A 4 Box 12.
15. NMC NAS 3/4/1 B 2 Box 2, OC Recruiting Natal and Zululand to DNEAS, 17 August 1942.
16. SADFDC, Adjudant-General (AG) (3) 154/667 Box 504, Resumé of a meeting called by Brig. Daniel to afford Col. Stubbs an opportunity to discuss with leading influential men the problems in connection with native recruiting in Natal, 2 March 1942; NMC NNAS 3/4/1 A 1 Box 2 and NTS Box 9130, File 69/363, Notes on meeting held in the Drill Hall Durban, 2 March 1942.
17. NMC NAS 3/21 A 6 Box 1, Col. E. T. Stubbs to Deputy Chief of Staff (DCS), 20 August 1942; NTS Box 9115, File 68/363, General Circular No. 24 of 1942 issued by H. Rogers (Acting Secretary for Native Affairs), 10 August 1942.
18. NTS Box 9629, File 511/400, Additional Native Commissioner, Rustenburg to H. Rogers, 11 March 1942.
19. NTS Box 9130, File 69/363, Notes on a meeting held in the Drill Hall Durban, 2 March 1942 and NMC NAS 3/4/1 B 4 Box 2, J. H. Dugard, Inspector of Schools Engcobo to Director of Information Non-European Section, 25 July 1942.
20. NMC NAS 3/21/C A 4 Box 15, Secretary for Defence to the Adjutant General, 5 August 1943.
21. SADFDC, Secretary for Defence Files (DC) 1473/32 Box 3090, Appeals from the following chiefs: Paswane Mphaphili (Vendaland); Mangope (Bahurutshe and Batsoana); Mshiyeni (Zululand); Abraham Moiboa (Bahurutshe); Albert John Lutuli (Umvoti Mission Reserve); J. K. Mankuroane (Matlhaping); NMC NAS 3/21 A 6 Box 12, Appeals by Chief Scanlen N. Lehane (Batlokoe tribe). (Accompany letter DNEAS to Editor, Bantu Press, 22 Sept. 1942); Jeremiah Moshesh (Basuto). (Accompanying letter DNEAS to Editor, Bantu Press, 4 Dec. 1942).
22. NMC NAS 3/4/1 B 4 Box 2, Lt-Col. H. S. Mockford for DNEAS to Secretary for Native Affairs, 3 August 1942.
23. NMC NAS 3/4/13 A 6 Box 51 and NMC NAS 3/4/1/B 8 Box 1, Capt. Rodseth to DNEAS, Report on visit of NMC Detachment to Nongoma, 7 July 1942.
24. NMC NAS 3/16/4 A 11 Box 40, Notes of a meeting in regard to recruiting for the NMC, 10 June 1941. See also NMC NAS 3/4/1 A 1 Box 2, Lt-Col.

H. S. Mockford to OC's 1–8 Bn. NMC, 27 Feb. 1942 and OC 3rd Bn. NMC to DNEAS, 15 April 1942; NMC NAS 3/4/1 B 5 Box 2, OC 4th Bn. NMC to DNEAS, 20 April 1942.

25. AG (3) 154/33/0 Box 154, DNEAS to DAG, 2 March 1942.
26. NMC NAS 3/1/17 A 3 Box 28, M. Mgali to Magistrate Kingwilliamstown. (Accompanying letter, OC 3rd Bn. NMC Woltemade to DNEAS, 16 Sept. 1942.)
27. NMC NAS 3/1/7 A 3 Box 28, Statement by Motwana Kantolo, 23 Oct. 1942.
28. NMC NAS 3/4/1 A 1 Box 3, C. H. Malcomess to Director of Information, 16 July 1942 and NMC NAS 3/4/1 A 1 Box 3, Chief Moroka to DNEAS, 25 Nov. 1942.
29. NMC NAS 3/4/1 B 5 Box 2, OC 3rd Bn. NMC to DNEAS, 15 April 1942. See also NMC NAS 3/4/13 B 9 Box 4, DNEAS to Secretary for Native Affairs, 19 May 1942.
30. NMC NAS 3/21/L A 6 Box 19, 'Mobilisation of Manpower' by H. Maxwell, undated. See also NMC NAS 3/4/1 A 2 Box 3 and NTS Box 9127, File 68/363/19, Report of W.M. Seymour to Magistrate Matatiele (Accompanying letter, Secretary for Native Affairs to DNEAS, 16 Jan. 1942) and NTS Box 9120 File 68/363/5, H. C. Lugg to Secretary for Native Affairs, 4 Oct. 1940.
31. NMC NAS 3/31 A 1 Box 55, D. L. Smit to H. S. Mockford, 9 Nov. 1940.
32. NTS Box 9128 File 68/363/20, Territorial News, 13 August 1942 (Accompanying letter, Sen. W. T. Welsh to D. L. Smit, 17 August 1942); NTS Box 9114 File 68/363, S. Young to Secretary for Native Affairs, 1 Nov. 1940; NMC NAS 3/1/7 A 3 Box 28, Sgt. D. A. R. Ndongo to Maj. C. C. Stubbs, 25 Sept. 1941; NMC NAS 3/1/7 A 3 Box 28, L/Cpl M. Mgali to OC 3rd Bn. NMC, undated (Accompanying letter, C. C. Stubbs to DNEAS, 16 Sept. 1942); AG (3) 154/667 Box 504, Resumé of meeting called by Brig. Daniel to afford Col. Stubbs an opportunity to discuss with leading influential men the problems in connection with native recruiting in Natal, 2 March 1942, Comment by Col. Stubbs.
33. NTS Box 9114 File 68/363, R. Fyfe King to D. L. Smit, 12 August 1940.
34. NTS Box 9130 File 69/363, H. C. Lugg to Secretary for Native Affairs, 27 August 1941.
35. NTS Box 9129 File 68/363/36, W. M. Seymour to the Magistrate Matatiele, 26 August 1946.
36. NTS Box 9129 File 68/363/36, Memorandum by D. L. Smit, 19 Nov. 1946.
37. NTS Box 9129 File 68/363/36, Schedule of blacks recruited by Chiefs of the Northern Areas. (Accompanying letter, Chief Native Commissioner Northern Areas to Secretary for Native Affairs, 13 Sept. 1946.)
38. DNEAS NAS 3/4/13 Box 6, OC Native Motor Transport Training Centre (NMTTC), suggestions for recruiting tour, undated; NMC NAS 3/4/13 B 10 Box 4, Chief Native Commissioner Kingwilliamstown to Secretary for Native Affairs, 9 July 1941; NMC NAS 3/4/13 B 10 Box 4, Secretary for Native Affairs to DNEAS, 11 July 1941; NTS Box 9127 File 68/363/18, Secretary, Sub-Committee for Non-European Progaganda: Report on contents of a letter dealing with Non-Europeans, 5 Sept. 1942; AG (3) 154/667 Box 504, DNEAS to AG, Report on conference to increase numbers

recruited in Natal, 4 March 1942 and NMC NAS 3/4/1 B 9 Box 1, Report of a conference at Bushbuckridge with Native Commissioner, 24 Oct. 1941.

39. NTS Box 9127 File 68/363/19, Report on recruiting by W. M. Seymour (Accompanying letter, Magistrate Matatiele to Chief Magistrate, Umtata, 22 Sept. 1942) and NTS Box 9130 File 69/363, E. H. Brookes to Secretary for Native Affairs, 17 June 1941.
40. NMC NAS 3/4/1 B 5 Box 2, Area Commandant NMC Training Areas Welgedacht to DNEAS, 23 May 1942 and NTS Box 9130 File 69/363, Acting Assistant Native Commission, G. V. Essery, Pinetown, report on visit by Chief Mshiyeni to Pinetown, 5 Sept. 1940.
41. NTS Box 9130 File 69/363, S/Sgt. R. E. Symons, F. Coy. 2nd Bn NMC to OC 2nd Bn NMC, Report on Recruiting Tour, 13 August 1942.
42. NMC NAS 3/4/1 B 5 Box 2, Report on Recruiting meetings held at Bloemfontein Township on the 30th March 1942, at No. 2 Township Kimberley on the 31st March 1942 and at Green Point Township Beaconsfield on the 1st April 1942.
43. NMC NAS 3/4/1 B 5 Box 5, Secretary for Native Affairs to DNEAS, 30 April 1942.
44. The Library, University of the Witwatersrand. Historical and Literary Papers Division, Ballinger Papers A 410 B 2.14.14, File 3 M. B. Mulandzi to M. Ballinger, 21 March 1944.
45. NTS Box 6813 File 28/318, Minutes of a quarterly meeting held at Moshedi, 10 Dec. 1940; NMC NAS 3/16/4 A 11 Box 40, Notes of a meeting held in regard to recruiting for the NMC, 10 June 1941, Comment by W. O. H. Menge.
46. NTS Box 9130 File 69/363, Magistrate Vryheid to Chief Native Commissioner, Pietermaritzburg, 19 Sept. 1942.
47. NMC NAS 3/16/4 A 11 Box 40, Notes of a meeting held in regard to recruiting for the NMC, 10 June 1941, Comment by W. O. H. Menge.
48. This term was used by D. Killingray with regard to recruiting in Ghana for the Second World War. D. Killingray, 'The colonial army in the Gold Coast: official policy and local response, 1890–1947' unpub. PhD thesis, University of London, 1982, p. 298.
49. NTS Box 9127 File 68/363/27, W. O. H. Menge to Magistrate Zeerust, 13 August 1941.
50. NMC NAS 3/1/7 A 3 Box 28, Statement by Pte E. Cliff, 12 Nov. 1942. See also NMC NAS 3/4/1 B 3 Box 2, 'Africans and the war', written by D. D. T. Jabavu and Z. K. Matthews (Accompanying letter, Controller of Censorship to Col. Werdmuller, Director of Recruiting, 30 June 1942) and NTS Box 9127 File 68/363/18, Report on contents of a letter dealing with Non-Europeans by Secretary Sub-Committee for Non-European Progaganda, 5 Sept. 1942.
51. NTS Box 9323 File 80/378, Draft speech by the Minister of Native Affairs, Nongoma, 19 June 1941 and NTS Box 9130 File 69/363, Speech by D. L. Smit to the Zulus at Pietermaritzburg, 14 June 1941.
52. A. H. M. Kirk-Greene, '"Damnosa Hereditas": ethnic ranking and the martial races imperative in Africa', *Ethnic and Racial Studies*, III, iv, (Oct. 1980), pp. 406–7.
53. Ibid., p. 408.

54. J. 'Bayo Adekson, 'Ethnicity and army recruitment in colonial plural societies', *Ethnic and Racial Studies*, II, ii (April 1979), p. 151.
55. NMC NAS 3/4/1 B 2 Box 2, 'Some views on the Recruiting of Natives' by Sgt. B. G. Tranchell, undated.
56. NMC NAS 3/21 B 3 Box 18, Letter no. 22 by Ndabazabantu, 27 June 1942.
57. NTS Box 9130 File 69/363, Magistrate, Richmond, Natal to C. P. Alport, Chief Native Commissioner, Natal, 15 Sept. 1942.
58. SADFDC, Chief of the General Staff Files (CGS) 32/3 V I File 1640, Extract from M.P.'s Conference No. 11 of 18 Nov. 1942.
59. NTS Box 9130 File 69/363, Leading article, 'Ilange lase Natal', 5 Sept. 1942.
60. University of Cape Town Libraries, Africana and Special Collections Department. Z. K. Matthews Papers BZA 78/9–78/13 B 4.34, 'Africans and the War', draft for publication in *Commonsense*, 1942.
61. NMC NAS 3/4/1 B 3 Box 2, Capt. H. B. Myburgh, OC 'D' Coy. 8th Bn. NMC to OC 8th Bn. NMC, 17 August 1942; NMC NAS 3/4/1 B 9 Box 1, Recruiting Officer NEAS to area Commandant NMC Training Areas Welgedacht, 1 Nov. 1941; University of Cape Town Libraries, Africana and Special Collections Department. W. G. Ballinger Papers BC 347 A 3 1940 and CAP, A 1 J. C. Smuts Papers, Vol. 145, no 44, Report of a tour of the Eastern Province in October and November 1940 by M. Ballinger for the information of the Prime Minister, the Rt. Hon. J. C. Smuts; NTS Box 9130 File 69/363, H. Balk, Native Commissioner Ndwedwe to C. P. Alport, Chief Native Commissioner,Natal, 15 Sept. 1942; NTS Box 9130 File 69/363, Magistrate Greytown to Chief Native Commissioner Pietermaritzburg, 15 Sept. 1942; NTS Box 9629 File 511/400, R. A. Midgley, Assistant Native Commissioner Groot Spelonke to Additional Native Commissioner Pietersburg, 9 July 1941 and NTS Box 6813 File 28/318, Minutes of a quarterly meeting held at Hartebeesfontein, 6 Dec. 1940.
62. NTS Box 9130 File 69/363, Native Commissioner Umzinto to Chief Native Commission Natal, 17 Sept. 1942; NTS Box 9130 File 69/363, Magistrate Greytown to Chief Native Commissioner Pietermaritzburg, 15 Sept. 1942; NMC NAS 3/4/1 B 9 Box 1, Conference at Bushbuckridge on 24 Oct. 1941; AG (3) 154/33/0 Box 154, R. D. Pilkington Jordan (Adjudant-General) to DCS, 20 Dec. 1941 and NMC NAS 3/28/15 A 5 Box 56, Report of a meeting at Native Commissioner's Office, Eshowe, 5 Feb. 1941.
63. University of Cape Town Libraries, Africana and Special Collections Department. A. B. Xuma Papers ABX 420304b, The African National Congress Deputation at Cape Town, 4 March 1942.
64. W. G. Ballinger Papers BC 347 A3 1940 and J. C. Smuts Papers A 1, Vol. 145, no. 44, Report of a tour of the Eastern Province in October and November 1940 by M. Ballinger for the information of the Rt. Hon. J. C. Smuts.
65. AG (3) 154/33/0 Box 154, R. D. Pilkington Jordan to DCS, 20 Dec. 1941 and NMC NAS 3/1/7 A 3 Box 28, S/Sgt. V. Seymour to Adjutant, 9th Bn NMC, 4 August 1942.
66. W. G. Ballinger Papers BC 347 A 3 1940 and J. C. Smuts Papers A 1, Vol. 145, no. 44, Report of a tour of the Eastern province in October and November 1940 by M. Ballinger for the information of the Rt Hon J. C. Smuts.

67. CGS 32/7 V I, Capt G. Sutter for OC 21st Field Regiment S.A.A. to D.F.A.A.T., 5 August 1941.
68. NMC NAS 3/21(A) Box 14, Undated pamphlet issued by the Non-European United Front (Transvaal).
69. AG (3) 154/33/0 Box 154, R. D. Pilkington Jordan to DCS, 20 December 1941.
70. Grundy, *Soldiers Without Politics*, p. 84.
71. The Library, University of the Witwatersrand. Historical and Literary Papers Division, South African Institute of Race Relations Papers (SAIRR), J. D. Rheinallt Jones Collection O. World War II AD 843 Box 109, L. M. Sediela to J. D. Rheinallt Jones, 14 December 1941.
72. A. B. Xuma Papers ABX 420304b, The African National Congress Deputation at Cape Town, 4 March 1942.
73. NMC NAS 3/4/1 A 1 Box 3, Draft of Secretary for Native Affairs, undated; NTS Box 9115 File 68/363, Hon Secretary Communist Party of South Africa to Secretary for Native Affairs, 19 June 1942. See also NTS Box 9130 File 69/363, Native Commissioner Verulam to C. P. Alport, 16 September 1942.
74. NTS Box 9127 File 68/363/27, F. M. S. Mapoch to Headquarters of Non-European Recruiting Office, 10 November 1941; NTS Box 6814 File 32/318, Minutes of a special meeting of Chiefs and Headmen held at Bushbuckridge, 11 November 1942; NTS Box 9130 File 69/363, Magistrate Ladysmith to Chief Native Commissioner, 16 September 1942 and NTS Box 9130 File 69/363, N. C. Babanango to C. P. Alport, 19 September 1942.
75. NMC NAS 3/4/1 B 5 Box 1, Sgt G. Sabela to Capt Franz, 24 June 1941.
76. UWH Box 1, J. W. Moll, 'Oorsig van die Geskiedenis van die Tweede Wêreldoorlog op landbougebied, 1952–53'.
77. NTS Box 9629 File 511/400, Additional Native Commissioner Louis Trichardt to H. Rogers, 5 March 1942.
78. NTS Box 9115 File 68/363, J. O. Cornell, Magistrate Qumbu to Chief Magistrate, Umtata, 25 November 1941; NTS Box 9130 File 69/363, Magistrate Greytown to Chief Native Commissioner Natal, 15 September 1942; NMC NAS 3/4/20 B 8 Box 7, Extract from report by S/Sgt R. E. Symons, recruiting in Nkandhla, Zululand, undated. Because of the possible fear aeroplanes could generate, it was omitted from any pictorial, photographic or visual propaganda. (NMC NAS 3/21 A 5 Box 12, J. Kreft, Deputy Director of Military Intelligence to Secretary for Defence, 13 February 1942.)
79. NMC NAS 3/4/20/1 B 9 Box 5, OC NMC Recruiting Natal and Zululand to DNEAS, 18 December 1942 and NTS Box 9128 File 68/363/20, S/Sgt R. E. Symons to OC 2nd Bn. NMC, 20 July 1942.
80. NTS Box 9127 File 68/363/19, Report on recruiting by W. M. Seymour (Accompanying letter, Magistrate Matatiele to Chief Magistrate Umtata, 22 September 1942.)
81. AG (3) 154/33/0 Box 154, R. D. Pilkington Jordan to DCS, 20 December 1941.
82. NMC NAS 3/4/1 B 3 Box 2, S/Sgt R. E. Symons to OC 2nd Bn NMC 13 August 1942; NTS Box 9127 File 68/363, Circular of Chief Magistrate of the Transkeian Territories to all magistrates in the Transkeian Territories,

4 July 1942 and NTS Box 9127 File 68/363/18, Minutes of an official meeting of departments dealing with propaganda, 12 June 1942.

83. NTS Box 9127 File 68/363/18, Minutes of an official meeting of departments dealing with propaganda, 12 June 1942.
84. NTS Box 9629 File 511/400, R. A. Midgley, Assistant Native Commissioner Groot Spelonke to Additional Native Commissioner Pietersburg, 9 July 1941.
85. NMC NAS 3/21 A 5 Box 12, OC 3rd Bn. NMC to DNEAS, 4 May 1942 and DNEAS NAS 1126/D Box 28, Director-General of Demobilisation to DNEAS, 1 November 1945.
86. CGS 32/7 V I, Capt G. Sutter to D.F.A.A.T., 5 August 1941.
87. NTS BOX 9127 File 68/363/19, Capt Rodseth to Secretary for Native Affairs, 13 November 1940; NTS Box 9114 File 68/363, S. Young to Secretary for Native Affairs, 1 November 1940 and AG (3) 154/667 Box 504, Resumé of a meeting called by Brig Daniel to afford Col Stubbs an opportunity to discuss with leading influential men the problems in connection with Native recruiting in Natal, 2 March 1942; NTS Box 9126 File 68/363/22, Note of a meeting with Chief Botha Sicgau, Chief Victor Poto, Chief Jeremiah Moshesh and Percy Sangoni by D. L. Smit, 24 April 1942.
88. NTS Box 9130 File 69/363, G. Whittaker, Native Commissioner, Bulwer to Chief Native Commissioner, Natal, 18 September 1942.
89. NMC NAS 3/21 A 4 Box 12, B. G. Paver to Director of Information, 19 December 1941.
90. Grundy, *Soldiers Without Politics*, pp. 28–9.
91. J. C. Smuts Papers, A 1 Vol. 155 no. 29, Report of the Witwatersrand Mine Natives Wages Commission on the Remuneration and Conditions of employment of Natives on the Witwatersrand Gold Mines and the Remuneration and Conditions of Natives at Transvaal undertakings of Victoria Falls and Transvaal Power Co., 21 December 1943 (Lansdowne Commission). See also NTS Box 7841 File 20/336, Assistant Native Commissioner, Whittlesea to Chief Native Commissioner, Kingwilliamstown, 15 August 1941; NTS Box 7848 File 45/336, Additional Native Commissioner Sibasa to Secretary for Native Affairs, 5 March 1942; NTS Box 7848 File 45/ 336, Additional Native Commissioner, Louis Trichardt to Secretary for Native Affairs, 11 March 1941; NTS Box 7847 File 41/336, P. W. Willis and Co. to the Controller of Food Supplies, 12 January 1944; NTS Box 9629 File 511/400, Memorandum by Maj. T. E. Liefeldt, 27 February 1942; SAIRR Papers J. D. Rheinallt Jones Collection S. 2 Senatorial Correspondence Box 4, H. Rogers to J. D. Rheinallt Jones, 16 June 1941; NMC NAS 3/4/1 A 1 Box 2, Maj. T. E. Liefeldt to DNEAS, 18 March 1942 and DC 1473/32 Box 3090, Appeal from Chief Paswane Mphaphuli, 1943–4.
92. NTS Box 7852 File 53/336, Sekretaris van Landbou en Bosbou aan Sekretaris van Naturellesake, 24 January 1942.
93. NMC NAS 3/4/1 B 2 Box 2, Lt Col R. Fyfe King to DNEAS, 28 September 1942.
94. SAIRR Papers J. D. Rheinallt Jones Collection S. 2 Senatorial Correspondence Box 4, Address by Urban and Rural Natives of the Bultfontein Area to J. D. Rheinallt Jones, 17 November 1940.

95. The Native Commissioner of Port Elizabeth noted that blacks from smaller towns were eager to enlist due to the fact that in these areas they were much more lowly paid than in the cities. (NMC NAS 3/4/13 B Box 4, Native Commissioner Port Elizabeth to Maj. Stubbs, Umtata, 22 September 1941.)
96. DNEAS NAS 3/4/3 Box 5, B. W. Mcanyangwa to General Smuts, 29 January 1945.
97. NTS Box 9653 File 520/400 (7), G. J. Kutshwayo, Mount Frere to Secretary for Native Affairs, 23 May 1940; DNEAS NAS 3/4/3 Box 5, D Ramakatore to DNEAS, 12 May 1944 and SAIRR Papers J. D. Rheinallt Jones Collection O. World War II Box 109, Address to NUSAS, 27 April 1940.
98. 'Forgotten Heroes of World War II' in *Springbok*, LXII, ix (September 1979), p. 7.
99. NTS Box 9114 File 68/363, Telegram from Secretary for Native Affairs to Chief Magistrates of Umtata, Pietermaritzburg and Kingwilliamstown, 7 August 1940 and SAIRR Papers ('B' Box) B 43.7.2, Memorandum on pay and allowances of Non-European soldiers with special reference to the African soldiers presented to the Secretary for Defence by the Home Front League of the Springbok Legion, August 1942.
100. UWH Box 159 Narep Unfo 13, Hallack, 'Record', p. 173. See also NMC NAS 3/40 A 1 Box 45, Training Inspectorate Report on NMC Training Area, East Rand conducted by Lt-Col J. V. Lyle during 24–27 November 1941.
101. NMC NAS 3/4/1 B 3 Box 2, 'Africans and the War', written by D. D. T. Jabavu and Z. K. Matthews. (Accompanying letter, Controller of Censorship to Col Werdmuller, Director of Recruiting, 30 June 1942.)
102. CGS Gp (2) G 1019/79A Box 645, Training Inspectorate Report on NMC, General Summary, East Rand Area, 13–19 March 1941.
103. NMC NAS 3/4/1 B 9 Box 1 DCS to Director of Recruiting, 5 December 1941; NMC NAS 3/4/1 B 2 Box 2, Lt Col R Fyfe King to DNEAS, 28 September 1942; NTS Box 9125 File 68/363/16, J. Simelane to Native Affairs Department, 26 August 1941.
104. DNEAS NAS 3/4/3 Box 5, B. W. Mcanyangwa to General Smuts, 29 January 1945; SAIRR Papers J. D. Rheinallt Jones Collection O. World War II Box 108, J. M. Thabakgale to J. D. Rheinallt Jones, 10 October 1941; NMC NAS 3/4/1 B 4 Box 2, J. H. Dugard, Inspector of Schools Engcobo to Director of Information, 25 July 1942; SAIRR Papers J. D. Rheinallt Jones Collection O. World War II Box 109, E. D. Shibambe to J. D. Rheinallt Jones, 6 August 1941; NTS Box 9260 File 16/371, Minutes of the 15th meeting of the Ciskei Missionary Council, 13 November 1940 and CAP, Department of Labour Files (ARB) Box 1730 File 1612/1/17/813, D. Mzinyali to Public Service Commission, 27 January 1947.
105. South African National Military History Museum. Library. E. T. Stubbs and H. S. Mockford, 'A Plan for the Development of Manpower, Bantu and NMC,' undated, pp. 48–51.
106. Ibid.
107. NMC NAS 3P/4/3 A 3 Box 3, H. G. Plaatje to J. C. Smuts, 16 July 1940.

8 The Second World War in Southern Cameroon and its Impact on Mission–State Relations, 1939–50

ANTHONY NDI

The Second World War threatened to be a major disaster for the British in Southern Cameroon.[1] The territory, officially a British Mandate of the League of Nations, presented some embarrassing features by 1939. Although an ex-German colony, German influence and not British transcended many facets of Cameroon colonial life.[2] Much of the commercial economy, particularly the cocoa, banana and rubber plantations and the import and export business remained in German hands. On the spiritual plane, all foreign nationals of the Basel Mission were either German or Swiss–Germans, as were all the German Baptist missionaries. A significant number of the Catholic missionaries were also German or Italian. German influence therefore was widespread. The British hold on Cameroon was light. Between the wars she played a minimum caretaker role and totally failed to create any serious economic, social, cultural or political impact on the territory or on its inhabitants. It is understandable therefore why the Administration became so nervous in 1939.

Before the war the British colonial administration never failed to demonstrate in every way its awareness at all times of its tenuous hold on the Mandated Territory. The administrative staff had been reduced in number,[3] hence the very heavy reliance on traditional rulers. The British colonial policy of indirect rule further estranged the colonial adminis-

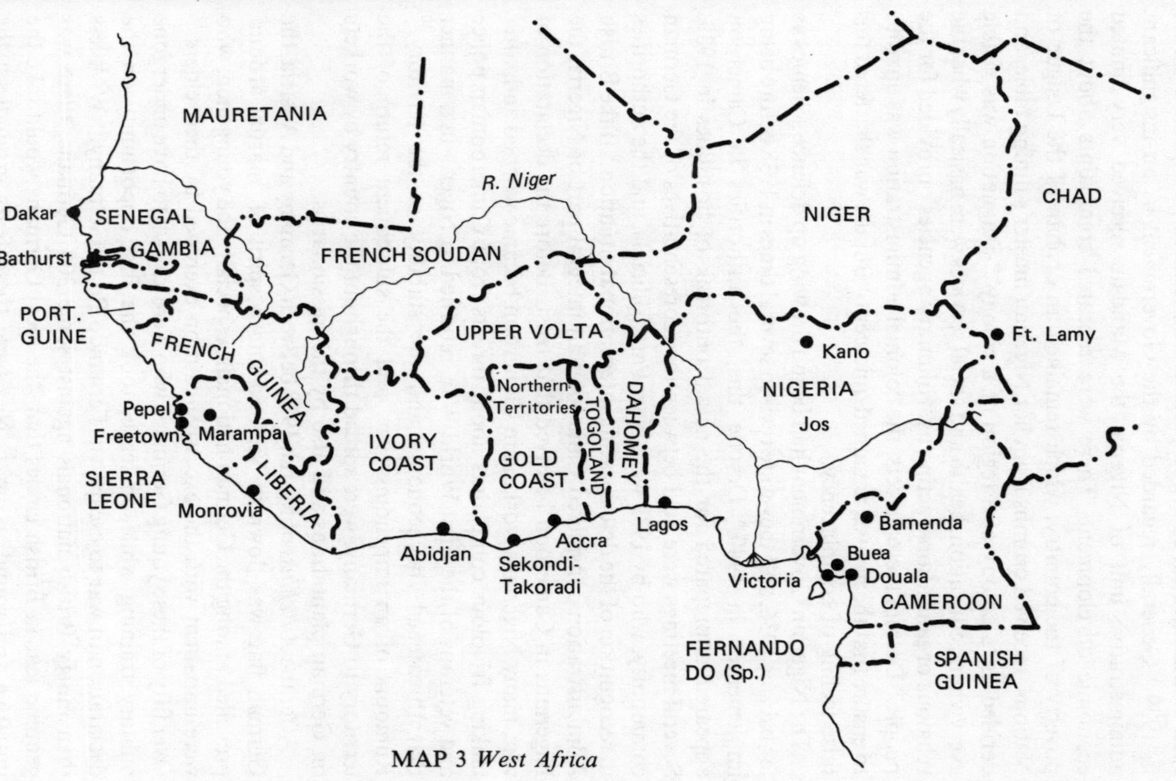

MAP 3 *West Africa*

trators from the people they claimed to be administering, while the new roles they assigned the traditional rulers caused resentment among their subjects. The infrastructure was basically what the Germans had left; road communications outside Victoria and Kumba were primitive even in 1939.[4] Generally regarded by the Government as an insignificant administrative unit of Nigeria, the Mandate received very limited economic development. There were repeated complaints about the poverty of the country, which remained an orphan of the League of Nations, received crumbs from her Nigerian master's dining table, and derided as 'a colony of a region of a colony'.[5] Stagnation was visible everywhere; education, health and social services were basically what the religious organisations, acting as 'voluntary agencies', provided for the people.[6] Despite these defects, the colonial administration was anxious to ensure that the natives remained quiescent.[7] But the war shattered this false feeling of complacency.

The Nigerian Government had begun drawing up defence schemes as far back as 1936, and they were revised several times in 1938 before being implemented in 1940.[8] Despite this, the authorities in Cameroon appeared unprepared for the actual outbreak of hostilities in 1939. Several meetings were held between the representatives of the German community, who by 1939 were Nazi Party officials, and the authorities in recognition of the deteriorating international situation.[9] If the British Administration considered Cameroon an integral part of Nigeria, the Nigerians in Cameroon betrayed that trust. Before the declaration of war, many Nigerians working in Cameroon became worried and, after making frivolous complaints about threats from Cameroonian police and veterans of the First World War, returned to Nigeria in a manner that threatened the economy and the stability of the territory.[10] Rumours of an impending war, and the subsequent return of the territory to Germany, were spread throughout the country by workers on German plantations and also by the missionaries.

After the *Anschluss* of March 1938 between Germany and Austria, the German flag was flown in Victoria and a spirit of 'martial ardour' prevailed among the German nationals, especially the young men, who were impatient with the excessive caution exercised by their elders.[11] Over fifty of these young Germans, who were known to have undergone military training while on leave, took the first opportunity on the declaration of war to escape via Fernando Po to Germany.[12] With less than ninety British nationals against some 300 Germans, there was genuine fear in British circles that 'the local Germans would take the initiative and round us up'.[13] Nor were these fears groundless: the

Germans were capable of much more that kept the British ill at ease. They possessed arms and ammunition far in excess of those normally required for self-defence and sporting activities, and were further alleged to be hoarding arms dumps along the creeks.[14] What largely restrained the Germans in Southern Cameroon was not fear of British security arrangements but a fundamental concern for their heavy investments in the plantations, which covered over 360 square miles, together with railways and rolling stock, light planes, dwellings and factories.[15]

At the outbreak of war the greatest threat to security in Cameroon came primarily from the manner in which the economy was managed. By 1925 the Germans had returned to recover their plantations, which had been forfeited during the First World War,[16] and they outnumbered the British. By the late 1930s the medium of a local Nazi Party hierarchy, at the head of which was Herr Luppe, appointed by the German Foreign Secretary. Nazi control over its members appeared total; their whole existence and operations were corporate and there was no means by which the Administration could isolate and deal with individual Germans. In Herr Luppe's own words, 'Every male German in the Cameroons with the exception of a few members of the various missions [was] a member of the NAZI Party'; and of his own authority he declared, 'As every German entering the organization undertakes the binding pledge to obey the Führer, I have full authority over all the members of the organization in Cameroons'.[17] This assertion was amply demonstrated at the various meetings and occasions over which he presided.[18]

Ernst Böhle, head of the Nazi party office dealing with Germans abroad, could hardly have made a better choice than Luppe to head the *Landesgruppe* in Cameroon. Shrewd, crafty, dogmatic in his goals and outwardly sincere, Luppe used his position to good effect. He pledged absolute loyalty and obedience to the British authorities on several occasions on behalf of his compatriots.[19] His ambition was to secure German ownership of the plantations which formed the backbone of the country's economy. Much of the technical manpower, capital, transport, and, even more strategically, a native labour force of over 25 000 was tied up in the Cameroon plantations.[20] German managerial skill was vital to the economy and it was from this strong position that the local Nazi leader subtly negotiated, virtually dictating, the terms of operation to the Government well into the thick of the war. Germans were treated with every courtesy and respect, an ironical situation in view of what was going on in Europe. In dealing with the Germans on the plantations, the British walked a real tightrope, for their very hold on the Mandated

Territory depended on how carefully they managed the planters, whose grip over the influential sector of the population was strong in every sense.[21]

On the other hand, four major considerations guided German attitudes in Cameroon and restrained them from taking a military option which was well within their reach. A first concern was to protect their plantations, which would have been sure targets in any hostilities. Secondly, was the unfounded allegation, probably propounded and circulated among the Germans by Herr Luppe himself and understandably encouraged by the British authorities, that a secret agreement existed between the British and German Governments by which Southern Cameroon would be returned to Germany regardless of the outcome of the war.[22] This idea, which was firmly held by Herr Luppe, stemmed from the belief that the issue of the ex-German colonies could only be settled in Europe or at the international level.[23] There was also great optimism among the Germans before the declaration of war that the British people were unlikely to take up arms against Germany. In Cameroon this manifested itself in the very harmonious and friendly relations between the two nationalities, an attitude that scared settlers in French Cameroon.[24] Lastly, all Germans were confident after hostilities had broken out that it was going to be a short war which Germany would win decisively.[25] Taking all these ideas into consideration, it would have been illogical for the Germans to do anything that would harm a territory whose fortunes they thought were inextricably bound up with their motherland.

Herr Luppe, a diplomat of sorts, ensured that his declarations of loyalty were usually double-edged, with something beneficial for Germany. With hindsight, it is now clear that his numerous meetings with the Administration after September 1939, at which he made these professions, were simply ploys to put the authorities off their guard, defuse tension and buy time while waiting for German victory.[26] However, as the war became protracted and ultimate German victory elusive, he resorted to mild threats. When the British authorities decided to cut down the number of Germans on the plantations to the barest necessary for full production, Herr Luppe suggested 30 per cent of the existing staff would be adequate.[27] But, even from this shaky position, he demanded that the British authorities should give a firm undertaking that they would never afterwards change their mind or withdraw the proposition, otherwise, he threatened, all the planters would pull out at once.[28] Had this perpetuity clause been endorsed, the Germans would have claimed legal possession of the plantations *ad infinitum*. For the time being, and until the British had secured substitutes from Jamaica to replace the planters, they continued to defer to Herr Luppe's blackmail.

Before the outbreak of war intelligence reports repeatedly indicated that the Germans were carrying out subversive activities. Herr Luppe was said to be transmitting secret information to Germany, to this the Administration continued to turn a blind eye in the hope of the greater advantage derived from maintaining the Germans on the plantations.[29] German nationals were also able openly to despatch code and cipher messages through government wireless and telegraph, a situation Brigadier D.P. Dickenson described as 'dangerous in view of the worsening international situation'.[30] Until Herr Luppe was caught outright, British officials tended to disregard negative reports about Germans.[31] Reporting to Berlin through the German consulate at Fernando Po in October 1939, Luppe made some striking disclosures. He observed with some satisfaction, the success made by the Germans in Southen Cameroon and boasted of:

> The impression on the natives that we are still here and that up till today business still continues to function is already constructed as an amazing success which will be for the greatness of Mighty Germany . . . Pictures of the Führer hang everywhere and everybody greets the other with 'Heil Hitler'.[32]

He concluded by describing Southern Cameroon as 'Your Cameroon'. This was the other side of Herr Luppe, which was unknown to many British officials.[33] As a result of the German victories in Europe in 1940 Germans in the Cameroon spoke openly about the colony being returned to the Reich and blatantly defied Government authority in direct contravention of the paroles they had signed.[34] But up to this point the Administration still felt constrained in dealing with the Germans, arguing that 'Hitler's portraits [did] no harm and to remove them would cause unnecessary irritation'.[35] Even after Herr Luppe had been caught red-handed with alarming disclosures and there was no alternative but to intern him, the authorities still dreaded the consequences of such an action on the planters. Surprisingly, he himself urged the deputy Nazi leaders to continue to cooperate with the British authorities.[36] Evidently the plantations were as dear to the Germans as they were invaluable to the British colonial administration, and, despite the fact that hands had been laid on their leader, the planters submitted to the Administration's bluff, though with bad grace.[37] It was this dualism of the plantations that settled the fate of Southern Cameroon and saved it from open hostilities.

The authorities regarded the internment of Herr Luppe, without any revolt or even 'passive resistance' from the Germans, as a great achievement, and Captain Denton, the Resident, declared with relief, 'it seemed . . . a challenge that we had got to meet sooner or later, the point at issue being: [were] the plantations to be run by Government or by favour of the Nazi Party?'[38] This achievement increased the self-confidence of the authorities,[39] and with the mounting bitterness of the war in Europe this invidious situation 'became harder to bear even for the most level headed'.[40] The Germans were told point-blank that Government would henceforth deal directly with individual planters and no longer through the Nazi Party. When planters resisted the authority of Mr Longe, the Supervisor of Plantations, appointed by the Custodian of Enemy Property, the decision was taken in June 1940 to intern all the Germans on the plantations, and officers were brought in from Nigeria to replace them.[41] This too was carried out without any immediate repercussions, perhaps because it was planned and executed with great precision.[42] However, it also resulted in large-scale lay-offs of labour, and to an increase in crime in the plantation villages as some of the unemployed 'preyed on innocent citizens'.[43] The only enemy aliens now at liberty in the country were the German and Italian missionaries and also German-speaking Swiss, who were often regarded with suspicion.

On the whole, the prosecution of the Second World War appears never to have elicited popular support among the people of Southern Cameroon, partly as a result of resilient German propaganda, but mostly because of the nature of British administration, which had never been inspiring. This was reflected in the poor response to recruitment and in the general attitude of the people towards the war.

With an estimated population of over 400 000, barely 3500 Cameroonians enlisted as soldiers.[44] The German plantations, which employed over 25 000 workers, were a more attractive alternative to military service. Both the army and the plantations basically required similar men. The basic qualities required by the army were that recruits should reach the prescribed age and standard was that he 'be a farm labourer, agriculturalist or hunter; used to an outdoor life and able to march barefooted'.[45] The initial recruiting drive was met with enthusiasm but as the war progressed the numbers dropped drastically. Recruitment of artisans and literaes remained poor throughout the war because of the slightly higher qualifications and the scarcity of institutions where such candidates could be trained in Southern Cameroon.[46] This factor became a source of great frustration and unrest after demobilisation, when many of the ex-servicemen could not find employment and better qualified men were imported from Nigeria to work on the plantation.[47] Senior non-commissioned ranks attained on the battlefield without basic educational qualifications raised high hopes of employment and of social status not easily obtained within civil structures and institutions.

Reviewing the recruitment situation well into the middle of the war, the Resident, Mr A. M. Muir, opposed the introduction of conscription in Cameroon, explaining that, of a gang of Cameroonians carefully recruited over night, there was always sure to be some 10 per cent missing in the morning:

> . . . and when we come to mobilize a reserve we should have to deal, not only with those who thought it dangerous and unpleasant to take part in any military operations, but with men who had no special aversion . . . only who thought they would come later on, as there was a new farm to be cleared or house to be built or their wife had had a baby. There would also be many who had left their villages after registration and could not be found.[48]

He considered registration as a necessary part of planning, but thought that 'any plan which counted on mobilisation according to schedule in Cameroons would be unreliable'. Cameroonians, he observed, were 'loyal', devoted and hardworking people but it was pointless asking them to register to fight in a war which they were told no longer threatened their country. Mr Muir considered it dangerous to introduce conscription in Cameroon

> . . . where the people have had the opportunity of comparing British and German administration, and find the salient feature of our rule, as compared with the German is the absence of compulsion. That is the difference we have emphasised, and which has counted much in our favour.[49]

Introducing conscription, Muir argued, would strike the natives as either a revolutionary alteration of policy or that the British were in desperate straits, and that there was 'little to choose between British and German masters'. He could also have added that the Administration was overstretched and that the Native Authorities were wholly incompetent to enforce conscription. The defect therefore lay more in the manner in which the people were administered than in alleged inherent tendencies. As the end of the war approached, 'several' Cameroonians deserted the army and could not be traced.[50] Cameroon soldiers also established a reputation as brave and courageous fighters on the battlefield, just as they were renowned ringleaders in disturbances in various parts of Nigeria.[51] On leave, and eventually when demobilised, they gained a notoriety throughout the country for their lawlessness in the local markets and bars.[52]

But the soldiers had many good qualities. For example, as a result of the correspondence encouraged by the Administration to raise the morale of the Cameroon soldiers fighting overseas,[53] they responded by contributing many useful ideas and even significant portions of their meagre savings towards post-war development projects in the country. Some saw themselves as 'the bright genii' and promised to 'come back to our homeland with experiences in foreign lands to start the construction of our Postwar Plan'.[54] Generally, their correspondence bore the impression of a global concern, since they saw Cameroon as a national unit, an attitude which found fulfilment in the parades they organised after demobilisation all over the country and which aided the rise of nationalism. In reply to a letter from the Resident, one soldier emphasised:

> Now that plans are being laid down for the development in the near future, I would like to call your attention to the idea of a *UNITED CAMEROON UNDER ONE RULE*. Though it is not a problem for the Resident to solve . . . it is worth saying something about. In comparison with the West African colonies, this country is still crawling in its infancy and illiteracy.[5]

The reasons he advanced for this state of affairs included the earlier partition of the territory, which led to changes of colonial masters, policies and boundaries that separated 'tribes and even relatives'. He concluded: 'The whole world is eagerly awaiting a new and better world to emerge after the war. I, as well as every fighting man and civilian of this country lay hopes for a better united Cameroons . . . after the war'.[56]

Hopes such as these, encouraged variously by the military authorities, the Colonial Administration and by programmes initiated by the Colonial Development and Welfare Acts, ended up inflicting great frustration and bitterness on the soldiers and civilians alike. Many of the pronouncements were simply propaganda and most of the programmes never evolved beyond the planning stage.[57]

Barely three years after the war the administration was concerned about the danger of subversive political activity among the ex-servicemen.[58] As the confidential report on Resettlement of Ex-servicemen in Cameroons Province commented in 1948: 'Ex-servicemen who have travelled abroad bring to the native communities acquired knowledge, breadth of mind, enterprise and initiative. . . . They form a useful nucleus in the rural communities of which the population mainly consists'.[59] In practical terms, they set up social standards for everything: dresses, dances, houses, the opening and building of schools, and organising cultural and welfare societies, which became springboards not only for socio-economic development but for political activity.[60] In the struggle for independence and re-unification of Cameroon, the Kamerun Exservicemen's National Union (KENU) played a notable part in the campaigns. They violently opposed integration with Nigeria, which was described as a 'devouring lion'. They further suggested that Cameroon receive a federal constitution and that a permanent seat be reserved in the legislature for ex-servicemen.[61]

It deserves to be stressed that both military and civilian colonial authorities took great pains to rehabilitate and secure employment of ex-servicemen. Demobilisation in Southern Cameroon proceeded without a hitch from the port of Victoria to the furthest post of dismissal in Bamenda.[62] Ex-servicemen were given priority for employment where openings existed, with attractive conditions of pay and promotion. Loan schemes and training facilities were arranged for those who seriously wanted to take up farming.[63] Quite often it was the general scarcity of jobs and, in particular, ex-soldiers' lack of pertinent qualifications, disdain for manual labour and apathy for civilian control, that was responsible for the massive unemployment among the veterans. Many found gainful employment in the Cameroon Development Corporation (CDC) plantations (established in 1947), with the Public Works Department, and as messengers in offices.[64]

Economic stagnation under British rule in the interwar years brought into sharp focus for many people the advantages of German colonial days, which now became in a sense the 'golden age of Cameroon'. This view was clearly enunciated and emphasised by the Chief Secretary to the Government, Lagos, in 1940, when he pointed out that 'there (was) a growing desire among the natives for the Germans to come to the colonies' because they believed 'in the alleged generosity of the Germans, better trade and better opportunities for the average native'. Even more significantly, he argued that 'no amount of expressed or implied loyalty to the British Government [would] undermine the growing convictions of better days which the natives believed they saw when they were in contact with the Germans'.[65] Abstract arguments about the just cause of the Allies and the unwarranted aggression of the Germans were immaterial to the average Cameroonian faced with privations that only worsened as the war progressed. Barely one year after the expulsion of the Germans from the plantations they were virtually closed down for lack of markets and shipping facilities. However, some 20 000 workers were thrown off, with untold consequences. Crime in the adjoining towns and villages rose to unprecedented proportions, resulting in numerous court cases, which consumed the valuable time of the skeletal administrative staff.[66] Prices soared, imported goods disappeared and basic necessities such as salt and soap were in short supply.[67] Cameroonians resorted to ancient methods of producing these commodities and, when the value of money further deteriorated, they reverted to trade by barter.[68] Later on in the war they were asked to produce wild rubber, and quite often, as with recruitment, the Native Authorities employed force. People in the Bamenda grasslands were known to trek eight days to and from their homes in the futile search for wild rubber.[69] Yet in addition to all this they were required to contribute 'generously' towards the 'Win the War Fund'. Large sums, relatively speaking, were raised but this was more out of fear, war weariness or compulsion and could not be taken to indicate native approval of the war.[79]

These measures could not have been calculated to make British rule in Cameroon any more attractive, and it is in this light that the offer by scores of Cameroonian veterans of the First World War to serve in the German army, toasts to the Führer at parties, the singing of the German national anthem, celebrations in honour of German victories in Europe, and other such 'treasonable' acts by prominent Cameroonians, can best be assessed.[71] The Chief Secretary, summarising the situation to June 1940, feared that 'if by any means the Germans were to come here . . . and try to take this place, I doubt what chances we have of gaining the cooperation of the natives'.[72] This was an accurate assessment of much native sentiment and could not be classified merely as an exaggeration of the real situation.[73] In fact, the apathy only heightened with the progress of the war. Although in its chequered history Cameroon went through only 30 years of German rule and over 45 of Anglo-Nigerian administration, the British Mandate period was also overwhelmingly dominated by German influence, though without legal title. Consequently, German influence sank deeper into the people, for it was these memories that were conjured up and became beacons for re-unification at independence in 1961.[74]

As early as 1939 the British Government decided to set up a Ministry of Information with the major objective of counteracting German propaganda, emphasising the ethical aspect of the war and projecting Britain as the champion of weak nations.[75] But little was done in Cameroon and, faced with German activity in Mamfe, the Divisional Officer, while requesting the internment of all Germans, warned that. 'After hostilities the next most powerful weapon against us is propaganda'.[76] German propaganda might lead to a 'native' revolt, which the administration dreaded even more than a German rising, because it could have unpredictable repercussions. With only one battalion (of 165 soldiers) and less than 200 policemen for the entire territory of 16 000 square miles of difficult terrain, at the best of times the administration was ill-equipped to handle any such situation.[77] Eventually the propaganda offensive was set up, with reading rooms organised in the major towns, where literature about the war was made available and talks and films shown.[78] Occasions for the 'Comforts Fund' and 'War Relief Week' were used to educate the people about the war. To raise the flagging loyalty of Cameroonians to the Union Jack it was arranged, for the first time ever, that the Governor of Nigeria should tour Cameroon in 1943 and 1944.[79] When suggestions were made to erect a war memorial for the dead of both world wars in Nigeria, a strong case was made for Nsanakang near Mamfe, 'the only part of the Colony and Protectorate where Empire troops have fallen in action'; the next site chosen was Victoria, also in Cameroon.[80]

Of the structures set up by the British Government to cater for post-war socio-economic and political development, the Colonial Development and Welfare Act of 1940, through its Development Committees, affected Cameroon in a profound way. Mr P. G. Harris, the Resident, was led, with good reason, to describe the inauguration of the Development Committee at Buea in 1944 as, 'the greatest thing that had ever happened to "sleepy southern Cameroons"'.[81] It was this committee that made a strong case for the Nigerian Government to acquire the German plantations, the backbone of the Cameroon economy, which had been virtually closed down, resulting in 'a most depressing effect on the morale of African and European employees'.[82] The plantations were bought up, consolidated, and became the Cameroon Development Corporation (CDC) in 1947, which has since then continued to boost the country's economy. With the assistance of the Colonial Development and Welfare Fund, some major roads were constructed, educational and agricultural institutions were set up, and sociological and anthropological studies essential for development were undertaken.[83] In 1944 Sir Arthur Richards made constitutional and political proposals that marked the first stages towards self-government for Nigeria, and hence Cameroon, for they accelerated nationalist sentiments which had been stimulated by the war. But the greatest significance of these post-war schemes lies in the fact that they helped stimulate an interest in nationalism and increasing demands for independence.

The political frontiers instituted by the British and French colonial masters in 1919 ignored the ethnic and geographical topography of Cameroon. A significant number of Southern Cameroonian soldiers, as well as several thousand workers on the German plantations, crossed into the British Mandate from French Cameroon.[84] But the warm relations that had existed between the colonial administrations of these sister territories froze and came to border on hatred with the approach of the war. In the French Cameroon the authorities were thoroughly disgusted with the scandalous latitude given to the Germans in British Cameroon.[85] Their official complaints that arms were being dumped from German ships at various points along the British Cameroon coast were dismissed by the British authorities as the traditional French anxiety and nervousness when Germans were concerned.[86] Actually, until an understanding had been reached between both administrations, the French officials considered 'British Cameroon to be occupied by a hostile power', fully in collusion with the Germans.[87]

Indeed, the French Cameroon authorities had good reason to be alarmed. Unlike the British, thousands of Frenchmen had taken up permanent residence in French Cameroon, investing heavily to buy out the German plantations.[8] Again, unlike British Cameroon, French Cameroon both in defence and civil matters was administered largely independently of Paris. Its military defences, as testified by Captain I. W. Wight, were very solid,[89] one reason why it was able to defy Vichy France and be among the first African colonies to be visited by General de Gaulle in his campaign for Free France. Hatred for the Germans was intense among many French settlers.[90] The German arms build-up and the way in which they fraternised with the British in British Cameroon led to French fears that they intended to stage a coup in Douala, from their stronghold across the border.[91] French Cameroon offers of military assistance to the British Cameroon authorities were initially treated with scorn, but as things got worse, Captain Wright was despatched from Nigeria to investigate the possibilities of collaboration with them. After the French defeat in mid-1940, it was the turn of the British military authorities in Nigeria to panic about an invasion from French Cameroon when Marshal Pétain declared for Germany.[92] However, after several meetings between the military and civilian authorities of both sides, an understanding was reached. For the rest of the war they worked in perfect harmony, exchanging military secrets and personnel; the French Cameroon military authorities even established military posts on British Cameroon soil, while a British naval control unit operated at Douala.[93]

Difficult as it had been handling Nazi sympathisers on the plantations, the British, for quite different reasons, found it was incomparably more delicate dealing with the enemy alien missionaries, who numbered about fifty in the territory. Most of them were clearly irreproachable characters and belonged to powerful international missionary organisations ready to defend their members to the last. In 1939 there were some 80 000 adherents of all categories attending the churches besides the several thousand children who benefited from the mission schools, maternity homes, clinics and child welfare centres. These were led by nearly 1000 helpers, mostly schoolteachers, catechists, pastors and evangelists, who were generally fervent followers and zealous propagandists for the missions. Any action taken against the missionaries had to be balanced against its impact on all these people and institutions. Originally it had been decided not to lay hands on the missionaries who were enemy aliens. They were merely required to sign 'a declaration of good behaviour and willingness to obey the orders of the government', and internment was not contemplated except for a breach of parole.[94] But decisions in Cameroon necessarily reflected the fortunes of the war in Europe, and when, in 1940, the Allies suffered major reverses, the aliens' situation had to be reviewed.

In dealing with the missionaries the Government was guided by certain factors, generally precedents from the First World War. In Southern Cameroon the missions were serious partners with the Government in development. This was a cardinal consideration in dealing with the missionaries. After the First World War, as a result of the expulsion of Germany missionaries (1916–25), the Government was faced with what they described as 'Political Ethiopianism' among Christians who yearned for the return of the missionaries.[95] This movement was strong enough to threaten the British hold on the territory and, because British missionary substitutes could not be found, the Germans were eventually permitted to return in 1925, firstly, to restore order among their followers, and, secondly, to restart the invaluable educational and medical services that had been arrested by the war. Consequently, in 1939, it was agreed through the International Missionary Council that if missionaries were expelled, adequate arrangements would be made to ensure that there were replacements to keep their work going so as to avoid international criticism and threats of revolts. But there were also bitter experiences of German missionaries who were paid money to subvert British authority through adverse propaganda, and of others who were directly engaged in sabotage during the First World War.[96]

Of the three main religious denominations in the territory, Baptist, Lutheran (Basel) and Catholic, the latter two had traditions of conflict with the Government. Originally it was the Baptist Missionary Society that had opened up southern Cameroon to serious European influence and, eventually, to an attempted British annexation in 1884. It was Alfred Saker, a British Baptist missionary who founded Victoria in 1858, and who for 22 years operated a Baptist theocracy there, with the chief missionary performing the functions of a governor.[97] Church and State were identical. In 1886 the British surrendered 'Victoria Colony' to the Germans, the London Missionary Society 'handed over'[98] to the Basel Mission, and Baptist influence also diminished, until revived after the First World War. It was the Basel Mission (BM) which came to wield enormous religious and political authority, as it was originally recruited by the German Government as a 'Colonial State Church' with a commission to project 'mission–nationalistic' policies.[99] Logically it would have been expected that the 'German' Basel Mission and the German Colonial Government would work hand in glove, but within the first decade serious disagreements set in. The Basel Mission violently objected to Government expropriation of native lands around Buea and defied its ruling that only the German language should be used in schools and churches.[100] By the outbreak of the First World War, state and church were operating at great variance, with an increasing tendency for the government to favour the Catholics, who had been kept out of Cameroon until 1890 because of Basel Mission opposition.[101] However, between the two world wars, the Basel Mission cooperated fully with the British administration, which had supplanted the Germans in 1916.

Paradoxically, it was from the Mill Hill Fathers of London, a British Catholic missionary organisation invited into Cameroon by the British colonial administration in 1922, after the expulsion of all German missionaries in 1915, that the British administration faced its greatest opposition between the wars. Attempts to get the Church Missionary Society and the Church of Scotland to replace the German Baptist and Basel missions failed.[102] The Hill Mill missionaries were therefore received in the great hope of *cujus regio, ejus religio*, and the fullest collaboration was expected between church and state. This indeed happened until 1925 when relations turned sour and were replaced by mounting hostility and recriminations.

The cause of the conflicts between the Catholic Mill Hill Fathers and the Government deserves further probing, because it illustrates how the exigencies of the Second World War helped to forge cordial relations between them, and also because the Catholics emerged as the most enduring mission body during the war. The Mill Hill missionaries, comprising British, as well as Irish, Dutch, German, Italian and Austrian nationals, were British only in name but widely international in character. In general they were also mostly youthful, inexperienced and totally out of sympathy with the British colonial policy of indirect rule.

Indirect rule, or 'Native Administration', was directly derived from Lugard's method in Northern Nigeria of governing through their 'Emirs' and 'Sultans', the equivalent of Chiefs and *Fons* in southern Cameroon. But Southern Cameroon, unlike feudal Northern Nigeria, presented striking peculiarities. The autocratic, semi-divine Bamenda *Fons* contrasted irrevocably with the acephalous, highly conciliar and more democratic politics of the forest zone. Despite this, the bigoted British administration, short-staffed and financially handicapped, was determined to see the system work, regardless of the vast tribal differences throughout the territory. Consequently it strove to uphold the power and authority of all types of chiefs and installed puppet ones where they did not formerly exist.[103]

Furthermore, the institution of chieftaincy, especially in Bamenda and parts of Mamfe, displayed certain features which were total anathema to the Catholic priests and their converts. For example, polygamy was its hallmark and the *Fons* exercised authority through secret fraternities and cults that the missionaries broadly regarded as the work of the devil. Intent that indirect rule should succeed, the administration conferred enormous powers, traditionally unknown, on the *Fons*, Village Heads and District Heads. In their capacities as Native Authorities and Presidents of Native Courts, they administered justice and local government in all their entirety.

This situation was exacerbated by the Mill Hill missionaries establishing mission settlements that their converts used as fortresses, and from them, acting as states within a state, scorned all traditional norms. They flagrantly defied the authority of the chiefs and administrative officers in the name of Christianity, which they saw as a liberating force from traditional supervision. The Native Authorities, wielding extensive political and judicial powers and backed by the administration, openly harassed the converts through the Native Courts and Village Councils. It was thus that the priests in supporting their followers collided head on with the administration.

The climax of these hostilities was reached in 1930. The Government threatened the Mill Hill missionaries with expulsion,[104] accusing them of brazen interference in the Native Courts, an utter disregard for the Native Authorities, brutal missionary methods, and the administration of corporal punishment for sexual offences.[105] Although conflict between the Mill Hill missionaries and the Government was reduced after a Concordat was agreed in October 1931, real harmonious relations only came in the wake of the Second World War. Reports in the late 1930s criticised the system of Native Administration and suggested reforms but the Second World War prevented their introduction, and British administrative and economic policies were further discredited. Ironically, during the war and thereafter, the Catholic mission emerged as the most enduring missionary body, providing vital educational, medical and social welfare services for the territory which even the Government could not afford.

On the whole, the Second World War hit the missions at a very crucial stage in their development and totally shattered all their plans and hopes for future expansion.[106] Government and missions cooperated in a symbiotic relation in which the latter acted as 'voluntary agencies', providing valuable educational and medical services complete with personnel and infrastructure while Government paid them with 'grants-in-aid'. Increasingly Government surrendered these functions to the missions,[107] and, while it got cheap services, the missionaries reaped souls.

Besides the Catholics, the Protestant missions also made great progress before the war. The Basel Mission, which resumed its work in 1925 with four members,[108] by 1936 already had forty-four missionaries and 27 000 members, and ran fifteen recognised primary schools with 6000 children.[109] Between 1927 and 1935 the German Baptist Mission (Neuroppin) and the Cameroon Baptist Mission (USA) took possession of their former stations, and by 1940 had ten missionaries in the field, some 6000 followers and five primary schools.[110] Including the forty-six Catholic priests and nine nuns, there were in all over 100 foreign missionaries scattered over southern Cameroon when war broke out in 1939.

Confidential reports indicated that further delays with interning enemy alien missionaries could lead to greater complications. There had been vague suspicions that Basel missionaries had Nazi sympathies, but the relevation was made by the Nazi leader himself. In a secret letter to Berlin, that was intercepted, Herr Luppe declared: 'I consider it most desirable that the missions which extend over the whole Cameroon should continue to work. I drawn attention to the fact that the leader of the Basel mission is the referee of the local Nazi organization'.[111] In soliciting financial assistance for the Basel Mission, 'since within there [was] a certain reliable recruitment which [was] of great value', he requested the German Government to 'address itself . . . immediately', to the Mission Directorate at Basel. These were indictments that gave rise to serious doubts about the missionary activities of the Basel Mission and later to a decision to prohibit the admission of Swiss missionaries and even for the proscription of the Basel Mission altogether.[112] There were equally damaging reports about the German Baptist missionaries, and their situation was further worsened by disunity among themselves and with the Cameroon Baptist Mission (USA).[113] One of the missionaries had served for 12 years in the 'New German Army' and risen to the rank of sergeant-major, and behaved very suspiciously,[114] while the Principal Missionary was described as a man of 'great immoralty'.[115] Thus the only group of enemy alien missionaries wholly absolved of Nazi sympathies were the Catholic priests, and their internment was an agonising decision.[116]

Eventually, instructions were received 'to intern all enemy missionaries except nuns'.[117] In effect this meant all but four of the Basel missionaries and all but three of the Baptist missionaries.[118] The Catholic mission lost only seven of its missionaries, and, already beginning from a vantage position, it came to have an edge over its rivals. The internees were taken first to Umuahia in Nigeria and eventually to Jamaica, where they remained for the duration of the war. Great care was taken throughout the whole process to minimise inconvenience so as not to provoke adverse international propaganda. On the contrary, unlike the First World War, many missionaries expressed gratitude to the British authorities for their kindness.[119]

In the circumstances, even given the large number of African helpers, four Basel and three Baptist missionaries without funds could barely keep the institutions alive. The dislocation was so severe initially that futile attempts were made to bring back some of the German missionaries. Catholic missionary activity, on the other hand, with only seven of their men removed, was the least disturbed. In fact, only two of their major mission stations were temporarily deprived of priests.[120] It is therefore not surprising that the Catholics made great strides during the war, and that their relations with the Native Authorities and consequently with the Government were finally improved and fully stabilised. The effect of the war was such that not a single brush with the missionaries and their zealous followers was reported anywhere. For the authorities their greatest anxiety was about the conclusion of the war and the development which was being offered by the missions, especially the Catholic mission.[121]

As pointed out earlier, the relations between the missions as a whole and the Government were born out of mutual self-interest and necessity. To the Government the missions were a cheap and easy means of development, while the missionaries merely sought an atmosphere in which they could pursue their three-fold mission of evangelising, educating and healing the people. Bishop Peter Rogan humorously put it in a circular to his priests in 1942, that '"as trade follows the flag" so schools, colleges, training centres, seminaries and novitiates follow the fortunes of the vicariate'.[122] It was a policy statement, and he achieved all these objectives, and more, for the Catholic mission during the hard times between 1939 and 1947. Government dependence on mission education was so overwhelming that it came under severe criticism at the United Nations Trusteeship Council.[123]

Right at the beginning of the war, when there was much retrenchment, the Catholic mission dared the unthinkable by opening the first secondary school in the country, a feat the Government was never able to perform throughout the colonial period.[124] In 1944 and again in 1947, when the effects of the war were still being felt, the mission opened two teachers' colleges, the first for men and the second for women, in response to the swelling primary school population.[125] As far as education and medical service went, the missions, especially the Catholic mission, led the Government from the Second World War until independence. Government appreciation and concern was expressed in several ways. When instructed to intern all enemy missionaries in August 1940, the Resident made a strong case in favour of retaining some German priests, not only because they were anti-Nazi but because they were valuable science teachers at the Catholic, and only secondary, school in Cameroon.[126] Very much the same thing happened with nine Catholic nuns, who, being Tyrolese with Italian passports, were enemy aliens and should ordinarily have been interned.[127] But they were permitted to stay largely because there were no substitutes for the selfless services they performed in child welfare, midwifery, health care and domestic science. Mr Harris, the Resident, fought a personal crusade for their total liberation during the war in recognition of this fact.[128] These services revealed the missions as visible agencies of development, even to the traditional rulers, at a time when all that people wanted was 'development'. The deaths of three missionaries during the war years were lamented as 'national' losses.[129] Cooperation between the chiefs and the missionaries in setting up schools and clinics brought about greater understanding and largely defused tension. In yet another dimension the missions were the easiest medium during the war through which Government could issue important instructions and distribute scarce commodities such as salt, potatoes and various seeds, to the people.[130] Such were the astonishing improvements in relations, especially between the Catholic mission and the Native Authorities, that in 1946 Mr A. F. Bridges, the Resident, reported 'cordial relations' where there had been incessant conflicts 15 years earlier.[131] Of Bamenda, the seat of these hostilities, Mr Brayne-Baker was very impressed to note further in 1952, that:

> Good relations between the Mission and the people including Chiefs have now been established in a way that could hardly have been anticipated twenty years ago . . . due to gratitude for real benefits that have been brought by the tireless work of the missions in the education and medical fields.[132]

As the war drew to a close, there was a sense of urgency everywhere, in the words of the Resident, 'to make up for the stagnation of the inter-war years'.[133] Workers from the plantations, demobilised soldiers, traders and graduates from the mission schools infiltrated society with new and disturbing ideas and fashions that rocked the traditional *status quo* which the British had struggled to preserve, while the missions complained about loose morals.[134] But these were merely the birth-pangs of political, social, educational and economic ferment that gripped the country as a consequence of the war. In 1947, right at its birth, the CDC workers organised a paralysing strike, the first in the territory's history, and a constitutional conference at Mamfe in 1949 resulted in an 'uncompromising demand for regional autonomy for Southern Cameroon'.[135]

The recovery of the missions was phenomenal. Even before the end of the war the Basel Mission had opened new schools, a teacher training college and, in 1949, the second secondary school in the territory.[136] The Cameroon Baptist Mission (USA) fully supplanted the German Baptist Mission with five new missionaries who took up their functions with great zeal. The Catholics progressed from strength to strength, while the Government surrendered more of its institutions to the missions and took up more of a supervisory role. Education was identified as the key to all progress, and by 1950, besides the various teacher training centres and secondary schools, a Technical College, Nursing School and Agricultural Centre were opened and the CDC began awarding scholarships for further studies. There were over 30 000 children in 400 primary schools. But the spirit of restlessness provoked by the war led to insatiable demands for more educational establishments and for faster economic and political development that were not even arrested by re-unification and independence 11 years late in 1961.

NOTES

ABBREVIATIONS

AR	Annual Report
BA	Buea Archives
DO	Divisional Officer
NC/NA	Native Court/Native Authority
SEP	Secretary Eastern Province
SEO	Senior Educational Officer
SSP	Senior Superintendent of Police

1. It was formerly part of the German colony of Kamerun occupied by Germany after 1884. After the defeat and expulsion of the Germans in 1916, Kamerun was provisionally partitioned between Britain and France. Britain's share (one-fifth) was further broken into British Northern Cameroons, administered as part of Northern Nigeria, and British Southern Cameroons, administered as part of Eastern Nigeria (1916–54). The various portions were administered as Mandates of the League of Nations from 1922 to 1946.
2. See Victor T. Levine, *The Cameroons from Mandate to Independence* (Los Angeles, 1964), p. 38.
3. There were repeated complaints about the inadequate staff from 1916 right through to 1961. *Annual Report*, 1947, BA Ba (1947) 4.
4. The Colonial Development and Welfare fund grant of £35,000 for the Mamfe–Kumba road was made in 1942, and the construction was completed in 1947. See Cameroons *Annual Report* for 1943, para. 519. Also, L. E. Vine, *The Cameroons*, pp. 25–36.
5. This became critical in 1948 with the rise of nationalism and the demand for provincial status for Bamenda. Ba (1948) 2nd *Annual Report*, 1948 by A. F. Bridges. See also, Edwin Ardner, 'The Kamerun Idea', in Claude E. Welch (ed.), *Dream of Unity*, (Ithaca, 1966), p. 161.
6. The Resident, A. F. Bridges, complained bitterly of British neglect of Cameroon in interwar years. Britain was severely criticised more publicly too. See, *Examination* of 1947 AR by Trusteeship Council, 4th Session, 27.1.49 BA Ba/1947/4.
7. The British posed throughout as the upholders of the traditional and cultural values of the people through the NAs and NCs. See also, Bamenda

Improvement Association's *petition* to Trusteeship Council, 24.10.49, Td 1949/2.

8. For example, G. C. Whiteley, Chief Commissioner to Chief Sec. 'Nigeria Defence Scheme: Internment', BA S 2/1938 vol. I Pa(1938)2.
9. Resident, Cameroons Prov. to Chief Sec. forwarding *minutes* of meeting with Senior Reps. of the German Community held at Buea 29 September 1938. BA S2 (1938) 162. Secret. Several of such meetings were held.
10. *Memo* from DO Victoria to Resident of 8.5.39 expresses anxiety of Nigerian nationals about their future. BA No. C73/1939/53 'Confidential'. Also, *Telegram* No. X/10/11 from Supt of Police, Buea, to Comm of Police, Lagos – Nigerian allegations unfounded, dated 20.6.39. See, also *AR*, 1940 by A. E. F. Murray, 1940, for effects of Nigerian withdrawals on economy.
11. W. E. Hunt, Officer administering the Govt, Lagos, to the Rt Hon Malcolm MacDonald, Sec of State for Colonies – *Reports on Situation in Cameroons*, dated 10.8.38. BA Pa(1938)2 S2/1938/vol. I. Also, Sanford H. Bederman, *The Cameroons Development Corporation*, (Cameroon, Bota-West, and London, Brown and Knight Ltd, 1968), p. 16. See also, Resident to Chief Sec of 10.5.38. BA S2/1938/3.
12. A. E. F. Murray, Notes for Cameroons Provincial *Report*, 1939. Fifty-two young Germans escaped with two motor barges to Fernando Po en route to Germany.
13. 'Secret', from DO Kumba to Resident, Sealy-King, of 2.9.38. BA S2/1938/5. Also, Sealy King to SSP Lagos, 26.9.38. BA S2/1938/93.
14. Resident, O. W. Firth to CSG, Lagos: 'Activities of Germans in British Cameroons', 30.6.38. BA P/100/9 secret. S2/1938/5. The Germans owned 56 revolvers, 144 rifles and 60 shot guns. From December 1937 to August 1938 there were 41 000 rounds of various ammunition imported by them. Supt of Police to Resident, 419/38. BA S2/1938/5.
15. Bederman, op. cit., pp. 13–19; Supt of Police to Resident, Inventory of German registered vehicles, arms, marine craft, etc., No. 4/935. BA S2/1938/5.
16. Supt of Police, ibid. Of the 264 000 acres advertised by Britain, the Germans bought back 207 000 acres and in 1938 there were 285 Germans to 86 British nationals. Le Vine, op.cit., pp. 121–5.
17. A lengthy exposition to the Resident about the Nazi Party in Cameroon–Calabar by Herr G. Luppe, dated 20.6.39. BA S2/vol. II/38 Pa/1939/3.
18. Herr Luppe held great sway over the planters, e.g. meeting at Ikone. See Memo from Supt of Police, Victoria, to the Comm. Police H/Q, Lagos, 17.6.39, No. V2/29 BA S2/vol. II/38 Pa(1939)3.
19. Herr Luppe, dated 20.6.39 to Resident. BA S2/vol. II/38 Pa(1939)3.
20. Report by Capt I. L. Wight, Brigade Major, of situation in Cameroon, April 1939, 'Native revolt would be worse than German revolt'. BA No. S2/vol. III/38 Pa (1938)4.
21. Ibid.
22. Memo from Supt of Police, Victoria, to Comm. H/Q, Lagos of 17.6.39 on Herr Luppe's address at a Nazi meeting: 'whether the British maintained control of Cameroons or not, the interests of the coys would remain unaffected'. BA No. V2/29 S2/vol. II/38 Pa(1939)3.

23. See Le Vine, op. cit., pp. 126–30.
24. British and Germans held a 'club night' together two months before the war. Supt. of Police Victoria to Commissioner of Police H/Q-Lagos, 17/6/39. BA. S2/vol. II/38 Pa(1939)3.
25. *Report* on Herr Luppe to Chiefsec by NC Denton. No. S190/113 of 26/10/39. BA. File No. 190/39 Pa(1939)6.
26. Ibid. Also, Resident to Chief Secretary, Lagos, 30/9/38, forwarding minutes of a meeting between the Acting Resident and Senior Representatives of the German Community held at Buea on 29/9/38. Such meetings 'greatly eased tension'. BA. S2(1938)162 Pa(1938)2.
27. He initially suggested the 30 per cent but later on claimed, it was decided by the Resident, who, unfortunately, had been transferred. See, Herr Luppe to Resident, 20/6/39. BA. S2(vol. II) 38 Pa (1939)3.
28. Ibid.
29. See Resident to Chief Secretary 8/11/39 explaining that 'Banana industry wholly depends on German goodwill'. BA. No. 32315/560 Pa(1939)1.
30. Brigadier, Commandment D. P. Dickenson, to Chief Secretary, Lagos, 13/04/39. BA. HQ/NR/5736/G Pa(1939)3.
31. DO, Victoria to Resident, 11/5/39, reports 'native' élite, 'pro-German activity' and mentions Chief Manga Williams and Inspector Mosi – no serious action was taken. BA. No. 73(1939)35 Pa(1939)3.
32. Herr Luppe's secret transmission to German Consul at Fernando Po intercepted, dated 21/10/39. BA. S190/96 Pa(1939)3.
33. Undertaking signed by Herr Luppe and forwarded to Chief Secretary, Lagos, 18/08/39. British officials seemed to trust him. BA. S2/vol. 4/39/567x Pa(1939) 6. Also Note 85 below.
34. Many examples, e.g., Report on Dr Charton by P.C. No. 3309 O. Nwabarra to Superintendent of Police Victoria 20/10/39. BA. Pa(1939)6.
35. Resident to Chief Secretary, 8/11/39. BA. S190/127 Pa(1939)6.
36. N.C. Denton, Resident, to Chief Secretary forwarding Luppe's letter to Herren Jacobi and Karstedt, 26/10/39. BA. S190/113 Pa(1939)6.
37. For example 'rudeness' to Mr Longe by Dr H. Weiler, 10/5/40. Ba No. 186/39/vol. II Sd/1940/2; Also Note 40 below.
38. N.C. Denton, Resident, to Chief Secretary 26/10/39. Ba S190/113 Pa(1939)6.
39. Ibid.
40. 'Political appreciation . . . regarding the Cameroons Plantations'. Secret, 1/6/40. BA Sd(1940)2.
41. Orders for officers on emergency duty by A. E. F. Murray, Resident, 3/6/40. BA. Sd 1940/2.
42. Ibid.
43. DO Victoria to the Resident; 229 criminal cases were tried in Victoria alone in 1940. 5/4/40. Ba No. v.872/13 Tc(1940)1.
44. Confidential, W. Fowler, DO, 'Resettlement of Ex-servicemen; Cameroons Province', 22/4/48, addressed to the Resident, para 2. BA v.1277 Pa(1948)1.
45. Circular No. HQ/NR/1985/5 (A) of 22/7/39 Kaduna: Recruitment – African Ranks, para 2 d. BA Pa(1936)6.
46. Government Technical College Ombe, the first Technical college, was opened in 1950.

47. J. S. Dudding, Area Resettlement Officer Eastern Province, to Chief Resettlement Officer Lagos, 10/9/48. V1277 BA Pa(1948)1. Besides several frivolous complaints, some veterans plotted to attack Barclays Bank, Victoria in 1952, DO Va, to Resident, 11/12/52. BA Pa(1952)1.
48. A. M. Muir, Resident, to Chief Secretary, Lagos, 7/4/41, 'Review of African Manpower', para 2. BA Ni, 271/35 Pa(1942)12.
49. Ibid., para 5.
50. See Note 44 above.
51. There were two major 'Disturbances of Soldiers' at Aba and Calabar reported by C. J. Pleass, SEP in 1943, the leaders and majority of whom were from Bamenda Division in Cameroons Province; 47 were imprisoned for various terms, 14/11/43. No. 18542/1/64. However, in 1948, Fowler argued that these outbreaks of disorders resulted from 'grave administrative ineptitude'. BA V1277 Pa(1948))1.
52. A generally held view confirmed by eight out of ten of contemporaries interviewed. However, some exservicemen interviewed maintained they were told in the army to use force where they had little or no money. Hence they seized chickens, wine and other commodities displayed for sale in the local markets and eloped with young girls. Folksongs were composed about them. They were both envied and dreaded.
53. The Residents (Administration) wrote circular letters also to the soldiers, keeping them informed about developments at home.
54. Reply to Resident from Paul Thomas Etong, No. 13011 CSM, 2410 Coy, African PC, ME Forces, 18/9/44. Ba Pa(1941)8
55. Reply to Resident from NA 87698 Sign. B.Njume, special Wireless Coy (D) WA signals, SE Asia command, dated 25/2/45. BA Pa(1941)8. His emphasis.
56. Njume, ibid. Many of the letters were written collectively e.g. one signed by Fineboy Forefore (Chairman) for 'all Cameroons [sic] Serving in South East Asia', dated 18/6/45. They sent £21 for the construction of Basel and Catholic Missions schools in Bamenda. BA. Pa(1941)8.
57. See minutes of the Eastern Area Development Committee No. C. 366 Pa(1944)4 Post-war planning. All veterans interviewed expressed disappointment.
58. Fowler, Resettlement of Ex-servicemen, 22/4/48, introduction. BA No. V. 1277 Pa(1948)1.
59. Ibid., para 4.
60. The Kamerun Ex-servicemen's National Union was formed in 1958 and projected itself right to the UN, e.g. Petition of 31/8/61, BA. T/Com 4/L68 Add 1. Pa(1960)2. They complained bitterly against the British Government, which had not paid them their retirement benefits, and about neglect by the Cameroon Government. (All fifteen interviewed expressed this); see also, 'Andrew Ngandi to Premier, S. Cameroons' of 12/6/61 D 24/6 Pa(1960)2 BA.
61. Their hatred for Nigeria is shown in 'A Guide for Rehabilitation", BA. P.377 Pa(1960)2 dated 10/7/60. Also letter to the Editor, *Cameroon Times* of 29/12/60 on the plebiscite and the role of ex-servicemen. BA. Pa(1960)2.
62. AR 1946 by Mr A.F. Bridges, Resident, para, 551. BA. Ba 1946/3.
63. Circular of 22/6/48 from T.V. Sorivenor, Chief Secretary, Lagos on 'Employment of Ex-servicemen', No. 43/1948. BA. Pa(1948)1. Also

Fowler, 'Resettlement of Ex-servicemen . . .', 22/4/48 V.1277 Pa(1948)1.

64. Fowler, ibid. Out of 3564 exservicemen in Cameroon, only 980 found jobs. All ex-servicemen interviewed were bitter about this.
65. Chief Secretary, Lagos to the Resident, 18/7/40 No. 200/96. BA. No. 2865 vol. 1 Pa(1940)1.
66. Criticism by A. F. Bridges, Resident, AR, 1947. BA. Ba(1947)4.; see, Note 43 Above. Also Welch, op. cit. p. 163.
67. *Annual Reports* for Cameroon 1941, 1942, 1943 and 1944 emphasize these shortages.
68. In the *AR* for 1944 for Bamenda it was reported, 'Owing to production drives and shortage of imported articles money has cheapened and in some areas people have resorted to exchange by barter', para 523. BA Ba Sd(1944)1.
69. Ibid. Compulsion was used.
70. Ibid. Bamenda Division, the poorest in the Province, raised £2566 out of £5227 in 1944. Yet Cameroon, the poorest of the five Eastern Provinces, contributed the highest amount. People like L. H. Cort, a victim of the London 'blitzes', worked very hard towards this achievement. See Cort to Harris, 13/11/44; Cameroons War Relief Fund 19/12/44. BA. V.894/1 (Pa(1944)8.
71. Numerous examples, e.g., declaration by 'German African Old Soldiers W.A.P.V.' [sic] for total loyalty to Hitler, 22/5/39. Also meeting of fifteen prominent Cameroonians, including Chief Manga Williams, reported on 11/5/39 at which the German national anthem was sung etc. No. 73.1939/55. Ba. Pa(1939)3.
72. Chief Secretary, Lagos to Resident, 18/7/40 No. 200/96 BA. Pa(1940)1.
73. In AR. for 1943 Mr P. G. Harris, Resident, referred to the 'general lack of interest in the war and the discouraging response to the Rubber Drive, para. 531.
74. See E.J. Welch (ed.), 'The Kamerun Idea', in *Dream of Unity* (London and Ithaca, Cornell University Press, 1966).
75. *Secret Circular No. 32* from the Governor, 2/9/39. BA. Pa(1944)3.
76. DO Mamfe to the Resident, on Mr Otto Born's activities, 18/9/39. S.l, vol. 11/39 BA. Pa(1939)6.
77. Resident, Sealy-King, to SSP on 'Nigeria Defence scheme', 26/9/38. BA. S2(1938)93. Under the terms of the Mandate the authorities were restricted to a military force capable of defending the territory.
78. See report on 'Comforts Fund for Nigerian Troops', 4/2/41 by the DO, Victoria. BA. Pa(1940)7.
79. They were HE Sir Bernard and Lady Bourdillon in 1943 and Sir Arthur and Lady Richards in 1944.
80. A. F. Bridges, Resident, to SEP, War Memorials, 22/2/46. BA. Pa(1946)1. Strong claims were made for Cameroon.
81. P. G. Harris, AR, 1944 para 1. BA. Ba(1944)1.
82. Minutes of the Third Meeting of the Eastern Area Development Committee, 21/2/46, para 27, 'Future of the Cameroons Plantations', BA. C366 Pa(1944)4.
83. Ibid. They included Bambui Agricultural Farm, Victoria Hospital, Bafut-Modele road etc., and, later, the invitation of Dr Phyllis Kaberry, the noted anthropologist.

84. There were 526 soldiers (see Note 44 above), while 17 per cent of labourers in 1947 came from French Cameroon besides those settled in S. Cameroon. Bederman, op. cit., p. 26.
85. Chief Secretary to Resident, defending German security, 31/10/38 No. 32315/105 BA. S2(1938)162.
86. DO, Bamenda to Resident, 22/07/38, 'Intelligence from Fr. Cameroons'. No. C21/13 BA. S2/1938/5. Also O. W. Firth to C.S.G., Lagos, 16/6/38 AB. S2/1938)5.
87. Capt., Brigade Major, I. L. Wight, 'Report on a visit to Duala on 23/24-3-39', HQ/NR/5736/G. BA. Pa(1939)3.
88. Superintendent of Police to Commissioner of Police Lagos, 30/6/38. BA. P(100)a S2/1938/5.
89. See, Note 87 above.
90. Ibid.
91. See Note 11 above.
92. Circular Telegram from Secretary of State for the Colonies to the Governor, 6/12/41, specifically referring to Cameroon. No. 37956/6 BA. Pa(1941)7. Also AR 1940, para 488, Free French families crossed frontiers to S. Cameroon.
93. *Code wire* from Consul General at Duala to Resident, against rents being charged French post at Mabetta while Naval Control (British) at Daula have a block of flats free, 14/12/42. No. 03019. BA. Pa(1941)14.
94. Resident to SEP, 15/12/39. BA. No. C184/24 Sd (1939)6.
95. Mr J. W. C. Rutherford, DO, made a detailed and historical report on 'Protestant Christianity in Mamfe Division', 16/4/33. BA. Sd/1920/1.
96. A Rev. Brother at Bonjongo attempted to blow up a British ship. See late Fr Woodman's private papers, Njinkom Parish Archives.
97. See Anthony Ndi, 'Alfred Saker . . . and the Founding of Victoria' (MA thesis, SOAS, London, 1977).
98. Ibid. Literally the LMS was 'bought over' by the BM. Also Werner Keller, *The History of the Presbyteria Church in West Cameroon* (Victoria, Presbook, 1969), pp. 12–13.
99. Erik Halldén, *The Culture Policy of the Basel Mission in the Cameroons 1896–1905* (Sweden, Uppsala, 1968), pp. 30–2, 66–7.
100. Ibid.
101. Ibid.
102. R. J. Hook, Resident to SEP, 10/12/45, 'Future of German and Italian Missionaries'. BA. No. 186/39/11/162 Ba(1942)2.
103. In the very first report written on Cameroon in 1916, the Resident, E. C. Duff, emphasised that the authority of important chiefs should be upheld. But his successors, e.g. Arnett, went even further. See Anthony Ndi, 'Mill Hill Missionaries and the State in Southern Cameroons, 1922–1962' (PhD thesis, London, 1983), ch. 5.
104. Ibid.
105. Memo. E. Arnett, Resident to the Registrar, Lagos, 16/11/28. BA. Sd(1926)2 Flogging was common in the NCs and, under the Germans, frequently used.
106. AR 1940 by A. E. F.Murray, para 495. BA. Sd(1940)1.
107. Francis Bernard Booth, 'A Comparative study of Mission and Government Involvement in Educational Development in West Cameroon,

1922–1969' (PhD thesis, Univ. of California, 1973), pp. 430–7.

108. The British ban on enemy missionaries expired that year but the earliest Basel missionaries came in under the auspices of the Société des Missions Evangélique de Paris, at Duala. Letter to Ruxton, Resident, 14/1/25. Ba Sd(1921)4.
109. Keller, op. cit., pp. 72 and 96.
110. Lloyd E. Kwast, *The Disciplining of West Cameroon*, (Grand Rapids, Michigan, 1971) p. 92.
111. See Note 32 above.
112. DO, Kumba to Resident, 1.11.45. To drive away the 'Germanic memories from the minds of the elder inhabitants the removal of the Basel Mission would be a progressive step'; of course it was overruled. No. KC 33/3. BA Ba(1942)2. See also SEP, R. F. A. Grey, to Resident, 29.12.45, against Swiss Missionaries (pro-German). BA. Sd(1946)1.
113. Herr Simoleit accused Rev J. Sieber of embezzling Mission funds but investigations found him an upright missionary, Sieber to Resident, 16.12.39; Simpson, SEO, to Resident on Simoleit, 4.1.40; Herr Wettstein quarrelled with Herr Schmid, refused to work or stay with him and ended up on the plantation, Simpson to Resident, 4.12.39. etc. BA. Sd(1939)6. Eventually, the Rev'ds Dunger and Gebauer (CBM, USA) disagreed over property of German Baptist Mission and Government was anxious as this hampered development. See SEO to Resident, 18.4.47. EA Sd(1940)1.
114. 'Herr Wettstein', W. Simpson, SEO to Resident 4.12.39. BA. Sd(1939)6.
115. Draft telegram of 31.8.40 at instance of Resident gave five reasons for Herr Simoleit's internment. He was the Principal Missionary. BA. Sd(1940)2.
116. The Resident, Sealy-King, to Chief Secretary, while asking for Rev Simoleit to be interned, pleaded for the release of the Rev Fathers Altnann, Kneidinger and Schmidt, 2.8.40. BA. Sd(1940)2.
117. Internment orders from Resident, A.M. Muir, 2.7.40. No. 186/38/11/TJ128 AB Sd(1940)2.
118. DO to Resident, 24.9.40, No. C 109/3 BA. Sd(1940)2.
119. Rev Father Figl to Mr Schofield, DO Mamfe, on behalf of himself and others, 5.8.40. BA. Pa(1939)3.
120. These were Babank: Tungo and Bafut.
121. Booth, 'Comparative study', pp. 308–9.
122. Circular letter by Bishop Peter Rogan, dated 24.1.42, Sasse, 'changes and appointments'. 'Vicariate of Buea must become self-contained . . . keep, train and ordain our boys'. Education costs in Nigeria were becoming prohibitive.
123. Examination of 1947 AR, at 4th Session of Trusteeship Council. BA Ba (1947)4.
124. 'Federal Bilingual Grammar School Buea', the first Government Secondary School, was opened in 1963, 25 years after Sasse College.
125. They were TTC, Njinikom (later ETC, Bambui, 1948) and Girls Training Centre, Fiango, Kumba.
126. St Joseph's College, Sasse, opened in 1939.
127. For example, Rev Simoleit's plea for the release of 'Deaconess Sister Frida Maier', when the Protestant equivalent of a 'nun' was rejected. Simoleit to Resident, 30.7.40 BA. Sd(1940)2.

128. The movement of the nuns had been restricted under the orders of the DO, Dr M. D. W. Jeffreys, in 1940, to within a radius of 1 mile from the Convent. But Mr Harris, the Resident, only discovered this in February 1944 and was much upset. He opened up a chain of correspondence with the various officials concerned, which led to the end of all the restrictions on the nuns. It was one of his greatest satisfactions before his sudden death in 1945. See BA. File No. 186/39/Vol. II Sd(1940)2.
129. They were Herr Sieber (Baptist), 1939; Father Gussenhover (Catholic) 1944; and Father Croon, 1946. In each case the Resident took the occasion to laud the efforts of the missionaries.
130. There were hundreds of circulars and instructions issued through the missions during the war.
131. See AR, 1946 by Mr A. F. Bridges, para 554. BA Ba(1946)3.
132. AR for Bamenda Province by Brayne-Baker, 1952. BA. E1952.
133. Mr A. F. Bridges, AR, 1947. BA. Ba(1947)4.
134. In Mankon in 1944 Fr W. Nabben reported 'a distinct laxity of morals' and suggested the 'war', 'soldiers on leave' and the 'opening up' of Bamenda new roads as causes. *Sacred Returns*, 1944, Mankon.
135. AR, 1949 by Mr D. A. F. Shute, Resident, para 612. BA. Ba(1949)1.
136. Basel Mission College, Bali (later 'Cameroon Protestant College, Bali, in 1957 as a joint Basel–Baptist Mission enterprise).

9 The Second World War and the Sierra Leone Economy: Labour Employment and Utilisation, 1939–45

GILBERT A. SEKGOMA

Micro-studies[1] on the economic impact of the Second World War on some important strategic African colonial outposts of the British Empire, such as Sierra Leone[2] and Kenya, have not received much attention from political scientists and historians. This neglect in the past could be attributed to the inaccessibility of official materials covering the critical years 1939–45. This chapter seeks to stimulate research on this crucial period of African history now that some materials are open to the public in British and other archives. It examines the impact of the Second World War on Sierra Leone's economy, with particular attention to labour utilisation. It reinforces the argument initially advanced by La Ray Denzer, L. Sptizer, M. Amolo and H. Conway that the colonial state used war-time emergency powers to crush the development of an independent labour movement. The paper also demonstrates the machinery of Britain's manipulation and domination of Sierra Leone's economy, and proceeds from two hypotheses: (i) that during the war, Sierra Leone's economy was further integrated into that of the metropole and the resultant linkages continued into the post-colonial period; (ii) that Sierra Leone's economy operated in an environment shaped indirectly by a war directly affecting the metropole, a world system,[3] moreover, in which Sierra Leone was only a peripheral part. This unstable situation had a profound and negative influence on the colony's economy.

After the outbreak of the Second World War, the British colonial empire was called upon to support the Imperial Government economically in the war effort. Economic sacrifices had to be made throughout the Empire in a bid to save money for the war. A circular from the Secretary of State for the Colonies, Lord Moyne, specifically instructed the various colonial administrations to raise taxation with a view to reducing consumption, to limit imports in order to curb expenditure and simultaneously provide more shipping space for war goods. Colonial administrations were also instructed not to grant licences for dollar goods where sterling goods could be obtained, and to exercise tight control on the use of existing stocks of imported materials. The colonial governments were also told to mount propaganda drives aimed at persuading people to invest money in the war savings schemes. The overriding factor was the paramount need to curb expenditure on luxury goods. The colonies were also to transfer a large part of their financial surpluses to the Imperial Government as free gifts. Finally, the colonial administrations were to maintain some reserves, which would be utilised for post-war reconstruction. Those reserves were invested in British Government securities or were lent to the Imperial Government free of interest. The repayment these monies was to be made after the war.[4] The plea from the Imperial Government for such stringent austerity measures on the part of the colonial empire, it would appear, was to make massive resources available for the war effort.

The colonial government in Sierra Leone welcomed these directives. It cooperated with the Imperial Government in building defences for the port of Freetown. The colonial state in Sierra Leone also contributed materially to the Imperial Government. In 1941 the sum of £250 000 was transferred free of interest. Commitment to the continuation of such assistance was also promised.[5] In fact the Sierra Leone Government started such contributions earlier. In 1940 it contributed 14.9 per cent of its extraordinary expenditure of £1 139 137 7s 6d to the war effort; in 1941, 14.5 per cent of that expenditure of £1 109 258 15s 0d was contributed; 15.5 per cent of its extraordinary expenditure of £1 684 500 was given in 1944; and 16.8 per cent of £1 992 000 in 1945.[6] These contributions were undoubtedly made at the expense of local infrastructural development. For instance, Sierra Leone's long-term agricultural development policy, a 5 to 10-year medical and health development programme, and a general policy for the development of education in the Protectorate, all due for implementation in 1940, were shelved as most resources were directed to the war effort.[7]

On the question of War Savings Schemes, propaganda drives to achieve this objective began in 1939. By August of the same year a

Savings Account was opened in the Post Office with an initial balance of £95 000. By the middle of 1941 the balance had reached £156 000 and was increasing at a high rate of about £5000 to £6000 per month. Sierra Leoneans were also manipulated into contributing to the Bomber Fund, which in 1941 had a balance of £26 000, and to the Torpedoed Seamen's Fund, which in 1941 amounted to £5900 and was expected to increase considerably.[8] All those balances were invested by the Crown Agents for the Colonies in British Government securities. To this extent, the siphoning-off of financial resources was not only limited to the government level, but also included the wider society of Sierra Leone.

The colonial state also imposed limitations on imports. As a result, liquor imports, particularly from the dollar area, were greatly reduced. Imports from South Africa were also reduced to one or two ships per month.[9] This trend also affected imports from Britain. The imperative for such a policy was not only dictated by a need to curb expenditure and save foreign exchange, but also by the overriding desire to provide shipping space for the transportation of war materials. However, the limitation of imports soon resulted in the scarcity of essential consumer goods. This had the effect of forcing up prices of whatever commodities were available. Consequently, by the end of 1941, the cost of living had increased to 175.57 percentage points from a base index of 100 percentage points in 1939. By the end of the war in 1945 the cost of living had rocketed to 233.7.[10] This inflationary trend demonstrates that the multiplicity of demands which were made by the colonial administration severely constrained the colony's economy.[11]

The war not only affected the financial and the cost of living aspects of the Sierra Leone economy; it also had a devastating effect on the development of an independent labour movement, thereby providing an opportunity for the exploitation of both industrial and agricultural labour by both the colonial administration and British capital. Immediately after the outbreak of the War, the Emergency Powers (Defence) Act was invoked throughout the British Empire.[12] In Sierra Leone the invocation of this Act was welcomed by the administration. Colonial states were now empowered to order the arrest and detention of any person, without reference to *habeas corpus*. The Sierra Leone Government, with the consent of the Colonial Office, used the Emergency Powers (Defence) Act in September 1939 to arrest and detain Wallace-Johnson, the Organising Secretary of the West African Youth League (Sierra Leone Branch) and organiser of trade unions.[13] The colonial state also ordered the arrest and detention of the Youth League's cadres and active trade union leaders. These included George

Cornwall, Nathaniel Thomas, Sidney Boyle, George S. C. Willoughby and George Pratt.[14] The Youth League and some trade unions, particularly the War Department Amalgamated Union, were left without leadership.

The Youth League, robbed of its dynamic leadership, was seriously weakened, and thus began to lose direction. However, the authorities were not satisfied that the Emergency Powers (Defence) Act provided them with enough powers to destroy the Youth League effectively. Subsequently, in 1940, the colonial government amended some features of the Emergency Powers (Defence) Act, and introduced new regulations which gave it powers to forbid public employees from membership of the Youth League. For instance, section 18 (2) as amended in 1940 noted that:

> If the Governor has reasonable cause to believe any person to have been or to be a member or to have been or to be active in the furtherance of the object of any such organization as is hereinafter mentioned and that it is necessary to exercise control over him he may make an order against that person directing that he be detained.
>
> The organizations hereinafter referred to are any organizations in respect of which the Governor is satisfied that either . . . (b) the persons in control of the organizations have or have had associations with persons concerned in the government of any power with which His Majesty is at war, and in either case that there is danger of utilization of the organizations for purposes prejudicial to public safety, the defence of the realm, the maintenance of public order, the efficient prosecution of any war in which His Majesty may be engaged, or the maintenance of supplies or services essential to the life of the community.[15]

Under these regulations the administration instructed all heads of departments to deal with all public employees who were members of the Youth League. The chief labour officer was also instructed to warn all union leaders against membership of the Youth League. Although the regulations were initially aimed at the Youth League, they were also applied to the trade unions because most of them had been formed by the Youth League, and most of their personnel were also members and leaders of the Youth League.

These war-time regulations suffocated both the development of a mass-based nationalist movement and that of labour movements independent of government influence. By 1942 the colonial state measures against labour, which were implemented from 1940, were showing signs of success. The Youth League was beginning to dwindle, and the colonial state managed to establish some control over most trade unions.[16] The ease with which the authorities defeated such forces of change reflected the stability, intent, and relative power of the colonial state in Sierra Leona. The Youth League and most trade unions founded in 1939 were in their infancy and had not established enough influence among the masses to withstand government repression.

The suppression and subsequent control of labour were achieved through a two-pronged policy, which was implemented from late 1940.[17] The policy comprised intimidation or actual detention of the radical labour leaders and rehabilitation for those union leaders who agreed to toe the government line. The intimidation or detention strategy was prosecuted convertly, while rehabilitation was carried out overtly. The rehabilitation option began to show signs of success in 1942, when the colonial administration sponsored the establishment of a Labour Advisory Board.[18] This Labour Advisory Board's constitution was weighted against trade unions; which did not have the right to appoint their representatives to the Board; instead each union had to submit names of its proposed representatives to the governor, who had the power to select unions that were to have representatives on the Board, as well as their representatives. Invariably the Governor's choices favoured 'responsible' unions, which included the Freetown Maritime Workers, represented by M. K. Paterson; the Sierra Leone Masons' Workers' Union, which G. C. Thomas represented; the Railway Workers' Union, with T. S. Johnson as its representative; and the African Commercial Clerks' Union, represented by C. M. A. Thomas.[19]

The employers' side of the Labour Advisory Board included G. A. G. Lane (Chief Justice) as chairman, the Director of Public Works, the General Manager of Railways, and the Director of Combined Services, who was also the local commander of the Royal Engineers. The Chamber of Commerce was represented by the agent for Messrs. G. G. Ollivant, the General Manager of the United African Company Limited, the Manager of Sierra Leone Coaling Company Ltd, and the General Manager of Sierra Leone Development Company Ltd, with the Chief Labour Officer as secretary. Commenting on the creation of this Labour Advisory Board, Acting Governor Blood noted that the idea was to create machinery that would afford Government a chance to control matters affecting labour, especially during the war time.[20]

The inclusion of trade unions in the Labour Advisory Board had little effect. Labour's numerical inferiority ruled out chances of its pushing through the interests of its members, even had the Board been in essence democratic. The Board therefore was simply a token established through which the administration and capital defined the framework within which labour was to operate.

The Labour Advisory Board was elaborated and perfected by Edgar Parry (then Chief Labour Officer) in 1943–4. Edgar Parry's scheme aimed at establishing structures through which the colonial state would have more influence over labour. The scheme basically hinged upon buying off union leaders and according them prestige, as well as sending them to London for some courses on labour organisation; Parry also added a new structure to the Labour Advisory Board, the Wages Board.[21] This instrument was aimed at winning token or limited concessions from employers through collective bargaining. In 1947 another structure was added, the Joint Industrial Councils in the construction and transportation industries.[22] Through these structures and other measures, the government managed to dominate and influence labour for some time.[23] This was also the case in the Gold Coast. A similar development also took place in Canada, where a new legislative machinery for collective bargaining was introduced. The only discernible difference in these developments was that in Canada union leaders forcibly demanded the institution of such structures,[24] while in the West African colonies, the administrations imposed such machinery in order to create organisations amenable to the colonial authoriies, in line with the imperial labour policy for the colonies. Jack Woddis pertinently summarized the major objectives of the colonial labour policy thus:

> a) To spread ideas of class collaboration,
> b) To prevent strikes,
> c) To safeguard profits,
> d) To help governments frame Trade Union legislation,
> e) To prevent Trade Unions taking an interest in political questions,
> f) To isolate colonial Trade Unions: from militant Trade Unions in other lands and especially from the W.F.T.U.,
> g) To denounce militant Trade Unionists and expose them to Government persecution.[25]

This framework was bequeathed to African governments at independence and is in some cases still the corner stone of labour policy.

Labour in Sierra Leone during the war not only lost the relative independence it had enjoyed, but was also subjected to new compulsory obligations. In late 1941 the Government passed the Defence (Compulsory Service) Amendment regulations under which some establishments were scheduled 'essential services' and the workers in those services could not go on a strike under any circumstances. They included the Railways Department, mining, the Freetown Fire Brigade, the War Department workers and the sanitation department.[26] The same Act also gave the Government the right to conscript all available manpower for the prosecution of the war or for other services which might be declared essential. It is instructive to point out that similar regulations were also introduced throughout the African colonial empire and in the Commonwealth as a whole. What is of interest to this study is the difference in application of these regulations in the colonial empire and the metropole.

In colonies such as Sierra Leone the Compulsory Service Regulations did not provide sufficient protection for workers in essential services. Whereas no worker in scheduled occupations could vacate his job without the express consent of the Director of Essential Services, Briggs, or the Governor, there were no specific provisions preventing employers from dispensing with the services of workers in reserved occupations.[27] This was certainly not the case in Britain, where no worker was permitted to leave a scheduled occupation without the permission of a National Service Officer, and employers were also forbidden by wartime regulations from laying off war workers without full and sufficient reasons. Moreover, if any worker became redundant, the Ministry of Labour was charged with responsibility to transfer such a worker elsewhere.[28] Such an arrangement also existed in Canada, but was implemented with less rigour.[29]

By 1942 the Compulsory Regulations were proving difficult to implement in Sierra Leone. The mining companies and other scheduled establishments dismissed some of their labourers over petty disputes, such as turning up late for work, not strictly obeying orders and absenteeism. This development was harshly received by the military establishment, whose major concern was with the maintenance of law and order as well as accelerated production. Consequently, the War Department pressed the Sierra Leone government to introduce tougher measures aimed at controlling labour and restricting employers from dismissing labour in scheduled operations. The military also wanted the registration of labour in order to form labour corps units, to identify labourers for essential work orders and other defence works for which it might be necessary to call on the aid of the general public.[30] From the military's point of view, all these recommendations were essential if any proper organisation and utilisation of labour were to be achieved.

This argument was supported by the colonial state. Governor Hubert Stevenson wrote to the Colonial Office that the labour situation in Sierra Leone was getting out of hand, and, as a result, output in many sectors had fallen to approximately 30 per cent of the pre-war levels. The governor also pointed out that lack of registration enabled essential workers to leave their employment and easily get jobs elsewhere. The situation was worst among the dockworkers – especially since Freetown port was a defended port – and also among railwaymen – another scheduled occupation.[31] The Port Development Committee, Labour Advisory Board and the Executive Council all strongly recommended the registration of labour and issuing of identification cards bearing signatures or fingerprints and records of employment. The Government hoped to use the scheme to control the movement of labour from the Protectorate to the Colony and to safeguard the continued production of export commodities and local food supplies, especially rice, and other raw materials essential to the war effort.[32] In Britain, in spite of emergency laws, control of labour was accomplished by direction rather than by compulsion, and while workers were made to realise the part they had to play in the overthrow of Nazi Germany, employers also demonstrated a sense of responsibility by cooperating and collaborating with workers towards the attainment of the common goal. The power of the British labour movement was also a factor here. For instance, the Joint Consultative Committee, consisting of equal numbers of the Trade Union Congress (TUC) and Employers Federation, was consulted on matters in which the interests of war-workers were affected. This helped to win the cooperation of labour and safeguard its interests.[33]

The Compulsory Service (Essential Works) Regulations came into force on 2 May 1942. These not only provided for the conscription and registration of labour, but also introduced a novel convention in West African military service. The regulations provided for the registration of women for call-up in non-combatant services, such as nursing, cooking, food production and all clerical work.[34]

By September 1942 the legal machinery which had been introduced for the utilisation of labour was beginning to show signs of success. The average number of workers employed in essential services was about 40 000 in the Colony and approximately 12 000 in the Protectorate. About 41 837 people were registered for call-up between June and September 1942. It was estimated that by the end of October 1942 about

78 000 people were registered, and the process was to continue as the war proceeded.

Conscription for military service began in November 1942. The army requirements for that month alone was 1054. By the beginning of April 1943 about 9450 men had been conscripted into the various services of the Imperial Army. Conscription included semi-skilled people.[35] This scheme was to continue for the duration of the war.

However, the heavy demands imposed on the Sierra Leoneans by the imperatives of the war were poorly rewarded. The remunerations of labour were meagre at a time when the cost of living was rising. Towards the end of 1939, mineworkers' wages were increased by one penny to tenpence a day. The Government also increased the wages of its labourers by a penny in 1940, to tenpence for those in Freetown and other towns, and ninepence for those working in the Protectorate. However, by 1942, the cost of living had risen to 175.57 per cent, and this development badly affected the workers. W. B. Birmingham notes a similar development in the Gold Coast during the war.[36]

By 1941, the Governor had reported a 60 per cent rise in the cost of living and noted that this had made it impossible for European workers in essential services to live comfortably. He thus requested the Secretary of State for the Colonies to give him permission to raise the salaries of European workers and also to pay them separation allowances.[37] What is of interest, however, is that the Governor did not indicate the extent to which the rising cost of living affected African labour in general. It may well be that the Government assumed that it would suppress all labour grievances through the use of war-time measures.

Although the control of labour was in many ways achieved, it was strongly challenged in 1942 by the Mineworkers Union, which staged a strike at the Marampa iron ore mines and at the railway terminus port of Pepel. The 1942 strike of Delco workers was by no means the first. A number of strikes had occurred earlier in the mining industry. In 1935 a strike took place at Marampa, and in 1937 strikes occurred at Marampa and at Pepel. In both strikes, the grievances of labour among other things included (1) low rates of pay and long hours of work (12 hours per day), (2) indecent treatment, (3) lack of roads, (4) poor medical attention, and (5) compulsory overtime. In both cases, the strikers returned to work following promises from management to investigate grievances.[38] However, the colonial Government did not consider the demand for increased wages seriously; writing to the Colonial Office, the Governor observed that:

> . . . there is no difficulty in getting labour at the rate of 9d a day plus two cups of rice without any sort of pressure. Even at this rate the labourers do not work every day so that they presumably find that they can manage well enough according to their diets on approximately twenty days' pay a month for 15/- plus the rice.[39]

Failure on the part of Delco to settle the demands of the workers satisfactorily led to another wave of strikes in 1938 at Pepel and at the Marampa iron ore mine in 1938 and May 1939. Pay increases and full payment during absences due to injury were the major demands of the workers. However, the dark hand of Wallace Johnson and his Youth League were alleged to have been another contributory factor. Workers returned to work in 1939 after the management had conceded a minimum daily wage for a labourer of 10d.[40]

The 1942 strike was thus deeply rooted in the pre-war system of industrial relations. However, it differed from the earlier strikes in the sense that labour was better organised and more aware of its ruthless exploitation by the mining company. The Youth League's activities had brought about this awareness. Labour chose this war-time opportunity to strike, when its labour was most needed for the extraction of iron ore, and the union demanded a pay increase in order to meet the rising cost of living, and increases in overtime payment. The union complained of difficulty in obtaining food at Marampa and Pepel to supplement the company's rice issues; then objected to the refusal of the company to grant passes to workers wanting to visit Freetown, and to the failure to issue protective clothing such as gumboots and waterproofs during the wet season to men working in the conveyor tunnels and on the conveyors. Finally, the union complained of the company's deduction of rent from its members' wages.[41]

The strike could have been averted had the Delco management shown interest in the workers' problems. In late January 1942 the general manager of the Sierra Leone Development Company, Lyell, showed indifference and took no immediate action to redress the workers' grievances, which had been building up since 1941. Instead, he tried to minimise those grievances and told the union representatives that the question of pay increases and rates of overtime would be referred to the company's head office in London. As for protective clothing, Lyell told the union leaders that the company would only supply it if the workers were willing to pay for it.[42]

These responses angered the union. The signs of impending labour unrest became evident on 30 January. The general manager of Delco thereupon informed the Chief Labour Officer of the situation at Marampa and Pepel. On 1 February the labour officer, Nisbet, arrived at Marampa, in the hope of saving the situation. After consultation with the general manager of Delco, Nisbet simply repeated the Company's position, suggesting that the demands for paying increases and rates of overtime work would be referred to London, and that the company would consider establishing a small store at Pepel for the sale of the more essential articles of diet and clothing. The management, he promised, would afford easier facilities for men to obtain passes to Freetown. The general manager conceded the free issue of gumboots and waterproofs to the tunnel gang and to the men working on conveyors, subject to the condition that the men would be liable for the value of any articles lost or becoming unserviceable through neglect. The Labour Officer also emphasised that the strike was illegal under war-time regulations and therefore all grievances should be settled amicably with the company. If that was impossible, the workers should refer the matter to the Labour Department.[43]

The major grievance of the workers was, however, low pay. Since this was not settled, and there was no hope of it being settled in the near future, the workers decided to stage a strike from 2 February 1942. Pickets were formed in all workplaces, including workshops, offices of the clerical staff and transport depots, and were so effective that virtually all work stopped.[44]

The news of the strike at Marampa and Pepel was received by the colonial administration with alarm. Iron ore was badly needed by the Imperial Government both for its revenue and in the manufacture of weapons. The Chief Labour Officer was quickly despatched to Marampa to solve the dispute and order the men to resume their work. When he arrived at Marampa on 3 February, the union leaders presented him with a demand for a minimum wage of 1/6d per day, on the grounds of increased cost of living and harder work consequent upon increased production. As indicated in Table 9.1 and Table 9.2, production had increased in 1940. Decline in production started in late 1941 because of the workers' response to the unsatisfactory working conditions that led to the 1942 strike. The graph also shows a downward trend to 1944, after which production picked up, save for a slight decline in 1946 caused by a strike in that year. On the whole, the trend in production was upward. The Labour Officer did not agree to the demands, but emphasised the illegality of the strike and ordered the workers to return. They defied the order and stated that they would only comply if their demands were met. The workers also resisted the Labour

TABLE 9.1 *Production trends at Marampa mine, 1933–50*

Year	*Tons*	*Year*	*Tons*
1933	24 550	1942	623 270
1934	229 465	1943	556 515
1935	433 540	1944	455 660
1936	566 595	1945	827 332
1937	633 983	1946	729 398
1938	861 955	1947	840 636
1939	828 560	1948	952 299
1940	689 290	1949	1 089 036
1941	1 029 970	1950	1 165 969

Officer's threats to use punitive action against them if they continued to refuse to return to work.[45]

The refusal of the mineworkers to resume work invited the wrath of the colonial state. The anti-aircraft squadron was called in at Marampa to guard vital installations and prevent labour from taking violent action. Contingency measures included the deployment of troops and police as well as court messengers in nearby areas, ready for use against workers, if they continued to refuse to go back to work. On 5 February Nisbet held another meeting with the workers in an attempt to break the strike. However, the workers were still not prepared to return to work. At that juncture, O'Dwyer, District Commissioner for Port Loko, signalled the police and court messengerse to surround the workers. The point was well summed up by O'Dwyer:

> It was evident to me that if they were allowed to move off, professedly to consult, they would never return, that the meeting would be dissolved and there would never be an opportunity for any arrests. The 4000 labourers at Marampa can dissipate themselves so quickly in Lunsar and surrounding villages that one wonders how and where labour was housed. I therefore called upon them to halt . . . This was the signal for messengers and police unobtrusively to surround the crowd.[46]

Despite the presence of the police, the meeting resulted in a stalemate, the workers refusing to return to work before their grievances were resolved.

Although no arrests of the union leaders were made, O'Dwyer ordered police, court messengers and the military to shepherd the

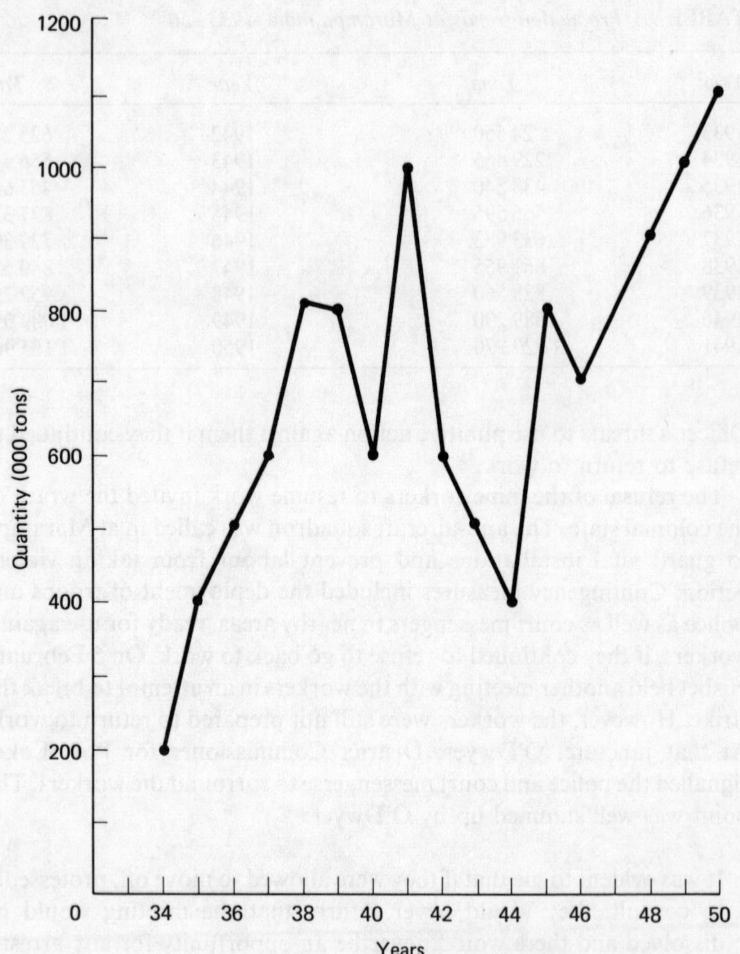

TABLE 9.2 *Graph of production trends at Marampa Mine (1933–50)*

workers to the workplace. Reporting to the Governor on this action, O'Dwyer noted:

> I therefore decided that the best course was for court messengers and police to escort them to the Hill, about 1½ miles. They moved off towards the mine. A number turned back and went into Lunsar town saying that they had not prepared for work that day and that it was

> necessary to change their clothes. Court messengers and police with Captain Craig and Mr Brothers followed them into Lunsar town, to rout out any other labourers from there and shepherd them towards the mine. Major Keating and myself followed the first batch with court messengers and police herding them. It was mid-day when we reached the mine.[47]

Thus did the authorities bring about an end to the Marampa–Pepal strike of 1942. The action taken by the authorities against labour was repressive. Apart from demonstrating that the interests of the workers were unprotected by the law, it also indicated that war-time emergency regulations bred an atmosphere in which the exploitation and suppression of labour were perpetuated.

After the resumption of work by labour, an Arbitration Tribunal was appointed to investigate the grievances of the mine-workers over the cost of living, basic wage rates, the issue of rent and conditions of the labour lines. In its investigations the Arbitration Tribunal found that there had been an increase of 50 per cent in the cost of living at Lunsar and the prices of some commodities had increased by 100 per cent since 1940. A cost of living index for Sierra Leone as a whole indicated an increase to 233.7 (from a 1939 base of 100) in 1945. An attempt by the Tribunal to ascertain whether the company lost money on labour costs was to no avail, since the company refused to disclose its labour costs and its general financial structure. Despite these findings, the Arbitration Tribunal recommended that there should be no increase in the basic wage. Instead, the Tribunal recommended a periodical (six-monthly) payment of a basic threepence per diem to workers earning below two shillings per day. This award took effect from March 1942. The decision of the Arbitration Tribunal not to recommend an increase in the basic wage rates of workers flew in the face of the fact that prices of basic commodities had risen while wages had relatively declined. This situation made it almost impossible for many of the total labour force of 4098 earning between sixpence and elevenpence per day at Marampa and Pepel to live comfortably. For instance, the average expenditure on food per month for a family of four was about £1.14.6, whereas the basic wage per month at elevenpence per day amounted to £1.7.6. The above expenditure did not include estimates for burials, fees to *poro* and *bundu* societies, clothing, pots and entertainments, although expenditure on these items was necessary. The wage structure apart from demonstrating labour exploitation and the hardship experienced by labour, also shows that the workers' opportunity to save was minimal.

The Tribunal also considered the issue of overtime payment. On this matter, the Arbitration Tribunal recommended that:

(a) Where an employee works on any day in excess of ten hours, exclusive of intervals for food and rest, he shall receive pay each hour in excess of ten and up to 8 p.m. at the rate not less than the hourly rate at which he was paid during the normal day.

(b) Where an employee continues such work after 8 p.m., then he shall receive pay of one and a quarter times the hourly rate at which he was being paid during the normal day.

(c) Where an employee is required to commence work before the work of 5 a.m. and continue without an interval, except for food and rest for ten hours after the normal hour of commencing work, then he shall receive pay for each hour worked before 5 a.m. at the rate of one and a quarter times the hourly rate at which he would be paid during the normal day. And for hours from 5 a.m. to the normal hour for commencing work, he shall receive pay at the rate of not less than the hourly rate at which he would be paid during the normal day.'[48]

On the problem of accommodation, the Arbitration Tribunal found the labour lines in poor condition; sanitary facilities were non-existent, the rooms small and dilapidated. The management of Delco promised to improve the situation. The Tribunal also found that the company deduction of rent of 1s 6d monthly from the wages was contrary to Rule 20 of the schedule of Employers and Employed Ordinance 1934 which ran: 'Save where agreement is made to the contrary, no deductions shall be made from the wages of a labourer for housing, fuel, medicine or medical attendance provided by the employer'.[49] Contrary to this regulation, Delco had made its own rules to the effect that: 'The rent of the house shall be payable monthly at the end of each month and shall be deducted by the company from the wages of the tenant taking it.'[50] The Tribunal overrules this practice. Some members of the Tribunal, such as Otto-During, considered that rent deduction by the company was illegal and therefore the company should be made to refund the money. Eventually, Otto-During was prevailed upon by other members, but it was recommended that workers should not pay rent in the Company's labour lines.

However, the Governor took exception to the latter recommendation. Governor Stevenson maintained that the company was justified in deducting rents from wages, because workers had a choice of either staying in the company's labour lines and paying rent or living in the surrounding villages.[51] It was ironic that European workers, who were actually better paid, stayed in company accommodation without paying rent. The European workers were paid Christmas allowances, moreover, while the African employees were not. This treatment of the African labour force by mining capital represented a brutal form of exploitation. A similar situation was summed up by the District Commissioner of Port Loko in 1939.

> This now makes the fourth strike in 7 years. The impression I get is that the company look upon their labour merely as an instrument for getting iron-ore out of that hill and shipping it home. The side issues, e.g. labour's welfare do not concern them.[52]

Labour exploitation is Sierra Leone also affected peasant producers. This did not occur in an economic vacuum. The development of commercial agriculture in Sierra Leone dates back to the late eighteenth century, and was largely the product of peasants' response to the market. However, colonization expanded and rationalised this staple economy. Consequently the colonial economy did not so much constitute a break but rather a continuation of existing phenomena. Colonial rule provided the political framework within which Sierra Leone was integrated into the capitalist economy. Thereafter, peasants' vulnerability to economic forces and dependence on the world market became the norm rather than the exception. This world market proved very unstable during the years of the Depression, and was further complicated by the imperatives of the war in the early 1940s.

Following the outbreak of the war, the Imperial Government in London instructed the administrations in West Africa to centralise the purchase and export of agricultural products. This development led to the establishment of a West African Produce Control Board (WAPCB).[53] The major objectives of the WAPCB were to control the export of agricultural produce to the Ministry of Food in London and to encourage production by guaranteed producer prices. In addition, local administrations were to deflate prices of commercial produce and introduce stringent price controls on all commodities. In effect, this trend affected most of the British African colonies, though in different degrees. Zwanenberg and King maintain that agricultural commodities in Uganda were bought at well below market purchase prices.[54] The situation was, however, different in Kenya, where the settlers actually benefited from higher prices at the expense of African labour and African production.

Sierra Leone was hard hit by this developing trend. The price of ginger was deflated from £54 (1938 price) to £11 per ton in 1939–40. However, after the fall of Burma and other Asiatic countries which produced this commodity, the price of ginger in the international market rose from £78 to £100 in 1943–44. In Sierra Leone the Government thereupon issued a defence order fixing the price of ginger in 1943 at £30 per ton.[55]

The price of palm kernels (the major export commodity next to minerals) was also slashed from £28 to £12 per ton. To this extent the imperatives of the war took precedence over the real needs of the peasant producers. The policy, however, boomeranged. The desire to lower prices of agricultural commodities negated the intent to save money for the war effort, on the one hand, and to maintain increased production levels on the other. The peasant producers' response to these price cuts, or to put it in other words, to this aggressive form of exploitation, was a partial withdrawal of their labour. The result was a perceptible decline of commodity production, as indicated in the Table 9.3.

Table 9.3 indicates a general decline of agricultural production during the war period. For instance, palm kernels, whose contribution to the total export tonnage in the pre-war years recorded 91.07 per cent, declined to 88.89 per cent during the war. A similar trend affected almost all agricultural products. In percentage terms kola nuts dropped from 2.35 per cent before the war to 1.94 per cent during the war. However, although ginger and piassava declined in absolute terms during the war, in relative terms they gained. This explains the increase in percentage terms of their contribution to the total export tonnage during the war. The trend after the war was generally upward, due to improved market prices. The decline in commodity production during the war could also be interpreted as peasants' refusal to support the war effort. However, efforts to explore this train of thought have been less productive, and future research in this area may uncover new evidence to advance our understanding of peasant action during the war.

The other contributory factor to the decline in commodity production may well have been the withdrawal of labour from agriculture to the various services in the war. However, this would be contradictory to the Fei-Renis model, which maintains that (i) labour can be withdrawn from agriculture without causing a perceptible decline in agricultural production, even if the level of technology remained unchanged; (ii) that this labour can be fed by the agricultural surplus if they moved to the urban sectors; (iii) that as long as surplus can be extracted from the agricultural sector, there will be sufficient food for internal consumption and export and thus economic transformation can take place and non-farm jobs can be created without causing any food shortages for the urban-labour force.[57] Whereas this model may be valid for dynamic economies, its

TABLE 9.3 *Production trends in agricultural commodities (tons) 1932–52*[56]

	Palm kernels	*% of total*	*Kola nuts*	*% of total*	*Ginger*	*% of total*	*Piassava*	*% of total*	*Total production*
Pre-war, 1932–8	512 970	91.07	13 252	2.35	12 796.1	2.27	24 216.1	4.30	563 234.2
War-time, 1939–45	310 171	88.89	6 779	1.94	11 611.6	3.33	20 363	5.84	348 924.6
Post-war, 1946–52	473 732	90.72	11 190	2.31	11 163.8	2.08	27 030.7	4.89	523 116.5
	1 296 873		31 221		35 571.5		71 609.8		1 435 275.3

applicability in situations like that in Sierra Leone is doubtful. In effect, what obtained during the war and afterwards in phases of urban migration disproves the assumptions of the model. Commodity production declined, despite the high demands for crops for export and to feed the urban population, together with the increased number of soldiers in Freetown. The model implies that the urban population would provide a ready market for agricultural produce, and this would stimulate production in the countryside. Although there was increased demand for agricultural produce during the period under consideration, this did not stimulate production, and does not do so to this day. The model therefore needs more variables to capture such situations. It would appear, however, that unfavourable market situations, coupled with inflationary trends during the war, played a dominant role in this development. This was well expressed by Acting Governor Blood, who wrote in 1941, that as long as the prices were controlled at virtually slump level in the interest of the British economy, production would continue to fall, and this would be accompanied by the declining standard of living of the African producers.[58] In the final analysis there was a loss of income for the colonial state and a smaller contribution for the war effort.

As regards rice, the staple food for Sierra Leoneans, the colonial administration imposed a quota on every producer chiefdom. That quota was to be sent to the government to feed the soldiers and the surpluses were to be exported.[59] Wallace-Johnson, writing in 1945 to the new British Prime Minister, Clement Attlee, maintained that the people in the hinterland gave up most of their harvest to the government agents because of fear of punishment. He also argued that such brutal methods as tying and flogging were often meted out to those who failed to meet the requirements of government quotas.[60]

Despite the stringent controls of produce prices, the costs of imported items rose steeply. As a result, peasant producers were exploited both by low produce prices, which were close to the cost of production, and through the high prices of imported goods. This unequal exchange of commodities hit not only the agricultural producers but the entire economy. At the end of the war the extraction of quotas from peasant production was replaced by the imposition of a 'target production' scheme. The major aim of this scheme was to increase production for exports and thus accumulate more funds to salvage Britain's war-torn economy. The failure or success of this policy can be discerned from the Table 9.4.

Excepting palm oil, which seems to have been a dismal failure, other

TABLE 9.4 *Production of major cash crops (tons), 1947–50*[61]

	1947	*1948*	*1949*	*1950*	*Targets (tons)*
Palm kernals	61 240	66 431	76 541	71 269	100 000
Palm oil	637	2 208	3 308	1 940	10 000
Kola	2 300	1 841	1 680	1 070	2 000
Cocoa	439	1 379	—	1 620	3 000
Ginger	1 451	1 319	1 395	2 251	2 000
Groundnuts	—	890	2 454	3 465	5 000
Beanseed	3	349	287	804	500
Piassava	2 958	2 160	2 785	5 348	4 000
Totals	69 028	76 577	88 450	87 767	
Estimated value	£1 815 899	£2 556 920	£3 086 296	£3 616 404	

products recorded well above 50 per cent of the target tonnages, and production of other crops, such as ginger, beanseed and piassava, reached well above production targets. Two factors accounted for this positive development. One had to do with the government's deliberate pressure on the peasants to produce for export. The other factor was the relatively favourable prices of most agricultural commodities. By 1949 local prices of agricultural products had risen by 31 per cent over those of the war years.[62] These increases in the prices of primary commodities were a direct reflection of relatively positive market situations, which was a result of the substantial amount of US money that was injected into Western economies as part of the economic recovery plans and the gradual phasing out of discriminatory trade practices.

However, despite the apparent boom in export trade, which actually affected all the British West African colonies, both the peasant producers and the colony's economy were exploited. The sterling balances of the West African Marketing Boards, of which Sierra Leone was a part, instead of being reinvested in individual colonies or handed over to the peasant producers who earned them, were invested in British securities to salvage the British economy.[63]

CONCLUSION

An analysis of the impact of the Second World War on Sierra Leone's economy validates our opening hypothesis. First, during the war, Sierra Leone's economy was further integrated into the metropolitan economy, and this accelerated the under-development and dependency of the colony's economy which continues even to this day. Evidence has been provided of how the Imperial Government imposed conditions that served to reinforce the integration of Sierra Leone's economy into that of the metropole. Some of those measures included emphasis on production for export, controls over foreign investment, and price controls of local products, which resulted in the adjustment of the economy to the needs of the metropole within the world market.

This situation somewhat invalidates A.G. Frank's hypothesis on Latin America, which posits that, 'the satellites experience their greatest economic development and especially their most classically capitalist industrial development if and when their ties to the metropolis are weakest'. Frank indicates that such development occurs during crisis periods – such as 'War or Depression'. These crisis periods embraced the Depression of the seventeenth century, the Napoleonic Wars, the First World War (1914–18), the Depression of the 1930s and the Second World War. Frank concludes that the effect of these crises was the *consequent loosening* of linkages between the centre and periphery, and subsequently the satellites were left relatively free to initiate autonomous industrialisation and growth.[64]

Certainly, this was not the case in Sierra Leone, and indeed most of the British African empire. Former linkages were strengthened and control of the colony's economy by the metropole became more aggressive. This indicates that during the war the metropolitan power needed the colonial resources for the war effort and the general survival of the capitalist system.

The latter situation is more or less analogous to that of Germany as analysed by Hans-Ulrich Wehler. Wehler argues that crisis periods actually had catalytic effects on Bismarck's imperialist policies.[65] In other words, crisis situations impelled Germany to integrate the economies of her potential colonies and her spheres of influence into that of the metropole. The major aim of this policy was to rescue the metropole's economy from the crisis. The result of such a policy on the periphery was invariably its under-development and dependency. This was the case in Sierra Leone and many other parts of the British colonial empire. Britain mounted a remarkably comprehensive and coercive effort to integrate the colonies' human and material resources into the imperial war effort. Sierra Leone was too valuable to be overlooked in this climactic military struggle. To this extent, Frank's thesis needs revision or modification when applied to many parts of the colonial empire.

Secondly, as argued earlier, the imperatives of the war compelled Britain to impose stringent controls on the colony's economy: limitation of imports in order to provide more shipping space for war goods and to avoid luxury expenditure; deflation of prices for locally produced primary commodities amidst spiralling cost-of-living indices; redirection of a large part of the colony's revenues to the war effort from local infrastructural development; and the more aggressive extraction of minerals (with little financial returns) for the benefit of the Imperial Government and British capital. All this severely constrained the colony's fragile economy. What aggravated the situation even more was the absence of a financially powerful local or settler bourgeoisie to seize this opportunity of dire strains to initiate some forms of import-substitution, as was the case in Kenya.[66] Where such a class existed to a significant degree (as in Kenya and Southern Rhodesia), it responded to the outbreak of the war by agreeing to help mobilise local resources for the imperial defence, but, as a *quid pro quo*, demanded increased scope for capital accumulation and political initiatives. In Kenya this agreement to be cooperative (in so far as it was given) included important political concessions. When confronted by an aggressive core of colonial entrepreneurs, the British government appears to have been inclined more toward accommodation than confrontation (although racial factors seem to have had a bearing on London's outlook, with white settlers encountering the least resistance). In contrast to Kenya and Southern Rhodesia, Sierra Leone found itself subjected to a policy of predatory mercantilism, a policy which brought significant material denial to local industrial workers and agricultural producers.

The increased proletarianisation and peasantisation of the Sierra Leonean labour force was accompanied by political suppression, as a result of the needs of the war, both for industrial and agricultural production for export for meagre remuneration. Labour utilisation under the war regulations was marked by the most serious form of exploitation. For instance, after the 1942 strike at Delco's iron ore mining and port installations at Marampa and Pepel, the general manager of Delco admitted that the company was making reasonable profits and that it would still realise a profit even if it were to pay its labourers a minimum wage of 1/6d per day. It is also important to note that the company paid a meagre royalty to the Protectorate. In 1946 this amounted to a mere £6519, out of an estimated value of about £1 million sterling for the 729 398 tons of iron ore produced that year.

The situation of the agricultural producers was little different. Following the outbreak of the war, the British Ministry of Food attempted to deflate the prices of all agricultural commodities. Under this measure agricultural producers' labour was exploited for the benefit of the British economy. This mode of exchange had negative effects on Sierra Leone's economy. To this extent, the impact of the war on Sierra Leone's economy thus indicates an accelerated process of colonial under-development by the metropole.

It was also during the war crisis that the colonial state became more effective on labour matters. Through the Department of Labour, the colonial state developed institutions and defined the framework within which labour could operate. This heralded the end of independent unions and simultaneously ushered in an era in which the evolution of 'acceptable unions' whose interests were limited to economism was encouraged by the colonial authorities. Lastly, this essay is not limited to one particulary understudied period and area of African colonial history, but also pertains to many other central – periphery relationships during the Second World War.

NOTES

1. Specific studies on the impact of the Second World War on either Sierra Leone or Kenya are scanty. However, there are some general works that deal with some historical and economic aspects of these countries during the period under consideration. These include Milcah Amolo, 'Sierra Leone and British Colonial Labour Policy, 1930–1945' (PhD thesis, Dalhousie University, Halifax, 1977), pp. 45–180; Leo Spitzer, *The Creoles of Sierra Leone: Response to Colonialism, 1870–1945* (Madison, Wis., 1974), pp. 186–350; Leo Spitzer and La Ray Denzer, 'I.T.A. Wallace-Johnson and the West African Youth League. Part II: The Sierra Leone Period, 1930–1945', *The International J. of Historical Studies*, vol. VI, 4 (1973), pp. 565–601; Anthony Clayton and Donald Savage, *Government and Labour in Kenya, 1895–1963* (London, 1974, pp. 265–89; R.M.A. van Zwanenberg with Anne King, *An Economic History of Kenya and Uganda, 1800–1970* (London, 1975, pp. 44–5, 125–9, 213–16; Nicola Swainson, *The Development of Corporate Capitalism in Kenya, 1918–1977* (London, Ibadan, Nairobi, 1980), 58–92; and Nicholas Westcott, 'The Impact of the Second World War on Tanganyika, 1939–1949' (PhD thesis, Cambridge University, 1982).
2. Freetown in Sierra Leone has the best protected natural harbour in West Africa. It was for this reason that it was chosen and declared a protected strategic port in West Africa. The Imperial Government also established a War Department in Freetown in preparation for the Second World War. Kenya, with its port of Mombasa, played more or less a similar role in East Africa.
3. For a definition and more sophisticated discussion of 'world system', see

Samir Amin, *Unequal Development* (New York, 1976), p. 73; and 'Accumulation on a World Scale', *Review of African Political Economy*, vol. 1, no. 1 (1974), p. 1.

4. CO 267/683/18836/44, Lord Moyne to the Colonial Administrations, 5 June 1941.
5. CO 267/683/18836/41; H.R.R. Blood to Lord Moyne, 8 August, 1941.
6. CO 272/118; (MFLM) Sierra Leone Blue Books, 1938–43.
7. H.R.R. Blood to Lord Moyne, 8 August 1941.
8. Ibid.
9. Ibid.
10. Hugh E. Conway, 'Industrial Relations in Sierra Leone: with special reference to the development of and functioning of Bargaining Machinery since 1945' (PhD thesis, University of London, 1968).
11. Blood to Moyne, op. cit., 8 August 1941.
12. CO 267/670/32210/2; Jardine to MacDonald, 5 September 1939.
13. For background information on the activities of Wallace-Johnson, see Leo Spitzer and La Ray Denzer, 'I.T.A. Wallace-Johnson and the West African Youth League. Part II'; also Leo Spitzer, *The Creoles of Sierra Leone: Responses to Colonialism, 1970–1945*, and Milcah Amolo, 'Sierra Leone and British Colonial Labour Policy'.
14. Ibid., Leo Spitzer, *The Creoles of Sierra Leone*, 216.
15. CO 267/683/18836/40, Colony of Sierra Leone: Public no. 66 of 1940; The Emergency Powers (Defence) Act 1939. The Defence (Amendment) no. 3 regulations, 1940.
16. CO 267/683/18836/41; H.R.R. Blood to Moyne, 21 June, 1941.
17. Ibid.
18. CO 267/682/32303/41; H.R.R. Blood to Moyne, 15 July, 1941.
19. Ibid.
20. Ibid.; also see Marcus Grant, 'History of Trade Unionism in Sierra Leone', paper prepared for Trade Union Leaders, Freetown (undated), p. 3. Hugh E. Conway, 'Labour Administration and Industrial Relations in Sierra Leone', Monograph, Fourah Bay College, pp. 3–5.
21. Ibid.
22. Ibid., H. E. Conway, 'Labour Administration and Industrial Relations in Sierra Leone', p. 4.
23. Ibid.
24. Laurel Sefton MacDowell, 'The Formation of the Canadian Industrial System during World War II', *J. of Canadian Labour Studies*, Vol. 3 (1978), pp. 175–6.
25. Jack Woddis, *The Mask is off: an examination of the activities of trade union advisers in the British Colonies* (London, 1954), pp. 11–12.
26. *The African Standard*, 1 August 1941.
27. CO 267/682/32306/42; Hubert Stevenson to A. J. Dawe, 4 April 1942.
28. *The Times* (London), 18 April 1942, pp. 18–32.
29. Stuart M. Jamieson, *Times of Trouble: labour unrest and industrial conflict in Canada, 1960–66: Study No. 22* (Ottawa, 1968), p. 279.
30. Hubert Stevenson to A. J. Dawe, op. cit., 4 April 1942.
31. CO 267/682/32306/42; Hubert Stevenson to Viscount Cranborne, 29 September 1942.

32. Ibid.
33. *The African Standard* op. cit., 3 April 1942; see also *The Times* (London), 18 April 1942, pp. 18–32.
34. Stevenson to Viscount Cranborne, op. cit., 29 September 1942.
35. CO 267/682/32306/42; extract from the conclusion of the 3rd meeting of the West African War Council, 6 October 1942. Also see CO 267/682/32306; Report on progress of registration and conscription, 30 September 1942.
36. W. B. Birmingham, 'An Index of Real Wages of Unskilled Labour in Accra', *The Economic Bulletin, Ghana* March 1960); see also Laurel Sefton, 'The Formation of the Canadian Industrial Relations System During World War Two', pp. 176–8.
37. Blood to Moyne, op. cit., 8 August 1941.
38. Hugh E. Conway, 'Labour Protest Activity in Sierra Leone during the early part of the 20th Century'.
39. *Sierra Leone Weekly News,* 10 September 1938. Monograph, Fourah Bay College, Freetown (September 1969) 16.
40. Ibid., 18.
41. CO 267/680/32199/42; Enclusure No. 1. 'Report on the Strike of Messrs Sierra Leone Development Company's Labour at Marampa and Pepel, 2 to 6 February 1942' in Stevenson to Cranborne, 22 October 1942.
42. Ibid.
43. Ibid.
44. Ibid.
45. Ibid.
46. Stevenson to Cranborne, op. cit., 22 October 1942.
47. Ibid.
48. CSO 36/42; Marampa Arbitration Tribunal 1942; Appendix Ex G., an assessment of the cost of living at Lunsar.
49. Ibid., Recommendations of Marampa Arbitration Tribunal, 1942.
50. 'Employers and Employed Rules' in *The Laws of the Colony and Protectorate of Sierra Leone*, Vol. 1 (1946), p. 1051.
51. Enclosure No. 3 in Stevenson to Cranborne, 22 October 1942.
52. Ibid., O'Dwyer, DC for Port Loko, quoted in Enclosure No. 2 by Chief Labour Officer.
53. Before the Second World War the export of produce from British West African dependencies was strictly in the hands of private enterprise. The major exporters were European and Levantine commercial houses, although West Africans acted mainly as middlemen and agents in the less accessible parts of the country. At the outbreak of the Second World War producers and exporters were faced with problems of transporting their produce because of hostilities. On the other hand, the British Government was interested in an increased and constant flow of primary products to the metropole. To implement this, a West African Produce Control Board was established in 1942, by the British Government. This board had to control the export of produce and encourage production. After the war, the Board was dissolved and a Department of Commerce and Industry was created to continue trade on behalf of British West African Colonies. This development was followed by the formation of separate boards in each colony in the late 1940s. In Sierra Leone the Sierra Leone Produce Marketing Board (SLPMB) was constituted in 1949.

54. Van Zwanenberg and King, *Economic History of Kenya and Uganda*, p. 215.
55. CO 267/687/32303/45; 'Wallace Johnson to Clement Attlee', in R.O. Ramage to G.H. Hall, 11 August 1945. This view was also expressed by Pa Morsay of Koidu Town, Gbensen Chiefdom in an interview, and Chief Sandy, of Sinah Town, Gbensen Chiefdom, December, 1982.
56. John Levi (ed.) *African Agriculture and Economic Action and Reaction in Sierra Leone* (Oxford, 1976), pp. 69–83; N.A. Cox-George, *Finance and Development in West Africa, the Sierra Leone Experience* (London, 1961), p. 275; D.T. Jack, *An Economic Survey of Sierra Leone*, mimeo (1958), p. 13; and Ralph Saylor, *Economic System of Sierra Leone* (Durham, NC, 1967), p. 38.
57. Gustav Ranis and John C. H. Fei, 'A Theory of Economic Development', *American Economic Review*, Vol. 51 (September 1961), pp. 533–65; also see John W. Mellor, 'Towards a Theory of Agricultural Development', in Herman M. Southworth and Bruce F. Johnson (eds), *Agricultural Development and Economic Growth* (New York: 1976–7), pp. 24–5.
58. Blood to Moyne, op. cit., 8 August 1942.
59. Wallace Johnson to Attlee, op. cit.
60. Ibid. Interview with Pa Fayiah Baker of Kissy Town – Koidu, Gbensen Chiefdom, December 1982; Bockarie Mbawa, Koidu Village, Gbane Karndor Chiefdom, December 1982.
61. CO 270/80; Agricultural Production in Sierra Leone, 1947.
62. CO 270/83; Sierra Leone Administration Reports (1949), pp. 27–30.
63. G. E. Metcalfe, *Great Britain and Ghana: Documents of Ghana History, 1807–1951* (London, 1964), p. 706.
64. Andre Gunder Frank, 'The Development of Under-development', in James D. Cockcroft *et al.*, *Dependence and Development: Latin America's Political Economy* (Garden City, 1972), pp. 10–11; and *Latin America: Underdevelopment or Revolution* (New York, 1969), ch. 1.
65. Hans-Ulrich Wehler, 'Industrial growth and Early German Imperialism', in Roger Owen and Bob Sutcliffe (eds), *Studies in the Theory of Imperialism* (London, 1976), pp. 80–1.
66. Zwanenberg and King, *Economic History of Kenya and Uganda*, p. 126.

10 Algerian Nationalism and the Allied Military Strategy and Propaganda during the Second World War: the Background to Sétif

MOHAMED KHENOUF and MICHAEL BRETT

In the history of Algerian nationalism, from its beginnings before the First World War down to the war of Algerian independence, 1954–62, the Second World War was a critical episode in which the demand for reform began to give way to the demand for independence. Two events stand out from the years 1940–5: firstly, the issuing of the *Manifeste*, a document claiming fully equal rights for the Muslim community, which was drawn up by the Muslim political leader Ferhat Abbas in 1943, and served as the basis for a Muslim front, the Amis du Manifeste et de la Liberté, created in 1944; and secondly, the communal massacres which began at Sétif and Guelma on VE day, 1945, killing scores of Europeans and thousands of Muslims, a foretaste of the violence to come.

The context for this radicalisation of the political opposition between the French and Muslim communities was the defeat of France in 1940, the occupation of French North Africa by American and British forces in late 1942, and the installation of a Free French government at Algiers in June 1943. The Allied occupation from November 1942 to June 1943 was an especially dramatic interlude, when the Vichy authorities in Morocco and Algeria were obliged to submit to Allied direction, and French North Africa itself was the main theatre of war before it became

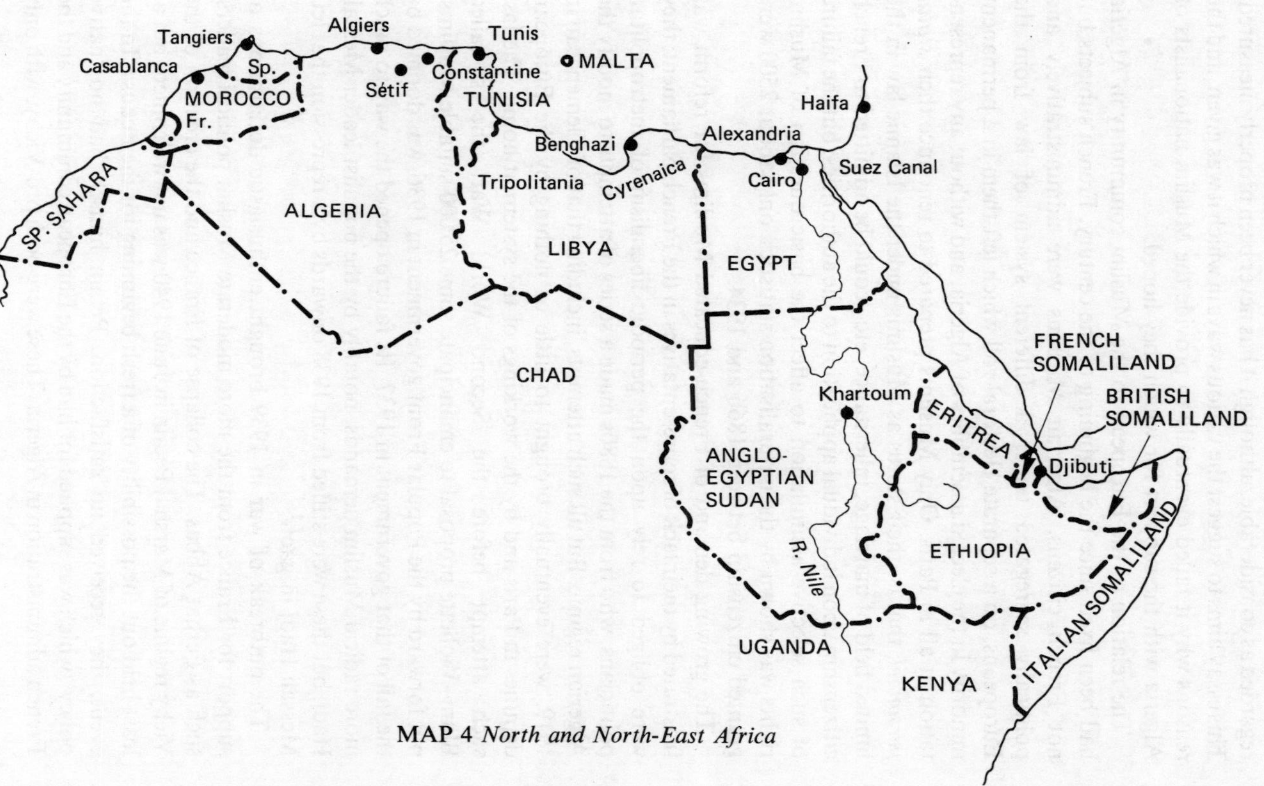

MAP 4 *North and North-East Africa*

a base for the invasion of Sicily. The encouragement given to the nationalists of Morocco and Algeria by the Allies has always been regarded as considerable, although it has never been properly measured. This essay aims to suggest the various ways in which it was given, and the reasons why it failed eventually to provide the Muslim nationalists of Algeria with the support for which they hoped.

The relation of the European to the Muslim community in Algeria had been fixed since the beginning of the century. French subjects but not French citizens, Algerian Muslims were administratively and politically segregated under a different system of law from the Europeans, on a separate electoral roll which left them in a permanent minority in the elected assemblies of Algeria, and without any representation at all in Paris. Only Muslims prepared to renounce their *statut personnel*, that is, their status as Muslims under the Islamic law in the limited field of marriage, inheritance, etc., could be admitted to French citizenship upon individual application to the authorities; but the failure of such selective assimilation to affect the basic question of Muslim rights was shown by the naturalisation statistics: only about 2500 were granted citizenship between 1866 and 1934.

The growing demand of French-educated Muslims for reform was frustrated by their lack of representatives in the French parliament; they were obliged to rely upon the periodic liberalism of metropolitan politicians, who from the 1880s made a series of attempts to modify the Algerian regime. But all such attempts, including that of Clemenceau in 1919, were eventually brought to little or nothing by the European deputies in Paris and by the workings of the system at home. The last such attempt before the Second World War, the so-called Blum–Viollette proposal to emancipate some 25 000 suitable Muslims, put forward by the Popular Front government in 1936, was doomed by the fall of that government in 1937. Its failure opened the way to much more radical Muslim demands, notably by the populist leader Messali Hadj, but these were stifled from 1938 onwards by a repression that left Messali Hadj in gaol.[1]

The outbreak of war in 1939 brought enthusiastic declarations of support for France from the more moderate Muslim political leaders, such as Ferhat Abbas. The collapse of France and the creation of the Vichy regime of Marshal Pétain in June 1940 was not welcomed, but at least held out the possibility of a fresh beginning for their cause. In the event, they received no satisfaction. Pétain himself had no 'native policy', which was supplied for him by the European community and the French administration in Algeria. These were both pro-Vichy, with only a tiny underground opposition. Strong Fascist sympathies were promoted by the heterogeneous origins of the European population in Italy and Spain as well as in France. The 'new French' of Spanish and Italian origins were intensely susceptible to the prestige of Franco and Mussolini. In the press, the editorials of the *Dépêche de Constantine*, for example, never failed in their enthusiasm for a victory of the Axis. This willing approval of the Axis cause was not confined to the opinion of the lumpen colonate. It extended to active collaboration on the part of the leaders of the French Algerian community: *grands colons* and shippers such as Schiaffino and Amédée Froger, who became commercial agents for the trade with Hitler's Germany, press bosses like Alain de Sérigny of the *Echo d'Alger*, and senior Algerian officials.[2] Their anti-Semitism, dating back to the Dreyfus affair in 1896, was gratified by the repeal of the Décret Crémieux of 1870, which had given French citizenship to the native Algerian Jewish community; a discriminatory *numerus clausus*, falling as low as 2.7 per cent, was imposed on Jewish schoolchildren and students. Their hostility to Muslim nationalism was reflected in the prison sentences ranging from 10 to 16 years passed in 1941 on Messali Hadj and other leaders of the radical Parti du Peuple Algérien (PPA) for conspiracy against the sovereignty of France.

Minor administrative changes were unimportant in the circumstances. During the 26 months of Vichy rule in Algeria, the country experienced a severe economic crisis especially affecting the Muslim population. Algeria was required under the armistice to supply large quantities of wheat in particular to metropolitan France and Germany; imports were minimal, and distributed in the first place to the Europeans by licensed importers. Prices rose while wages fell; a black market sprang up, starvation set in for the poor, and typhus broke out. About 200 000 cases were registered in 1942, a year in which the harvest fell disastrously to half its level in 1939. The apparent indifference of the bulk of the Muslim population to the war in 1940 turned increasingly to hostility towards France and the Regime. Paradoxically, this hostility was expressed in a certain enthusiasm for Hitler and the Axis, which paralleled that of the *colons*: German and Italian propaganda, which offered one thing to the Vichy French, offered another thing, liberation, to France's North African subjects.[3]

This enthusiasm became pro-American after the Allied landings in North Africa in November 1942. Through Admiral Darlan, Vichy agreed to the cooperation of the French authorities in Morocco and Algeria with the Allies, at the price of the German occupation of the whole of metropolitan France. With Pétain's government thus effectively at an end, Darlan himself was assassinated at Algiers in December, and General Giraud took command of the French forces and the French administration in North Africa. An opponent of Vichy, he was likewise opposed to De Gaulle and the Free French. Though a patriot, he was not a politician, and strove as far as possible to subordinate the political problems of North Africa to the war effort. With the battle for Tunisia in progress and the invasion of Sicily in preparation, this naturally took priority throughout the months of his authority, when the Allied High Command under General Eisenhower dominated the scene. The resident French administration, with its Vichy sympathies, was dismayed, but the Muslim population welcomed the situation, both for the prospect of a return to plenty with American aid, and for the opportunity to raise once again the question of political reform.

On 20 December 1942 Ferhat Abbas sent a first message to the 'responsible authorities', requesting the calling of a conference of all Muslim leaders to elaborate an improved social, political and economic status for Algerian Muslims in exchange for an active participation in the war effort. The request was unacceptable to Giraud as well as to Darlan, since it would have involved the British and Americans in the internal affairs of France, rather than as partners of a sovereign French government, and was rejected. Nevertheless the desirability of reform was acknowledged, and the first step was taken with the appointment of Marcel Peyrouton in January 1943 as Governor-general of Algeria. Robert Murphy, President Roosevelt's head of civilian affairs in North Africa, was instrumental in bringing the new regime and the moderate Muslim leadership together to work out a programme. In February, Ferhat Abbas produced his *Manifeste*, calling for full equal rights for the Muslim community, which was presented to Peyrouton at the end of March and accepted as a basis for discussion. In April a *Commission d'études économiques et sociales musulmanes* was set up for the purpose. The specific reforms the French were prepared to contemplate, however, fell short of the demands of the *Manifeste*, and far short of those of a second document, the *Additif au Manifeste*, which Ferhat Abbas produced in May with the approval of the elected Muslim members of the *Délégations financières*, the Algerian assembly. This called for the eventual separation of Algeria from France, in effect for independence.

The two sides came openly into conflict in June. Giraud was then replaced by De Gaulle, a leader far more determined to exclude the Americans and the British from interference in France's internal affairs, and to maintain the integrity of the French empire. General Catroux, who replaced Peyrouton as Governor-general of Algeria, rejected the

Additif, though like the *Commission d'études*, he pronounced himself in favour of reforms within the existing constitution.[4] The split continued to widen. In September the Muslim section of the *Délégations financières* was temporarily dissolved, Abbas and Sayeh Abdelkader were placed under house arrest, and other signatories of the *Manifeste*, notably Dr Bendjelloul and Dr Tamzali, were made to apologise and give an assurance of their loyalty. In December 1943, in an important speech at Constantine, De Gaulle promised a series of reforms along the lines of those proposed by the Popular Front government of 1936. An initial measure was introduced in March 1944, among other things abolishing the legal, civil inequality of Muslims, and granting citizenship to a few selected categories of persons; a much wider extension of the franchise was to be the work of the national Constituent Assembly after the war. But although these reforms were supported by Muslim politicians such as Bendjelloul, they failed to carry with them the bulk of Muslim opinion. The response of Ferhat Abbas was to found, a week after the March ordinance, a political party, the Amis du Manifeste et de la Liberté, to press for something grander than mere assimilation.

This outcome of a dialogue initiated by the Allied landings in November 1942 was a great advance upon the blocked position under Vichy; nevertheless it fell far short of Muslim aspirations, encouraged by the Anglo-American liberation, and expressed in the *Manifeste* and in the *Additif*. Looking at the result from the point of view of the Allied intervention, there can be no doubt that its ambiguity was at least partly the result of a fundamental ambiguity in British and American policy. On the one hand was the desire to win the war by a militarily and politically effective campaign; on the other was the desire to win the peace with a humane settlement based initially upon the principles of the Atlantic Charter, and eventually upon those of the United Nations. In North Africa, and in Algeria in particular, these desires came into conflict as regards the native Muslim population. On the one hand, Muslims were perceived as the victims of French colonial oppression, in danger of turning to the Germans; for immediate military as well as long-term political purposes they had to be won over to the Allied cause with the promise of a better future. On the other, they were recognised to be French subjects, the responsibility of a properly constituted French government belonging to the Western alliance. Such a government was formed first by Giraud and then by De Gaulle, and for the sake of the war effort it was necessary for the British and Americans not to interfere with its handling of the problem. This was true to some extent even during the Vichy period, for unlike the British, the Americans had recognised Pétain's government and maintained relations with it. Historians of the Second World War generally agree that the decision to maintain relations with Vichy was motivated by strategic considerations and that it may have contributed to the success of the Allied landings in North Africa. Nevertheless, even before these landings in November 1942, American support for Vichy had led to controversy within the American administration on the Muslim question, since the American consuls in Morocco and Tunisia, notably Hooker Doolittle, were vehement in their denunciations of French treatment of the natives.[5] From November 1942 onwards the matter was of practical importance.

Generally speaking, the United States avoided any strong commitment to the cause of Muslim liberation in French North Africa. Not only the French but the British were apprehensive. In a letter dated 9 August, 1942 to President Roosevelt, Prime Minister Churchill wrote about the Atlantic Charter that:

> We considered the wording of that famous document line by line together, and I should not be able, without mature consideration, to give it a wider interpretation than was agreed between us at the time. Its proposed application to Asia and Africa requires much thought.[6]

Thus although the political importance of the Atlantic Charter, together with its propaganda value, was boundless, the Allies had no precise plan to implement it. In North Africa, following the landings in November 1942, their presence was officially said to be 'for the purpose of preventing the domination of this territory by German and Italian forces, and for carrying on the war for the defeat of the Axis power'.[7] After the successful conclusion of the landings, code-named Operation Torch, these military considerations continued to govern US policy. Two years later, in a letter to Eisenhower and Murphy dated 11 December 1944, Cordell Hull, the American Secretary of State, made it clear that the American government 'regarded the whole North African situation from the military point of view, and consequently civil questions were subordinate except as they contributed to military effectiveness'.[8]

In the critical year 1943, however, the matter was not so simple. British documentation reveals not only a concern to avoid annoyance to the French, but a desire for a distinct British voice in Anglo-American propaganda. A document sent by Harold Macmillan, Resident Minister in North Africa, to the Foreign Office concerning the appointment of a senior political warfare executive at Algiers shows that a fight over publicity existed in North Africa between an Allied Headquarters dominated by the Americans and the British Ministry of Information. The document says that:

> There are several reasons why we think that British publicity must be handled by representatives of the Ministry of Information and not by Political Warfare Officers.
>
> i. The PWE officers in North Africa do not constitute a British unit but are simply members of the joint British-American team, and neither this team nor British members of it can be expected to perform purely British publicity.
>
> ii. British publicity would start on the wrong footing if it relied on such an impermanent organisation as Allied Force Headquarters of which the PWE is a part.

Macmillan was in any case clearly doubtful about army methods for high political purposes:

> iii. It is in principle undesirable to rely entirely on political warfare methods for putting the British case across.[9]

A second Foreign Office document, in the form of a memorandum from Algiers, develops this theme while showing concern about the audience. It laments the lack of experts on Arab affairs in North Africa, and the weakness of Allied propaganda as compared to that of Germany:[10]

> From the beginning our propaganda to natives of North Africa has laboured under a double handicap. We have had very inadequate distribution (mainly through Tangiers), and we have had to bear French susceptibilities constantly in mind . . . There is nothing that the Germans can give them that we cannot, and yet we don't seem to pay enough attention to that side.

To remedy the situation, it proposes the setting-up of a small organisation composed of experts on Arab affairs to accomplish the following tasks:

> i. Supply intelligence appreciations by means of comprehensive weekly telegrams, including native reactions to enemy propaganda.

ii. Establish printing facilities for leaflets based on the news of the day.
iii. Establish direct contacts with French broadcasters in charge of Arabic programmes.
iv. Establish direct contact with the local Arabic press.
v. Start the machinery of the all-important 'oral' propaganda.

It concludes:

> We fully realise the great difficulties which are certain to arise with the French as well as with the Americans. All we can say is that the potential dangers of inactivity are far greater.[11]

The 'oral' propaganda to which this document alludes took the form of contacts between Allied personnel, mainly army officers, and North African Muslims who might be thought to represent the Muslim people. No doubt it also concerned itself with the dissemination of rumours. But it was backed up by the broadcasts of the BBC North African Service. The standing directive for this North African Arabic Service was approved by a joint committee composed of Political Warfare Officers, representatives of the Ministry of Information and BBC staff on 27 August 1943.[12] It was approved and issued after the coming to power of De Gaulle and his Free French government in North Africa. However, in its first chapter, entitled 'Appreciation', the document stresses the propaganda objectives for the Vichy period prior to the Allied landings, of which there were two. The first, which continued to be valid after De Gaulle took power, was a long-term objective with the aim of convincing the listeners that Britain and America would win the war. The second, however, changed. It became:

> . . . a short-term objective with the aims of convincing listeners that they could only expect increased hardship – material and otherwise – from continued enemy domination; of explaining HMG's blockade policy; of stressing the material help extended to the natives by Britain and espeically the U.S.A.; and finally of *creating and sustaining in natives of all classes an attitude of passive hostility to Vichy and the enemy alike.*

With the rise of De Gaulle, a third objective appeared:

> To help restore native confidence in the new France and to restore French prestige in North Africa, and to help consolidate the position of the *Comité Français de la Libération Nationale*.

But the political problems generated by the Giraud–De Gaulle rivalry, by the faction-fighting within the CFLN, and by the growing demands of Muslim nationalists, needed the strictest guidance. On the question of political propaganda the directive stated: 'All references to the Atlantic Charter, other than hard news, must be avoided, since its application to French North Africa raises controversial questions.' However, references to the Atlantic Charter were certainly made, and its eventual application discussed between Ferhat Abbas and Robert Murphy during the numerous meetings they held.[13] Broadcasters were further warned to

> . . . avoid comparing educational and cultural progress in the Eastern Moslem world with that of French North Africa, especially as social and cultural conditions in the latter territory noticeably differ from those in the Middle East.

In dealing with economic and military matters propaganda 'should be limited to the three themes of food, clothing and military successes'.

It will be seen that the constraints of policy upon propaganda were considerable. There was to be no reckless extravagance in the appeal to the Muslim population of Algeria, and North Africa as a whole. Nevertheless, certain positive objectives did remain, and remained constant. The first was naturally to convince the listener of the certain victory of the Allies. Second was the need to convince this listener that it was to his advantage that the Allies, representing the United Nations, should be victorious, and that he, together with the whole of the local population, should actively collaborate with the Allies for this purpose. Finally there was the need to emphasise the economic advantages to which French North Africa could look forward, not so much during the war as in the immediate post-war period. This last theme was intimately linked to the question of Allied, especially American, aid to North Africa, a question important not only for its material consequences but for its effect upon the minds of the Muslim population.

The American programme of economic assistance to French North Africa during the war has been described by James J. Dougherty in his book *The Politics of Wartime Aid*, based on his study of US archival material.[14] It began in 1941 under a special agreement with the Vichy government, which Britain strongly opposed, and which failed to provide more than a small fraction of estimated requirements of petroleum products and other goods.[15] Thus, as Dougherty puts it:

> Despite a formal agreement and continued promises, North Africa never received sufficient assistance to bolster her sagging economy. Thus, in November 1942, when the lend-lease administration assumed the responsibility for the economic rehabilitation of the area, the shortcomings of the previous inaction were most evident; agency officials encountered a stagnated economy on the verge of total collapse.[16]

The turning-over of the aid programme to the Lend-Lease administration following the Allied landings in November 1942, however, represented a new departure. It was Roosevelt's intention to make of French North Africa, as the first liberated territory, an example of what the United Nations could and would do to abolish hunger and want. Moreover, from a military point of view it was thought essential for the success of the campaign in Tunisia to avoid the hostility of a starving and rebellious local population in Morocco and Algeria. Instead, North Africa and its peoples were required to contribute to the war effort, and that in turn meant rebuilding the North African economy over and above the subsistence level to the point at which it could produce a surplus for countries whose liberation was yet to come.[17]

The aim was ambitious, the achievement much more modest. The necessary administrative machinery was lacking. The aid programme began on a civilian basis, with a joint American and British North African Economic Board responsible to a Combined Committee for North and West Africa in Washington. But procurement of goods in the United States was made difficult by the vagueness of the orders, supply hampered by the priority of military over civilian goods in shipping across the Atlantic, and distribution frustrated by the need to rely upon the so-called *groupements*, the Vichy French import agencies, which continued to discriminate against the Muslim population. Thus although the supply of aid goods jumped from November 1942 onwards, the quantities fell persistently short of what was agreed – 66 000 out of at least 90 000 tons in the first three months, for example. Moreover:

> In February 1943 John O'Boyle, a lend-lease observer, reported that the large native population was receiving a rather small share of the

> goods. Since the French refused to sell European goods to native retailers, any Arab or Jew who desired European clothing could only purchase such materials through the flourishing Black Market . . . Although the high commissariat, the British and the Americans all possessed the authority to inspect the system, it proved virtually impossible to eliminate irregularities.[18]

At the end of 1943, the programme was finally turned over to the army in the form of the Allied High Command, and procurement improved as the French set up their own organisation to specify their requirements. But Dougherty's verdict is one of failure. Aid was sacrificed for the sake of the military operation, which requisitioned and took out of Algeria in particular far more than aid put in. As a result, in 1944 the population was little better off than in 1942, ill-prepared for the consequences of the failure of the 1943 harvest.[19]

It seems clear that the level of supply was insufficient, not only to meet the physical needs of the people at whom it was aimed, but to achieve the desired psychological result envisaged in the Allies' propaganda aims. But there were ways in which many of these people did benefit from the Allied presence, of which the aid programme was a relatively minor part. An incalculable quantity of Allied material reached the population by illicit means. Goods were stolen in transit, but more important was the willingness of Allied troops to let the local population have anything from food and cigarettes to petrol, equipment, and even arms. All such items found their way on to the black market, and inevitably enriched the few at the expense of the many. More open and more equitable was the employment provided by the military, which yielded relatively high wages to large numbers of people. All such activities brought personal contact between the Muslim population and the newcomers, from which Muslims undoubtedly drew their own conclusions about themselves, the French, the Americans and the British. Whether these conclusions were wholly in accordance with the aims of Allied propaganda or not, the French authorities in Algeria were certainly alarmed.

The archives of the Wilaya of Constantine give the view of these developments through the eyes of the French provincial administration. This remained in place throughout the war, and in outlook, like the bulk of the European population, remained Vichyist. It was deeply distrustful of the Anglo-Americans. With regard to their overt pronouncements and activities, a report on British propaganda among Muslims, issued by the *Centre d'information et d'études* on 29 March 1943, states:

> Undoubtedly there are signs of propaganda, saying that English rule in Muslim countries is more liberal than French rule. England does not concern herself with internal government in an occupied country. Rule in the British Empire is extremely supple and bears lightly on the ruled. Egypt, for instance, has kept its independence, and Egyptian fellah . . . their land, in contrast to what has happened in French North Africa.

Such propaganda obviously aimed at undermining French rule in North Africa and would, if the report be true, have conflicted with the objectives of British propaganda established by the Ministry of Information in consultation with Algiers and the Foreign Office. The French may have gleaned their indications from, among other possible sources, remarks and statements by British officers of the Allied forces' psychological warfare branch, of whom the report goes on to say that

> Some contacts with important native chiefs or elected representatives have been established by the PWB (Psychological Warfare Branch) of Constantine.

Other British soldiers were apparently much more sympathetic to the French; thus:

> Other representatives of the British Army, in contact with colonists, seem on the contrary to have developed anti-Arab views. According to information received, some officers have declared, for example, that if it had been up to them, Dr Bendjelloul would have been shot.[20]

One notes the element of hearsay as well as the different audience and presumably different set of officers.

Of the American members of the psychological warfare branch, another document issued by the *Centre d'information* says:

> American officers or agents belonging to the PWB sought out educated Algerian Muslims who were sympathetic to the claims of their co-religionists and engaged them as correspondents for the journal *El Houda* (The Good Way), which was published in Arabic in New York.[21]

This publication, *El Houda*, had been regularly taken by the Sheikh Abdelhamid Ben Badis, the founder and leader up to his death in 1940 of the *Association des Oulémas*, which championed the Arab and Islamic character of Algeria against French influence. A native of Constantine, his movement was particularly strong in that region.

The more generally unsettling effect of the American presence was noted among the Muslim units of the French forces in a report of the Gouvernement-général, 15 May 1943:

> Bitterness can already be seen among French-trained native troops and non-commissioned officers. Comparisons, to the disadvantage of the French, are made with the Allied Armies.
>
> i We know that the Americans employ, in Algiers, two Muslim officers – Lt Seblini, originally from Syria, who broadcasts on Radio Algiers, and Second Lt Mostapha Guellouz, originally from Tunisia.
>
> ii There is a rumour in Morocco that the Americans have a Muslim general in their Air Force.
>
> iii The press and radio have reported recently that General Omar Bradley has been appointed to command the Second Corps of the American Army in Tunisia in place of General Patton. Such an appointment has caused the Muslims to comment unfavourably on our own position.[22]

Presumably the Arab name Omar gave the impression that Bradley too was a Muslim. The examples quoted in the document show just what reaction might be expected to one of the strong recommendations in the BBC directive, namely, that cases of Muslims who contributed to the Allied war effort should be publicised in Allied propaganda in the belief that Muslims in North Africa would follow the lead of brother Muslims elsewhere. The French quite clearly regarded anything of the kind as highly subversive, apparently with reason.

They were equally concerned about the wages and working conditions of Algerian workers in a British camp at Biskra. A report issued by the *Brigade de surveillance du territoire de Constantine* states:

> The Muslim workers in the camp, numbering about 100, are paid 83 francs per day with meals. They work up to 5 o'clock and sleep in town. Through Aid Seghir they are each given 5kg of sugar, butter, beef dripping, chocolate and cigarettes.[23]

These British wages of 83 francs a day compare favourably with those of 65 francs a day fixed by the French administration, quite apart from the occasional extra gifts for the families of their Muslim workers.

The general shortage of food was to nobody's credit, but, even so, the French took the blame. A report from Captain Birchemal of the psychological warfare branch, contained in the Constantine archives, shows the importance attached by the Americans to a proper distribution of the goods they supplied:

> The principal food of the natives consists of cereals – wheat, semolina or a mixture of wheat and barley called 'boumerlout'. It is clear that there is insufficient for the mass of the people, and this is the cause of the present discontent . . . The amounts distributed have been cut from 4kg to 2kg per person per month, which has caused further trouble, while raising prices in the black market.[24]

When Muslims came to him to complain of the shortages, the US Vice-Consul, Utter, informed them that they were due to the bad management of the administration.[25]

The archives contain a number of files dealing with the relation between representatives of the Allied forces and Algerian nationalists. They note meetings between them, and express French disquiet. At the same time, there is at least one report by the Gendarmerie of Constantine of the sale of firearms by two American soldiers to Algerian Muslims.

How far were French fears justified? By their propaganda and their presence had the Americans and the British raised the expectations of French Muslim subjects to a dangerous level? The French could count it a victory that in the end their Allied partners had left Algeria firmly in their hands. The British and the Americans, for their part, could congratulate themselves that, having done so, they were not to be disappointed in their hopes of political liberalisation by General De Gaulle, who showed himself at Constantine ready for reforms blocked since the fall of the Popular Front in 1937. Unfortunately for all of them, Muslim opinion had by 1944 moved far beyond its position in 1936, and was unwilling to accept no more than the limited extension of the franchise decreed in March as a first instalment of wider reforms to be decided after the war. The Amis du Manifeste et de la Liberté, founded by Ferhat Abbas as a national front for some kind of independence, was rapidly overtaken in popularity and ambition by the banned Parti du Peuple Algérien, which campaigned almost openly for the release of its imprisoned leader, Messali Hadj, and for outright independence.

Equally important was the failure of Lend Lease not merely to revive the economy but to prevent famine conditions from late 1943 to early

1945. This should have dealt a severe blow to American credibility, but it is far from clear that it did. Hardship in 1944 may well have aggravated the contrast between the Algerian reality and Algerians' perceptions of a better world outside, briefly glimpsed at first hand in 1943, and sharpened the propaganda effect of the American presence and the rumours to which it gave rise. By comparison, the calculated pronouncements of official propaganda may have counted for less than the popular image.

Whatever the reason, there is no doubt that by the end of the war, Algerian Muslim aspirations were far higher than the French, of all shades of opinion, were prepared to tolerate. Famine came to an end in the spring of 1945 with a general increase in food supplies. Widespread popular support for the Parti du Peuple Algérien nevertheless continued to grow, becoming not only radical but insurrectional. As a result, the war itself ended in tragedy in the course of the VE Day celebrations, when on 8 May police fired on a demonstration at Sétif waving a red, white and green nationalist flag. What had been intended by the Party leadership as a peaceful provocation turned then into attacks throughout the region on Europeans, of whom about 100 were killed. In the course of systematic police and military repression and reprisals, some thousands of Muslims perished.[26]

NOTES

1. The best general history of Algeria in this period is Ch.-R. Ageron, *Histoire de l'Algérie contemporaine*, Vol. II (Paris, 1979). A lively introduction to the rise of Algerian nationalism is Ch.-A. Julien, *L'Afrique du Nord en marche*, 3rd ed. (Paris, 1972). The most substantial account is M. Kaddache, *Histoire du nationalisme algérien*, 2 vols (Algiers, 1980).
2. Public Record Office, Kew (PRO) WO 175/60, Army intelligence bulletin of November 1942, shows that British intelligence shared this view of French colonists and French civil servants.
3. On this Vichy period, cf. Ageron, *Histoire*, 549–58.
4. Ibid., p. 563, rejecting Ferhat Abbas' version that the *Additif* was accepted by the *Commission* with the government's approval.
5. James J. Dougherty, *The Politics of Wartime Aid* (Westport and London, 1978), pp. 124–5, 127–8.
6. Francis L. Loewenheim, Harold D. Langley and Manfred Jonas, *Roosevelt and Churchill. Their secret wartime correspondence* (New York, 1975), p. 234.
7. PRO FO.660/1, file 13.
8. Cordell Hull, *The Memoirs of Cordell Hull* (New York, 1948) II, p. 1201.
9. PRO FO.371/36180, file 36.

10. For a study of German propaganda during the war see Ch.-R. Ageron, 'Contribution à l'étude de la propagande allemande pendant la deuxième guerre mondiale', *Revue d'Histoire Mondiale* (January 1977), pp. 16–32.
11. PRO FO.371/36181, memorandum from Maknis to Mark, Algiers, 9 February 1943.
12. PRO FO.371/36249, series 1943/13.
13. Cf. A. Naroun, *Ferhat Abbas ou les chemins de la souveraineté* (Paris, 1961), p. 93.
14. See note 5, above.
15. Dougherty, *Politics of Wartime Aid*, pp. 27–47 and 233–5.
16. Ibid, p. 19.
17. Ibid., pp. 68–9.
18. Ibid., p. 86.
19. Ibid., pp. 116–18.
20. Wilaya of Constantine Archives (WCA), Fond SLNA/DSFA, File 12, 29 March 1943.
21. WCA, Fond SLNA/DSFA, File 70, 15 November 1943.
22. WCA, Fond SLNA/DSFA, File 16, 15 May 1943.
23. WCA, Fond SLNA/DSFA, File 140, 27 September 1943.
24. WCA, Fond SLNA/DSFA, File 55, 16 September 1943.
25. WCA, Fond SLNA/QES, File 18, 24 April 1943.
26. For the Sétif massacres, cf. Robert Aron, François Lavagne, Janine Feller, Yvette Garnier-Rizet, *Les origines de la guerre d'Algérie* (Paris, 1962), pp. 91–169, and Kaddache, *Histoire*, II, pp. 695–718. The event is usually taken to mark the beginning of the movement away from legitimate political activity towards organised rebellion by the Muslim nationalist movement.

Index